540

The
Pleasure-
Dome

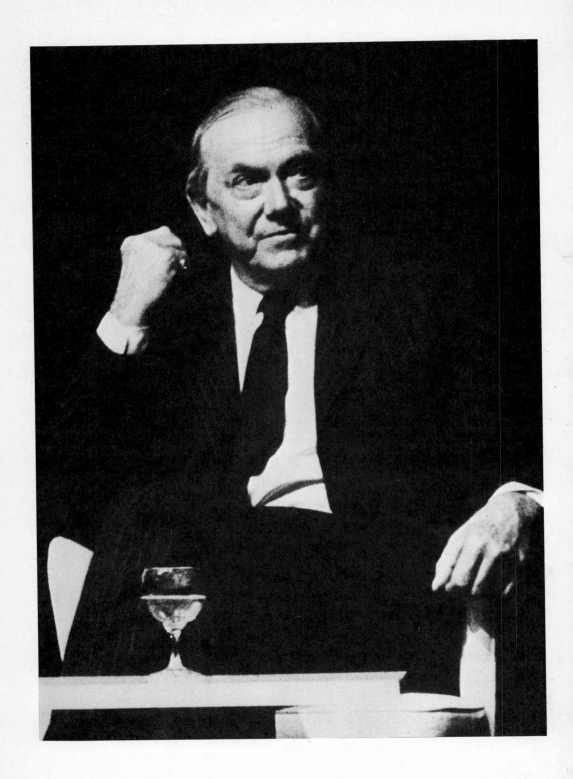

The Pleasure-Dome

Graham Greene

The Collected Film Criticism 1935–40
Edited by John Russell Taylor

'It was a miracle of rare device,
A sunny pleasure-dome with caves of ice.

Oxford   New York   Toronto   Melbourne
OXFORD UNIVERSITY PRESS
1980

Oxford University Press, Walton Street, Oxford OX2 6DP

OXFORD LONDON GLASGOW
NEW YORK TORONTO MELBOURNE WELLINGTON
KUALA LUMPUR SINGAPORE JAKARTA HONG KONG TOKYO
DELHI BOMBAY CALCUTTA MADRAS KARACHI
NAIROBI DAR ES SALAAM CAPE TOWN

® *Graham Greene 1972*

ISBN 0 19 281286 6

First published by Martin Secker and Warburg Ltd. 1972
First published as an Oxford University Press paperback 1980

Printed in Great Britain by
Lowe & Brydone Printers Limited, Thetford, Norfolk

INTRODUCTION

Four and a half years of watching films several times a week ... I can hardly believe in that life of the distant thirties now, a way of life which I adopted quite voluntarily from a sense of fun. More than four hundred films – and I suppose there would have been many many more if I had not suffered during the same period from other obsessions – four novels had to be written, not to speak of a travel book which took me away for months to Mexico, far from the Pleasure-Dome – all those Empires and Odeons of a luxury and a bizarre taste which we shall never see again. How, I find myself wondering, could I possibly have written all these reviews? And yet I remember opening the envelopes, which contained the gilded cards of invitation, for the morning Press performances (mornings when I should have been struggling with *Brighton Rock* and *The Power And The Glory*) with a sense of curiosity and anticipation. These films were an escape – escape from that hellish problem of construction in Chapter Six, from the secondary character who obstinately refused to come alive, escape for an hour and a half from the melancholy which falls inexorably round the novelist when he has lived for too many months on end in his private world.

The idea of reviewing films came to me at a cocktail-party after the dangerous third Martini. I was talking to Derek Verschoyle, the Literary Editor of *The Spectator*. *The Spectator* had hitherto neglected films and I suggested to him I should fill the gap – I thought that, in the unlikely event of his accepting my offer it might be fun for two or three weeks. I never imagined it would remain fun for four and a half years and only end in a different world, a world at war. Until I came to re-read these notices the other day I thought they abruptly ended with my review of *The Young Mr Lincoln*. If there is something a little absent-minded about that review, it was because, just as I began to write it on the morning of 3 September 1939, the first air-raid siren of the war sounded and I laid the review aside so as to make notes from my high Hampstead lodging on the destruction of London below. 'Woman passes with dog on lead,' I noted, 'and pauses by lamp post.' Then the all-clear sounded and I returned to Henry Fonda.

These were not the first film reviews I wrote. At Oxford I had appointed myself film critic of the *Oxford Outlook*, a literary magazine which appeared once a term and which I edited. *Warning Shadows, Brumes d'Automne, The Student of Prague* – these are the silent films of the twenties of which I can remember whole scenes still. I was a passionate reader of *Close Up* which was edited by Kenneth Macpherson and Bryher and published from a château in Switzerland. Marc Allégret was the Paris Correspondent and Pudovkin contributed articles on montage. I was horrified by the arrival of 'talkies' (it seemed the end of the film as an art form), just as later I regarded colour with justifiable suspicion. 'Technicolor,' I wrote in 1935, 'plays havoc with the women's faces; they all, young and old, have the same healthy weather-beaten skins.' Curiously enough it was a detective story with Chester Morris which converted me to the talkies – for the first time in that picture I was aware of *selected* sounds; until then every shoe had squeaked and every door-handle had creaked. I notice that the forgotten film *Becky Sharp* gave me even a certain hope for colour.

Re-reading these reviews of more than thirty years ago I find many prejudices which are modified now only by the sense of nostalgia. I had distinct reservations about Greta Garbo whom I compared to a beautiful Arab mare, and Hitchcock's 'inadequate sense of reality' irritated me and still does – how inexcusably he spoilt

1

The Thirty-Nine Steps. I still believe I was right (whatever Monsieur Truffaut may say) when I wrote: 'His films consist of a series of small "amusing" melodramatic situations: the murderer's button dropped on the baccarat board; the strangled organist's hands prolonging the notes in the empty church .. very perfunctorily he builds up to these tricky situations (paying no attention on the way to incon-sistencies, loose ends, psychological absurdities) and then drops them: they mean nothing: they lead to nothing.'

The thirties too were a period of 'respectable' film biographies – *Rhodes, Zola, Pasteur, Parnell* and the like – and of historical romances which only came to a certain comic life in the hands of Cecil B. de Mille (Richard Cœur-de-Lion was married to Berengaria according to the rites of the Anglican Church). I preferred the Westerns, the crime films, the farces, the frankly commercial, and I am glad to see that in reviewing one of these forgotten commercial films I gave a warm wel-come to a new star, Miss Ingrid Bergman – 'what star before has made her first appearance on the international screen with a highlight gleaming on her nose-tip'.

There were dangers, I was to discover, in film-reviewing. On one occasion I opened a letter to find a piece of shit enclosed. I have always – though probably incorrectly – believed that it was a piece of aristocratic shit, for I had made cruel fun a little while before of a certain French marquis. Thirty years later in Paris at a dinner of the *haute bourgeoisie* I sat opposite him and was charmed by his conversa-tion. I longed to ask him the truth, but I was daunted by the furniture. Then, of course, there was the Shirley Temple libel action. The review which set 20th Century-Fox alight cannot be found here for obvious reasons. I kept on my bath-room wall, until a bomb removed the wall, the statement of claim – that I had accused 20th Century-Fox of 'procuring' Miss Temple 'for immoral purposes'. Lord Hewart, the Lord Chief Justice, sent the papers in the case to the Director of Public Prosecutions, so that ever since that time I have been traceable on the files of Scotland Yard.

From film-reviewing it was only a small step to script-writing. That also was a danger, but a necessary one as I had a family to support and I remained in debt to my publishers until the war came. I had persistently attacked the films made by Alexander Korda and perhaps he became curious to meet his enemy. He asked my agent to bring me to Denham and when we were alone he asked if I had any film story in mind. I had none, so I began to improvise a thriller – early morning on Platform 1 at Paddington, the platform empty, except for one man who is waiting for the last train from Wales. From below his raincoat a trickle of blood forms a pool on the platform.

'Yes? and then?'

'It would take too long to tell you the whole plot – and the idea needs a lot more working out.'

I left Denham half an hour later to work for eight weeks on what seemed an extravagant salary, and the worst and least successful of all Korda's productions thus began. So did our friendship which endured and deepened till his death, in spite of two bad screenplays and my reviews which remained unfavourable. There was never a man who bore less malice, and I think of him with affection – even love – as the only film producer I have ever known with whom I could spend days and nights of conversation without so much as mentioning the cinema. Years later, after the war was over, I wrote two more screenplays for Korda and Carol Reed, *The Fallen Idol* and *The Third Man*, and I hope they atoned a little for the prentice scripts of which I prefer to forget even the titles.

If I had remained a film critic, the brief comic experience which I had then of Hollywood might have been of value to me, for I learned at first hand what a director may have to endure at the hands of a producer. (One of the difficult tasks of a critic is to assign his praise or blame to the right quarter.)

Mr David Selznick, famous for having produced the world's best-selling film, *Gone With The Wind*, held the American rights in *The Third Man* and, by the terms of the contract with Korda, the director was bound to consult him about the script sixty days before shooting began. So Carol Reed and I journeyed west. Our first meeting with Mr Selznick at La Jolla in California promised badly, and the dialogue remains as fresh in my mind as the day when it was spoken. After a brief greeting he got down to serious discussion. He said, 'I don't like the title.'

'No? We thought . . .'

'Listen, boys, who the hell is going to a film called *The Third Man*?'

'Well,' I said, 'it's a simple title. It's easily remembered.'

Mr Selznick shook his head reproachfully. 'You can do better than that, Graham,' he said, using my Christian name with a readiness I was not prepared for. 'You are a writer. A good writer. I'm no writer, but you are. Now what we want – it's not right, mind you, of course it's not right, I'm not saying it's right, but then I'm no writer and you are, what we want is something like *Night in Vienna*, a title which will bring them in.'

'Graham and I will think about it,' Carol Reed interrupted with haste. It was a phrase I was to hear Reed frequently repeat, for the Korda contract had omitted to state that the director was under any obligation to accept Mr Selznick's advice. Reed during the days that followed, like an admirable stonewaller, blocked every ball.

We passed on to Mr Selznick's view of the story.

'It won't do, boys,' he said, 'it won't do. It's sheer buggery.'

'Buggery?'

'It's what you learn in your English schools.'

'I don't understand.'

'This guy comes to Vienna looking for his friend. He finds his friend's dead. Right? Why doesn't he go home then?'

After all the months of writing his destructive view of the whole venture left me speechless. He shook his grey head at me. 'It's just buggery, boy.'

I began weakly to argue. I said, 'But this character – he has a motive of revenge. He has been beaten up by a military policeman.' I played a last card. 'Within twenty-four hours he's in love with Harry Lime's girl.'

Mr Selznick shook his head sadly. 'Why didn't he go home before that?'

That, I think, was the end of the first day's conference. Mr Selznick removed to Hollywood and we followed him – to a luxurious suite in Santa Monica, once the home of Hearst's film-star mistress. During the conferences which followed I remember there were times when there seemed to be a kind of grim reason in Mr Selznick's criticisms – surely here perhaps there *was* a fault in 'continuity', I hadn't properly 'established' this or that. I would forget momentarily the lesson which I had learned as a film critic – that to 'establish' something is almost invariably wrong and that 'continuity' is often the enemy of life.* A secretary sat by Mr Selznick's side with her pencil poised. When I was on the point of agreement Carol Reed would quickly interrupt – 'Graham and I will think about it.'

There was one conference which I remember in particular because it was the last before we were due to return to England. The secretary had made forty pages of notes by this time, but she had been unable to record one definite concession on our side. The conference began as usual about 10.30 p.m. and finished after 4 a.m. Always by the time we reached Santa Monica dawn would be touching the Pacific.

* Jean Cocteau has even argued that the mistakes of a continuity girl belonged to the unconscious poetry of a film.

'There's something I don't understand in this script, Graham. Why the hell does Harry Lime. . . ?' He described some extraordinary action on Lime's part.

'But he doesn't,' I said.

Mr Selznick looked at me for a moment in silent amazement.

'Christ, boys,' he said, 'I'm thinking of a different script.'

He lay down on his sofa and crunched a Benzedrine. In ten minutes he was as fresh as ever, unlike ourselves.

I look back on David Selznick now with affection. The forty pages of notes remained unopened on Reed's files, and since the film proved a success, I suspect Selznick forgot that the criticisms had ever been made. Indeed, when next I was in New York he invited me to lunch to discuss a project. He said, 'Graham, I've got a great idea for a film. It's just made for you.'

I had been careful on this occasion not to take a third Martini.

'The Life of St Mary Magdalene,' he said.

'I'm sorry,' I said, 'no. It's not really in my line.'

He didn't try to argue. 'I have another idea,' he said. 'It will appeal to you as a Catholic. You know how next year they have what's called the Holy Year in Rome. Well, I want to make a picture called The Unholy Year. It will show all the commercial rackets that go on, the crooks . . .'

'An interesting notion,' I said.

'We'll shoot it in the Vatican.'

'I doubt if they will give you permission for that.'

'Oh sure they will,' he said. 'You see we'll write in one Good Character.'

(I am reminded by this story of another memorable lunch in a suite at the Dorchester when Mr Sam Zimbalist asked me if I would revise the last part of a script which had been prepared for a remake of *Ben Hur*. 'You see,' he said, 'we find a sort of anti-climax after the Crucifixion.')

Those indeed were the days. I little knew that the reign of Kubla Khan was nearly over and that the Pleasure-Dome would soon be converted into an enormous Bingo hall, which would provide quite other dreams to housewives than had the Odeons and the Empires. I had regretted the silent films when the talkies moved in and I had regretted black and white when Technicolor washed across the screen. So today, watching the latest socially conscious serious film of Monsieur Godard, I sometimes long for these dead thirties, for Cecil B. de Mille and his Crusaders, for the days when almost anything was likely to happen.

Graham Greene

The Bride of Frankenstein/The Glass Key/No More Ladies/Abyssinia

Poor harmless Mary Shelley, when she dreamed that she was watched by pale, yellow, speculative eyes between the curtains of her bed, set in motion a vast machinery of actors, of sound systems and trick shots and yes-men. It rolls on indefinitely, that first dream and the first elaboration of it in her novel, *Frankenstein*, gathering silliness and solemnity as it goes; presently, I have no doubt, it will be colour-shot and televised; later in the Brave New World to become a smelly. But the one genuine moment of horror, when Mrs Shelley saw the yellow eyes, vanished long ago; and there is nothing in *The Bride of Frankenstein* at the Tivoli to scare a child.

The Bride of Frankenstein: Elsa Lanchester, Colin Clive

This is not Mrs Shelley's dream, but the dream of a committee of film executives who wanted to go one better than Mrs Shelley and let Frankenstein create a second monster from the churchyard refuse, a woman this time, forgetting that the horror of the first creation is quite lost when it is repeated, and that the breeding of monsters can become no more exciting than the breeding of poultry. In a prologue to the film Mrs Shelley tells Byron and her husband, who has been writing poetry rapidly by the fireside, that she has imagined a sequel to her novel. 'To think,' says Byron, 'that this little head contains such horrors.'

But it is unfair to Mrs Shelley to include the old school tie among the horrors in her little head. Baron Frankenstein wears it with his Harris tweeds, and his school crest is embroidered on his dressing-gown. Mr Colin Clive acts the part with a sturdy old Rugbeian flavour ('This heart won't do,' he says to a rather scrubby fag, 'fetch me another'), which was more suitable to *Journey's End* than a Gothic romance. This is a pompous, badly acted film, full of absurd anachronisms and inconsistencies. It owes its one moment of excitement less to its director than to the strange electric beauty of Miss Elsa Lanchester as Frankenstein's second monster. Her scared vivid face, like the salamander of Mr De La Mare's poem, her bush of hardly human hair, might really have been created by means of the storm-swept kites and the lightning flash.

It has been a week, as far as fiction is concerned, of the second-rate and the transient. *The Glass Key*, at the Plaza, unimaginatively gangster, and *No More Ladies*, at the Empire, slickly 'problem', though brightened by the acting of Mr Charles Ruggles, have come and gone and call for no comment. The best film in London is *Abyssinia* at the Rialto, the finest travel film I have seen, made by a Swiss expedition and explained in an admirably plain commentary. Here is the last medieval State in all its squalor (the flies swarming round the eyes and nostrils as though they were so much exposed meat in a butcher's shop), its dignity (the white-robed noblemen flowing into the capital followed by their armed retainers, the caged symbolic lions, and the Lion of Judah himself, his dark cramped dignity, his air of a thousand years of breeding), its democratic justice (the little courts by the roadside, on the railway track; the debtor and creditor chained together; the murderers led off to execution by the relatives of the murdered). This film, alas, may prove the last record of independent Abyssinia. It leaves you with a vivid sense of something very old, very dusty, very cruel, but something dignified in its dirt and popular in its tyranny and perhaps more worth preserving than the bright slick streamlined civilization which threatens it. I don't refer particularly to Italy, but to the whole tone of a time whose popular art is on the level of *The Bride of Frankenstein*.   *The Spectator*, 5 July 1935

The Bride of Frankenstein (USA, Universal, 1935). Director: James Whale. Boris Karloff, Colin Clive, Valerie Hobson, Elsa Lanchester, Ernest Thesiger, Una O'Connor.
The Glass Key (USA, Paramount, 1935). Based on the novel by Dashiell Hammett. Director: Frank Tuttle. Edward Arnold, George Raft.
No More Ladies (USA, M-G-M, 1935). Director: Edward H. Griffith. Joan Crawford, Robert Montgomery, Charles Ruggles, Franchot Tone, Edna May Oliver.
Abyssinia (Switzerland, Praesens Film, 1935). Director: Walter Mittelholtzer.

St Petersburg/Paris Love Song/The Phantom Light

A new Russian film. How exciting it seemed in the days when questions were asked in Parliament, when *The Times* refused to review the Film Society, when pictures banned by the censors were passed by Labour councils and bright, knowing people went to Whitechapel to see the best films. But the old tricks are beginning to pall: the romantic use of scenery, the long whiskers of depraved aristocrats shot from one angle, the short whiskers of simple peasants shot from another. Here again are the satirical photographs of heavy statues, though the Communist cameraman is finding it increasingly difficult to get a new slant on the horses and the emperors. The moral of *St Petersburg*, of course, is just as impeccable as the moral of *Mother*: the poor musician who can't get a hearing in the capital is Good, and the rich insensitive patrons of music are Bad. You can tell how bad they are by their jewels, their busts, the cherubs and the chandeliers and the pictures of naked women. For a Communist is nothing if he is not a Puritan. At the end of the film the poor musician hears his song sung by convicts on their way to Siberia, and knows that he has done something for Russia.

It is a naïve, jerky, sentimental film, sometimes genuinely moving, sometimes absurdly inept. Like most Russian films it is best when it is most savagely satirical, and the scenes in which the rich old patron listens with a scared, covetous appreciation to the new revolutionary tune, and in which the Duke of Baden's violinist catches the dowagers in the boxes and stalls with his mannerisms and little tricky melodies, are admirable. It is the serious Socialist idealism that is embarrassing, the sentimental simplification of human nature, the Dickensian plot. O, we feel inclined to protest, we know that you are on the right side, that your ideals are above reproach, but because you are virtuous, must there be no more cakes and ale?

Paris Love Song is all cakes and ale. You wouldn't think that Mr Milestone, the director, was a Russian, so deftly has he caught the gay, the shameless Lubitsch manner. It is a silly, charming tale of an Italian count who goes up the Eiffel Tower to pretend to commit suicide, and finds at the top a young woman who intends to commit suicide. They agree, of course, to make their lovers jealous, and their lovers come together in the same conspiracy. Mr Milestone has made out of this nonsense something light, enchanting, genuinely fantastic. Miss Mary Ellis's is the best light acting I have seen since Miss Francis appeared in *Trouble in Paradise*. She is lovely to watch and to listen to; she has a beautiful humorous ease. It is a pity that a film a thousand miles away from any human moral standards should have had tagged to its end a dismal sermon on true love and marriage to satisfy the new purity code. Only the cinema is able in its most fantastic moments to give a sense of absurd unreasoning happiness, of a kind of poignant release: you can't catch it in prose: it belongs to Walt Disney, to Clair's voices from the air, and there is one moment in this film when you have it, as the Count scrambles singing across the roofs to his mistress's room; happiness and freedom, nothing really serious, nothing really lasting, a touching of hands, a tuneful miniature love.

A Georgian poet once wrote some dramatic lines about a lighthouse, where, if I remember right, three men had died and six had gone mad. 'Three men alive', it went on, 'on Flannan Isle, Who thought on three men dead.' There was something too about 'A door ajar and an untouched meal And an overtoppled chair.' That roughly is the plot of the English melodrama, *The Phantom Light*. It is an exciting, simple story of wreckers on the Welsh coast. Mr Gordon Harker gives his sure-fire Cockney performance as the new keeper unscared by ghost-stories or by the fate of his predecessors, and there is some lovely use of Welsh scenery. That fine actor, Mr Donald Calthrop, is fobbed off in a small part. Mr Calthrop has seldom been lucky in his parts. There is a concentrated venom in his acting, a soured malicious spirituality, a pitiful damned dog air which puts him in the same rank as Mr Laughton.   *The Spectator*, 12 July 1935

St Petersburg (USSR, Soyuzfilm, 1934). Directors: Grigori Roshal, Vera Stroyeva. B. Dobronrauov, K. Fariassoua. [US title: *Petersburg Nights*.]

Paris Love Song (Paris in Spring) (USA, Paramount, 1935). Director: Lewis Milestone. Mary Ellis, Tullio Carminati, Ida Lupino.
The Phantom Light (GB, Gaumont British, 1935). Director: Michael Powell. Gordon Harker, Binnie Hale, Ian Hunter.

Becky Sharp/Public Hero No. 1/Barcarole

Becky Sharp, the American film version of *Vanity Fair*, is a triumph for colour, for the scarlet cloaks of the officers galloping off under the lamps from the Duchess of Richmond's ball, for the black Napoleonic shadows passing across the white-washed farm, the desolate rush of the dancers streaming away in panic when the guns sound below the horizon. It is absurd, this panic; it isn't true; it isn't as dramatic as the truth, but the winking out of the yellow candle flames, the surge of blue and grey across the dark hall, the windy encroachment of nocturnal colour, give so much delight to the eye that it would be ungrateful to complain of the silly climax in Bath, the indecisive acting of Miss Miriam Hopkins as Becky. The colour is everything here; the process has at last got well away from blurred mauve wind-flowers and Killarney lakes, and admits some lovely gradations, from the bright dresses to the delicately suggested landscapes on the walls. The only complaint I have against Technicolor is that it plays havoc with the women's faces; they all, young and old, have the same healthy weather-beaten skins.

But one must remember that colour has been tried out on the easiest kind of subject; the fancy dress. It would have been harder to produce *Barcarole* in colour, infinitely harder to produce a realistic film like *Public Hero No. 1*. If colour is to be of permanent importance a way must be found to use it realistically, not only as a beautiful decoration. It must be made to contribute to our sense of truth. The machine-gun, the cheap striped tie, the battered Buick and the shabby bar will need a subtler colour sense than the Duchess of Richmond's ball, the girls of Miss Pinkerton's Academy, the Marquess of Steyne's dinner for two. I can't help remembering how bright and new were all the dresses in *Becky Sharp*. Can Technicolor reproduce with the necessary accuracy the suit that has been worn too long, the oily hat?

Public Hero No. 1 is a conventional but exciting film of a police spy's war against gangsters, in which Mr Chester Morris makes a welcome reappearance in a tough melancholy part punctuated with machine-gun bullets. Just as in *G Men*, the realistic subject of 'men on a job' is spoilt by a romantic situation (the spy falls for the gangster's innocent sister). Mr Lionel Barrymore gives one of the best performances of his career as a drunken crook doctor, a pathetic, farcical figure, who bled gin when the police shot him down.

But I prefer the high tragedy mood of *Barcarole*. This film is made all of one piece. It doesn't mix the romantic and the realistic, but is all romance in the Elizabethan, or perhaps only the Rostand, manner. The story doesn't concern you too closely, so that you can leave the theatre feeling fine and sad, as if your human nature had been paid a very pretty compliment. You have had a taste, between the *News of the Week* and the *Silly Symphony*, of the Soul, Love, the Point of Honour, before the lights go on and the second house streams up the aisle, of Jealousy, Sacrifice, great abstract eternal issues, or perhaps only of ingenious artificial situations. A young reckless womanizer is trapped one night at his club into a bet with a Mexican that he will win his wife before morning. There will be a duel in any case: if he loses his bet the Mexican will fire first. The young man falls in love and rather than cheapen

Becky Sharp: Cedric Hardwicke, Miriam Hopkins

the woman pretends that he has lost the bet. The unity of a few hours of the Venetian night is beautifully preserved: the tenderness and the despair grow under your eyes in the dance-hall, in the horrible little wine-shop by the canal, as time ticks by. But the film owes most to the acting of Pierre Richard Willm as the lover, with his sharp, handsome young-old face (he makes death real, as he sweats there in the wine-shop in fear of what he's recklessly pledged himself to suffer), of Edwige Feuillère as the gentle cat-like girl, and Roger Karl as Zubaran, the tortured husband with the psychic sense which has enabled him to read a violent end on the young man's features.   *The Spectator*, 19 July 1935

Becky Sharp (USA, Pioneer Pictures, 1935). Director: Rouben Mamoulian. Miriam Hopkins, Cedric Hardwicke, Nigel Bruce, Frances Dee, Alan Mowbray, Alison Skipworth, Billie Burke.
Public Hero No. 1 (USA, M-G-M, 1934). Director: J. Walter Ruben. Lionel Barrymore, Jean Arthur, Chester Morris, Joseph Calleia.
Barcarole (Germany, Ufa, 1934). Director: Gerhard Lamprecht. Pierre Richard Willm, Edwige Feuillère, Roger Karl.

The Voice of Britain/Mimi

The superb complacency of the BBC was never more delightfully parodied than in the title of the official film made by Mr John Grierson and the GPO Film Unit: *The Voice of Britain*. It is certainly the film of the month if not of the year; but I doubt if the BBC realize the devastating nature of Mr Grierson's amusing and sometimes beautiful film, the satirical background to these acres of dynamos, the tall steel towers, the conferences and contracts, the enormous staff and the rigid technique of a Kremlin which should be sufficient to govern a nation and is all directed to this end: Miss Nina Mae McKinney singing 'Dinah', Henry Hall's Dance Orchestra playing 'Piccadilly Riot', a spot of pleasure, a spot of dubious education, and a spot, just a spot, of culture when Mr Adrian Boult conducts the Fifth Symphony.
     This was the most cynical moment of a witty film: Mr Adrian Boult agonizing above his baton, and then his audience – a man turning the pages of his book beside the loud-speaker, a man eating his dinner, nobody giving more than his unconscious mind to Beethoven's music. The picture too of the cramped suburban parlour, the man with his paper, the woman with her sewing, the child at his homework, while 'Piccadilly Riot' reverberates noisily back and forth across the potted plant between flowered wallpaper and flowered wallpaper is even more memorable than the lovely shots of sea and sky and such lyric passages as Mr Chesterton driving gently like a sea-lion through the little tank-like studios. For this is the BBC's chief contribution to man's life: noise while he eats and reads and talks. I wish Mr Grierson had included a few shots from the damper tropics where the noise of the Empire programmes is not disguised at all as entertainment or education, but is just plain wails and windy blasts from instruments hopelessly beaten by atmospherics. At enormous expense from its steel pylon at Daventry the BBC supplies din with the drinks at sundown.
     James once wrote of *La Dame aux Camélias*: 'The play has been blown about the world at a fearful rate, but it has never lost its happy juvenility, a charm that nothing can vulgarize. It is all champagne and tears – fresh perversity, fresh credulity, fresh passion, fresh pain.' Something of the same quality belongs to *La Vie de Bohème*. It too has been blown about the world and the studios at a fearful rate, and there still seems to me to linger in this slow decorative English version a little of the happy juvenility. *Mimi* owes much to Miss Doris Zinkeisen's dresses and

to the acting of Mr Douglas Fairbanks Junior, more perhaps than to Miss Gertrude Lawrence's pinched out-of-place charm, but even without them I would have enjoyed the sense of a period when you had to load your dice to win your tears, when the heroine must die quite fortuitously of consumption on the night of her lover's success. What safety, prosperity, happiness must have been theirs, one exclaims, for them to have taken such an innocent delight in turning the screw of human misery. *The Spectator*, 2 August 1935

The Voice of Britain (GB, GPO Film Unit for BBC, 1935). Director: John Grierson.
Mimi (GB, British International, 1935). Director: Paul L. Stein. Douglas Fairbanks Jr, Gertrude Lawrence, Richard Bird.

The Trunk Mystery/Hands of Orlac/Look Up and Laugh/The Memory Expert

Every now and then Hollywood produces without any blast of publicity a comedy of astonishing intelligence and finish. *The Trunk Mystery* is one of these: it ought to take its place immediately with the classics. A young Wyoming farmer (Mr Franchot Tone), who has come to New York in the hope of finding a brunette to marry, happens to look through the connecting door of his hotel room and sees a dead body on the floor. By the time the manager has been found, the body has disappeared and no one will admit that he can have seen it. With the help of a telephone girl, played in her best silly boy-crazy way by Miss Una Merkel, he sets out to solve the mystery. There *is* a body, death is somewhere in the background, but what matters is the witty dialogue, the quick intelligent acting of Mr Tone and Miss Merkel, who juggle death so expertly and amusingly between them. One is used to death as a horror, one is used to it as a cypher (the body found stabbed in the library in Chapter One): death as a joke is less familiar; it bathes the film in an atmosphere fantastic, daring and pleasantly heartless.

Hands of Orlac is one of those horror films that Mr Shortt,* the head of that curious body of film censors rumoured to consist of retired Army officers and elderly ladies of no occupation, has declared his intention of banning. I don't quite know why. If a horror film is bad, as *The Bride of Frankenstein* was bad, it isn't horrible at all and may be quite a good joke; if it is a good film, why should Mr Shortt narrow so puritanically the scope of an art? Can we no longer enjoy with clear consciences the stories of Dr M. R. James? It may be sexual perversity which leads us to sneak *The Turn of the Screw* out of a locked drawer, when all the house is abed, but must our pet vice be denied all satisfaction? Guiltily I admit to liking *Hands of Orlac* because it *did* make me shudder a little when Dr Gogol grafted the hands of a guillotined murderer on to the smashed stumps of Orlac, the great pianist whose hands had been destroyed in a railway accident, and because Herr Karl Freund's romantic direction did 'put across' the agreeable little tale of how the dead murderer's fingers retained a life of their own, the gift of knife-throwing, an inclination to murder. It would have been a thousand pities, too, if Mr Shortt's rigid good taste had prevented us enjoying the performance of Mr Peter Lorre as Dr Gogol. Mr Lorre, with every physical handicap, can convince you of the good-ness, the starved tenderness, of his vice-entangled souls. Those marbly pupils in the pasty spherical face are like the eye-pieces of a microscope through which you can see laid flat on the slide the entangled mind of a man: love and lust, nobility and perversity, hatred of itself and despair jumping out at you from the jelly.

* The Rt Hon. Edward Shortt, then Chairman of the British Board of Film Censors.

The Trunk Mystery: Franchot Tone

Mr J. B. Priestley is an admirable writer of light films. The Lancashire farces he constructs for Miss Gracie Fields have a pleasant local flavour, their plots are genuinely provincial. In *Look Up and Laugh*, Miss Fields, an actress on holiday, leads the stallholders of an old market in a lively battle against the local council and the owner of a big store who threatens to close the market down. One doesn't demand a high standard of realism in a farce, but *Look Up and Laugh* is distinguished from *The Memory Expert*, a slow worthy comedy in the same programme with Mr W. C. Fields, by the sense that a man's observation and experience, as well as his invention, has gone to its making. *The Spectator*, 9 August 1935

The Trunk Mystery (*One New York Night*) (USA, M-G-M, 1935). Director: Jack Conway. Franchot Tone, Una Merkel.
Hands of Orlac (*Mad Love*) (USA, M-G-M, 1935). Director: Karl Freund. Peter Lorre, Frances Drake, Colin Clive.

Hands of Orlac: Frances Drake, Peter Lorre

Look Up and Laugh (GB, Associated Talking Pictures, 1935). Director: Basil Dean. Gracie Fields.
The Memory Expert (*The Man on the Flying Trapeze*) (USA, Paramount, 1935). Director: Clyde Bruckman. W. C. Fields, Mary Brian, Kathleen Howard, Walter Brennan.

Der Schimmelreiter/Star of Midnight

Der Schimmelreiter is a film which can be confidently recommended to the middle-aged; its dignified progress demands no quickness of the cinematic sense. Solidly constructed and excellently photographed, it reminded me of the ponderous, talented novels of Sigrid Undset. It cannot meet such a film as *Star of Midnight* on equal terms because it represents a quite different conception of art, sailing majestically like an Armada galleon through the fleet of bright, agile, intelligent films, sniped at and harassed and unable to reply.

The story is of Friesland peasant-farmers, some time during the last century, and the continual threat of the sea. You watch them at their feasts, their weddings and their funerals; they have the grossness and dignity of their animals; they are more genuine and less self-conscious than the characters of *Man of Aran*, which exploited the same kind of primitive life at the edge of land. Hauke, a farm-hand, who had gained the richest farm by marriage, was elected to the honour and responsibility of keeping the dikes in order. The farmers had become slack, and Hauke was determined to show that he deserved his position. When he planned a new dike to reclaim the foreshore, they opposed him with their inertia and their superstition. The moral is not clear, for to build the new dike Hauke neglected the old; in the autumn storms the waves swept in and he saved the village only by cutting his own seawall and drowning himself and his farm. There was something about floods which appealed to the Victorian temperament (only Herr Freud could explain why), not the gigantic floods of China or the Mississippi, but little domestic floods which gave opportunities for sacrifice and the ringing of church bells and drenched golden hair. There is something of this atmosphere about *Der Schimmelreiter*; it takes one back to *The Mill on the Floss*, to *High Tide on the Coast of Lincolnshire*, and *The Sands of Dee*; the wind that blows so sombrely, banking the clouds over these drab Friesian fields, has shaken the windows of many Victorian parsonages. The moral, as I say, is confused, as confused as the religious beliefs of Charles Kingsley, but that only adds to the period flavour: you get a vague impression behind the poverty, the rigour of life and the greedy feasting, of nobility and profundity.

But of a film one expects something more agile: a speed which cannot be attained on the stage or in a novel. *Star of Midnight*, a light, quick, sophisticated comedy, in which Miss Ginger Rogers takes Miss Myrna Loy's place as Mr William Powell's partner, has no content which one would trouble to read in a novel or to praise in a play. It is all suavity and amusement, pistol-shots and cocktails; but I am uncertain whether the Victorian profundity of the German film has any more to offer, that there is really more behind the whiskers than behind the polish. And this genre of humorous detective films, *Star of Midnight*, *The Trunk Mystery*, *The Thin Man*, has no superiors in streamlined craftsmanship.

The Spectator, 16 August 1935

Der Schimmelreiter (Germany, R. Fritsch-Tonfilm, 1934). Director: Curt Oertel. Mathias Wieman, Marianne Hoppe, Eduard von Winterstein.
Star of Midnight (USA, RKO, 1935). Director: Stephen Roberts. William Powell, Ginger Rogers.

Where's George?/The Great God Gold/Boys Will Be Boys/The Murder Man

This week's Grim Subject is Fun: that boisterous national form of humour which can be traced up from the bear-pit by way of the Shakespearian clowns, Fielding, Hood, Dickens, until its sentimental culmination in popular rough-diamond prose, a clatter of beer-mugs on a bar, a refined belch or two (fun has grown progressively more refined since Fielding's day), the sense of good companionship.

This is the class to which *Where's George?* naturally belongs: the story of a hen-pecked husband in a Yorkshire town whose only friend was a dumb animal until all the good fellows who formed the local Rugger team persuaded him to break from home, play in the great match and win for the team. But a curious thing has happened: into this badly acted and carelessly directed film a real actor has been introduced, Mr Sydney Howard, and, comic actor though he is, he bursts like a realist through its unrealities. He can do very little with the stale gags they have given him; even the Rugger game, which might have been thought foolproof, was made as tame as table tennis; what emerges is a character of devastating pathos: Mr Howard, faintly episcopal, in endless difficulties with his feet and hands, minding the kettle in the little cramped kitchen. We are whipped back, past the

Where's George?: Sydney Howard

beer-drinkers and the punsters and the picaresque, to the bear-ring itself which began it all, to see the awkward beast driven in circles. But it isn't easy any longer to laugh at the bears and cheer the dogs on.

In the same programme is an excellent American melodrama of the depression, *The Great God Gold*, a story of the shady business racketeers who make money out of receiverships as the big firms fail. There are no stars, but a team of very able actors reproduce with delightful vividness the *bonhomie*, the plate-glass manner, the annihilating lack of trust. Even the hats have been carefully chosen: the crookeder the deal, the more flowing the brim.

Boys Will Be Boys, an adaptation of Beachcomber's chronicles of Narkover, is very amusing. Mr Shortt has found this realistic study of our public schools too subversive for a Universal Certificate. Mr Will Hay as Dr Alec Smart, appointed Headmaster on the strength of a forged testimonial, is competent, but the finest performance is that of Mr Claude Dampier as the half-witted Second Master whose uncle, the Chairman of the Governors, stops at nothing, not even at a false accusation of theft, to make room for his nephew's advancement. Realistic may perhaps seem not quite the right word to describe a film which ends magnificently in a struggle between the Rugger teams of past and present Narkovians for the possession of a ball containing Lady Dorking's diamond necklace. But Beach-comber in his fantasy of a school of crooks run by crooks has only removed the peculiar morality of the public schools just a little further from the standards accepted outside. It bears the same relation to truth as *Candide*. A free fantastic mind has been given just so many facts to play with; nothing is added or subtracted; but the bricks have been rearranged. The school cloisters particularly appealed to me with their tablets to old Narkovians who had passed successfully into gaol. The criminal features of the boys were excellently chosen, and the only jarring element in the quite Gallic consistency of the film was the slight element of good nature in the boys' gang warfare.

The Murder Man shows the life of the finished Narkovian. A business crook is murdered and the guilt of the crime is fastened on his equally dishonest partner. The man is innocent; and the interest of the film lies in the character of the crime reporter whose evidence is sending him to the chair. There is no more reliable actor on the screen today than Mr Spencer Tracy. His acting of these hard-drinking, saddened, humorous parts is as certain as a mathematical formula, but this film gives him the chance, in a grimly moral scene with the innocent man he has hunted down, of showing the reserve of power behind the ease.

The Spectator, 23 August 1935

Where's George? (GB, British & Dominions, 1935). Director: Jack Raymond. Sydney Howard.
The Great God Gold (USA, Monogram, 1935). Director: Arthur Lubin. Sidney Blackmer, Martha Sleeper.
Boys Will Be Boys (GB, Gaumont British, 1935). Director: William Beaudine. Will Hay, Claude Dampier, Gordon Harker, Jimmy Hanley.
The Murder Man (USA, M-G-M, 1935). Director: Tim Whelan. Spencer Tracy, Virginia Bruce, Lionel Atwill.

The Crusades

Mr Cecil de Mille's evangelical films are the nearest equivalent today to the glossy German colour prints which sometimes decorated mid-Victorian Bibles. There is the same complete lack of a period sense, the same stuffy horsehair atmosphere of beards and whiskers, and, their best quality, a childlike eye for details which enabled one to spend so many happy minutes spying a new lamb among the rocks, an un-obtrusive dove or a mislaid shepherd. As the great drawbridge falls from the besieger's tower on to the walls of Acre, you cannot help counting the little cluster of spent arrows quivering under the falling block; when Richard of England takes the Cross from the hairy hermit, the camera, moving its eye down the castle walls, stays on a couple of pigeons nesting in a coign of masonry. But one chiefly enjoys in Mr de Mille's films their great set-pieces; he handles, as no other director can, an army of extras. It is not a mere matter of spending money. The cavalry charge out-side Jerusalem, the storming of Acre: these are scenes of real executive genius. No clanking of tin swords here, but a quite horrifying sense of reality, as the huge vats tip the burning oil down on to the agonized faces of the men on the storming-

The Crusades: Loretta Young, Henry Wilcoxon

ladders, or when the riders meet at full gallop in the plain with a shock which jars you in the stalls.

But these moments occupy perhaps twenty minutes of a very long film. For the rest of the time we must be content with a little quiet fun at the expense of Clio, not always clean fun, although Mr Shortt has given this film the Universal Certificate he denied to *Boys Will Be Boys*. Richard Cœur-de-Lion, in Mr de Mille's pious and Protestant eyes, closely resembled those honest simple young rowing-men who feel that there's something wrong about sex. Richard took the Cross rather than marry Alice of France, and when the King of Navarre forced him at Marseille to marry his daughter (the alternative was to let his army starve), he merely sent his sword to the wedding ceremony, which was oddly enough carried out in English by an Anglican – or possibly American Episcopalian – clergyman in the words of the Book of Common Prayer. There is, indeed, in spite of the subject, nothing Romish about this film, which has the air of having been written by the Oxford Group. Only when his wife had been captured by Saladin did Richard allow himself to pray, but he found prayer as effective as did the author of *For Sinners Only*, and his wife, whom he had learnt to love, was restored to him. Richard shyly confessed, 'Last night ... last night ...', and Berengaria encouraged him with bright tenderness, 'You prayed?' But Richard wouldn't go quite as far as that. 'I begged,' he said, 'I begged ...', as the great Buchman heart melted at last and Berengaria slid to dry-dock in his arms.

Neither of the two principal players, Miss Loretta Young and Mr Henry Wilcoxon, really gets a chance in this film. The programme says all there is to be said about them. Mr Wilcoxon is 'six feet two inches tall, weighs 190 pounds. He was nicknamed "Biff" as a child.' Miss Young 'is five feet three and weighs 105 pounds'. The information is not as irrelevant as it sounds, for the acting can roughly be judged in terms of weight. Mr Wilcoxon leads over the hairy hermit, played by Mr C. Aubrey Smith, by six pounds, and Miss Katherine de Mille, who has an agreeably medieval face, as Alice of France beats Miss Young by ten pounds. (To quote the programme again. 'She avoids starches, sugars and fats; eats all greens and only enough meat to get the necessary proteins.')

As for the other Groupers, there was a delicious moment when I thought the Earl of Leicester said 'Aye, Colonel', to Richard when he was told to attack, but I think the din before Acre may have confused my ears. The Earl was made up distractingly to resemble Mr George Moore. He had one of the few English names in a finely orchestrated cast which included Sven-Hugo Borg, Fred Malatesta, Vallejo Gantner, Paul Sotoff, Hans von Twardowski, and the name I liked best, Pedro de Cordoba. One had to judge these actors by their names as their weights were not given.   *The Spectator*, 30 August 1935

The Crusades (USA, Paramount, 1935). Director: Cecil B. de Mille. Henry Wilcoxon, Loretta Young, Katherine de Mille, C. Aubrey Smith, Ian Keith, Joseph Schildkraut, Alan Hale.

Dood Wasser/Me and Marlborough

Mr Alexander Korda's company, London Film Productions, has lately started a 'national investigation' in the course of which the naïve question is asked, 'Do you prefer films that are purely entertainment, or films with a serious message?' In the childlike eyes of the great film executives *Dood Wasser*, I suppose, would be classed with the serious messages (though what this one is it might be hard to say), while

Me and Marlborough, one of the silliest films yet produced in this country, would be regarded as 'purely entertainment' (though in what the entertainment consists it would be harder still to discover). It may be thought very unlikely that many film magnates would be able to think of 'a serious message', but, if it may prevent more films of the *Me and Marlborough* type being produced, let us vote against entertainment and bear with fortitude the triangles, the divorce cases, the Great Marriage Problems of our celluloid Bjørnstjerne Bjørnsons. If by some happy accident they produce one film as exciting and genuinely entertaining as *Dood Wasser*, we shall be amply justified.

Dood Wasser is a story of the reclamation of the Zuyderzee and the opposition of the Vollendam fishermen, who see their catches getting yearly smaller. Its opening, a documentary prologue which presents the reclamation without the human factor, is an exciting piece of pure cinema. The geometrical instruments, the blueprints, maps and diagrams, the dance of numerals, the sad triumphant voice singing behind the figures, behind the diagrams of cranes and dredges: this is something neither the stage nor prose can present. It reminded me, in its dramatization of statistics, of Mr Eliot's 'Triumphal March' with its catalogue of armaments:

> 28,000 trench mortars,
> 53,000 field and heavy guns,
> I cannot tell how many projectiles, mines and fuses. . . .

It is very seldom that the cinema has made this lyrical use of a human voice divorced from the singer's image. Certainly it has never been used more effectively even by M. Clair or in the lovely opening to *F.P. 1*, where the aeroplanes dived and turned against a background of chorus and cloud.

The story which followed, exhibiting the human stupidities and the tragic fidelities behind the bare Blue Book report, is produced rather slowly, but it has some of the magnificent drive one felt behind the classic Russian films, behind *Earth* and *The General Line*: no tiresome 'message', but a belief in the importance of a human activity truthfully reported. The old fisherman with the horny tortoise face, who was ready to blow up the new dike rather than become a farmer, is given the importance of a general creed; he represents all the fatal courage, honesty and loyalty that may exist in a stupid brain. The photography is uneven: at moments it is painfully 'arty', deliberately out of focus, but it will be a long while before I forget the boisterous fair, the balloons and masks and buffoonery, the low roofs of the merry-go-rounds under the low cloudy sky when the deep animal stupidity of the Vollendam fishermen reached its climax.

The title of this Dutch film, of course, is not encouraging, and it may seem a little kill-joy to find more pure entertainment in its slow serious march than in the bright coy antics of Miss Cicely Courtneidge as a woman who disguises herself in men's clothes in order to follow her husband to the wars. She is not an actress who can suggest pathos or romantic love, and though Mr Victor Saville's direction has a smooth well-groomed air, while Mr Tom Walls plays Marlborough with dignity, I found myself too embarrassed by Miss Courtneidge's facial contortions to appreciate their share. Miss Courtneidge is used to throwing her effects to the back row of a theatre gallery, and the camera is not kind to her exaggerations.

The Spectator, 6 September 1935

Dood Wasser (Holland, Nederlandsche Filmgemeenschap, 1934). Director: Gerard Rutten. Jan Musch, Teo de Maal, Betsy Ranucci-Beckman, Arnold Marle.
Me and Marlborough (GB, Gaumont British, 1935). Director: Victor Saville. Cicely Courtneidge, Tom Walls.

September 1935

On Wings of Song/Peg of Old Drury/Break of Hearts

I'm afraid we are in for a run of films presenting the Loves of the Artistes. This week we have a singer's love-story, an actress's love-story, a musician's love-story. The great film executives have decided that Art is trumps (alas! that the final 'e' which so neatly distinguishes the artiste from the artist cannot be tacked on to that word Art). We have in one film extracts from *La Bohème*, in another speeches from Shakespeare, in the third a few minutes of *Tristan*. Personally, I preferred to any of these snippets the sight of Miss Anna Neagle in breeches and a three-cornered hat.

There is something rather pompous about the appearance of Miss Grace Moore on the screen: the profound silence of an audience that has never found it necessary to cease its chatter before fine direction or fine acting; the immense queues of elderly ladies in peasant blouses and little jackets who have slipped away from their art pottery to see something they really can enjoy; the stuffy reverence like that of a pit before a Bernard Shaw play. Miss Moore, of course, has a lovely voice and a figure unlike the usual *prima donna*'s, but her acting is quite undistinguished. The success of her films as films and not as potted operatic extracts has so far been the success of her leading men. Mr Tullio Carminati gave that dull and worthy film *One Night of Love* the little sparkle it possessed, and now Mr Leo Carillo takes all the honours in *On Wings of Song* as the cheap, vulgar, pathetic little Italian racketeer who ruins himself for love of music and love of the singer and nearly throws his life away before a gunman's automatic rather than miss her appearance at the Metropolitan. I seem to remember Mr Carillo before in small gangster parts; here he gives one of the finest performances of the year: to my mind one of the three finest performances, to be remembered with Mr Charles Laughton as Ruggles of Red Gap and with Mr Richard Barthelmess in *Four Hours to Kill*.

Neither Sir Cedric Hardwicke's smooth, well-bred playing of Garrick, nor Miss Anna Neagle's lively Peg Woffington is of that high standard, though I never tired of Miss Neagle's physical appearance, which was as pretty as a Chelsea figure. The whole film indeed is very pretty, with the sentiment neatly handled. But prettiness is a quality one wants, if at all, in small quantities. One wonders why the names Peg Woffington and Garrick have been attached to these characters; there is, of course, no historical truth to be found anywhere in the deft, neat tale. Peg Woffington lived before the days when 'the mummer' (to quote George Moore) 'grew ashamed of his hose and longed for a silk hat, a villa, and above all a visit from the parson'. She shares with Mrs Barry the distinction of having been one of our most sexually promiscuous actresses; *she* didn't die gracefully as the curtain fell on *As You Like It*; *she* didn't dream of domestic love with Garrick somewhere in Surrey. She had more life, more pleasing commonness one suspects, than this too sweet, too roguish figurine. But I am ungrateful: I have seen few things more attractive than Miss Neagle in breeches.

And so to the loves of the great orchestral conductor (Mr Charles Boyer) and the budding, the dewy composer (Miss Katharine Hepburn). These are both actors of very great talent, Mr Boyer condemned by some grim Dante of a film executive to suffer and be redeemed by love and suffer again in endless circles, Miss Hepburn to be so young, unsophisticated, idealistic, so very, very Barrie. Mr Boyer in *Break of Hearts* is an artistic philanderer, a character one doesn't associate with great

On Wings of Song: Leo Carillo, Grace Moore

Peg of Old Drury: Anna Neagle

conductors so readily as with crooners, who falls in love and marries and is faithless, loses his wife and loves her and takes to drink and is saved by her love. These two actors are talented enough to keep some of our interest even in a story of this kind: indeed, Miss Hepburn always makes her young women quite horrifyingly lifelike with their girlish intuitions, their intensity, their ideals which destroy the edge of human pleasure. *The Spectator*, 13 September 1935

On Wings of Song (*Love Me Forever*) (USA, Columbia, 1935). Director: Victor Schertzinger. Grace Moore, Leo Carillo, Michael Bartlett.
Peg of Old Drury (GB, British & Dominions, 1935). Director: Herbert Wilcox. Anna Neagle, Cedric Hardwicke.
Break of Hearts (USA, RKO, 1935). Director: Phillip Moeller. Katharine Hepburn, Charles Boyer, John Beal.

The Black Room

Mr Boris Karloff has been allowed to act at last. Like the late Lon Chaney, he reached stardom with the sole assistance of the make-up man. Any face would have done as well on a big body, and any actor could have produced the short barks and guttural rumbles, the stiff, stuffed sawdust gestures, which was all his parts required of him. A Karloff scenario must have made curious reading. Were those grunts phonetically expressed? One pictures the Karloff arriving in his luxurious car for a hard day's grunting at the studio, the hasty study of the part in the dressing-room while one eye is blacked out and all his teeth disappear, the dreadful moment when the distinguished actor forgets his part, whether this time he has to bark or rumble, at last the stately gollywog entrance under the lights. . . . But in *The Raven* Mr Karloff was allowed a few minutes of ordinary speech before his face was mutilated and his tongue paralysed and we discovered that he had an expressive voice and a sense of pathos. In *The Black Room* he is given a long speaking part at last.

I liked this wildly artificial film, in which Karloff acts both a wicked central European count and his virtuous, cultured twin of the Byronic period. A curse rests on the family to the effect that the younger twin will kill the elder in 'the black room' of the castle. The room is bricked up by their father, but there is a secret entrance known to the elder brother, the wicked Count, who lives in the traditional atmosphere of boarhounds and wenches (when he finishes with a girl he flings her body down a kind of *oubliette* in the black room). At last, to escape the wrath of the peasants and the curse as well, he murders his younger brother, who is distinguished from him physically by a paralysed arm, and takes his place. The story follows a natural Gothic course, the deception is discovered at the altar when he is about to marry the young, pale, 'proper' heroine, he is pursued to the castle by the enraged peasants, takes refuge in the black room and is knocked into the pit by his brother's dog, falling on the dagger which sticks up through the rotting corpse. Karloff is not quite at ease with virtue, suavity and good looks, but he gives a very spirited performance as the wicked Count and carries the whole film, so far as acting is concerned, on his own shoulders.

The direction is good: it has caught, as Mr James Whale never did with *Frankenstein*, the genuine Gothic note. Mrs Radcliffe would not have been ashamed of this absurd and exciting film, of the bones in the *oubliette*, the scene at the altar when the dog leaps and the paralysed arm comes to life in self-defence, of the Count's wild drive back to the castle, the lashing whip, the rearing horses, the

The Black Room: Boris Karloff

rocketing coach, the strange valley of rocks with its leaning cross and neglected Christ, the graveyard with its owls and ivy. There is much more historical sense in this film than in any of what Miss Lejeune calls, with curious lack of humour, the 'scholarly' works of Mr Korda. A whole literary period comes to life: Wyatt might be raising the huge tower of Fonthill, Monk Lewis writing of the false, fair Imogine ·and her ghostly betrothed (another part for Karloff):

> His vizor was closed, and gigantic his height;
>   His armour was sable to view;
> All pleasure and laughter were hush'd at his sight;
> The dogs, as they eyed him, drew back in affright;
>   The lights in the chamber burnt blue!

The Spectator, 20 September 1935

The Black Room (USA, Columbia, 1935). Director: Roy William Neill. Boris Karloff, Katherine de Mille, Marian Marsh, Alan Mowbray, Thurston Hall.

Jazz Comedy/Two for Tonight

Jazz Comedy is the best thing that has happened to the cinema since René Clair made *The Italian Straw Hat*. Alexandrov, who has been awarded a Soviet Order for his direction, has produced, just as Clair did then, out of the smallest resources and apparently with poor-quality film, a picture of almost ecstatic happiness. It is a freer happiness than Clair's, rougher, less sophisticated: behind Clair's films is always a sharp, smooth, satirical Gallic air, the faintest odour of the most expensive hair-oil; you never get further away from Paris than the dry herbage outside the gramophone factory where the ex-convict listened to the song from the horn of a convolvulus.

But Alexandrov's story of a shepherd who was mistaken by a rich snobbish woman for a famous conductor and who later, after a series of wild accidents and coincidences, became the head of a jazz orchestra in Moscow, has a simple irrelevance quite unlike Clair's tight expert tales. The opening sequence, when the shepherd leads out his flocks and herds, of sheep and goats and cows and pigs, to graze by the seashore, is the most lovely a moving camera has yet achieved, as it follows him with the quickness of his long stride over hills and rocks, streams and verandas, while he sings, knocking the tune out on the slats of a bridge or the bars of a paling. And if something of the kind has been done before, in *Congress Dances* and Walt Disney's cartoons, to convey a sense of lyrical happiness, this at any rate is completely original: Alexandrov's use of a moving camera to convey the grotesque in his long panorama of a crowded bathing beach. The wealthy woman in pyjamas swaying her munificent hips along the shore in pursuit of the famous conductor is followed by the camera behind a close-up frieze of enlarged feet stuck out towards the lens, of fat thighs, enormous backs, a caricature of ugly humanity exposing pieces of itself like butcher's joints in the sun.

I have no wish to criticize this film, but simply to rejoice in its wildness, its grotesqueness, its light, taking tunes, a sense of good living that owes nothing to champagne or women's clothes. If Alexandrov sometimes seems to dwell too long on an incident, at least no one has shown a richer comic invention, for, like Clair and Chaplin, this director has worked to his own scenario; it is to Alexandrov we owe the conception as well as the execution of the magnificent sequences when the shepherd pipes to the rich woman's guests and the notes bring all his animals trampling out of their enclosure, up the steps of the hotel, in at the windows, to eat and drink the feast laid out in honour of the conductor. The tottering tipsy bull, with the dignity and lack of humour of a King's Bench judge, who is laid to sleep in the woman's bed, and the pig who lies down in a dish and the drunken guest who tries to carve it belong to a fantasy more robust than Clair's.

This is genuine cinema: few English titles are needed: there is action all the time, a minimum of speech. *Two for Tonight* depends on dialogue. It is a very amusing and well-written entertainment; Mr Bing Crosby is attractively commonplace among the stars; Miss Mary Boland and Mr Lynne Overman are two of the most reliable players. . . . So this picture forces one to write, in terms of actors and authorship. The camera has played a very small part in the entertainment. Even a spirited battle in a restaurant with soda-water siphons could have been transferred at a cost to the stage; and the studies of a theatrical magnate, of an Austrian producer turned manservant, of a madman with a passion for noughts and crosses would have been even more amusing behind footlights.

Sometimes one is inclined to believe that characters can all be left to the stage; the cinema generalizes. It is not one man called Kostia who sings his way through *Jazz Comedy*, but all brave, coarse and awkward simplicity.

The Spectator, 27 September 1935

Jazz Comedy (USSR, Mosfilm, 1934). Director: Grigori Alexandrov. Leonid Utyosov, Lubov Orlova, Maria Strelkova, Yelena Tyapkina.
Two for Tonight (USA, Paramount, 1935). Director: Frank Tuttle. Bing Crosby, Mary Boland, Lynne Overman.

Song of Ceylon

Dog, I suppose, ought not to eat dog, otherwise I should be inclined to cast a malicious eye towards my fellow film-reviewers who have gone into such curious Gothic attitudes of reverence before what must be one of the worst films of the year, *The Dark Angel*, writing of 'classic tragedy' and the 'great' acting of Miss Merle Oberon. It is the ballyhoo, of course, which has done it: the advance gossip and the advertisements, the crowds outside the cinema on the opening night, the carefully drilled curiosity as to what Mr Sam Goldwyn had done to Miss Oberon's eyebrows. . . .

Song of Ceylon, on the other hand, made by the GPO Film Unit and directed by Mr Basil Wright, is introduced as a second feature into the Curzon programme with little notice from the ecstatic connoisseurs of classic tragedy, although it is an example to all directors of perfect construction and the perfect application of montage. Perfection is not a word one cares to use, but from the opening sequence of the Ceylon forest, the great revolving fans of palm which fill the screen, this film moves with the air of absolute certainty in its object and assurance in its method.

It is divided into four parts. In the first, *The Buddha*, we watch a long file of pilgrims climb the mountain-side to the huge stone effigies of the god. Here, as a priest strikes a bell, Mr Wright uses one of the loveliest visual metaphors I have ever seen on any screen. The sounding of the bell startles a small bird from its branch, and the camera follows the bird's flight and the notes of the bell across the island, down from the mountain-side, over forest and plain and sea, the vibration of the tiny wings, the fading sound.

The second part, *The Virgin Island*, is transitional, leading us away from the religious theme by way of the ordinary routine of living to industry. In *The Voices of Commerce* the commentary, which has been ingeniously drawn from a seventeenth-century traveller's account of the island, gives place to scraps of business talk. As the natives follow the old ways of farming, climbing the palm trees with a fibre loop, guiding their elephants' foreheads against the trees they have to fell, voices dictate bills of lading, close deals over the telephone, announce through loud-speakers the latest market prices. The last reel, *The Apparel of a God*, returns by way of the gaudy gilded dancers in their devil masks to the huge images on the mountain, to a solitary peasant laying his offering at Buddha's feet, and closes again with the huge revolving leaves, so that all we have seen of devotion and dance and the bird's flight and the gentle communal life of harvest seems something sealed away from us between the fans of foliage. We are left outside with the bills of lading and the loud-speakers.   *The Spectator*, 4 October 1935

Song of Ceylon (GB, Ceylon Tea Propaganda Board, 1935). Director: Basil Wright.

Anna Karenina/The Informer

A new film with Greta Garbo: the event is exciting, of course, but it has very little to do with the art of the cinema. The film does not need great actresses so much as great directors, and it is no reflection on Hollywood to say that no one there knows what to do with Garbo, with her awkward ungainly body, her hollow face strong and rough as an Epstein cast. *Mata Hari, Grand Hotel, The Painted Veil*: these are typical of the slick commercial products to which she has been expected to adapt her powerful personality. The result has generally been unfortunate. Power misapplied is apt to be a little absurd. Garbo's great talent might appear less confined on the stage.

In *Anna Karenina* she has been better served than in most of her films. Guilt and misery and passion, these suit the melancholy grandeur of her voice. Very nearly all her acting is in her voice: watch her among a crowd of other actresses in the mazurka, she is stiff, awkward, bony, rather grotesque among the graceful bodies, the lovely shoulders; but listen to her as she bends over her croquet-ball playing a game with her lover before all the gossips in St Petersburg and you are in the presence of deep authentic pain. The word 'doom' is frequently in the mouths of these characters, but there is no other actress on the screen who would not have made the idea of doom false and preposterous, who would have convinced us, as she does from her first appearance on the Moscow platform, her face emerging from the engine's steam, to the last scene when we watch her brain stagger with the thudding wheels, that she has been driven to her fate.

What can the cinema do with an actress of her quality and kind? The film, if it is to be true to itself, must depend first on picture and movement and only secondarily on dialogue: it is a director's art, neither an author's nor an actor's. The stage technique forced on the other players in *Anna Karenina* by the personality of Greta Garbo, the slowing of the film to allow time for the incredibly lovely voice, the harsh suffering face, to make their points, calls for a standard of acting they cannot meet, with the exception of Mr Basil Rathbone, who as Anna's husband draws an intense bitter portrait of a man living for appearances alone. Mr Fredric March, so satisfactory in ninety-nine films out of a hundred because he is arranged in the right patterns by his directors, left to his own resources is unconvincing.

It is Greta Garbo's personality which 'makes' this film, which fills the mould of the neat respectful adaptation with some sense of the greatness in the novel. No other film actress can so convey physical passion that you believe in its dignity and importance, and yet there is no actress who depends so little on her own sexual charm. Sitting in the corner of a freezing railway carriage, with the ugly shadows of the single globe deepening the crevices of her face, she is more like a man than a woman. What beauty she has is harsh and austere as an Arab's; and I was reminded of Mr Yeats's lines on Dante's mask:

> An image that might have been a stony face,
> Staring upon a bedouin's horse-hair roof
> From doored and windowed cliff, or half upturned
> Among the coarse grass and the camel dung.

Mr Liam O'Flaherty's novel of the Irish Rebellion has been filmed a second time. It is superb material for the screen; very few words are needed for this drama; terror is not a subtle sensation; it can be conveyed very much easier by images alone than scruples, guilt, tenderness. You only need the Black and Tan patrols through the Liffey fogs, the watching secretive figures outside the saloons as the drunken informer drifts deeper and deeper with his cronies into the seedy night life of Dublin. Mr Victor McLaglen has never given an abler performance, and the film, even if it sometimes underlines its points rather crudely, is a memorable picture of a pitiless war waged without honour on either side in doorways and cellars and gin-shops. *The Spectator*, 11 October 1935

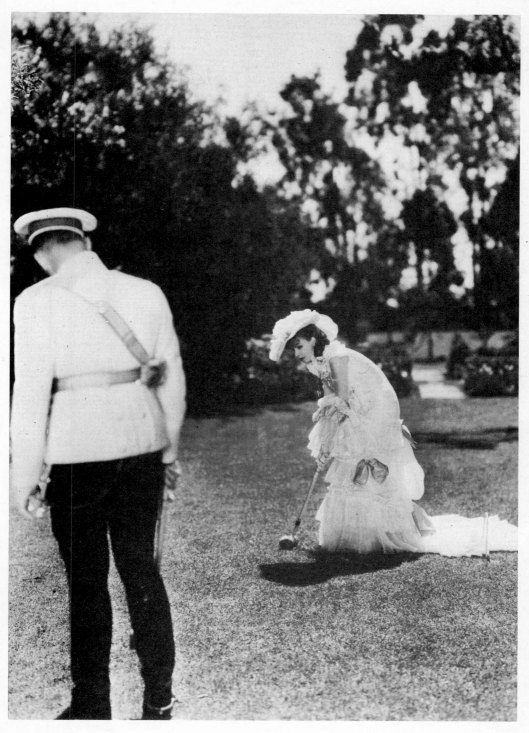

Anna Karenina: Greta Garbo

Anna Karenina (USA, M-G-M, 1935). Director: Clarence Brown. Greta Garbo, Fredric March, Basil Rathbone.
The Informer (USA, RKO, 1935). Director: John Ford. Victor McLaglen, Heather Angel, Preston Foster, Margot Grahame, Wallace Ford, Una O'Connor.

A Midsummer Night's Dream

I sometimes wonder whether film-reviewers are taken quite seriously enough. Criticism, of course, may not be quite in our line, but the production of *A Midsummer Night's Dream* has demonstrated beyond doubt that no one can shake a better tambourine or turn a better table. We are superb mediums, or is it an intuitive sympathy with the poet which enables a Mr Luscombe Whyte (to be remembered for his appreciation of Sam Goldwyn's 'classic tragedy', *The Dark Angel*, and to be distinguished from Mr Pedro de Cordoba who was a Crusader) to tell us that Shakespeare 'had he lived now' would have approved of Herr Reinhardt's film version of his play? 'He had a mind which must have chafed at the limitations of candle-lit, small stages and curtains. He would have conjured up mad woods with twisted trees, peopled with fantasies clothed in visibility.' A pregnant sentence, that, straight from the ouija-board.

Unfortunately, the mediums differ. Mr Sidney Carroll tells us with an even greater air of authority that Shakespeare would *not* have liked the film. It is his obligation, he says, 'as a man of English descent on both sides for generations to try to protect our national poet dramatist from either idolatry or desecration'. As I have said, apart from criticism, there is little we film-critics cannot do.

Alas! I failed to get in touch with Shakespeare (my English descent is less pure than Mr Carroll's), but I feel quite sure that Anne Hathaway, 'had she lived now', would have thought this a very nice film (I am uncertain of the Dark Lady of the Sonnets). She would have liked the chorus of budding Shirley Temples drifting gauzily up the solid Teutonic moonbeams, and I am sure she would have liked the Bear. For Herr Reinhardt is nothing if not literal, and when Helena declares, 'No, no, I am as ugly as a bear; For beasts that meet me run away for fear', we see a big black bear beating a hasty retreat into the blackberry bushes. All the same, I enjoyed this film, perhaps because I have little affection for the play, which seems to me to have been written with a grim determination on Shakespeare's part to earn for once a Universal Certificate.

But Herr Reinhardt, lavish and fanciful rather than imaginative, is uncertain of his new medium. Although in his treatment of the Athenian woodland, the silver birches, thick moss, deep mists and pools, there are sequences of great beauty, there are others of almost incredible banality. After an impressive scene when Oberon's winged slaves herd Titania's fairies under his black billowing cloak, we watch a last fairy carried off over a slave's shoulder into the night sky. It is very effective as the slave sinks knee deep into the dark, but when the camera with real Teutonic thoroughness follows his gradual disappearance until only a pair of white hands are left twining in the middle of the Milky Way, the audience showed its good sense by laughing.

Much of the production is poised like this on the edge of absurdity because Herr Reinhardt cannot visualize how his ideas will work out on the screen. We are never allowed to forget the stage producer, a stage producer, though, of unlimited resources with an almost limitless stage. At every passage of dialogue we are back before footlights and the camera is focused relentlessly on the character who speaks. The freer, more cinematic fairy sequences are set to Mendelssohn's music, and this is the way Shakespeare's poetry ought surely to be used if it is not to delay the action. It must be treated as music, not as stage dialogue tied to the image of the speaker like words issuing from the mouth of characters in a cartoon.

The acting is fresh and vivid for the very reason that it lacks what Mr Carroll calls 'proper Shakespearian diction and bearing'. I do not want to be ungrateful, the film is never dull, and the last sequences, when the human characters stream up the stairs to bed, and the fairies flood in and fill the palace in their wake, was a lovely and effective visualization of 'the sweet peace', 'the glimmering light', 'the dead and drowsy fire'. *The Spectator*, 18 October 1935

A Midsummer Night's Dream (USA, Warner Bros, 1935). Director: Max Reinhardt. James Cagney, Joe E. Brown, Mickey Rooney, Victor Jory, Anita Louise, Dick Powell, Olivia de Havilland.

Joan of Arc/Turn of the Tide/Top Hat/She

The German film, *Joan of Arc*, is of greater interest to students of Nazi psychology than to film-goers. One would have thought it almost impossible to produce so dull a film on so dramatic a subject (a subject which defeated even Mr Shaw's talent for triviality). It is very noisy, rather like the Zoo at feeding-time, which gives an odd impression in bright, dapper Curzon Street, and it is quite as inaccurate as any Hollywood spectacle of *The Crusades* order but not so funny. The author, Herr Gerhard Menzel, we are told, has 'made intensive studies in France, with the result that new light has been shed on some of the most famous figures of history'. But I hardly think that any research can have helped him to reject Joan's meeting with Charles VII at Chillon in favour of Joan appearing to Charles VII, in beleaguered Orleans of all places, and saving him from an infuriated rabble.

Other inventions are less ingenuous. But the pure Nordic mind, whether in its politics or its poetry, is doomed to be a little absurd, and Herr Menzel's new light on a Charles who lets Joan die 'for the sake of France', a Charles intended to be a noble, lonely, rather Machiavellian Führer is as ridiculous in effect as Schiller's conception (he was too sensitive to let her burn) of a Joan who died on the battlefield. Perhaps one should not condemn Fraulein Angela Salloker for her quite nerveless playing, for it is one of the purposes of this Nazi film to belittle a rival national saviour. The real hero is Charles with his Nazi mentality, his belief in the nobility of treachery for the sake of the nation. The purge of 30 June and the liquidation of Tremouille, the burning Reichstag and the pyre in Rouen market-place – these political parallels are heavily underlined. The direction is terribly sincere, conveying a kind of blond and shaven admiration for poor lonely dictators who have been forced to eliminate their allies.

Turn of the Tide, an unpretentious and truthful film of a Yorkshire fishing village, of rivalry over the crabpots, is one of the best English films I have yet seen, apart from the 'documentaries' in which this country has long led the world. It has been compared to *Man of Aran*, but it is on a quite different plane from Mr Flaherty's bogus and sentimental picture. Mr Flaherty's direction is hopelessly 'literary', he lays 'beauty' on inches thick, he contributes just about as little to the film as the author of *The Fountain* to the novel. But Mr Norman Walker is concerned with truth; he doesn't trouble about silhouettes on skylines, and the beauty his picture

29

Turn of the Tide: Joan Maude, Niall MacGinnis, John Garrick, Sam Livesey

catches is that of exact statement. The ordinary life of a fishing village, the competition between lifeboat and salvage tug, the changing market prices, satisfy him: he doesn't have to *invent* drama as Mr Flaherty does, who painfully reconstructed a type of fishing which the Aran islanders had not practised in living memory.

Top Hat is a vehicle, a little better than *Roberta*, for Mr Fred Astaire's genius. It doesn't really matter much that the music and lyrics are bad. Mr Astaire is the nearest approach we are ever likely to have to a human Mickey Mouse; he might have been drawn by Mr Walt Disney, with his quick physical wit, his incredible agility. He belongs to a fantasy world almost as free as Mickey's from the law of gravity, but unfortunately he has to act with human beings and not even Miss Ginger Rogers can match his freedom, lightness and happiness.

The Wag of the Week is Mr Shortt, of our Board of Film Censors, who has

Top Hat: Fred Astaire

granted to this quite pleasantly bawdy film the Universal Certificate he has refused to the earnest manly Boy Scout virtues of Rider Haggard's *She*. I cannot write reasonably about this film, for few books at one time excited me more than *King Solomon's Mines* and *Allan Quartermain*. *She* always bore its symbolism a little heavily: at that age one was not so interested in the lovely immortal woman and the flame of life as in the great ice-barrier, the avalanche, the cannibals in the caves, but to an unrepentant Haggard fan it does sometimes seem to catch the thrill as well as the childishness of his invention.   *The Spectator*, 25 October 1935

Joan of Arc (*Das Mädchen Johanna*) (Germany, Ufa, 1934). Director: Gustav Ucicky. Angela Salloker, Gustav Gründgens, Heinrich George.
Turn of the Tide (GB, British National, 1935). Director: Norman Walker. Geraldine Fitzgerald, Wilfrid Lawson.
Top Hat (USA, RKO 1935). Director: Mark Sandrich. Fred Astaire, Ginger Rogers, Edward Everett Horton, Eric Blore, Helen Broderick.
She (USA, RKO, 1935). Directors: Irving Pichel, L. C. Holden. Helen Gallacher, Helen Mack, Nigel Bruce, Randolph Scott.

Barbary Coast/Episode/The Passing of the Third Floor Back

Barbary Coast is melodrama of the neatest, most expert kind, well directed, well acted and well written. The wit, vigour and *panache* of Mr Ben Hecht and Mr MacArthur have raised nearly to international halma form (in Mr Aldous Huxley's phrase) a conventional film story of a girl who comes to San Francisco one fog-bound night in the 1840s to marry a gold-prospector and finds that he has been murdered. She stays to become the mistress of his killer, the Big Shot, and falls in love with a young prospector who reads Shelley and wants to write poetry. The Big Shot, himself pursued by Vigilantes, follows his mistress with the intention of killing her lover, but, taking pity on them both, goes to meet his lynchers. The story, it will be seen, belongs to the 'far, far better' school, but the character of the Big Shot has a sourness, of the girl an unscrupulousness, which is fresh and interesting. The conventionality of the plot has provided a challenge to the director and the authors to make something real out of the hocus-pocus.

They have succeeded triumphantly. There are moments as dramatically exciting as anything I have seen on the fictional screen. *Sous les Toits de Paris* contained a sequence in which Préjean was surrounded by a gang with drawn razors in the darkness of a railway viaduct; the smoke blew continually across, and the dialogue was drowned in the din of shunting trucks. The steamy obscurity, the whispers, the uproar overhead combined to make the scene vividly sinister. There is a moment in *Barbary Coast* that takes its place with Clair's, when the Big Shot's gunman, on his way to commit another murder in the San Francisco of which he has long been one of the undisputed rulers, feels the pistols of the Vigilantes against his ribs. They walk him out to the edge of the acetylene-lighted town along streets ankle-deep in mud, holding a mock trial with counsel and witnesses as they go; the low voices, the slosh of mud round their boots, the rhythmic stride are terrifying because they have been exactly imagined, with the ear as well as the eye.

The Austrian film *Episode* has nothing comparable to offer, nothing even to equal the acting of Mr Edward G. Robinson and Miss Miriam Hopkins and half a dozen less-known players in their small vivid parts in *Barbary Coast*. I cannot

Barbary Coast

understand the enthusiasm for Fraulein Paula Wessely, star of the slow decorative *Maskerade*. This stocky, rather graceless actress may be said, I suppose, to act naturally, rather in the same way that a Roedean girl may be said to play hockey naturally, but if one wants art to *imitate* the natural, to be conscious and precise in its effects, one will surely prefer Miss Lynn Fontanne or half a dozen other natural-istic actresses to Fraulein Wessely, whose air of healthy prudery I always find peculiarly odious. The background to this rather silly comedy about a rich old philanderer, his sons' tutor and an art student who wishes to keep from her widowed mother the fact that they have been ruined is supposed to be the Vienna of 1922, the Vienna of the inflation: but so tragic a breakdown of the framework of life deserves a less perfunctory, a less humorous and sentimental treatment.

To my surprise I enjoyed *The Passing of the Third Floor Back*. The pious note has been toned down, the milk of human kindness in the original play has been agreeably watered, and the types in the small London 'private hotel' are observed with malicious realism. Unfortunately, sweetness and light do break in, and the director cannot convey these qualities with the same truth as the cans of cooling water, the interminable uncarpeted stairs, the jangle of bells and nerves. The excursion steamer, on which the Stranger takes everyone for a trip to Margate, is as

33

chromium-plated as a millionaire's yacht and carries a chorus of Goldwyn girls in bathing-costumes. This is to be a little too cynical. The right sense of sudden and happy release can surely sometimes be caught among the winkles and blare and sweat of an August holiday.   *The Spectator*, 1 November 1935

Barbary Coast (USA, Samuel Goldwyn, 1935). Director: Howard Hawks. Miriam Hopkins, Edward G. Robinson, Joel McCrea.
Episode (Austria, Viktoria-Film, 1935). Director: Walter Reisch. Paula Wessely, Georg Tressler, Karl Ludwig Diehl.
The Passing of the Third Floor Back (GB, Gaumont British, 1935). Director: Berthold Viertel. Conrad Veidt, Anna Lee, Rene Ray.

The March of Time

The March of Time is the title of an American news series, and this first instalment ought to shock the complacency of British news directors. No attempt has ever been made over here really to edit news films; a football-match, minor royalty opening a housing estate, the launching of a ship, a wharfside fire: scraps of unimportant material are flung without arrangement on to the screen. A tremendous organization has been built up to bring the exposed film to the laboratory in the shortest possible time. A British heavy-weight takes the count somewhere in the Middle West, and a fleet of aeroplanes, acting in conjunction with Atlantic liners, bring the film to London at enormous expense in record time. But this is not news by any journalistic standard: the story is at least six days old and as dead as last season's tunes. Of course, if Sir Josiah Stamp were to break a bottle of wine over a new railway engine at Euston, it would be possible to exhibit the completed film in every cinema in London before the locomotive was dry, but that event might well be considered insufficiently important to upset the weekly programmes already showing, and we should have to wait for Sir Josiah Stamp quite as long as we have to wait for the boxer. So in spite of the aeroplanes most of the items in a news programme have ceased to be news by the time they are shown, however hastily and perfunctorily exhibited.

The producers of *The March of Time* have realized this. They have realized too that some forms of news do not grow cold in twenty-four hours. Their fortnightly programmes can be compared with an authoritative article by a special correspondent rather than with a haphazard page of photographs from the *Daily Mirror*. Their method is to connect newsreel shots with studio reconstructions, to make a vivid, and often politically partisan, story. The law of libel is not so dreaded in America as in England, or the bitter exciting film, which I saw privately, of the activities of the armaments ring could not have been made. But no less exciting and now publicly shown at three London cinemas is the account of the Croix de Feu, the French Fascist organization. The film opens with the riots of February 1934, and gives some idea of the extent of the bloodshed and the ferocity of the fighting. It was from these riots that the Croix de Feu gathered strength, and in *The March of Time* we can watch the recruiting, the processions of private cars driving out from Paris at night to secret meetings in the countryside, we can listen to Colonel de la Rocque's torch-lit violence.

But there is great danger that news films may not be allowed the same political freedom as the Press; the British Board of Film Censors have been known in the past to impose a political censorship over fictional films, and they have tried their hands with curious results on *The March of Time*. The sequences of the Paris riots have been severely cut, and the film has been made Fascist in tone by the removal of the telling final shot which gave the source from which the Croix de Feu derives its funds.

It should not be forgotten, therefore, that the Board are merely the employees of the film industry, and that their decisions have no legal sanction except where it has been granted them by local authorities. They could if necessary be dismissed by the industry acting as a whole, or news films could be taken altogether out of their hands. The law of libel will always safeguard individuals better than the Board. Unfortunately, film companies have never shown a talent for co-operation or they would not have imposed on themselves so curious a form of censorship, a censorship working by a set of rules so absurd that it has imposed on *The Thirty-nine Steps* a certificate for adults only and granted to the domestic indecencies of *The Crusades* a Universal Certificate. This means that in many districts a parent is not allowed to give his own child permission to see Mr Hitchcock's blameless film of Lord Tweedsmuir's patriotic 'thriller'. *The Spectator*, 8 November 1935

The March of Time (USA, 1934 on). Produced by Louis de Rochemont with *Time* Magazine.

Last Love/Moscow Nights/Oil for the Lamps of China

Last Love has a pleasant unpretentious air of truth about it, which is very rare in films about singers or composers. One knows what treatment they generally receive on the screen, how nobly and dolefully the Schuberts and Chopins sacrifice themselves for former room-mates. Even the story of *Last Love*, of the middle-aged 'finished' composer who returns to his home in Vienna after ten years in America, who falls in love with a Japanese student, writes his last opera for her to play in and watches at rehearsal her growing love for the young conductor, might have been made for Herr Tauber. But once accept the romantic plot and the rest is genuine: a creative career from a professional angle. Herr Albert Bassermann as the elderly composer gives one of the best performances I have seen this year. This is not a man romantically 'inspired', but a man with a profession, a man who works; watch the pleasure and cunning in his face as he recognizes a good trick, a technical dexterity. His acting in the wintry scene of the small country inn, where his new tenderness comes to a head and he drinks with the village musicians, conducting over the beer-mugs, and the girl breaks into a spontaneous tipsy song and he feels the fun of life return because he has ideas again after ten years of sterility, is very moving. Miss Michiko Meini, who plays the Japanese student, has a charming voice. To a European the Oriental face doesn't, thank God, register emotions in the way we are used to, and the faint flicker across the broad rice-white surface of love, pain, tenderness helps the film to maintain, even at its less plausible moments, a pleasant muted quality.

Moscow Nights, Mr Anthony Asquith's new film, is completely bogus. Moment-arily forgetting *The Dark Angel*, I wondered, as I came out from the assembly of peeresses and minor royalty and the high shriek of friend recognizing friend into the blue glare of searchlights, whether this was the worst, as well as the most bally-hooed, film of the year. Mr Asquith was once a promising director, though he was always more tricky than imaginative. Now his bag of tricks seems empty. This absurd romantic spy-drama of wartime Russia opens with Volga boatmen and carries on with every worn-out property of a Hollywood Russia, even to the gipsy orchestras. The direction is puerile, no one can drop a tray or a glass without Mr Asquith cutting to a shell-burst. But he has been well served by his players, by M. Harry Baur as an awkward pathetic war-profiteer, by Miss Athene Seyler as an old genteel spy who haunts the hospitals, and Mr Laurence Olivier as an embittered front-line officer who loves a young society nurse engaged to the profiteer. The acting of Miss Penelope Dudley-Ward, who plays the girl's part, belongs to another class altogether, to country-house charades. It is an error of taste to star this player above such brilliant professionals as Miss Seyler and Mr Hay Petrie, who makes a more vivid impression in the few feet of film allowed him and with his two words of dialogue than Miss Ward in all her reels.

The subject of *Oil for the Lamps of China* is excellent: the ballyhoo of sham idealism with which the young recruits of an American oil company are inoculated before they are dispatched to China, the appeals to their loyalty, the assurances that 'the company always takes care of its men'; and then the truth, the sacrifices they are expected to make without return, the appointments filled by intrigue in New York, the inventions stolen by their superiors, and finally, when they grow old, the studied attempts to rob them of their pensions by forcing them to resign. It is a pity that so interesting a theme should have been passed first through the mind of a good, sincere and sentimental woman and then through the mind of a perhaps less sincere but certainly not less sentimental Hollywood scenario-writer.

The Spectator, 15 November 1935

Last Love (*Letzte Liebe*) (Austria, Morawsky-Film, 1934). Directors: Rudi Loewenthal, Fritz Schultz. Albert Bassermann, Michiko Meini, Hans Jaray.
Moscow Nights (GB, Denham Productions, 1935). Director: Anthony Asquith. Laurence Olivier, Penelope Dudley-Ward, Harry Baur, Athene Seyler, Hay Petrie. [US title: *I Stand Condemned*.]
Oil for the Lamps of China (USA, First National, 1935). Director: Mervyn LeRoy. Pat O'Brien, Josephine Hutchinson, Jean Muir.

Arms and the Girl/Accent on Youth

Arms and the Girl may have set out, in the simple rather adolescent American manner which seems insolubly linked with high cheekbones, fraternities and curious shoes, to argue that a soldier's uniform has more sex-appeal than a pacifist's red tie, but it has developed *en route* into one of the best comedies of the screen since *It Happened One Night*. These two films have a very respectable ancestry, the Restoration duel of sex, Dryden's quarrelling lovers, the philosophy of love so beautifully stated in *The Mock Astrologer*:

> Celimena, of my Heart
> None shall e'er bereave you:
> If with your good Leave I may
> Quarrel with you once a Day,
> I will never leave you.

A general's daughter in love with a college pacifist is kidnapped by her father and dumped safely out of the way, without the money to return, in Mexico. There she gets drunk with an American private soldier, they haven't the money to pay for the drinks, and by the time the soldier has come to his sober senses, he has deserted, smashed a Government car, rushed the boundary, stolen a motor caravan and finds himself driving towards California with a girl whose politics he can't stand, who loathes the sight of a uniform and who wants to go west to her pacifist at Washington and not east. Miss Barbara Stanwyck as the malicious-tongued aristocratic Red and Mr Robert Young as the reckless irritated private soldier give admirable performances. The tradition of sparring lovers usually survives in the form of facetiousness, a dreadful intellectual slap and tickle, but the dialogue of *Arms and the Girl* does belong, however great the difference of quality, to the same unsentimental genre as Wildblood's and Jacintha's

> 'Twas a meer Trick of Fate to catch us thus at
> unawares: To draw us in, with a what do you
> lack, as we pass'd by: Had we once separated
> tonight, we should have had more Wit, than ever
> to have met again tomorrow.

But for painful contrast: 'You are the type of girl a man can imagine in his own home – married I mean.' This lover's speech from *Accent on Youth* belongs to another world, and so do the direction and the acting of this dreary comedy. There is one good scene at the end of the picture, but I wouldn't advise any but dog-lovers to wait so long. *They*, of course, will enjoy Mr Herbert Marshall's usual canine performance of dumb suffering.   *The Spectator*, 22 November 1935

Arms and the Girl (*Red Salute*) (USA, Reliance, 1935). Director: Sidney Lanfield. Barbara Stanwyck, Robert Young.
Accent on Youth (USA, Paramount, 1935). Director: Wesley Ruggles. Sylvia Sidney, Herbert Marshall.

The Last Outpost

The Last Outpost, which will be shown shortly at the Plaza, is a curious mixture. Half of it is remarkably good and half of it quite abysmally bad. One can even put one's finger on the joins, and it will be well worth a visit if only because it indicates what might be made of the short-story form on the screen. It consists of two stories unrelated except for the coincidence of characters. The first, which lasts for about half an hour, is a very well-directed and well-acted war-story of a British Secret Service agent and his success in warning a defenceless tribe against a Kurd attack and inducing them to move with their flocks over a flooded river and across a snow-bound range of mountains to safe pastures. It is one of those stories of dogged physical endeavour that the film does so well. It belongs to the order of *Grass* and *The Covered Wagon*. Mr Claude Rains as the Secret Service agent in Turkish uniform and Mr Cary Grant as the incurably light-minded and rather stupid British officer whom he rescues from the Kurds both act extremely well. Mr Rains's low husky voice, his power of investing even commonplace dialogue with smouldering conviction, is remarkable. He never rants, but one is always aware of what a superb ranter he could be in a part which did not call for modern restraint but only for superb diction. I should like to see him as Almanzor or Aurengzebe, for he could catch, as no one else could, the bitter distrust of the world, religious in its intensity, which lies behind the heroic drama.

37

November 1935

The Last Outpost, if it had stopped on the mountain pass above the pastures with the officer on the way down to hospital and the comforts of Cairo and the secret agent turning back towards the enemy, would have been a memorable short film. Mr Charles Barton, the director, has obviously used old documentaries: the crossing of the flooded river is not a Californian reconstruction, and all through this first section the camera is used with fine vigour to present a subject which could not have been presented on the stage.

I cannot see why we should not have serious films of this length as well as farces, short stories as well as novels on the screen. The essential speed and concision would be an admirable discipline for most directors, who are still, after seven years of talkies, tied to stage methods, and we might be saved from seeing such a good film as this padded out to full length by the addition of a more than usually stupid triangular melodrama of jealousy and last-minute rescue in the Sahara, where needless to say Mr Rains sacrifices his life at the end for his wife's lover, so that all may end in the fixed, almost Oriental, short-hand of military melodrama, 'It is better so', clasped fingers and topees off and fading bugle-calls.

The Spectator, 24 November 1935

The Last Outpost (USA, Paramount, 1935). Directors: Louis Gasnier, Charles Barton. Cary Grant, Claude Rains, Gertrude Michael.

La Bandéra/Come Out of the Pantry

The camera swings down from the night sky above the Paris roofs to a narrow ill-lit street where a drunken girl is dancing with her lover. A man slips out of a doorway and she clutches him. Only after he has pushed her aside and disappeared into the warren of dance-halls and one-night hotels does she see the blood he has left smeared across her blouse.

La Bandéra: Jean Gabin

38

This is the effective opening of *La Bandéra*, a French film of the Spanish Foreign Legion into whose anonymous ranks the murderer escapes after he has been robbed of all his money in a shabby Spanish port. It is an excellent illustration of the main advantage the film possesses over the ordinary stage play; the means it has to place the drama in its general setting. We have almost given up hope of hearing *words* with a vivid enough imagery to convey the climate of the drama. *La Bandéra* on the stage would be only one more melodrama of African heat and brutality and death, an intelligent melodrama saved from triteness by the character of the police spy, admirable and despicable, with his strung nerves and body of childish delicacy, who pursues the murderer even into the hard dangerous exile of the Legion. But the camera, because it can note with more exactitude and vividness than the prose of most living playwrights the atmosphere of mean streets and cheap lodgings, gives the story background and authenticity. We recognize the truth of the general scene and are more prepared to accept the truth of the individual drama.

But it is astonishing how seldom in English films a director uses the camera in this way to establish a scene, a way of life, with which he and his audience are familiar. Miss Lejeune's remark, quoted at the end of this article, is an example of the social snobbery which hampers the English cinema. The material of English films, unlike French or American, is nearly always drawn from the leisured class, a class of which the director and his audience know really very little. Mr Hitchcock sometimes indulges in crime or 'low life', but it is with the 'amused' collector's air of a specialist in sensation. An English film as a rule means evening gowns by Hartnell, suitcases by Asprey. An excursion steamer to Margate (*vide The Passing of the Third Floor Back*) becomes a luxury liner full of blondes in model bathing-dresses. Even in the worst French films one is not conscious of this class division, the cafés and dance-halls are of the kind familiar to the majority of the audience. The snobbery of such a film as *Come Out of the Pantry*, in which a duke's son plays the part of a footman and shows himself so 'amusingly' sociable in the pantry, would be quite meaningless to any but an English audience.

It is not that one wants English directors to 'go' proletarian (I remember with discomfort how Mr Anthony Asquith, of all people, was set to direct a film about workers on the Underground); one must accept this English class division which prevents the scenario-writer or director from treating naturally and truthfully more than a very limited material, but let that material at any rate be drawn from his own experience, which is probably neither that of the very rich nor of the very poor.

The Spectator, 6 December 1935

BON MOT OF THE WEEK
By sheer diligence and enthusiasm the cinema, which 25 years ago was producing such morsels as 'What Drink Did', has now arrived at the point when the Queen, the Prince of Wales, and the President of the United States are all prepared to patronize its shows within a fortnight.
(C. A. Lejeune.)

La Bandéra (France, Société Nouvelle de Cinématographie, 1935). Director: Julien Duvivier. Jean Gabin, Annabella, Pierre Renoir, Viviane Romance. [US title: *Escape from Yesterday*.]
Come Out of the Pantry (GB, British & Dominions, 1935). Director: Jack Raymond. Jack Buchanan, Ethel Stewart.

Riders to the Sea

The cinema, as much as poetry in the eighteenth century, needs patrons. Little good work can come from commercial companies under the pressure of popular taste. The early Russian films showed the immense superiority of the State-aided over the popularly supported, and to see again such an old silent film as *The New*

Babylon, which the Forum recently revived, is to be painfully aware that the modern commercial picture has not merely learned nothing in the last six years, it has even forgotten what it once seemed to be learning from the Russian cinema. Nor need one go as far as Russia to see the effect of State patronage. Mr Alexander Korda's publicity cannot blind our eyes to the fact that the only important films being made in England today come from Mr Grierson's system of film units. Of course the commercial cinema has had its fine moments: *The Front Page, City Streets, En Natt*, one could name a dozen films, but they seem to have crept into the cinema accidentally, while the big executives were dozing. Their makers have received so little encouragement that it was necessary for Mr Hecht and Mr MacArthur, the authors of *The Front Page*, to break away from Hollywood to produce *Crime Without Passion*. So one has nothing but praise for the courage and generosity of Miss Gracie Fields who has financed an independent film version of Synge's *Riders to the Sea*, played by the Abbey Theatre players and produced for the most part in Connemara. The intention is admirable, but the result shows one danger of private patronage. I doubt if the best work has ever been produced in complete independence of a public. Even Mr Grierson has his public, a public of several millions, though his films may sometimes not be distributed at all in the ordinary way through cinema circuits. Popular *taste* makes a thoroughly bad dictator, but the awareness of an audience is an essential discipline for the artist.

There is something altogether too private about this Synge film, a touch of mutual admiration about the continual close-ups of the individual players, a self-conscious simplicity. The camera is always delayed for Synge's words, when in a true film the words are less important than the camera. I confess I am not an admirer of Synge's plays, of the idea that style is a decoration, something you can apply to your subject, instead of being an economy and exactitude. The attempt to express exactly an emotion or a half-conscious state, of course, may take the writer into queer places, but in Surrealist prose or in the pages of *Anna Livia Plurabelle* one can recognize the attempt as one cannot in Synge's incantatory style. But I do not think that even Synge's admirers will enjoy *Riders to the Sea*. Something has gone badly wrong with the continuity; the loss of act divisions has upset the sense of time. Though the movements of the actors, between the set speeches which are nearly always delivered in close-up, are intolerably slow, so that most of the film seems to have been spent in getting from door to fire and back again, the events outside the fishing cottage follow quite another order of time, without interval or preparation. No sooner has one lost son been keened for than the dreary band of mourners enter to announce another death. What the film might have done, and the stage could not do so well, was to show us the manner of those deaths; it might have given us with its larger scope in space and time the sense of the poor hard lives before and after: a reason for their deaths. As it is the deaths do not matter, they are merely an excuse for dirges as resonant, and as hollow, as a church bell's.

The Spectator, 20 December 1935

Riders to the Sea (GB, Flanagan-Hurst, 1935). Director: Brian Desmond Hurst. Abbey Theatre players.

The Ghost Goes West

M. René Clair made his name by a very individual form of fantasy. He was a realist, with a social conscience, dealing satirically with French types and scenes which he knew intimately. He was not a humorist in the modern English sense of a man who shares the popular taste and who satirizes only those with whom the majority are already displeased. His satire was so far from being safe and acceptable that his early film, *The Italian Straw Hat*, roused enough opposition to keep him out of the cinema for some years. I use the past tense. It is typical of the British film industry, whose leading showman if not producer is Mr Alexander Korda, that M. Clair should be brought to this country to direct a Scottish film full of what must be to him rather incomprehensible jokes about whisky and bagpipes, a humorous fantasy without any social significance, realistic observation, or genuine satire: it appeared first as a short story in *Punch*.

The story is of the Glowrie ghost, who is condemned to haunt an impoverished castle in the Highlands until, by forcing a Maclagan to admit that one Glowrie is worth seven of his clan, he has recovered the honour he lost two hundred years ago on the battlefield. The ghost is the double of the present Glowrie, who sells the castle to an American millionaire in order to pay his bills and falls in love with the daughter. The girl, of course, confuses the free amorous eighteenth-century ghost with his rather shy descendant, the millionaire decides to build the castle up stone by stone in Florida, a rival manufacturer turns out to be of Maclagan blood, and the complications are as gently and traditionally obvious as coloured Christmas illustrations. The only opportunities for satire are at the expense of rich and tasteless Americans, as safe a form of weekly family fun as were war-profiteers a few years ago and as Cubists still seem to be today.

And yet I have never believed more firmly in Clair's genius than I did during this film. The silly story, the gross misuse of Clair's peculiar qualities, were forgotten in my admiration for his camera sense. In no other film this year has there been the same feeling of mobility, of visual freedom. And the actors responded with unforced lightheartedness. Mr Eugene Pallette as the American millionaire gave the finest performance of his career, and Mr Robert Donat as the ghost and his descendant acted with invincible naturalness.

It is only in memory that the silly tale begins to outweigh Clair's direction, for it is so much easier to carry a subject in the mind than a treatment. But even in the cinema there were moments when one realized the conflict between the scenario and Clair's poetic talent; these were the moments of which *this* ghost was unworthy, when we were much closer to Elsinore than pasteboard Glowrie, to Purgatory than the brandy flames of the seasonal pudding. One remembers the long drift of white cumulus while the voice of the dead father condemned the cowardly ghost; the moment on the ramparts at midnight when the great lace sleeve fell in close-up across the corner of the screen and with all the sudden shock of a striking clock one knew the ghost was there, just beyond the dark edge of one's vision; the seconds when the camera slowly climbed the long worm-eaten cobwebbed stairs and paced beside the cracked panelling.

So, curiously enough, the silly tale gave one a chance to see a more deeply imaginative Clair than had his own scenarios. The Scottish holiday may well prove valuable for his future. Surely no artist can continue indefinitely to write as well as direct, to double the creative demand on his nerves. One has seen the effect on Mr Chaplin, and Clair's films since *A Nous La Liberté* have become rather tired and repetitive.   *The Spectator*, 27 December 1935

The Ghost Goes West (GB, London Films, 1935). Director: René Clair. Robert Donat, Jean Parker, Eugene Pallette, Elsa Lanchester, Everly Gregg.

The Guv'nor/Midshipman Easy/Treasure Island

Mr George Arliss, who has dressed up as Disraeli, Voltaire, Richelieu, Wellington, Rothschild, now dresses up as a French tramp, and I suppose those who like Mr Arliss will like his latest film. They may not be disturbed by the thought of how little this tramp has in common with the broken-shoed stragglers they may meet making a daily monotonous march back and forth between the workhouses of Oxford and Chipping Norton, with no more freedom than the length of a chain. He belongs, of course, to the 'bird-song at morning, star-shine at night' school, and his admirers need not fear that he has lost any of his usual refinement or sentiment, his cultured English accent, the Universal Certificate. I do not know why he has to be a French tramp unless for this reason: that his accent need not be coarsened; unless too it is felt that the general Yuletide air of sweetness and light might have been broken if the wicked capitalists had been English.

I am not an admirer of Mr Arliss, but I found this film rather more tolerable than his recent appearances as the family Wellington, the family Voltaire. The story, if it had been more consistently worked out, would have had quite a Clair ring. The tramp's name is Rothschild, and there is at least a hint of satire when the unscrupulous banker appoints him to the board of his bankrupt firm to restore public confidence for long enough to enable him to withdraw his own interests after enriching himself with a shady financial *coup*. The effect of the name is immediate; the old tramp has only to telephone for a little corn with which to feed the city pigeons and the Stock Exchange responds. Clair, one feels, would have made more of such incidents, nor would he have allowed the gross inconsistency which robs the film even of a fantastic reality. For the firm of Rothschild, who are so careful of the family name that when the tramp is arrested for poaching they secure his release and give him money to keep him out of the courts, apparently make no attempt to interfere with his activities as director of a great bank.

The film soon proceeds on more conventional Arliss lines. The banker's plot is so elementary that the tramp easily tumbles to it, and Mr Arliss defeats the wicked capitalist in favour of – not the honest worker, or even the honest Green Shirt or the honest collectivist, but of a pair of good women capitalists whose ignorance of the business in which they are the main shareholders is regarded as a rather disarming innocence (so far have we gone from any genuine social criticism). Mr Arliss, of course, goes back to the road where 'all days are good days when the sun is shining'.

Midshipman Easy can be unreservedly recommended to children. It is the first film of a new English director, Mr Carol Reed, who has more sense of the cinema than most veteran British directors, certainly than Mr Wilcox or Mr Basil Dean. It is simply and dramatically cut, it contains the best fight I can remember on the screen, and I can imagine no child too sophisticated to be excited and amused. Hughie Green gives an excellent performance as the courageous, argumentative and rather absurd Easy whose father has brought him up, on the principles of Godwin, to believe in human equality, and Mr Harry Tate's boatswain is deliciously mellow.

If this film is not quite on the same level as *Treasure Island*, which the Royal Court Cinema has very sensibly revived for Christmas, the fault does not lie with either the director or the actors. The story of *Treasure Island* has a deeper, a more

The Guv'nor: George Arliss

Midshipman Easy: Hughie Green

poetic value: the capture of the Spanish merchantman, the fight with the Italian convicts, these are exciting inventions: but the buried treasure, the desert island, the horrifying murder of the faithful sailor, the persons of Long John and blind Pew, all these have symbolic value. *Treasure Island* contains, as *Midshipman Easy* does not, a sense of good and evil. Even a child can recognize the greater dignity and depth of this Scottish Presbyterian's *Mansoul* written in terms of an adventure-story for a boys' magazine. *The Spectator*, 3 January 1936

The Guv'nor (GB, Gaumont British, 1935). Director: Milton Rosmer. George Arliss, Gene Gerrard, Frank Cellier, Patric Knowles, Viola Keats. [US title: *Mr Hobo*.]
Midshipman Easy (GB, Associated Talking Pictures, 1935). Director: Carol Reed. Hughie Green, Harry Tate, Margaret Lockwood.
Treasure Island (USA, M-G-M, 1934). Director: Victor Fleming. Wallace Beery, Jackie Cooper, Lionel Barrymore.

Reifende Jugend/The Bride Comes Home

There is a delightful moment in *Reifende Jugend*, a film which is described as 'a psychological study of three girls who enter a boys' school to prepare for their final examination', when the Headmaster tells the Science Master, who confesses to him that he has fallen in love with one of the girls: 'Be patient. Remember that after the examination she is no longer a pupil.' In another scene one of the senior class discloses a plot to steal the examination papers. 'Tonight the Head's room will be searched.' 'Suppose he finds nothing?' the other boy says. 'Then he will study the blotters with a mirror.' These two pieces of dialogue give a rough idea of the spirit of this entertaining film: the charmingly realistic attitude of the Headmaster towards the sexual problem, the serious, absurd, emotional, Teutonically thorough schoolboys. It is an odd film because the situations seem fantastic to English eyes, and the bare summary which the management of the Forum supplies does justice only to this oddity:

One of the girls is loved by both the Science Master and a pupil. Intense rivalry exists between them, and the boy threatens to expose the master unless he helps him through his exam. The master ignores this threat, consequently the boy fails. The Headmaster, suspecting something questions the boy, who refuses to implicate the master; the Headmaster, touched by the boy's strength of character, persuades the Board of Examiners to pass him, asserting that strength of character and personal worth are more effective than examination papers.

It certainly doesn't do justice to the light lyrical treatment of some of the scenes, the truthful, unsentimental but not unkindly picture of emotional awkwardness.

Compare this film with that embarrassing play, *Young Woodley*. Mr Van Druten put an exaggerated value on adolescent emotion; it was a play about adolescence written by an adolescent, and he tried to make the boy's passion dignified and tragic. But the truth is seldom tragic, for human beings are not made in that grand way. The truth may be sad, but it is nearly always grotesque as well, and the value of this film is that it catches the absurdity just as effectively as it catches the freshness. Herr Heinrich George gives a charming performance as the realistic, coarse, kindly Headmaster and the acting of Fraulein Hertha Thiele, as unemphatic as her pale ashen hair, needs no recommendation to those who remember her in *Mädchen in Uniform*.

Miss Claudette Colbert has been three times lucky – in *It Happened One Night*, her best film, which has been revived this week at the Royal Court Cinema, in *She Married Her Boss*, and now in *The Bride Comes Home*, a comedy of fiery-tempered and incompatible lovers who fight their way into marriage. For it is exceptionally lucky in the cinema to be given a chance to develop your proper talent, and the fact that Miss Colbert is the most charming light-comedy actress on the screen did not prevent Hollywood from starring her as Cleopatra, so that she might have complained with Nell Gwyn:

> . . . I walk because I die
> Out of my Calling, in a Tragedy.
> O Poet, damn'd dull Poet, who could prove
> So senseless! to make Nelly die for love.

The Bride Comes Home: William Collier, Robert Young, Edgar Kennedy, Fred MacMurray, Claudette Colbert, Kate Mackenna

None of the earlier films has a more memorable sequence than that of the nocturnal marriage by a small-town judge, the American equivalent of the Gretna Green blacksmith. The whole scene, the little hideous parlour, the cracked harmonium, the flowery mechanical service composed by the judge himself, is satirical comedy of a very high order. *The Spectator*, 10 January 1936

Reifende Jugend (Germany, Carl Froelich Film, 1933). Director: Carl Froelich. Albert Florath, Heinrich George, Paul Henkels, Albert Lieven, Hertha Thiele.
The Bride Comes Home (USA, Paramount, 1935). Director: Wesley Ruggles. Claudette Colbert, Fred MacMurray, Robert Young.

Second Bureau/Sans Famille

One is inclined to exaggerate the value of another country's films, just as much as of its fiction, for only the selected few reach us. Those who think of the French cinema in terms of Clair and a few super-realists may learn a salutary lesson this week.

Second Bureau is a rather dull film, a long packed melodrama of the French and

German Secret Services. It begins brilliantly enough with shots of blossoming trees and pastoral landscape, a trench in a field filled with yapping, snapping dogs of every breed (one dachshund sits aloof with an air of melancholy poetic foresight), four men in lounge suits wearing gas-masks and carrying small attaché-cases. One of them takes a bomb out of his case and throws it, the gas fumes spread, the field flowers wither, a pigeon falls dead from the sky, the yapping rises agonizingly and subsides, a single bark, and three grotesque masked men gather round the fourth with congratulations. The film, alas! does not maintain this sinister and satiric level. Two secrets stolen from the Germans, a double-crossing agent, a motor chase, a beautiful woman spy who falls in love with the Secret Service officer she has been sent to trap, two murders and an attempted suicide: the film is too thick with drama. The clever atmosphere of routine destruction in the opening sequence is quite lost.

It is a great pity, for what an amusing film of the Secret Service could be made if the intention was satiric and not romantic, the treatment realistic and not violent. One remembers Mr Maugham's Ashenden bored at Geneva, his official existence 'as orderly and monotonous as a city clerk's', and Mr Compton Mackenzie's office in Athens. There is a moment in *Second Bureau* when the French officer watching the German woman in the hotel lounge thinks of her with a handkerchief over her eyes bound to a post. This is an example of the film's unnecessary melodrama. After all it is peacetime. There is no reason why anybody should suffer more than a few years' imprisonment, and isn't there material enough in that? In the man who sketches near a dockyard and is arrested in a suburban teashop and put away for a couple of years? The true drama is the lack of drama, the pettiness of the actual climax against the background of arming nations, the meagreness of the information to be stolen, the smallness of the money earned, the unimportance of the agent. *Second Bureau* gains nothing by its violence because there is no room to make the violence convincing. One enjoys parts of the film for their touches of truth, not the acting of the stars but of M. Pierre Larquey as the silly pathetic under-officer Colleret, who is ruined by the spy, with his spray of cheap scent, his childish boasts and humble love; of M. Jean-Max as the double-crossing agent, an exiled Russian, a bored womanizer full of a self-pity for the past, a self-pity as mechanical as the gallantry.

Sans Famille, directed with deadly seriousness, is very funny indeed. It is the story of how Lady Milligan's baby is kidnapped at the instigation of her wicked brother-in-law so that he may inherit her property, her husband having just died. It is a bad bargain because immediately after the child has disappeared she tells him she is expecting *un autre enfant*. He means the child to be murdered, but the kidnapper instead takes it across the Channel and leaves it on the steps of Notre-Dame. The boy is adopted by peasants and then by a strolling singer, once a famous operatic star, who dies in a snowstorm, of which the constituent feathers are only too visible. The child makes his way to an appallingly foggy London and the arms of his mother. The chief fun is provided by the London police. They chase juvenile offenders with drawn truncheons, but even when they are inactive there is something subtly wrong about them. They are small men with sloping shoulders and enormous helmets which fall low over their eyes, and they have a dumb beaten-dog air as they creep through the thick fog past public houses where the London burglars dance apache dances with their women.

The Spectator, 17 January 1936

Second Bureau (*Deuxième Bureau*) (France, Compagnie Française Cinématographique, 1935). Director: Pierre Billon. Jean Murat, Véra Korène, Jeanine Crispin.
Sans Famille (France, Société Agatos, 1935). Director: Marc Allégret. Robert Lynen, Dorville. [US title: *No Relations*.]

The Case of the Lucky Legs/Charlie Chan in Shanghai

It is curious how little the cinema has done for the detective public; perhaps that public is not large enough to tempt the film magnates, consisting, as it chiefly does, of crossword-puzzlers and tired intellectuals. There have been a few unsuccessful attempts to transfer Sherlock Holmes to the screen, there was even a rather deplorable effort by an English company to film an adventure of Lord Peter Wimsey, but the only sustained detective characters on the screen are Mr Warren William's Perry Mason, Mr Warner Oland's Charlie Chan, and Mr William Powell's suave suede impersonations in such agile and amusing films as *The Thin Man*, revived this week at the Royal Court Cinema, and *Star of Midnight*. Of course, the cinema cannot go in for the really dry, donnish game; the type of detection which depends on a Bradshaw's timetable has to be excluded, for a cinema audience cannot be expected to carry a series of mathematical clues in mind. Detection is almost necessarily the weakest part of a detective film; what we do get in the Perry Mason films is a more vivid sense of life than in most detective stories, the quality we get in some of Mr David Frome's novels, in all Mr Dashiell Hammett's, and in a few of the early works of Miss Sayers.

The Case of the Lucky Legs: Warren William, Allen Jenkins

Charlie Chan in Shanghai: Warner Oland

Perry Mason is my favourite film detective; he is curiously little known, perhaps because his films, as 'second features', are usually not shown to the Press. *The Case of the Lucky Legs* is an admirable film, but it is thrown in as makeweight at the Regal to the appalling film, *I Give You My Heart*. Perry Mason is a hard-drinking and not very scrupulous lawyer. He owes something to the character established by Mr William Powell: there is the same rather facetious badinage with a woman assistant, but he is, I think, a more genuine creation. Mr Powell is a little too immaculate, his wit is too well turned just as his clothes are too well made, he drinks hard but only at the best bars; he is rather like an advertisement of a man-about-town in *Esquire*, he shares some of the irritating day-dream quality of Lord Peter Wimsey. I find the cadaverous, not very well-dressed Perry Mason more real in his seedy straw hat with his straggly moustache; one does not find him only in the best bars; he is by no means irresistible to women; his background is the hiss of soda rather than the clink of ice. He is far more likely on the face of it to be a successful detective than Mr Powell's character because he belongs to the same class as his criminals. Often, indeed, as in his latest case, they are his clients. For I can never really believe that a good detective will be found in the Social Register or that Lord Peter would be capable of detecting anything more criminal than a theft by a kleptomaniac duchess. To those who do not yet know Perry Mason I recommend *The Case of the Lucky Legs* as good Mason if not good detection, better, I think, than *The Case of the Curious Bride*.

Charlie Chan does a good deal more honest detection with finger-prints than Mason, and his break-up of a big dope-smuggling gang in Shanghai is a well-made, if conventional piece of genuine Chan. A much more desirable person, of course, this slow, astute Chinaman with his rather lovable turns of broken English than the shady lawyer. But the lawyer is better fun.   *The Spectator*, 31 January 1936

The Case of the Lucky Legs (USA, Warner, 1935). Director: Archie L. Mayo. Warren William, Patricia Ellis.
Charlie Chan in Shanghai (USA, 20th Century-Fox, 1935). Director: James Tinling. Warner Oland, Irene Harvey.

Dr Socrates/The Man Who Broke the Bank at Monte Carlo/ The Imperfect Lady

There are occasions when I envy dramatic critics; Mr Agate after a bad week can fill up a column with what somebody else once said about Rachel. But Garbo, the screen's only classic, is alive, and frankly there is no film this week worth writing more than a few lines on. *Dr Socrates* is a third-rate gangster film, *The Man Who Broke the Bank at Monte Carlo* is a mildly agreeable comedy marred by the intrusion of White Russians into the plot (I can never appreciate the pathos of princes who have become taxi-drivers and drink coffee essence instead of champagne; unlike other taxi-drivers they have *had* their champagne), and *The Imperfect Lady*, Miss Cicely Courtneidge's first American film, is to be avoided at any cost.

Miss Courtneidge's performances in revue I remember enjoying with some reluctance fifteen years ago: it was in the theatre that she learnt to fling her odd facial contortions to the back of the gallery, and no film director has proved himself capable of softening the exaggerations she learnt then. Her last English film, the deplorable *Me and Marlborough*, revealed that Miss Courtneidge, like so many comedians, was going the Pagliacci way; the smile in future would not, alas, hide the tear. Pathos has nearly ruined Mr Chaplin, who is an artist of genius; what it has done for Miss Courtneidge is rather horrible to watch. Needless to say, too, that before the end of *The Imperfect Lady* Miss Courtneidge is given an opportunity to dress up as a young soldier and sing a patriotic song. Gallantry is out of place in a review, but I will content myself with suggesting that Miss Courtneidge's career has been a longer one than Miss Jessie Matthews's and that male impersonation is really only permissible to the young.

Mr Ronald Colman, who breaks the bank on behalf of his fellow White Russians and whom the directors of the casino feel it necessary to lure back to the tables by any means and at any cost for the sake of the advertisement, is an actor of the opposite type. He is an excellent director's dummy. He has no personality of his own, only an appearance, and for that reason he is an almost perfect actor for the fictional screen. There was a time when Russian directors made a great point of using non-professional material and Mr Colman may be said to have all the merit of the moujik and this advantage as well: that he can obey with a rather more lively intelligence.

I say the almost perfect actor because there is still room in the cinema for the actor of genius, for the great personality, for Garbo as well as for Joan Crawford. I sometimes think that Mr Paul Muni, the 'star' of *Dr Socrates*, is of this rank. As with Garbo, you get an impression of immense force in reserve, an unexpressed passion of life. It is a quality of character rather than of acting. Miss Courtneidge acts, acts all the time; it is as tiring to watch her as to watch the defeated boat-race crew strain raggedly after Cambridge up the Thames. Neither Garbo nor Muni acts in this sense; they exist vividly and without apparent effort. This is the old romantic style of genius, one feels, not the infinite capacity for taking pains, but a luck, a gift, a passion they were born with. *Dr Socrates* is not one of Muni's successful films; it is not another *I am a Fugitive* (that performance of agonizing power he has never quite repeated), nor even a *Black Fury*, but a trivial themeless film about a small-town doctor who, by persuading them that their leader has typhoid, puts a band of gangsters out of action with morphia injections. This climax should have been exciting, but there were too many beds, too many doped gangsters, it was only funny. But even in this poor film Muni establishes a background: the accident and death which shook his nerve and ruined his career. That is what a director's dummy cannot do: he exists in the action and not outside it; though the chief problem for the film-writer, just as much as for the novelist, must always be to represent 'the dark backward and abysm of time'.   *The Spectator*, 7 February 1936

Dr Socrates (USA, Warner Bros, 1935). Director: William Dieterle. Paul Muni, Ann Dvorak, Barton Maclane.
The Man Who Broke the Bank at Monte Carlo (USA, 20th Century-Fox, 1935). Director: Stephen Roberts. Ronald Colman, Joan Bennett.
The Imperfect Lady (*The Perfect Gentleman*) (USA, M-G-M, 1935). Director: Tim Whelan. Cicely Courtneidge, Frank Morgan.

Modern Times

I am too much an admirer of Mr Chaplin to believe that the most important thing about his new film is that for a few minutes we are allowed to hear his agreeable and rather husky voice in a song. The little man has at last definitely entered the contemporary scene; there had always before been a hint of 'period' about his courage and misfortunes; he carried about with him more than the mere custard-pie of Karno's day, its manners, its curious clothes, its sense of pathos and its dated poverty. There were occasions, in his encounters with blind flower-girls or his adventures in mean streets or in the odd little pitch-pine mission halls where he carried round the bag or preached in pantomime on a subject so near to his own experience as the tale of David and Goliath, when he seemed to go back almost as far as Dickens. The change is evident in his choice of heroine: fair and featureless with the smudged effect of an amateur water-colour which has run, they never appeared again in leading parts, for they were quite characterless. But Miss Paulette Goddard, dark, grimy, with her amusing urban and plebeian face, is a promise that the little man will no longer linger at the edge of mawkish situation, the unfair pathos of the blind girl and the orphan child. One feels about her as Hyacinth felt about Millicent in *The Princess Casamassima*: 'she laughed with the laugh of the people, and if you hit her hard enough would cry with their tears'. For the first time the little man does not go off alone, flaunting his cane and battered bowler along the endless road out of the screen. He goes in company looking for what may turn up.

What *had* turned up was first a job in a huge factory twisting screws tighter as little pieces of nameless machinery passed him on a moving belt, under the tele-vised eye of the manager, an eye that followed him even into the lavatory where he

Modern Times: Charlie Chaplin, Paulette Goddard

snatched an illicit smoke. The experiment of an automatic feeding machine, which will enable a man to be fed while he works, drives him crazy (the running amok of this machine, with its hygienic mouth-wiper, at the moment when it has reached the Indian corn course, is horrifyingly funny; it is the best scene, I think, that Mr Chaplin has ever invented). When he leaves hospital he is arrested as a Communist leader (he has picked up a red street flag which has fallen off a lorry) and released again after foiling a prison hold-up. Unemployment and prison punctuate his life, starvation and lucky breaks, and somewhere in its course he attaches to himself the other piece of human refuse.

The Marxists, I suppose, will claim this as *their* film, but it is a good deal less and a good deal more than Socialist in intention. No real political passion has gone to it: the police batter the little man at one moment and feed him with buns the next: and there is no warm maternal optimism, in the Mitchison manner, about the character of the workers: when the police are brutes, the men are cowards; the little man is always left in the lurch. Nor do we find him wondering 'what a Socialist man should do', but dreaming of a steady job and the most bourgeois home. Mr Chaplin, whatever his political convictions may be, is an artist and not a propagandist. He doesn't try to explain, but presents with vivid fantasy what seems to him a crazy comic tragic world without a plan, but his sketch of the inhuman factory does not lead us to suppose that his little man would be more at home at Dneipostroi. He presents, he doesn't offer political solutions.

The little man politely giving up his seat to the girl in the crowded Black Maria: the little man when the dinner-bell sounds tenderly sticking a spray of celery into the mouth of the old mechanic whose head has been caught between the cog-wheels: the little man littering the path of the pursuing detectives with overturned chairs to save his girl: Mr Chaplin has, like Conrad, 'a few simple ideas'; they could be expressed in much the same phrases: courage, loyalty, labour: against the same nihilistic background of purposeless suffering. 'Mistah Kurtz – he dead.' These ideas are not enough for a reformer, but they have proved amply sufficient for an artist.   *The Spectator*, 14 February 1936

Modern Times (USA, Charles Chaplin, 1935). Director: Charles Chaplin. Charles Chaplin, Paulette Goddard.

I Dream Too Much/Anything Goes/Faust/Hohe Schule/Captain Blood

Here are a pack of films to choose from; but I confess that though one or two of them offer a few moments of meagre entertainment, there is not one I would pay money to see.

I Dream Too Much irritated me the most because it disappointed me the most. About fifteen years ago the composer, Mr Jerome Kern, enjoyed the same popularity as Mr Cole Porter does today. Were the tunes of *The Cabaret Girl*, which once seemed so richly, sensually sentimental, as pompous and middle-aged as these numbers? There is a tiresome pseudo-serious air of domestic drama (a great singer's love-life) about this film that always seems to surround Metropolitan Opera singers when they go to Hollywood. *I Dream Too Much* might really have been written for Miss Grace Moore – a pity, because Miss Lily Pons has a less ponderous personality. As it is, a performing seal supplies the only light, I was about to say the only human, touches in this worthy picture of gay (oh, tiresomely, trillingly gay) abandon in Montparnasse attics followed by marital squabbles in luxurious reception-rooms. Nor have American directors yet learnt how ugly the close-up of a woman singing must invariably be; we are treated to many dreadful shots of a cavernous mouth projecting high notes like shells from a trench mortar.

Anything Goes was very nearly as disappointing, for I had enjoyed the London stage version and Mr Cole Porter's music. Mr Charlie Ruggles's performance as Public Enemy No. 13 who escapes in an Atlantic liner from America, disguised as a clergyman, is a very faded affair after Mr Sydney Howard's. Mr Bing Crosby's moony methods, too, slow up a picture which should rattle quite as fast as a sub-machine gun. There are several new and undistinguished songs, the lovely lush sentimentality of 'All Through the Night' is missing, and a really dreadful woman singer murders the Audenesque charm of 'You're the Top'.

Then there's *Faust* at the Academy. I think this is the worst colour film I have ever seen. The characters, with their faces out of focus, move with slow primeval gestures through a thick brown fog – the scarlet cap of Mephistopheles occasionally gleaming out of the obscurity with the effect of a traffic-signal. They weave their arms in a curious shorthand which I suppose opera-goers understand, beating their breasts, dragging their feet (this at any rate is understandable) through the Spectra-colour gloom.

In the same programme is *Hohe Schule*, a silly Austrian film about a count who does High School riding on the variety stage wearing a little black mask: he had been cashiered from the Army during the war for duelling (his secret motive

53

was quite unbearably high-minded) and he falls in love with the sister of the man he has killed. I have a fondness for Herr Rudolf Forster's middle-aged and unresilient charm, his heavy period moustaches, his well-bred voice, but breeding in this film has gone berserk, and there is something indescribably absurd about the Count's riding act, his shiny boots, his immense moustaches and rigid back and overpowering air of disguised nobility, as his horse dances delicately on hoof-tip round and round and round the stage.

That seems to leave *Captain Blood* unaccounted for, and really I enjoyed *Captain Blood* the most. After three film versions everyone must know Mr Sabatini's romantic tale of Protestant slaves and chaste pirates, wicked West India governors, bad King James and good King William. Here is a fine spirited mix-up with clothes and wigs which sometimes hark back to the sixteenth century and sometimes forward to the period of Wolfe. One is hardly surprised, therefore, by the magnificently wrong characterization of dull grim virtuous James as a wicked witty debonair eighteenth-century aristocrat, and one is quite prepared for the culminating moment when the Union Jack breaks proudly, anachronously, forth at Peter Blood's masthead.   *The Spectator*, 21 February 1936

I Dream Too Much (USA, RKO, 1935). Director: John Cromwell. Lily Pons, Henry Fonda, Eric Blore, Osgood Perkins, Lucille Ball, Mischa Auer.
Anything Goes (USA, Paramount, 1935). Director: Lewis Milestone. Bing Crosby, Ethel Merman, Ida Lupino, Charles Ruggles.
Faust (GB, 1936). Director: A. E. C. Hopkins. Anne Ziegler, Webster Booth, Dennis Hoey.
Hohe Schule (Austria/Germany, ABC-Film/Tobis Sascha, 1934). Director: Erich Engel. Rudolf Forster, Angela Salloker.
Captain Blood (USA, Warner Bros, 1935). Director: Michael Curtiz. Errol Flynn, Olivia de Havilland.

Things to Come/Bonne Chance

'I've been timid, O'Man. I've been holding myself in. I haven't done myself justice. I've kept down the simmering, seething, teeming ideas. . . .' The voice of Mr Polly's friend Parsons came irresistibly to my mind as the vast expensive Korda-Wells film of the future ground noisily on its way, as I watched the giant aeroplanes, the streamlined tanks, the bright complex meaningless machinery of Mr Wells's riotous fancy. The reformed clothes, the odd rather Grecian dresses with square shoulders and pouter-pigeon breasts, this whole vision of a world peopled by beautiful idealistic scientists would certainly have appealed to the rapturous literary provincial Parsons, the inventor of the Port Burdock school of window-dressing. Parsons too was an idealist.

Nevertheless, a third of this film is magnificent. No one but the author of *War in the Air* could have created so vividly, with such horribly convincing detail, the surprise air raid with which the great war of 1940 opens: the lorry with loudspeakers in Piccadilly Circus urging the crowd to go quietly home and close all windows and block all apertures against gas, the emergency distribution of a few inadequate masks, the cohort of black planes driving over the white southern cliffs, the crowd milling in subways, the dreadful death cries from the London bus, the faceless man in evening dress dead in the taxi. But from this point the film steadily deteriorates, though the world's reversion to barbarism, the plague, the small parochial dictator who carries on twenty years later the same war with the same slogans against his parish neighbour, like a medieval Della Scala, has the acuteness and authenticity of a lesson properly drawn from history. It is with the intrusion of Mr Wells's 'Great Conspiracy', an organization of airmen working together from a base in Basra to clean up the world, that the film begins to lose all its interest in the clouds of Mr Wells's uncontrolled fancies, vague, optimistic, childlike. 'I am Wings over the World,' the strange airman persistently and irritatingly replies to the robber leader's question, 'Who are you?' As Mr Polly remarked when he saw Parsons's window-dressing, 'The High Egrugious is fairly On.'

The unreligious mind when it sets about designing a heaven for itself is apt to be trivial, portentous, sentimental. Out of the simmering, seething, teeming ideas of Mr Wells there emerges, after the reformed dresses, the underground city, the new machinery, the classless society, the television, the tiny wireless sets worn on the wrist, the endless little mechanical toys, the realization that something after all is still missing. It never ceases to come as a shock to a mind like Mr Wells's that a man can still be unhappy when he has leisure, food, comfort, and the best modern dynamos. But it comes as even more of a shock to his audience that Mr Wells can think of no less old-fashioned a way of appeasing this sense of dissatisfaction than by shooting two of his characters at the moon ('The best of life' – nobody in this film speaks less bookishly than that – 'lies nearest to the edge of death'), and the film closes with a sky of stars and some hollow optimistic phrase about the infinite spaces and the endlessness of man's future progress. It is in such smug and sentimental terms that the characters in this film always speak. Only Mr Polly, I think, could find the right words to describe their embarrassing eloquence. 'Sesquippledan,' one can almost hear him saying, 'sesquippledan verboojuice. Eloquent rapsodooce.'

When the noise and the shouting has subsided it may be possible to suggest that M. Sacha Guitry's *Bonne Chance* is worth a dozen *Things to Come*, whether you consider it as cinema, as entertainment or even as social criticism. It is a charming silly film in the Clair genre, a lyrical absurdity. It reminds one again that

Bonne Chance: Jacqueline Delubac, Sacha Guitry

only the cinema and music among the arts have been able to convey this sense of poignant happiness, the quickness and lightness and transience of a sensation you cannot call by any name so heavy as joy: 'the phoenix hour': the nearest to a Utopia poor mankind is ever likely to get.   *The Spectator*, 28 February 1936

Things to Come (GB, London Films, 1936). Director: William Cameron Menzies. Raymond Massey, Ralph Richardson, Cedric Hardwicke, Sophie Stewart, Ann Todd.
Bonne Chance (France, Maurice Lehmann/Fernand Rivers, 1935). Director: Sacha Guitry. Sacha Guitry, Jacqueline Delubac.

Rose of the Rancho/Jack of All Trades

Miss Gladys Swarthout is the latest singer from the Metropolitan Opera House to 'go movie' and to my mind, which cares little for music, the most agreeable. *Rose of the Rancho* is a very long way indeed from being a good film, but at least it is without the bogus seriousness, the artiness, the pomposity of Miss Grace Moore's and Miss Pons's pictures. There is nothing operatic about it: no love-life of a *prima donna*, no blithe Dôme or wistful Rotonde, no first appearance in New York threatened by unhappy Romance. It is just a commonplace Western (the scene is actually New Mexico) with galloping horses and last-minute rescues and masked riders and a secret Federal agent who falls in love with the bandit. One could do very happily without the music altogether, for Miss Swarthout is quite as attractive as any other star dummy, whether she is wearing a mantilla as Queen of Santa Something *festa*, or, as the mysterious leader of the patriotic brigands, black riding-breeches. And one could do very happily, too, without Mr John Boles. I find Mr Boles, his air of confident carnality, the lick of black shiny hair across the plump white waste of face, peculiarly unsympathetic; and never more so than in this film as he directs his lick, his large assured amorous eyes, towards Miss Swarthout and croons:

> I call you a gift from the angels,
> For I feel in my heart you're divine.

That is about the standard of the lush last-century melodies which interrupt rather oddly the gunshots, the beating hoofs, the traditional American dialogue that one begins after a while to welcome rather wearily like very old friends whose conversation one has exhausted – 'Siddown won't you – Thenks.' 'A wise guy, huh?'

Mr Hulbert is another actor for whom I feel a perhaps unfair repugnance. The beginning of *Jack of All Trades*, however, shows him at his best, as he gate-crashes into a job with a big financial house by inventing on the spur of the moment a *plan*, the magic contemporary word. No banker dares to confess that he has heard of the Plan for the first time, and the scene at the board meeting, when Mr Hulbert, asked to explain it in connection with Rationalization (another magic word he doesn't know the meaning of), carries the directors with him by reciting Henry V's speech before Agincourt, is excellent and pointed fooling. Afterwards the film degenerates into nothing but the jutting jaw and the permanent grin, the same memory that one takes away from all Mr Hulbert's films, a nightmare memory, for what could be more horrifying than a jaw and a grin moving through restaurants and along streets, in and out of offices, down subways, an awful eternal disembodied Cheeriness?

I wish there existed an organization with the means to anthologize the excellent sequences that can so often be found in the worst films and save them from oblivion. Mr Hulbert's scene at the board meeting might find a place, and the fight in *'Frisco Kid*, shown last week at the Regal, would certainly deserve to be included. *'Frisco Kid* was a stale sentimental worthless film with the same kind of tough, period subject, without the style, as *Barbary Coast*, but the fight between Mr James Cagney and a one-armed sailor with a hook was the most brutal and convincing I can remember seeing on the screen. Another sequence well worth saving occurred in a silly English musical farce shown last week at the Plaza, *Public Nuisance Number One*: the singing by Miss Frances Day of a delightful skit on a Victorian ballad: 'I had a dog. It got lost in a fog' (it thoroughly puzzled an audience which took the canine sentiment quite seriously). Admirably directed, admirably acted, this sequence was worth sitting through all the long weary film to see. It was even worth bearing with patience Mr Riscoe's contorted music-hall face which thrust every joke down one's gullet with the relentless energy of the machine that corks the bottles in a lemonade factory. Miss Frances Day, with her ashen hair, her humorous elongated face, her lovely witty and malicious eyes, given a Capra to direct her or a Guitry to write for her, would rival in one's affections Miss Claudette Colbert or Mlle Jacqueline Delubac.   *The Spectator*, 6 March 1936

Rose of the Rancho (USA, Paramount, 1936). Director: Marion Gering. Gladys Swarthout, John Boles, Charles Bickford.
Jack of All Trades (GB, Gainsborough, 1936). Director: Robert Stevenson. Jack Hulbert, Betty Astell, Robertson Hare, Gina Malo. [US title: *The Two of Us*.]

Crime et Châtiment/Veille d'Armes

I suppose it may be considered a laudable ambition to try to translate Dostoievsky's novels into film terms, but *Crime et Châtiment*, just as much as *The Brothers Karamazov* a year or two ago, suggests that such an attempt is almost bound to fail. It is the superficial violence of these novels which attracts the film director. 'Here,' one can imagine him arguing, 'are tales of murder. The cinema has always been successful at conveying violence, and what a remarkable film will be the result when our murder is a really classic one.' I have long suspected that a high-class murder is the simple artistic ideal of most film directors, from Mr Hitchcock upwards.

And the murder, of course, *is* admirable: the director and the cameraman and the scenario-writer do their usual work to admiration. They are remarkably faithful, too, to the original murder, even to the tinny sound of the old money-lender's bell, to Raskolnikov's decayed, absurd and mournful 'topper'. For this is a more than usually intelligent film (once granted the initial mistake), and what of the novel's theme *can* be converted into visual terms has been converted. Raskolnikov's unbalanced pride is well suggested: in the mockery of a hat, in his crazy isolation as he makes his way through the friendly evening crowds to the scene of his crime; and of his sensitive conscience you can have no doubt watching M. Pierre Blanchar's hollow handsome haunted features.

But after all there is more to Dostoievsky's story than a case of conscience;

Raskolnikov is a more subtle figure than Eugene Aram and a more general one. The director has not met his first difficulty: the fact that the book is written from inside Raskolnikov's brain. M. Chenal's camera takes its stand on the outside, the world's side. It would have been far better to have dropped the realistic approach altogether, to have battered the real theme into us with soliloquies, with aerial voices, with dream imagery, with every kind of superrealist trick. There would be no place in such a film, of course, for anything but the barest bones of the objective plot, but even M. Chenal has found it necessary to omit most of the sub-plot, though he has left a few untidy and bewildering pieces behind. And what is more unsatisfactory still, he has treated the character of Sonia with such curtness and false delicacy that an audience unacquainted with the book will find it very hard to understand her presence at all.

'Do not despise life', and again 'I look upon you as one of those men who, with a smile, would permit their executioners to tear their bowels out, provided they had found their fetish.' The magistrate Porphyrius thus stated the theme of the book, when he suggested to Raskolnikov that by confessing he would renounce his crazy egotistic Napoleonic fetish, which had proved in the act of murder so bestial, and discover 'the ordinary current of life'. Raskolnikov's worship of the prostitute, Sonia, his patient endurance of the Siberian prison, were not meant to be a spectacular atonement for his crime but a private means of one day attaining the ordinary, the humble, the communal happiness. He had no chance of freedom: proofs of his guilt were in Porphyrius's possession; but in the film the magistrate has no proofs; he presents him with the melodramatic choice between confession and liberty. M. Harry Baur's Porphyrius is a lovely performance, the finest I have seen in the cinema this year, with his tortoise movements, his streak of cruelty, his terrible good humour; it is a pity that the drama should have been narrowed down to one murderer's guilty conscience.

This narrowing, of course, is the usual commercial process. When you have narrowed your theme sufficiently you have obtained a fiction which has no disturbing features, the pure commercial article like that ably served at Studio One. A French naval captain's wife, hidden in her lover's cabin during a battle, is the sole surviving witness of the enemy signals, the only witness who can clear her husband from the charge of losing his ship by negligence. A rather less usual case of conscience, this, and the theme narrowed to the safe absurd commercial limit.

The Spectator, 13 March 1936

Crime et Châtiment (France, Compagnie Générale de Production Cinématographique, 1936). Director: Pierre Chenal. Pierre Blanchar, Harry Baur.
Veille d'Armes (France, SEDIF, 1935). Director: Marcel L'Herbier. Annabella, Victor Francen.

The Milky Way/Strike Me Pink/Night Mail/Crime and Punishment

The gag-makers have been very well employed on the latest Harold Lloyd film. The great Lloyd factory has never constructed a better picture, and one is more amazed than ever at the good fortune of this youngish man whose chief talent is not to act at all, to do nothing, to serve as a blank wall for other people to scrawl their ideas on. He is a very amiable blank, he doesn't mind others acting, and Mr Adolphe Menjou in *The Milky Way* acts with the toughness and energy he showed in *The Front Page*. Mr Menjou in this kind of part is unbeatable, the part of a crooked boxing manager who nurses, by means of phoney fights, the publicity

The Milky Way: Harold Lloyd, Adolphe Menjou

value of Lloyd – 'the fighting milkman' – in order to collect the big money when he matches him against his other protégé, the world champion. It is odd, as one watches Mr Menjou stride noisily and victoriously through this picture, ranting, raving, wheedling, double-crossing, to remember his first 'break' when Mr Chaplin starred him as a suave elegant vicious 'man of the world' in *Woman of Paris* and condemned him to years of miscasting. Mr Menjou runs away with the film: he doesn't need gags: he doesn't need to smuggle a foal into a taxi and disguise its neighs with his own: he doesn't need to boomerang bowler-hats. These gags are for the star, and so with the gag-makers at the top of their form and Mr Menjou at the top of his, we have the best 'Harold Lloyd' to date.

Mr Eddie Cantor is another matter altogether. He too has a fine team of gag-men behind him (one pictures these anonymous creatures as belonging to the same intellectual genre as the inventors of practical jokes which fill the windows of the Holborn shops at Christmas-time: the buns that squeak, the flies sculptured with Oriental nicety on real lumps of sugar, the rubber plate-lifters). But Mr Cantor does not depend entirely on his gags; he is an actor of distinction with his dim plaintive voice, his revolving eyes, his reckless gleam. He tries hard to raise himself to the Chaplin level, to represent a whole class, a philosophy, but he will never be quite good enough for that, his idea of the *victorious* little man is too patently

Strike Me Pink: Eddie Cantor

optimistic and untrue. Nevertheless, one will have to wait a very long time for any film funnier than this one. Mr Cantor is appointed, after taking a correspondence course in character development ('Are you a Man or a Mouse?'), to the management of an amusement park. His predecessors have been put on the spot by gangsters who wish to install crooked betting-machines, and the scene between Mr Cantor and the gunman who has taken the same correspondence course but has stopped at an earlier chapter is superb.

Night Mail, directed by Mr Basil Wright and Mr Harry Watt for the GPO Film Unit, is one of the best films to be seen in London. It isn't a complete success; the opening sequences seem to lack design – and clarity (the pictures taken from the air are of poor quality and the eye doesn't immediately recognize them for what they are). But the final sequences as the train drives at dawn through the northern moors, the sheep-dog racing the train and the rabbits scurrying to cover, set to the simple visual verses of Mr Auden, are extraordinarily exciting. This use of verse has been rather obtusely criticized, notably by Miss Lejeune, whose comments show an amazing lack of cinema *ear*. To criticize Mr Auden's words (timed selective commentary made to match the images on the screen) as if they were lyric poetry is absurd.

The American *Crime and Punishment*, in spite of the fine acting of Mr Peter Lorre, is a dreadful contrast to the French. In the dark intense French picture there was at least something of Dostoievsky's religious and unhappy mind. This gleam-ing lunch-bar-chromium version – which opens at the University with Raskol-nikov receiving his degree and listening to the Vice-Chancellor's earnest American abstractions about Youth and Alma Mater and the Future – is vulgar as only the great New World can be vulgar, with the vulgarity of the completely unreligious, of sentimental idealism, of pitch-pine ethics, with the hollow optimism about human nature, of a salesman who has never failed to sell his canned beans.

The Spectator, 20 March 1936

The Milky Way (USA, Paramount, 1936). Director: Leo McCarey. Harold Lloyd, Adolphe Menjou, Verree Teasdale, Helen Mack, Dorothy Wilson.
Strike Me Pink (USA, Samuel Goldwyn, 1935). Director: Norman Taurog. Eddie Cantor, Ethel Merman, Sally Eilers.
Night Mail (GB, GPO Film Unit, 1936). Directors: Basil Wright, Harry Watt.
Crime and Punishment (USA, Columbia, 1936). Director: Josef von Sternberg. Peter Lorre, Edward Arnold, Marian Marsh, Mrs Patrick Campbell.

Rhodes of Africa/October

Sober, worthy, humourless, *Rhodes of Africa* unrolls its eleven well-bred reels with all the technical advantages of 1936. It is a good film, judged by the ordinary standard, well photographed, well directed, well acted, particularly by Mr Oscar Homolka as Kruger, with some fine shots of African scenery. It is the kind of respectable picture (there was another some years ago of Livingstone) which reminds one a little of a biography by a modern Liberal: someone kindlier, more trustworthy, infinitely more charitable but not less dull than Lord Morley, with the anarchistic point of view of a man who never makes a moral condemnation. *October*, another historical picture made as long ago as 1928 by Eisenstein, is a curious contrast, restless, excited, crackling with venom: this is certainly not fair, certainly not Liberal (the sub-titles spit out 'Mensheviks' as one might exclaim 'Rabbits!' whenever these toothy well-meaning politicians in pince-nez pass across the screen).

Nobody concerned with the English film, neither its German director, Mr Berthold Viertel, nor its American star, Mr Walter Huston, has any passionate conviction whether for or against Rhodes and his work in Africa. Miss Peggy Ashcroft as a most unlikely woman novelist – one imagines she is intended for Olive Schreiner – rebukes Rhodes for his treatment of the Matabele in her usual gentle, carefully enunciated, Shakespearian tones, flickering her young romantic Juliet lashes at stated intervals with the effect of too much punctuation; but the emphasis otherwise is all on the good side of human nature: Barney Barnato, Kruger, Jameson, Rhodes himself, the King of the Matabele – there is something to be said, that is the impression, for all of them; the kindly optimistic Liberal tempera-ment does not recognize the Fall of Man. After ten days I can remember very little of this film but a sense of gentle titillation, of being scratched agreeably in the right spot.

But the talkies have come, and stereoscopy and colour no doubt will come, without destroying the vivid memories of *October*: Kerensky hounded from the capital by a camera which never fails to record with merciless caricature the gleam of gaiters, the Napoleonic gesture, the neurotic hands, the thin frightened defiant egotistical face, the braces hanging over the chandelier in the Tsar's bedroom; the macabre and comic Battalion of Death, large ungainly women in uniforms as shapeless as policewomen's, adjusting their stockings and brassières as they sprawl across the billiard-tables in the Palace, or wandering hand in hand, like affectionate hippopotami, through the great tank-like rooms; the huge crowds fleeing, in the July days, before Kerensky's machine-guns; the women in lace petticoats and picture hats stabbing out the eyes of the young agitator with their parasols; the scene, which recalls the Odessa steps sequence in *The Cruiser Potemkin*, when the bridges are raised between the workers' quarters and the city, and the ancient unhorsed cab is balanced for a while high above the river before it rushes down the long perpendicular slide.

To me the most vivid impression of revolution (and one which only a participant would have thought of presenting) was the committee-room door swinging continually open, the people pushing in and out, the telephone bells ringing, the crowded secretarial rooms, the shouting to make yourself heard, the little rabbitty scared people getting up and proposing resolutions. Compared with *Mother*, *October* is almost comedy; Kerensky inspecting the Tsar's footmen, weeping among the sofa cushions, playing with the royal decanters, is a figure for laughter; the film has something of that air of happiness Trotsky described in his history: 'the colossal task, the pride in success, the joyful failing of the heart at the thought of the morrow which is to be still more beautiful than today'. I suppose somebody once felt that about Rhodes too, about his Cape to Cairo ambition, the amalgamation of diamond-mines; a good film might have been made about it all in those days; now as an Empire we are too old, the pride isn't there, the heart seems to have failed once too often. *The Spectator*, 27 March 1936

Rhodes of Africa (GB, Gaumont British, 1936). Director: Berthold Viertel. Walter Huston, Peggy Ashcroft, Oscar Homolka. [US title: *Rhodes*.]
October (USSR, Sovkino, 1928). Director: Sergei Eisenstein. Nikandrov, N. Popov.

Merlusse/The Day of the Great Adventure/Desire

French schoolboys supervised in their small asphalt yard, in their cold stone dining-hall, in their dormitory where a master sleeps in a square muslin tent: Nordic schoolboys (strictly speaking Polish, but their blond hair, their simple handsome brutish faces are exactly those of German boys) washing their shoulders in the snow, pillow-fighting in a mountain hut, skiing alone across the wastes. The contrast is extreme, and I cannot help preferring the French.

Merlusse, directed by Marcel Pagnol with a cast of which only the principal player has appeared on the screen before, is a slight sentimental tale of a one-eyed master feared by the boys and distrusted by his colleagues, who on Christmas-night finds a way to the affections of the twenty boys left by their parents at the school. We are told that it is a true story of the Marseille Lycée where Pagnol was once a master and where the scenes are taken. But that matters less than the fine acting of Henri Poupon as Merlusse ('Codfish'), with his terrible dead twisted eye, his scrubby beard, his starved paternity, and his secret terror of the boys he has to control. Pagnol's direction has a simpleness, a directness that are admirable.

As for the children, how much more agreeable and varied they are, how much less aggressively healthy and priggish and normal than the Boy Scouts who in the Polish film hunt down a gang of cocaine-smugglers in the Tatra Mountains. These scrubby, rather miserable, and not too clean children, smoking illicitly round the corner of the asphalt yard, boastful over first love-letters, not above getting somebody else to leave a drawing-pin on the master's chair, overgrown louts and curly Fauntleroys, a nigger, an Asiatic, a Jew, these might well include in their number a

Desire: Marlene Dietrich

Rimbaud, a Cézanne; but as for the Boy Scouts with their communal song, their unnaturally developed sense of honour, their portrait of Lord Baden-Powell, their parade at evening to salute with raised arms the Flag, the best that any of these can become, one feels, is a Hitler – or not even a Hitler, but a Hitler's lieutenant to be purged on some thirtieth of June. This film has been awarded medals at Venice and Moscow. Stalin's youth and Mussolini's youth both found it, I suppose, inspiring, but in this country, happy thought; it is still possible to find their well-drilled morality a little absurd. Particularly delightful to the comic sense is the moment when three Scouts, who for the most honourable and civic reasons have found it necessary to violate their Scout oaths, surrender their whistles to the Scout Captain. Their whistles are accepted, but a telegram from Warsaw at the last moment directs the Captain to return them. Yes, it is still possible for us to laugh, but not with too great an assurance; it is these and not the French who are nearer to the English public-school spirit, and it is an Englishman's portrait, not Pilsudski's or Hitler's, which hangs on the wall.

Desire – ridiculous and misleading title – is the best film in which Miss Marlene Dietrich has appeared since she left Germany, and the most amusing new film to be seen in London this week. Produced, though not directed, by Lubitsch, this comedy of an international jewel thief who smuggles her stolen pearls across the French frontier in the pocket of an American 'hick' on a holiday (one of Mr Gary Cooper's best performances), and who while she tries to retrieve them falls in love with the hick, has all the absurd delicious trimmings one expects in a Lubitsch film. Best of all is the sinister old female crook who remarks, 'If I *were* your grandmother, you'd offer me some brandy.' Miss Dietrich is allowed to act in this film, even to sing, and what memories of the cheap alluring cabaret figure, the tilted top hat, that husky voice recalls. But since those days Miss Dietrich has been so tidied groomed, perfected that one simply cannot believe that she exists at all – though there are moments in *this* film when Absolute Beauty very nearly wavers into the relative, the human, the desirable.   *The Spectator*, 3 April 1936

Merlusse (France, Films Marcel Pagnol, 1935). Director: Marcel Pagnol. Henri Poupon.
The Day of the Great Adventure (Poland, Panta-Film, 1935). Director: Josef Lejtes.
Desire (USA, Paramount, 1936). Director: Frank Borzage. Marlene Dietrich, Gary Cooper.

Liebesmelodie/Pot Luck/If You Could Only Cook/One Way Ticket

It has been a dead week so far as new films are concerned: after so many successes one must expect a few rather empty weeks, for there are not enough cinemas free with Charlie Chaplin, Harold Lloyd and Eddie Cantor still holding out at the Tivoli and London Pavilion, not to speak of the dull and depressing Cassandra in Leicester Square. All but the last of the new films are comedies; they are not bad comedies judged by the depth to which the cinema can fall, but they look rather small in company with Chaplin and Cantor. Each contains a player whom I find peculiarly antipathetic, however well directed: Fräulein Marta Eggerth in the first, Mr Ralph Lynn in the second and, most of all, Mr Herbert Marshall in the third.

Liebesmelodie is one of those devastatingly gay films of Austrian life: one's spirit withers as the glasses fill. Only too soon, one feels certain, they will be splintered on the floor in gallant and noisy toasts; the director will begin to cut his picture rapidly at fancy angles; the gipsy violinist will reach the table of the revue star who will then (improbable generosity!) burst into unpaid song. Then for contrast comes, of course, the trip into the Hungarian countryside (the revue star has long dreamed of an old farmhouse) and we begin to recognize the grim inevitability of that kiss on a haycock, the quaint national costumes of the peasants going by to a wedding. But there are consolations (though perhaps I ought not to count among them the odd use of incestuous love as a comic idea): the admirable performances of Herr Leo Slezak, who may be remembered as the old composer in *Musik im Blut*, now an old Hungarian landowner threatened by a relic of his immoral youth, and of Herr Hans Moser as his badgered and despairing moral bodyguard.

There are consolations too in *Pot Luck*: Mr Tom Walls as a retired detective-inspector of Scotland Yard acts with his usual ease, and Mr Robertson Hare is admirably true to form as the diffident owner of an old abbey in which a gang of art thieves have their secret hide-out. This is the best *directed* film Mr Walls has made, but one misses the slightly salacious humour of the earlier pictures: there is too much melodrama, too little Hare, and, of course, as always to my mind, too much Lynn, too much of the scaly tortoise face and hollow imbecility.

The Regal programme will have changed by the time this review appears, and I do not think anyone need await the release of *If You Could Only Cook* with any impatience. It is produced by Mr Frank Capra, who made *It Happened One Night*, and it bears a few agreeable Capra touches, a few situations which might have had wit if the main performance had been less earnest, less conceited, less humourless than that of Mr Marshall, who plays the part of a millionaire on holiday posing as a butler. Not a bright situation, though Mr Capra, with the help of such players as Mr Leo Carillo, Miss Jean Arthur and Mr Lionel Stander, might have made something of it. But fantasy droops before Mr Marshall, so intractably British in the American scene. He does, I suppose, represent some genuine national characteristics, if not those one wishes to see exported: characteristics which it is necessary to describe in terms of inanimate objects: a kind of tobacco, a kind of tweed, a kind of pipe: or in terms of dog, something large, sentimental and moulting, something which confirms one's preference for cats.

One Way Ticket is a rather sentimental melodrama about a prison officer's daughter who helps a convict to escape. It is well acted and has one excellent sequence: the prison break when the captain of the guard (played by Mr Walter Connolly) mows down with a machine-gun two of his own men who are held as hostages in the floodlit yard. This picture will pass an hour at a local cinema better than many more pretentious pictures. The most conventional American melodramas usually have a bite about them: they criticize as well as thrill, and that makes even *One Way Ticket* more convincing and entertaining than the polished fairy-tales of Mr Hitchcock. *The Spectator*, 10 April 1936

Liebesmelodie (Austria, Standard-Film, 1935). Director: Viktor Tourjansky. Marta Eggerth, Leo Slezak, Hans Moser.
Pot Luck (GB, Gainsborough, 1936). Director: Tom Walls. Tom Walls, Ralph Lynn, Robertson Hare.
If You Could Only Cook (USA, Columbia, 1935). Director: William Seiter. Herbert Marshall, Jean Arthur, Leo Carillo, Lionel Stander.
One Way Ticket (USA, Columbia, 1935). Director: Herbert Biberman. Lloyd Nolan, Peggy Conklin, Walter Connolly.

Kliou the Tiger

'Into her unfinished basket Dhi – the daughter of the Quan – was weaving dreams of her beloved one.' That is the kind of film the Marquis de la Falaise has brought back with him from Indo-China. Oh, the appalling conceit, one longs to exclaim, as the horrid Technicolor browns and greens stain the screen, of these travellers with movie cameras who, not content to photograph what they see, presume, on a few months' acquaintance, to write a tale of native life, to say *what* dreams. . . .

This to my mind is the worst type of travel film. Better the travelogue, the 'views of old Japan', the cherry tree blossoming to point the wisecrack. Far better, of course, the plain statement of fact, such a film as Mr Smythe's *Kamet*. Best of all – there has been only the one of this kind – *Song of Ceylon*, where the plain statement has the intensity of poetic experience. Mr Basil Wright was content to accept the limitations of ignorance, of a European mind, to be 'on the outside, looking in'; the film is a visual record of the effect on a sensitive Western brain of old, communal, religious appearances, not of a life which Mr Wright pretends to *know*.

'Thrice five suns had risen over Klien-hara, since last the forest had swallowed them up.' The Marquis de la Falaise is speaking again, and, of course, the caption is followed promptly by the sixteenth sun, an improbable ochre dawn. . . .

But perhaps what annoys one most in this cheap vulgar film is the waste of good material – not such good material as Mr Zoltan Korda brought back from Nigeria to waste in *Sanders of the River*, for the Marquis has no eye whatever for the significant (an elephant or a tiger is always more important to his melodramatic mind than the men and women of the Moi tribe, though equally good shots of tigers could have been made in Hollywood; indeed . . . but to that doubt later), still fairly good material: the houses on stilts, the poor patches of cultivation at the hill foot, gentle lovely youth, ugly diseased age and a little of the ordinary life that goes between. The Marquis has preferred to dramatize, to use what – for want of a more accurate word – we must call 'imagination'. 'Into her unfinished basket . . . ' and the strange faces can hardly restrain their smiles at the curious awkward emotional Western thoughts they are made to express. But first the prologue: the lonely French outpost on what we are told is the edge of 'tiger-infested' jungle, 'fever-ridden' swamps where live 'the mysterious' Moi, 'a very savage and dangerous tribe': the Marquis emerging in shorts and topee from a shrubbery and recounting to the lonely officer over a sundowner his traveller's yarn, which consists of the love-story of Dhi, the daughter of the Quan, and Bhat, the hunter. The Quan is mauled by Kliou the tiger, and a medicine-man tells the tribe that unless the tiger is killed, the Quan will die. So Bhat goes out with his spear to hunt the man-eater and win his bride.

And now we come to the Problem of the Tiger so admirably photographed (the other wild animals, even the elephants, the pythons, the water-buffalo, 'most treacherous of horned beasts', present no such difficult dilemma). We are told that for filming in Technicolor 'long-focus lenses cannot be used, so the pictures showing close-ups of tigers were genuine close-ups – not pictures taken hundreds of yards away. The Marquis vouches for the authenticity of every shot, the entire picture having been filmed in the jungle without any studio or specially staged scenes being added. The tigers are real tigers [certainly one had not thought of them as stuffed], photographed in their natural surroundings.' So definite a statement leaves us with a painful dilemma: we see the tiger leap upon the Quan, we seem to see the man mauled. None of the scenes, we have been told, were staged; the Marquis with eighteenth-century imperturbability must have continued to shoot his film within a few feet of the struggle. How are we to help doubting either his accuracy or his humanity? And the little well-shaven gentleman in shorts and topee emerging from that fever-ridden swamp has all the appearance of a kindly man.   *The Spectator*, 17 April 1936

Kliou the Tiger (*Kliou the Killer*) (USA, Barret, 1936). Director: Marquis de la Falaise.

Follow the Fleet/The Peace Film

It needs an effort of the mind to remember that Mr Fred Astaire was not invented by a film director and drawn by a film draughtsman. He is the nearest we are ever likely to get to a human Mickey, near enough for many critics to have noted the resemblance. If one needs to assign human qualities to this light, quick, humorous cartoon, they are the same as the early Mickey's: a touch of pathos, the sense of a courageous and impromptu intelligence, a capacity for getting into awkward situations. Something has to be done, and Mickey without a moment's hesitation will fling his own tail across an abyss and tread the furry unattached tightrope with superb insouciance. Something has to be done, and Mr Astaire bursts into a dance which in its speed and unselfconsciousness seems equally to break the laws of nature. They are both defending Minnie, though Miss Ginger Rogers will never quite attain Minnie's significance (she is too brazen and self-sufficing for the part), and there is no villain type, no huge black Pasha cat continually to threaten her with ravishment: the plots of Mr Astaire's films are more everyday; one might almost say more decent, more 'family'.

That is a pity, for he doesn't belong to this unfantastic world: he ought not to double his story with the sentimental romance of a Paris dressmaker, formerly of the tedious Russian nobility, and an American hick (*Roberta*), or of the nice homing girl and the untrustworthy sailor in the present film. He has never again been quite so good as in *Gay Divorce*, not merely because he had Mr Cole Porter's music to dance to and the enchanting 'Night and Day' to sing, but because then the tale – of the professional co-respondent – had the right fantastic note. Our divorce laws *do* belong to Mickey's gravitationless world (no wonder that our national humorist should feel that they are inconsistent with this – the sensible, the middle-class, the *Punch* – globe).

But his new film, I think, is the best since *Gay Divorce*. Not that there is any merit to the story of this hoofer enlisted in the United States Navy who meets his former dancing partner when on shore leave. Nor does Mr Randolph Scott as a Juanesque sailor provide less heavy entertainment than he did in *Roberta*, though his new partner, Miss Harriet Hilliard, with her Sylvia Sidney eyes and her husky voice, is infinitely to be preferred to Miss Irene Dunne. I think one reason why one so enjoys this film is that the human Mickey is more suitably clothed in the simple impersonal sailor blue and white than in 'top hat, white tie and tails'. There is something curiously ill at ease about the cinema's – and the music-hall's – attitude to evening dress, something horrifyingly doggish. (One remembers Mr Jack Hulbert and Miss Cicely Courtneidge twirling canes and raking unnaturally glossy hats.) Nothing is less graceful for a Mickey to dance in: the tails twist round the performer in Laocoön coils. Mr Astaire dressed in a seaman's inhuman uniform does drop one more terrestrial envelope, comes nearer to soaring in those regions where once Mickey soared. Alas! where he soars no longer. Mickey in his Technicolor days has been refined out of all knowledge; no longer does Minnie struggle on the edge of the great cat's couch, and the very capable Fleischer cartoon, *The Little Stranger*, in the same programme as *Follow the Fleet*, should be a warning to Mr Disney that if he relies only on agreeable colour, on pictorial prettiness, there will soon be others to equal him.

The British Board of Film Censors have once more supplied the best joke of the

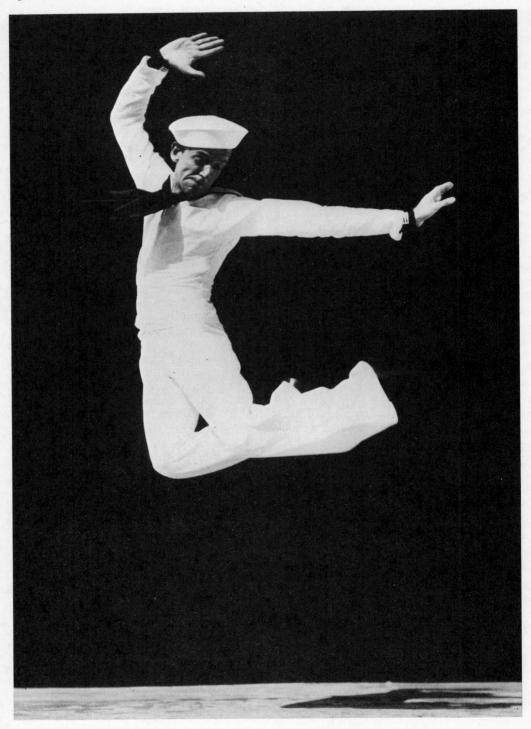

Follow the Fleet: Fred Astaire

week by carefully preserving the devil from disrespect. This funny but really rather deplorable Board have substituted a sharp metallic click for Satan's name when Miss Hilliard sings the refrain of a charming sentimental song, 'Get thee behind me ——'. Nor is it really to the credit of the Board that they have rendered a service to the cause of collective security by the publicity their absurd Fabian tactics have given to the 'Peace' film, an admirable little three-minute picture, which for its point and economy, its clever simultaneous use of image, caption and voice, deserves to be reckoned the best film of the week.   *The Spectator*, 24 April 1936

Follow the Fleet (USA, RKO, 1936). Director: Mark Sandrich. Fred Astaire, Ginger Rogers, Randolph Scott, Harriet Hilliard.
The Peace Film (1936).

These Three/The Student of Prague

I have seldom been so moved by any fictional film as by *These Three*. After ten minutes or so of the usual screen sentiment, quaintness and exaggeration, one began to watch with incredulous pleasure nothing less than life: a genuine situation, a moral realism that allows one of two school-mistresses, whose lives and careers have been ruined by the malicious lie of a child, to murmur before the rigid self-righteousness of the wealthy grandparent: 'It is the very young and the very old who are wicked.'

These Three: Miriam Hopkins, Merle Oberon

The Student of Prague: Anton Walbrook

The credit, of course, rests primarily with the American theatre, with *The Children's Hour*, but the forbidden subject of the play has been adapted with very little loss of truth: only the beginning and the ending have been blurred and softened for the film public. Miss Merle Oberon and Miss Miriam Hopkins as the two school-teachers act admirably from the moment when the playwright really takes control, from the moment of entanglement in their horrible situation, and Mr Joel McCrea gives one of his amiable, if slightly monotonous, performances. These three represent innocence in an evil world – the world of childhood, the world of moral chaos, lies, brutality, complete inhumanity. Never before has childhood been represented so convincingly on the screen, with an authenticity guaranteed by one's own memories. The more than human evil of the lying sadistic child is suggested with quite shocking mastery by Bonita Granville. This character raises the film from the merely anecdotal, however ingenious and moving the anecdote; it has enough truth and intensity to stand for the whole of the dark side of childhood, in which the ignorance and weakness of the many allows complete mastery to the few. The eleven-year-old actress Marcia Mae Jones gives an almost equally fine performance as one of the weak, whose theft of another girl's bracelet puts her in the power of the blackmailer. The audience laughed when the smudged feeble child repeated to her schoolfellow and torturer under threat of betrayal a solemn 'knightly' oath of vassalage, but it was a terrifying and admirably chosen example of the taboos which exist at that age in that egotistic world, compared with which the adult appears almost kindly and honest. 'It is the very young and the very old who are wicked': there is nothing incredible in the grandparent's support of the lying child, for human sympathies have to die as well as be born.

Of *The Student of Prague*, Dr Robison's last film, one can say at any rate that it is on the right side. It may be dull, but this allegory of the divided personality, of the student who, by the enchantment of an evil and jealous doctor, leaves his dreaming good-natured self behind in the mirror and steps out of his room, undivided, acquisitive and cruel, is on the side of the imagination in an unimaginative industry. Dr Robison from his first film, *Warning Shadows*, was one of the few directors who could mark a picture with his own personality (Lubitsch, Lang, Pudovkin, Clair . . . the list soon peters out). There is no mistaking his slow decorative methods, the curious ballet-like quality he procured by the constant smooth panning of his camera. But dull the film undoubtedly is: a curiosity, a relic of the classical German film of silent days. This doctor 'out of hell', this Faust driven to suicide by remorse, this fair angel, the innkeeper's virtuous daughter with the horseface of awful Teutonic integrity: one admits their right in such a legend to feel, not as human beings do feel, but as they ought to feel, granted the faith behind the symbol. But one cannot believe that this neo-Gothic fantasy really represents any faith; the allegory doesn't satisfy, the sense of evil, one suspects, is there for merely decorative purposes. Nor does the acting help. *The Student of Prague* of silent days was more memorable; the magnificent fox-hunt when the hounds wheeled across the fields as the enchanter turned his hand; the moment when Conrad Veidt as the damned student went down through the woods to the duel he had no intention of fighting, and met his other self mounting the hill with the damp blade that showed he had been more punctual at the appointed place.

The Spectator, 1 May 1936

These Three (USA, Samuel Goldwyn, 1936). Director: William Wyler. Merle Oberon, Miriam Hopkins, Joel McCrea, Bonita Granville.
The Student of Prague (*Der Student von Prag*) (Germany, Cine-Allianz, 1935). Director: Arthur Robison. Adolf Wohlbrück [Anton Walbrook], Dorothea Wieck, Theodor Loos.

Anne-Marie/Tudor Rose

Anne-Marie is a quite amazingly silly film about a girl (Annabella) in an aeroplane firm and the five aces who instruct her in flying: silly but with some amiable qualities. The five aces, in order to keep the girl's mind off an inventor with whom she is falling in love, arrange that one of them shall write her anonymous and passionate letters: the girl, without that ration of sexual interest, cannot be trusted to take her pilot's certificate successfully and afterwards win one of the innumerable records which it is the main livelihood of these pilots to accumulate.

There is very little to be said for this odd plot: the five aces give a rather embarrassing exhibition of dumb masculine affection, and there is no discoverable theme, unless it is a remark of the inventor who protests to the five tough comrades against their involving a woman 'in the terrible games of men'. The terrible games are the record flights: long distance, height, endurance, we have all heard of those, but there is no end to the crazy and childish ingenuity of these professional record-breakers with their closed circuits over so many kilometres with such and such a machine.

But the film, as I have said, has redeeming qualities. The scenario, written by M. Antoine de Saint-Exupéry, the author of *Vol de Nuit*, has a pleasantly technical atmosphere: the dialogue jangles agreeably with gadgets. But it is chiefly worth seeing for an exciting and beautifully directed melodramatic climax, when the girl, attempting a night record, becomes lost in the neighbourhood of Angoulême with a failing petrol-supply in the path of a fleet of military planes: the shots of this dark formation passing overhead between the massing night clouds are finely dramatic. The fleet, of course, is averted just in time from Angoulême, and in an amusing and exhilarating final scene the inventor and the five aces storm the municipal electricity works and signal in morse with the lights of the whole city to the lost plane.

Tudor Rose is one of the more distressing products of the British screen: the fault is not in the director, who has made a smooth, competent, if rather banal, picture, but in the vulgarity of the scenario. The story of Lady Jane Grey is surely dramatic enough to be converted truthfully into film material, but this sentimental pageant in fancy-dress could have displayed no more ignorance of the period if it had been made in Hollywood. There is not a character, not an incident in which history has not been altered for the cheapest of reasons. Edward VI is shown as a preparatory schoolboy who wants to get out in the garden and play with a gun: the weakling Lord Guildford Dudley becomes a tender and romantic 'boy husband': Lady Jane Grey herself, perhaps the nearest approach to a saint the Anglican Church has produced and a scholar of the finest promise, is transformed into an immature child construing – incorrectly – Caesar's *Gallic War* and glad to be released from tiresome lessons. This, I suppose, is the Dark Age of scholarship and civilization, and one ought not to expect anything better from celluloid artists than this sneering attitude to the learning of the Renaissance. The dialogue in English films is notoriously bad, from Mr Wells downwards, but I have seldom listened to more inchoate rubbish than in *Tudor Rose*. The style chops and changes; sometimes, when the Earl of Warwick (so the Duke of Northumberland remains throughout this film) or the Protector Somerset is speaking, the dialogue is written in unconscious blank verse; at other times it consists of the kind of flat simplified colloquialisms that Mrs Naomi Mitchison has made popular in historical novels.

The Spectator, 8 May 1936

Anne-Marie (France, Majestic, 1935). Director: Raymond Bernard. Annabella, Pierre Richard Willm, Jean Murat.
Tudor Rose (GB, Gainsborough, 1936). Director: Robert Stevenson. Nova Pilbeam, Cedric Hardwicke, John Mills. [US title: *Nine Days a Queen*.]

The Trail of the Lonesome Pine/Secret Agent

The only film I have seen with real excitement during the last fortnight was made in 1915. D. W. Griffith's *The Birth of a Nation*, shown in the first of the Everyman Theatre's admirable historical programmes, has hardly dated at all; it is still in advance of the popular film as it exists today. Some of his technical devices, of course, have been adopted, though not the most striking, his way of escaping the ugly artificiality of the screen by fogging part of his film, so that the characters do not move up and down within a fixed rectangular frame but appear, as it were, out of the unfocused corners of the eyes with an effect of startling realism. A superb sense of reality dictates all his devices and is Griffith's main characteristic. Compare the dresses in this film with those of any modern 'period' picture – *The Barretts of Wimpole Street* or *Little Women*: those are 'fancy-dress' in their newness, their archness, their exaggeration, but it needs an effort of the mind to realize that Griffith's film, with its dowdy convincing costumes, its daguerreotype air, was not made in the 1860s. Note too the realistic sense of place: how deeply we get to know the Southern house in Piedmont, seeing it first in its spruce pre-war days and then through all the stages of its decay, and note the careful documentation of Griffith's history, how continually we are told that such and such a scene is a historical facsimile – the circumstances of Lincoln's assassination, for example, which we follow minute by minute, so that even the shifting of a chair has its historical guarantee. And then remember the contemporary film: *Tudor Rose* and *Henry VIII*.

Realism, of course, is not everything, but for a long while the popular film director must expect to be judged by his ability to give an illusion of reality.

On the unrealistic screen colour is already acceptable, but *The Trail of the Lonesome Pine* shows no appreciable advance in realistic colour. It is just bad bright picture-postcard stuff, and if one sometimes forgets its picture-postcard quality, it is only because the images move, change, distract, the story (quite a good one of Kentucky hill feuds) interests, and the actors (Miss Sylvia Sidney in particular) charm. But picture-postcard the colour is, and a still would disclose how crude. The film has one merit: the director by trying to use the ordinary dissolve and obtaining only a distressing blur has demonstrated how many technical devices making for speed we must be prepared to sacrifice for the yet doubtful benefit of Technicolor.

There were those at the Everyman who found the occasional jerkiness of movement and Griffith's pre-war sentiment comic, and one wished them as sharp to detect the cruder absurdities of the contemporary film, for then Mr Hitchcock's latest picture might have been punctuated, and its dullness enlivened, by laughter: laughter at the secret agent who loudly discusses his instructions in front of the hall porter of a Swiss hotel and who brandishes his only clue to a murder in a crowded casino, laughter at the representation of a Secret Service which so

74

arranges things that its agent's photograph appears in every paper, laughter in fact at Mr Hitchcock's inadequate sense of reality. It is all a great pity; a pity because of the immense wasted talent of Mr Peter Lorre, and because Mr Hitchcock too has talent. How unfortunate it is that Mr Hitchcock, a clever director, is allowed to produce and even to write his own films, though as a producer he has no sense of continuity and as a writer he has no sense of life. His films consist of a series of small 'amusing' melodramatic situations: the murderer's button dropped on the baccarat board; the strangled organist's hands prolonging the notes in the empty church; the fugitives hiding in the bell-tower when the bell begins to swing. Very perfunctorily he builds up to these tricky situations (paying no attention on the way to inconsistencies, loose ends, psychological absurdities) and then drops them: they mean nothing: they lead to nothing. As for Mr Maugham's *Ashenden*, on which this film is said to be based, nothing is left of that witty and realistic fiction.

The Spectator, 15 May 1936

The Trail of the Lonesome Pine (USA, Paramount, 1936). Director: Henry Hathaway. Fred MacMurray, Henry Fonda, Sylvia Sidney.
Secret Agent (GB, Gaumont British, 1936). Director: Alfred Hitchcock. Madeleine Carroll, John Gielgud, Peter Lorre, Robert Young, Lilli Palmer.

Klondyke Annie/Professional Soldier

'Ah'm an Occidental wooman, In an Awriental mood.' The big-busted carnivorous creature in tight white sequins sits as firmly and inscrutably for inspection as the fat tattooed women in the pleasure arcades. The husky voice drones, the plump jewelled fingers pluck, the eyes slant, and immediately we are in the familiar atmosphere – not the atmosphere of San Francisco's China Town where the beautiful white lily is in danger of mutilation at the hands of her Oriental lover, behind the bead curtains, among the burning censers – but the friendly, smoky, alcoholic atmosphere of a Private Bar, hung with advertisements for Guinness and Black and White, where for some years now it has always been possible to observe a small group of middle-aged, bowler-hatted businessmen knotted at the far corner away from the youngest barmaid: 'Have you heard this one? Why is Mae West like ——'

One cannot but pay tribute to a personality so outrageously suggestive to the middle-aged. I am completely uncritical of Mae West; I enjoy every one of her films, aware all the time, whether the scene be the Bowery, the Klondyke, Texas or a New York drawing-room, of that bowler-hatted brigade gathered invisibly like seraphs about her stout matronly figure. It is with sorrow, therefore, that I have read the unfavourable notices of her latest picture, in which, escaping from the police (she has stabbed her Chinese lover), she puts on the dress of a dead Salvationist and brings prosperity to a Klondyke settlement house by instilling some vigour into the services. I should be sorry if anyone wasted money owing to my minority opinion; but I did not, as some did, find the satire on religious revivalists in bad taste; I thought the whole film fun, more fun than any other of Miss West's since the superb period piece, *She Done Him Wrong*, but then it never occurred to me that Miss West's conversion was intended to be taken seriously. I liked, too, Mr McLaglen's performance as the dumb dog of a coasting skipper who saves her from the Canadian police ('You're what makes me tick,' he declares with genuine eloquence), and I liked the whole parody of a Salvationist settlement: the unattractive soapy virtues. It is always necessary to review a Mae West film in terms of personalities. The director's job is confined to winning a particularly hazardous kind of obstacle race, to guessing correctly how much the censors will stand, to knowing when to fade out.

Professional Soldier should be carefully avoided. It is a silly and sentimental story of an American mercenary soldier who is hired by virtuous revolutionaries to kidnap the child king of a Ruritanian State and hold him out of harm's way until the revolution has been successful. The child, of course, wins the mercenary's heart, and, when he falls into the wrong hands and is facing a firing-squad, the American successfully breaks gaol, seizes a machine-gun and rescues him single-handed from a regiment of regulars. Mr McLaglen does his best, but Master Freddie Bartholomew never begins to act. He has never begun as far as I know. He recites his words by rote in whatever part he plays, and his directors help him to exercise a lustrous and repulsive charm. The setting and costumes in these Ruritanian stories have a character of their own: plumes and barley-sugar pillars, unbecoming trousers and ornate mantelpieces. *The Spectator*, 22 May 1936

Klondyke Annie (USA, Paramount, 1936). Director: Raoul Walsh. Mae West, Victor McLaglen.
Professional Soldier (USA, 20th Century-Fox, 1935). Director: Tay Garnett. Victor McLaglen, Freddie Bartholomew.

The Robber Symphony/The Littlest Rebel/The Emperor's Candlesticks

Herr Friedrich Feher's *The Robber Symphony* is certainly the most interesting film of the last twelve months, heretical though it is, a picture cut to synchronize with the music. Containing moments of really sensitive direction, it goes on for nearly two hours, restless, scatterbrained, amusing, boring, cheap, lyrical, farcical. The story is derived rather obviously from *Emil and the Detectives*, but with a super-realist atmosphere foreign to the agreeable common sense of that fantasy.

I think one might be more ready to surrender to its charm if one did not detect a certain complacency, a conscious withdrawal from the corruption of the com-mercial film, in its painstaking irresponsibility. Virtue can afford to be charitable, and all those who have occasionally enjoyed the corrupt pleasures, the bright facile excitements of popular entertainment will feel as if an old friend (vicious, of course, but not always unamusing) has been too priggishly reprimanded. There is a didactic note, that is the trouble, in a film which promises to be peculiarly care-free and irrational from the moment when a symphony orchestra of a hundred musicians in curiously shaped bowler-hats begin to play the overture. The story is excellent, leading improbably up to the superb sequence of four player-pianos dragged across the Alps behind a monstrous wine-barrel containing a gang of robbers in pursuit of a fifth player-piano, in the mechanism of which, unknown to the boy in charge of it, lies a stocking filled with gold pieces. The gold pieces have been stolen by the Robber with the Straw Hat (an admirable piece of grotesque miming by Mr Michael Martin-Harvey) and deposited in the piano, which belongs to a family of strolling musicians. The robbers pursue it to a mountain village where the Man with the Straw Hat holds the attention of the people with a rope-walking act, while the others produce four identical pianos drawn by four identical donkeys with the complex idea of confusing the boy and stealing his piano. This whole sequence is delightful: one of the best pieces of direction and invention I have seen, genuinely irresponsible, but even here it is the music which dictates the pace, and as a result the mind moves quicker than the camera. To the credit of the

The Robber Symphony

The Littlest Rebel: John Boles, Shirley Temple

music, though, it may be said that one is seldom conscious of the silence of the actors.

Herr Feher calls his picture the first 'composed' film, but in so far as his experiment is original, it is barren. In order to synchronize pictures with music in this way he found it necessary to shoot 600,000 feet of film; the synchronization is perfect but the cost is enormous, and the object – I do not quite know what the object is. Herr Feher composed the music, wrote the story, directed the film, but the music (of which I am no proper judge) surely does not require illustration. There seems to be a confusion of thought which prevents the picture – or the music – being quite the masterpiece which had been intended – intended, for there is no doubt about the bardic self-confidence of the director.

To return to our corrupt friend – never more so than at the New Gallery where Miss Shirley Temple appears in a very sweet and very simple tale of the American Civil War which culminates, as these dramas always do, with an appeal to Abraham Lincoln to save somebody – in this case a father, in Mr Drinkwater's play a son, in *The Birth of a Nation* a lover – from being shot. I had not seen Miss Temple before: as I expected there was the usual sentimental exploitation of childhood, but I had not expected the tremendous energy which her rivals certainly lack. A film like this makes one sympathize with Herr Feher's Puritanism: it is a little too enervating. If one must have disreputable enjoyments, let them have the glitter of *The Emperor's Candlesticks*, an absurd Edwardian tale of Polish plotters and secret documents hidden in stolen candlesticks, of a beautiful police agent and an idealistic revolutionary, acted in his usual sad, worried and endearing way by Herr Karl Ludwig Diehl. Good direction, fair acting and the attractively Baker Street dresses make this a pleasant film to doze at. *The Spectator*, 24 May 1936

The Robber Symphony (GB, Concordia, 1936). Director: Friedrich Feher. Hans Feher, Magda Sonja, Webster Booth, George Graves.
The Littlest Rebel (USA, 20th Century-Fox, 1935). Director: David Butler. Shirley Temple, John Boles.
The Emperor's Candlesticks (*Die Leuchter des Kaisers*) (Austria, Gloria-Film, 1935). Director: Karl Hartl. Sybille Schmitz, Karl Ludwig Diehl.

The Marriage of Corbal

What is an English film? There are times when one cannot help brooding with acute distress on the cheap silly international pictures exported under that label. *The Marriage of Corbal* is a fairly harmless example. It is incredibly silly and incredibly badly written but there is a kind of wide-eyed innocence about this story of the French Revolution which is almost endearing. But an English film? Is that a fair description of a picture derived from a novel by Rafael Sabatini, directed by Karl Grune and F. Brunn, photographed by Otto Kanturek, and edited by E. Stokvis, with a cast which includes Nils Asther, Ernst Deutsch and the American, Noah Beery? The result is appalling: the dialogue is the worst I have heard these twelve months, the scenario the silliest, and as for the acting – let me be charitable to Mr Hugh Sinclair and the young 'dumb' newcomer, Miss Hazel Terry, and put some of their faults down to Herr Grune and his international assistants.

England, of course, has always been the home of the exiled; but one may at least express a wish that *émigrés* would set up trades in which their ignorance of our

The Marriage of Corbal: Hazel Terry, Hugh Sinclair

language and culture was less of a handicap: it would not grieve me to see Mr Alexander Korda seated before a cottage loom in an Eastern county, following an older and a better tradition. The Quota Act has played into foreign hands, and as far as I know, there is nothing to prevent an English film unit being completely staffed by technicians of foreign blood. We have saved the English film industry from American competition only to surrender it to a far more alien control.

It is not that there are no English technicians capable of producing films of a high enough standard to take their place in the international markets (an absurd idea when we think of *Song of Ceylon, The Voice of Britain, The Turn of the Tide, Night Mail, Midshipman Easy*). Aesthetics have nothing to do with the matter. In the last eleven months I have reviewed 124 films, of which only 13 conveyed any kind of aesthetic experience and another 48 were reasonably entertaining: the other 63 films were trash. The reason why English technicians are seldom employed is more likely to be financial: it is not English money that calls the tune, and it is only natural that compatriots should find jobs for each other. And so the big film families are founded, a system of nepotism which recalls the less savoury days of the Papacy, and as for 'the art of the cinema' it remains almost as unrealized as in the days of *The Great Train Robbery*. The peepshow, the fun-fair, the historical waxworks are triumphant.

And there is something unusually sinister about *this* collection of waxworks: it does in some moods appear to be a chamber of horrors. The wax corpse with the painted wound is often grotesque, and the anonymous letters one receives – I remember a particularly ill-scented specimen from High Wycombe – are amusing, if one ignores the animality and the ignorance of their source. But the chamber contains darker shadows: what is one to think of a Board of Film Censors (with at least one judge of over eighty years) which allows a far greater latitude to the big American companies than to its own less wealthy countrymen? And there is only too obviously a sinister side to many newspaper criticisms. Even the hardened Press audience at *The Marriage of Corbal* gave way to impatient laughter at the inflated dialogue, the grotesque situations, and yet when I examined the notices later, I found the film had made the contrary impression to what I had supposed. 'Second thoughts are best' – that, of course, is one proverb, but 'money speaks' is another.

Watching the dark alien executive tipping his cigar ash behind the glass partition in Wardour Street, the Hungarian producer adapting Mr Wells's ideas tactfully at Denham, the German director letting himself down into his canvas chair at Elstree, and the London film critics (I speak with humility: I am one of them) exchanging smutty stories over the hock and the iced pudding and the brandy at the Carlton, I cannot help wondering whether from this great moneyed industry anything of value to the human spirit can ever emerge.   *The Spectator*, 5 June 1936

The Marriage of Corbal (GB, Capitol, 1936). Directors: Karl Grune, F. Brunn. Nils Asther, Hazel Terry, Hugh Sinclair, Noah Beery.

The Country Doctor

The Country Doctor is an honest film. The picture of the small Canadian timber station, shut off in winter from the outside world, and the elderly G.P. who has practised there for thirty years, paid more often in kind than in cash, and who has never troubled, or had the necessary ready money, to take out his licence to practise, is admirably genuine: the camera – rare occasion in the cinema – doesn't lie, and Mr Jean Hersholt gives one of the most sympathetic performances I have seen this year as the patient courageous doctor, out of date through no fault of his own, with a core of obstinacy, a determination to make the rich corporation which owns the land build him a proper hospital. After an epidemic of diphtheria, in which many of the workers' children have died for want of proper equipment, the doctor goes to Montreal to interview the Managing Director. He is told, as usual, to fill up form 48 and his request will be considered in due course; but with patient determination he follows the Director to a public dinner given by the medical association, the rich city specialists, and makes his protest. He has done no good. The corporation takes its revenge; their lawyers discover he has no licence, he is forbidden to practise and is about to leave the settlement altogether when a wretched father, whose wife spawns by calendar every fall, implores his help. The successful birth of quintuplets makes the doctor a national hero; for their sake he gets the hospital for the lack of which children have died every year for thirty years, and the Managing Director (a fine satirical portrait, this, of brutal complacency) receives the compliments of the Governor-General.

The theme is serious, the treatment has unusual edge; no one, after seeing this picture will complain again that the Dionne quintuplets and Dr Dafoe have received more than their due of attention. And perhaps it would be too austere to criticize the picture because it does not quite maintain its seriousness and realism. The scene of the birth, with the policeman protesting to the unlicensed doctor with every fresh arrival that he is only 'piling on the evidence', is not in the best of taste, perhaps, and the human values are quite forgotten, but it is undeniably comic. It would be harsh too to expect the director to cut his admirable sequence of the quintuplets playing with Mr Hersholt on the floor of the new hospital. From the point of view of a balanced film there is too much of them, but this again is to judge from the austerest angle, for the sequence is extraordinarily funny, and the professional actor sprawling on the floor with these reckless carnival characters can only suggest in his expression a bewildered admiration at their virtuosity, their impromptu and perfectly timed performance: a performance which reminded me of Buster Keaton's solemn slapstick, as a quintuplet with an air of methodical pedantry upset each chair in the room in turn.   *The Spectator*, 12 June 1936

The Country Doctor (USA, 20th Century-Fox, 1936). Director: Henry King. The Dionne Quins, Jean Hersholt, June Lane.

Dangerous/Big Brown Eyes

Miss Bette Davis won some kind of a gold medal for her acting in *Dangerous*: the cinema is a shady business and one would like to know more about that medal, who gave it, how many carats, who the judges were: but at least it indicates that the publicity hounds have recognized her disturbing talent. Her performance in *Of Human Bondage* was wickedly good – up to a point, the point when passion got a little tattered, and even the most inconsiderable films – *Border Town* and others of which I have forgotten even the names – seemed temporarily better than they were because of that precise nervy voice, the pale ash-blonde hair, the popping neurotic eyes, a kind of corrupt and phosphorescent prettiness. *Dangerous*, like the others, is a picture to see for her sake, although the story is poor, the ending atrociously sentimental (*Dangerous* and *Show Boat* tie for the worst endings of the week), and although alas! Miss Margaret Lindsay is also in the cast, as if to reassure people that, whatever the censor may say, this film is U.

Hollywood has never forgotten its startling discovery that raffishness – the wild parties, the drugs and bathing belles and suicides and Fatty Arbuckle – was bad business. There is nothing now it takes to its heart so firmly as gentility: so that Miss Kay Francis is advertised as a woman who can wear the best clothes; Mr C. Aubrey Smith, that amiable and bush Wellington, is made to remind us, even in *The Crusades*, of the straight bat of his cricketing past, and Miss Lindsay is starred less as an actress than as a nice eligible girl, comradely and refined, who can pour out tea as if she really belonged to a tea-drinking nation. Miss Lindsay as the deserted but understanding fiancée provides the antidote to Miss Davis as the great actress who has become a drunken and friendless failure because of her intense selfishness which ruins every play she acts in or any man she likes. A highly coloured situation, this, which does little justice to Miss Davis's talent for vivid realism: we are aware all the time that she is acting, acting for the highest honours, for the questionable carats, acting with immense virtuosity, from the moment when the successful young architect (Mr Franchot Tone) spots her in the speak-easy. For Hollywood has a way of refining even Miss Davis: another performance so horrifyingly natural as her mean greedy little waitress in *Of Human Bondage* and her film career would have been ruined: and so with great ingenuity Hollywood adopts the homeopathic method, doubles the gin, multiplies the drink stains, intensifies the squalor, until you can safely cease to believe, until Miss Davis's latest picture becomes as curious, absurd and period as 'Sell No More Drink to My Father'.

Dangerous, then, is unusual, but only because of Miss Davis: a far more competent picture (though I would rather watch Miss Davis than any number of competent pictures) is *Big Brown Eyes*, a misleading title for a fast well-directed and quite unsentimental gangster film, pleasantly free from emotion – for emotion on the screen is nearly always false emotion. The chief players are Miss Joan Bennett and Mr Cary Grant, but they don't matter much: it is a director's picture.

The Spectator, 19 June 1936

Dangerous (USA, Warner Bros, 1935). Director: Alfred E. Green. Bette Davis, Franchot Tone, Margaret Lindsay, Alison Skipworth.
Big Brown Eyes (USA, Paramount, 1936). Director: Raoul Walsh. Joan Bennett, Cary Grant.

Show Boat/The Moon's Our Home

The latest version of *Show Boat* is very lavish. It runs for two hours, contains more than a dozen of Mr Jerome Kern's melodious songs, and is directed by Mr James Whale with a fine moneyed smoothness. Merely to illustrate one song, 'Ole Man River', he uses half a dozen sets and fifty people, and because there are times, particularly after several drinks, when one can watch money being squandered without a pang, *Show Boat* for three-quarters of its length proves good entertainment, sentimental, literary, but oddly appealing.

The story, by this time, is about as well known as that of *King Lear*: of the troupe of actors in Victorian days (the period is obscure, for the Zinkeisen dresses seem to span more than a human life-time) who tour the Mississippi in their own paddle-steamer; of the young girl, daughter of the old manager, who runs away with the handsome graceless gambler. He has played the hero's parts for a season on the river, and he abandons her with her young child in the great city; abandons her, of course, for the noblest reasons, because he feels himself unworthy of her love and does not wish to involve her in his ruin. She gets an engagement at a Chicago music-hall, becomes a world-famous singer, retires in time to watch from a box her daughter make a triumphant début on the New York stage, and since her husband, no older in appearance except for a few graceful grey hairs and a studiously shabby coat, turns out to be a doorkeeper in the same theatre, the family are reunited at curtain fall. Veterans complain that the ending has been altered by Mr Whale, and certainly the extreme sentimentality and improbability of that reunion a little jars with the quite restrained and agreeable sentimentality of the rest. For there are moods of generosity towards life when the sentiment, the idealism, the earnest rather throaty melodies of *Show Boat* have charm: everything is for the best in the best of all possible worlds; everyone is a little blurred with

Dangerous: Bette Davis, Franchot Tone

nobility, partings are 'such sweet sorrow', tears rainbowed, and life – don't so much as whisper the ugly word. For the first night was Gala: the three little pigs again defeated the big bad wolf in the latest silly symphony: the *Queen Mary* was the finest ship ever built, and we watched the ticker-tape falling for her in Broadway and heard the sirens blasting her towards the quay; and at the end of it all (the management's little surprise) we squealed with delight when first Mr James Whale, and then Miss Irene Dunne (the highest squeals), and last Mr Paul Robeson (the longest squeals) stepped in person before the screen. They had arrived in the *Queen Mary* just in time for Gala Night, and for two hours we too had lived on the *Queen Mary*, the Show Boat, level, in an atmosphere of immense expenditure, of boat-deck sentiment, of decorations lavish if not in the best of taste, of a huge machine grinding efficiently on, 'sweet sorrow' at last at Ellis Island.

In reality, though, I cannot help preferring *The Moon's Our Home*, a trivial charming comedy about people young and too famous, about a popular film star and a traveller who writes books (a character very delicately and sympathetically caricatured with his too vocal contempt for convention and his inappropriate memories, which wreck the wedding-night). They meet and marry in a holiday mood, but marry nevertheless for ever – under their real, not their invented public names, so that she does not know he writes (she hates his books) and he does not know she acts (he hates film stars). Miss Dorothy Parker has helped with the

83

dialogue, the best recommendation of any comedy, but it is to Miss Margaret Sullavan and Mr Henry Fonda, as much as to anyone, that we owe the sense of something fresh and absurd and civilized, like a sixteenth-century epithalamium for a pair who will always be young and extravagant and at odds together in a Penshurst world. It isn't, of course, as good as all that; nothing is as good as all that in the cinema, but the great commercial wheels don't grind here quite so effortlessly; a little satire, a little imagination, a little feeling for human inconsistency, has got into the works.   *The Spectator*, 26 June 1936

Show Boat (USA, Universal, 1936). Director: James Whale. Irene Dunne, Allan Jones, Charles Winninger, Paul Robeson, Helen Morgan.
The Moon's Our Home (USA, Paramount, 1936). Director: William Seiter. Margaret Sullavan, Henry Fonda, Charles Butterworth.

Fury/The Story of Louis Pasteur

Fury is Herr Fritz Lang's first American picture. The importation of continental directors is always a nervous business, Hollywood offers so much in the way of technical resources (so that a witty playboy like Lubitsch gains by the translation), so little help, among the yes-men and the entertainment racketeers, to the imagination. *M*, until *Fury* Herr Lang's best film, the study of a child-murderer, could hardly have passed the Hollywood executives; *Metropolis*, *The Spy*, *Dr Mabuse*, these melodramatic pictures of Herr Lang's apprenticeship, on the other hand, might possibly have been made with even more chromiumed efficiency in America; and I visited *Fury* in some trepidation lest Herr Lang had been driven back to melodrama (melodrama, of course, infinitely more expert than, say, Mr Hitchcock's). But *Fury*, the story of how a mob in a small Southern town lynches an innocent man who has been arrested under suspicion of kidnapping, is astonishing, the only film I know to which I have wanted to attach the epithet of 'great'. There have been other films – *Kameradschaft* comes first to mind – where a generous theme, a sense of spiritual integrity, has somehow got conveyed *in spite of* the limitations of the screen, but no other picture which has allowed no value to slip, which has conveyed completely by sound and image better than by any other medium the pity and terror of the story. (The last third of the picture leading up to a neatly contrived happy ending is not on the same level, though the picture never falls below finely directed melodrama.)

Mr Spencer Tracy as the victim, a garage-keeper, a simple honest kindly creature saving up to be married; Miss Sylvia Sidney as his girl, a teacher in the Southern town; Mr Edward Ellis as the Sheriff, harsh, upright, ready to defend his prisoner to the last tear-gas bomb, with his own life if necessary, but belonging nevertheless to the same township as the mob, knowing it as individuals, each in his home, his office, his barber's chair, refusing at the trial which follows the lynching to identify a single culprit: all these give their finest performances. Miss Sidney in particular. She has never more deeply conveyed the pain and inarticulacy of tenderness. No film passion here, no exaggeration of the ordinary human feeling, as the two lovers shelter under the elevated from the drenching rain, say good-bye at the railway station with faces and hands pressed to wet fogging windows: it is the ordinary recognizable agony, life as one knows it is lived. And the same power to catch vividly the truthful detail makes the lynching of almost unbearable horror. I am

Fury: Spencer Tracy

trying not to exaggerate, but the brain does flinch at each recurring flick of truth in much the same way as at the grind-grind of an electric road-drill: the horrible laughter and inflated nobility of the good citizens, the youth leaping on a bar and shouting 'Let's have some fun', the regiment of men and women marching down the road into the face of the camera, arm in arm, laughing and excited like recruits on the first day of a war, the boy singing out at the Sheriff, 'I'm Popeye the Sailor-man', at last the first stone, until the building is ablaze, the innocent man is suffocating behind the bars, and a woman holds her baby up to see the fire.

Any other film this year is likely to be dwarfed by Herr Lang's extraordinary achievement: no other director has got so completely the measure of his medium, is so consistently awake to the counterpoint of sound and image. Even *Louis Pasteur*, an honest, interesting and well-made picture, suffers by comparison, and seems half-way to the stage. It would suffer more disastrously if it were not for the acting of Mr Paul Muni. Lucky the film-goer who has been able to see in one week the work of the greatest director and of the greatest living actor. The range of this Protean figure (for unlike Mr Laughton he seems to lose voice and appearance in his part) is amazing: the convict in *I Am A Fugitive*, the Polish miner in *Black Fury*, the half-caste racketeer in *Border Town*, Louis Pasteur. With his whole body he establishes not only the bourgeois, the elderly, the stubborn and bitter and noble little chemist, but his nationality and even his period. *The Spectator*, 3 July 1936

Fury (USA, M-G-M, 1936). Director: Fritz Lang. Spencer Tracy, Sylvia Sidney, Walter Abel, Bruce Cabot, Edward Ellis, Walter Brennan.
The Story of Louis Pasteur (USA, Warner Bros, 1936). Director: William Dieterle. Paul Muni, Josephine Hutchinson, Anita Louise.

One Rainy Afternoon/Janosik/The Phantom Gondola

One Rainy Afternoon might so easily have been a good film, something light and absurd and happy in the early Clair tradition. Perhaps it *was* a good film once, somewhere far back, before the director, Mr Rowland Lee, knew that it existed, before Mr Francis Lederer, who has never plugged his Dodie charm, his Autumn Crocus accent, more strenuously, had so much as read his part, before the scenario-writers had begun to insert the gags; very far back indeed, before the author knew that his tale would be bought by Pickford-Lasky Productions, there surely existed in his mind a good film: a film about an unsuccessful actor in Paris who was trying his best to carry on an intrigue with a Cabinet Minister's wife, an intrigue which involved endless taxi-drives, round and round cinema blocks, until the films had begun and the foyers were empty: so that it was always the middle of films he saw, never, as he complained, the happy endings. One day in the dark auditorium there was a muddle, he kissed the girl next him and it wasn't the Minister's wife. The girl screamed, the Purity League representative insisted on a prosecution, and the absurd irresponsible tale took wings.

But, alas, the wings didn't work. Too many people had to join in the fun, and by the time the executives of Pickford-Lasky (twelve are mentioned in the programme besides the director) had really set to work, the light silly charming tale of a wet afternoon, a too careful mistress, a dark cinema and a kiss had become as seriously gamesome as tip and run played by fathers on holiday at the sea. Mr Lee has given a useful demonstration of how not to direct this kind of story: he has been remorselessly logical when he should have been crazy; his only idea of humour is speed and noise, not speed of thought or situation, but just literal speed of walking and talking. Mr Lederer's mechanic charm I find embarrassing, like the boast of a womanizer in a public bar, but in the grim hurly-burly Miss Ida Lupino's fair sulky features, the impression she can give of something Cockney and cheap and endearing, is as refreshing as a natural voice at a stage party. Miss Lupino as yet is a dummy, but she is one of the more agreeable screen dummies to whom things are made to happen, and I feel some remorse when I think of the shootings and strangulations she will have to endure next year in a story of my own.

At least *One Rainy Afternoon* was a good film until they began to make it: so much cannot be said of the Czechoslovakian film at the Academy or the French film at the Curzon. The Czech film is historical: a tyrannical landowner, a serf who takes to the mountains and robs the rich so that he may give to the poor: this theme should retain its appeal until the Millennium, but it is treated in such a romantic rollicking tuneful way that we are reminded of *The Maid of the Mountains*, until the effective final sequence of Janosik's capture and his cruel death, hung like butcher's meat with a spike in his ribs. Romance and robber tunes and lyrical shots of a long-legged Fairbanks hero don't go with the spike.

The Phantom Gondola has exactly the opposite fault. A cheap, trivial and pretentious story by a popular writer of rather low reputation (M. Maurice Dekobra, author of *His Chinese Concubine* and *The Madonna of the Sleeping Cars*) has been directed with enormous gravity and the kind of Art which goes with Venice, sunsets and huge expensive palazzos. It is one of the only two films this last year I have found myself unable to endure till the end (the other was *The Tunnel*), and so I cannot say how this tale of a mysterious and very aristocratic Englishwoman who steals a telegram from the study of the Turkish Ambassador, in order to prove her love for a still more mysterious Italian Count, ends. I couldn't wait long enough to learn his object, or to discover the name of the mournful Asiatic female with a good deal of sensual charm who followed him around and peered through windows. For never has a melodrama proceeded so slowly, with such a saga-like tread. *The Spectator*, 10 July 1936

One Rainy Afternoon (USA, Pickford-Lasky, 1936). Director: Rowland V. Lee. Francis Lederer, Ida Lupino.
Janosik (Czechoslovakia, Lloyd-Film, 1935). Director: Mac Fric. Palo Bielik, Zlata Hajdukova.
The Phantom Gondola (*La Gondole aux Chimères*) (France, Film Expert, 1936). Director: Augusto Genina. Marcelle Chantal, Roger Karl, Henri Rollan.

Poppy/Living Dangerously/Charlie Chan at the Circus

It is the loud check trousers we first see, a pair of shoes which have known their best days, and as the camera travels up to the extraordinary swollen nose, the little cunning heartless eyes, the period top hat, we become aware of the W. C. Fields voice, that low rich grumble rather like the noise of a distant train, which will presently swell, we know from experience, into loud rotund periods, the words a little misapplied – 'Forgive my redundancy, dear madam, forgive my redundancy.' Mr Fields's latest incarnation is Professor Eustace McGargle, a travelling quack, a three-card man (he uses one of his cards to stuff a hole in his daughter's shoe), temporarily down on his luck. The story is an old and sentimental one: how the Professor, with the help of a forged marriage certificate and the services of a crooked country solicitor, Mr Whiffen, claims for his innocent young daughter the local Pakenham fortune, how he is double-crossed by Whiffen, escapes with difficulty from the Sheriff, and how his daughter, who is not really his daughter at all, turns out to be the genuine heiress. Professor McGargle, of course, in the accepted Chaplin tradition, moves on – in the Mayor's best hat, with one of the Mayor's cigars in his mouth and the Mayor's best silver-knobbed cane in his hand.

But the story doesn't really matter, for Mr Fields has never acted better. There is no touch of sentimentality in *his* performance. When he says good-bye for the last time to his adopted daughter with spurious tears in the old boar eyes, his final word of advice is, 'Never give a sucker an even break.' The scenarist has had the good sense to leave Mr Fields's villainy undimmed by any genuine affection. He

Poppy: Rochelle Hudson, W. C. Fields

wins our hearts not by a display of Chaplin sentiment, not by class solidarity (he robs the poor as promptly as the rich), but simply by the completeness of his dishonesty. To watch Mr Fields, as Dickensian as anything Dickens ever wrote, is a form of escape for poor human creatures: we who are haunted by pity, by fear, by our sense of right and wrong, who are tongue-tied by conscience, watch with envious love this free spirit robbing the gardener of ten dollars, cheating the country yokels by his own variant of the three-card trick, faking a marriage certificate, and keeping up all the time, in the least worthy and the most embarrassing circumstances, his amazing flow of inflated sentiments. There is something in Mr Fields's appearance which has always reminded me of Mr Baldwin (or at any rate of Low's cartoon of Mr Baldwin), but it is Mr Fields's most delightful characteristic that his lips are never, for one moment, sealed, for he fills up even the blanks in the script with his rumble of unintelligible rotundities.

The other two films on my list will have left the Regal by the time this notice appears, but it is quite worth watching for them at local cinemas. *Living Dangerously* is an English melodrama with an American star, Mr Otto Kruger, the story of a doctor 'framed' by his partner, who accuses him of sexual relations with his wife while treating her professionally. He is struck off the register by the General Medical Council and goes to America with the woman. The husband follows them and tries to blackmail him, and the film begins with the murder of the blackmailer and ends with the District Attorney helping the doctor to make his 'self-defence' plea convincing. It is not a very satisfying film, but it is above the usual standard of English pictures, and the scene of the trial before the General Medical Council, where no witnesses are sworn and any lies can be told in the box without fear of perjury, is excellent. We are used to America criticizing her institutions on the screen, but it is unusual in this country for a picture with some bite and bitterness to get past the censor.

As for Charlie Chan he needs no recommendation. The films in which he appears are all genuine detective films as distinct from thrillers, they are always well made and well acted. The new picture is particularly agreeable, for we see Mr Chan for the first time in a domestic setting and meet not only his amorous eldest son but his complete family of fourteen.   *The Spectator*, 17 July 1936

Poppy (USA, Paramount, 1936). Director: A. Edward Sutherland. W. C. Fields, Rochelle Hudson, Richard Cromwell.
Living Dangerously (GB, British International, 1936). Director: Herbert Brenon. Otto Kruger.
Charlie Chan at the Circus (USA, 20th Century-Fox, 1936). Director: Harry Lachman. Warner Oland, Keye Luke, George and Olive Brasno.

The Petrified Forest

'Dramatize, dramatize.' Those were the words which used to ring in James's ear whenever some anecdote at a dinner-table touched his creative brain, but how seldom are they heard by even the most distinguished contemporary dramatists. Mr Sherwood, for instance. . . . I seldom go to the theatre, but even I have heard of Mr Sherwood as a playwright of uncommon ability, and it was with great hope that I visited *The Petrified Forest*. The opening movement of his drama is very promising: the lonely filling-station on the edge of the Arizona Desert; the old garrulous owner who had once been shot at for fun by Billy the Kid and had kept a soft place in his heart for killers ever since: his grand-daughter with her taste for poetry who feels her life drying up in the dust-storms: her father, an officer in the Vigilantes, trying to get excitement from his fake uniform and bogus drills: the huge dumb hired hand with his eyes on the girl: and then the arrival of the educated down-and-out, the girl's outbreak of sudden starved love, his departure with his food unpaid for and a dollar the girl had given him from the till, and finally disaster breaking in with a killer and his gang on the run from Oklahoma, and the down-and-out's deliberate return.

There is good dramatic material here, but Mr Sherwood doesn't see his play as certain things happening but as ideas being expressed, 'significant' cosmic ideas. As for the plot, the drama, these are rather low-class necessities, like the adulteries in Mr Charles Morgan's novels. The down-and-out, so that he may express the ideas, must be an unsuccessful author, the filling-station girl – to interest him – a painter of untrained talent, for whose Art he sacrifices his life (Mr Sherwood is nothing if not literary). The hero leaves the girl his life-assurance money and then forces the killer to shoot him, though why, if he hadn't a cent in his pocket, was the life-assurance for five thousand dollars fully paid up, or if that be explainable, why had this homeless and friendless tramp not cashed it for its face value? But first all through a long evening, with the sad simian killer (the best character in the play) sitting above with his beer and his pistol, the self-pitying post-war ideas have to be bandied about. 'Dramatize, dramatize,' one longs to remind Mr Sherwood, as more and more the concrete fact – the gun, the desert, the killer – gives place to Life, Love, Nature, all the great stale abstractions. It is as if Othello had met the armed men outside his door not with 'Put up your bright swords or the dew will rust them', but with some such sentence as: 'Nature, my men, is having her revenge. You can't defeat Nature with your latest type of swords and daggers. She comes back every time in the shape of neuroses, jealousies . . .' and had let Desdemona and the affairs of Venice, Iago and the one particular handkerchief vanish before Women, Life, Sex. . . .

So this drama slackens under the weight of Mr Sherwood's rather half-baked philosophy. The moral is stated frequently, with the tombstone clarity of a leading article, when it ought to be implicit in every action, every natural spoken word, in the camera angles even (but this is not a film but a canned play). There remain in this picture a few things to enjoy: the killer himself, with his conventional morality, his brooding hopelessness, his curious kindness, is memorable, but not so memorable nor so significant (the word which I am sure means most to Mr Sherwood) as the murderer in *Four Hours to Kill*. That killer was a profound and legendary figure, this one the ingenious invention of a clever writer. Miss Bette Davis gives a sound performance, Mr Leslie Howard faithfully underlines the self-pity and the bogus culture of a character embarrassing to us but obviously admired by his creator, and everyone works hard to try to give the illusion that the Whole of Life is symbolized in the Arizona filling-station. But life itself, which crept in during the opening scene, embarrassed perhaps at hearing itself so explicitly discussed, crept out again, leaving us only with the symbols, the too pasteboard desert, the stunted cardboard studio trees.   *The Spectator*, 24 July 1936

The Petrified Forest (USA, Warner Bros, 1936). Director: Archie Mayo. Bette Davis, Leslie Howard, Humphrey Bogart, Genevieve Tobin, Dick Foran.

Laburnum Grove/Ourselves Alone

Here at last is an English film one can unreservedly praise. How pleasant for that stubborn grain of national feeling which would, I suppose, endure for centuries, like the embryo tail, even in a bright Genevan international day. I refer to Mr Carol Reed's *Laburnum Grove*, not to Mr Brian Desmond Hurst's *Ourselves Alone*, one of the silliest pictures which even an English studio has yet managed to turn out. This latter picture has been extravagantly praised, even compared favourably with *The Informer*, and yet I defy any normal person (among whom one has long ceased to number the boisterous good fellows of the London Press) to find more than one effective sequence, more than one good sentence, in this sentimental and melodramatic story of the Irish Rebellion. The dialogue and the script are not the fault of Mr Desmond Hurst, who has indeed directed one good scene, when the Black and Tans search a public house and the Irish women hide the Sinn Fein revolvers under their skirts and a sentimental ballad-singer sings plaintively on, while the camera makes a complete circle of the room, from the singer's face back to the singer's face, picking out the right authentic details on its way. This scene has unmistakable quality and promise; otherwise *Ourselves Alone,* following Mr Desmond Hurst's previous picture, *Riders to the Sea*, might make one despair of this director, who cannot yet manage his actors (Mr John Lodge and Mr John Loder have never acted less convincingly) and who shows little idea of timing.

Mr Carol Reed is a director of very different quality. *Laburnum Grove* maintains the promise of his first picture, *Midshipman Easy*. Both films are thoroughly workmanlike and unpretentious, with just the hint of a personal manner which makes one believe that Mr Reed, when he gets the right script, will prove far more than efficient. *Laburnum Grove* set him and Mr Anthony Kimmins, the author of the screenplay, a difficult problem, for it is much harder to adapt a play to the screen than a novel. Mr Priestley's suburban fairy-tale of the respectable amateur gardener of Ferndale, who confessed cheerfully over the supper-table to his family that he was really a successful counterfeiter wanted by the Yard, was admirably suited to the three acts of the stage. Nine directors out of ten would simply have canned the play for mass consumption: Mr Reed has made a film of it. One remembered the opening sequence of *Midshipman Easy*, the camera sailing with the motion of a frigate before the wind down the hedge and the country lane to Easy's home, when the camera in Mr Reed's new film led us remorselessly down Laburnum Grove up to the threshold of the tall grim granite church at the bottom. Mr Priestley has been allowed to tell his agreeable and amusing story in much the same order and the same words as on the stage; but Mr Reed's camera has gone behind the dialogue, has picked out far more of the suburban background than Mr Priestley could convey in dialogue or the stage illustrate between its three walls: the hideous variegated Grove itself, the bottled beer and the cold suppers, the crowded ferny glass-house, the little stuffy bedrooms with thin walls, and the stale cigarette smoke and Bertie's half-consumed bananas. Suburbia, one of the newest suburbias, where the gravel lies lightly still over what was grass and clover, insinuates itself into every shot. There isn't a wasted foot, and Mr Desmond Hurst could take a lesson from Mr Reed in something as elementary as moving his characters from one room to another. Mr Desmond Hurst's camera wanders after the story, some way behind, so that when a character is being politely ushered through a door, the spectator is already in the passage waiting for the next action and chafing at the delay. Mr Reed's camera acts with a kind of quick shrewd independence of the dialogue, and presents its own equally dramatic commentary, so that the picture of suburbia seems to be drawn simultaneously from two angles – which is as near as the screen can come as yet to stereoscopy.　　　　　　　　　*The Spectator*, 31 July 1936

Laburnum Grove (GB, Associated Talking Pictures, 1936). Director: Carol Reed. Cedric Hardwicke, Victoria Hopper, Edmund Gwenn.
Ourselves Alone (GB, British International, 1936). Directors: Brian Desmond Hurst, Walter Summers. John Lodge, John Loder.

Under Two Flags/Captain January

How Ouida would have loved the abandon of this picture, the thirty-two thousand rounds of ammunition shot off into the Arizona Desert, the cast of more than ten thousand (we are told that twenty thousand salary cheques were paid out, which seems a bit on the mean side), the five thousand pounds which insured Miss Claudette Colbert, Mr Ronald Colman, Mr Victor McLaglen and Miss Rosalind Russell against camel bites – a curious item this, for none of these players, as far as I could see, came within half a mile of a camel – and, in the words of the programme:

'a fort 200 feet square, an Arabian oasis with eight fair-sized buildings, and a forest of transplanted date palms, two Arabian cities and a horse market and a smaller fort'. The absurdities are for once not Hollywood's: the picture does momentarily lift one into the odd dream-world of a passionate and inexperienced lady novelist resident in Italy. When Lady Venetia meets Sergeant Victor of the Foreign Legion (formerly a Guards officer and, as the newspapers put it, a West End Clubman) at the oasis at midnight and remarks, while the vox humana moans resonantly on, 'What perfect silence. One can hear the leaves move', Ouida, I am sure, would not have complained, for the vox humana must have been her perpetual background too: whether she was writing of boat-races ('no one rowed faster than . . .') or penning fiery letters to *The Times* on the subject of cruelty to animals, she must have lived at an emotional pressure to which only a Wurlitzer organ could do credit.

It was many years since I had seen the play, acted by half-starved barnstormers in a Welsh village, and I had forgotten the superb climax. Victor's company, down to their last rounds, are besieged by ten thousand Arabs in their desert fort. Help may reach them by the next noon, but they cannot withstand another attack: the Arabs' onslaught must somehow be delayed, and Victor, dressed in Arab robes, sidles across the sand-dunes to the enemy. He asks to be led to Sidi-Ben-Youssiff, and in the Arab leader's presence flings off his burnous. 'Don't you recognize me? I was at Magdalen when you were up at Balliol', and the Arab chief, taking a longer look, begins to recall those forgotten Oxford days. 'Of course. We met first, didn't we, at one of Professor Lake's breakfast-parties. . . .' But I couldn't help being a little shocked when next morning Sidi-Ben-Youssiff, whom Victor had deceived into delaying the attack with a trumped-up story of British troops in his rear (one was loth to distrust the word of a man one had met at Professor Lake's breakfast-table), announced the Legionary's fate. 'You remember those soccer games we used to play. Well, this time my men are going to play on horseback and you will be the ball.' This surely is the Brasenose, not the Balliol, manner.

My admiration for Miss Claudette Colbert is unbounded, even when she has to play Cleopatra or the Empress Poppaea or Cigarette, the mascot of the Legion. In this part she is as convincingly the passionate but pure cocotte who dies of her wounds, after a mad gallop with windblown fringe and in enchanting trousers to save the company, as Mr Colman is an Oxford graduate in reduced circumstances. It is evident that Ouida's reputation for daring has reached her contemporaries on the British Board of Film Censors, for they have given the film an Adult Certificate, or perhaps it is the result of six chaste, sandy kisses exchanged in the desert between the mascot and the Magdalen man.

Captain January, the latest Shirley Temple picture, is sentimental, a little depraved, with an appeal interestingly decadent. An orphan salvaged from the sea is brought up by an old lighthouse-keeper. A wicked school-inspector wants to remove the child to an institution, and the exciting climax of the film is the competitive examination, on which the child's fate depends, between Miss Temple and the Inspector's spotty nephew. Shirley Temple acts and dances with immense vigour and assurance, but some of her popularity seems to rest on a coquetry quite as mature as Miss Colbert's and on an oddly precocious body as voluptuous in grey flannel trousers as Miss Dietrich's.   *The Spectator*, 7 August 1936

Under Two Flags (USA, 20th Century-Fox, 1936). Director: Frank Lloyd. Ronald Colman, Claudette Colbert, Rosalind Russell, Victor McLaglen.
Captain January (USA, 20th Century-Fox, 1936). Director: David Butler. Shirley Temple, Guy Kibbee, Slim Summerville.

Captain January: Shirley Temple

Rhythm on the Range

Bing Crosby as a cowboy: Bing Crosby crooning a prize bull to sleep on a freight car: Bing Crosby more than ever like Walt Disney's Cock Robin: it needs some stamina to be a film reviewer. Only the conviction that a public art should be as popular and unsubtle as a dance tune enables one to sit with patient hope through pictures certainly unsubtle but not, in any real sense, popular. What a chance for the creative artist, one persists in believing, to produce for an audience incomparably greater than that of all the 'popular' novelists combined, from Mr Walpole to Mr Brett Young, a genuinely vulgar art. Any other is impossible. The novelist may write for a few thousand readers, but the film artist *must* work for millions. It should be his distinction and pride that he has a public whose needs have never been met since the closing of the theatres by Cromwell. But where is the vulgarity of this art? Alas! the refinement of the 'popular' novel has touched the films; it is the twopenny libraries they reflect rather than the Blackfriars Ring, the Wembley Final, the pin saloons, the coursing.

93

> I'm not the type that I seem to be,
> Happy-go-lucky and gay,

Bing Crosby mournfully croons. That is the common idea of popular entertainment, a mild self-pity, something soothing, something gently amusing. The film
executive still thinks in terms of the 'popular' play and the 'popular' novel, of a
limited middle-class audience, of the tired businessman and the feminine reader.
The public which rattles down from the North to Wembley with curious hats and
favours, tipsy in charabancs, doesn't, apparently, ask to be soothed: it asks to be
excited. It was for these that the Elizabethan stage provided action which could
arouse as communal a response as bear-baiting. For a popular response is not the
sum of private excitements, but mass feeling, mass excitement, the Wembley roar,
and it is the weakness of the Goldwyn Girls that they are as private an enjoyment
as the Art Photos a businessman may turn over in the secrecy of his study; the weakness of Bing Crosby's sentiment, the romantic nostalgia of 'Empty saddles in the
old corral', that it is by its nature a private emotion.

There are very few examples of what I mean by the proper popular use of the
film, and most of those are farces: *Duck Soup*, the early Chaplins, a few 'shorts'
by Laurel and Hardy. These do convey the sense that the picture has been made
by its spectators and not merely shown to them, that it has sprung, as much as
their sports, from *their* level. Serious films of the kind are even rarer: perhaps
Fury, *Le Million*, *Men and Jobs*, they could be numbered on the fingers of one
hand. Because they are so rare one is ready to accept, with exaggerated gratitude,
such refined, elegant, dead pieces as *Louis Pasteur*: the Galsworthy entertainments
of the screen: or intelligently adapted plays like *These Three*.

'People want to be taken out of themselves,' the film executive retorts under the
mistaken impression that the critic is demanding a kind of Zolaesque realism – as if
Webster's plays were realistic. Of course he is right. People are taken out of themselves at Wembley. But I very much doubt if Bing Crosby does so much. 'They
don't want to be depressed', but an excited audience is never depressed: if you
excite your audience first, you can put over what you will of horror, suffering,
truth. But there is one question to which there is no answer. How dare we excite
an audience, a producer may well ask, when Lord Tyrrell, the President of the
British Board of Film Censors, forbids us to show any controversial subject on the
screen?

Perhaps I ought to add that *Rhythm on the Range* is quite a tolerable picture
with a few scenes which do deserve to be called popular cinema and an excellent
new comedian, Mr Bob Burns. I think one might even find a place, in one's ideal
popular cinema, for Mr Crosby: he represents permanent, if disagreeable, human
characteristics of nostalgia and self-pity: I would have him bobbing about at the
back of the scrimmage like a worried referee – or like an Elizabethan clown
crooning his lugubrious reminders.   *The Spectator,* 14 August 1936

Rhythm on the Range (USA, Paramount, 1936). Director: Norman Taurog. Bing Crosby, Frances
Farmer, Bob Burns, Martha Raye.

Everything is Thunder/Die Kribbebijter

A Canadian officer escapes from a German prison camp, after killing a sentry who
has double-crossed him, is sheltered by a prostitute in Berlin, and finally escapes
with her across the frontier with the help of bootleggers who smuggle butter from
Holland to Germany. This English film is good entertainment, very ably directed

and admirably acted by two of its three international stars. Mr Douglass Montgomery as Captain McGrath, the escaper, gives a nervous, hunted, goose-fleshed performance, and Mr Oscar Homolka as the police detective, who is also one of the prostitute's lovers, breathes into a film that grows at times dangerously lyrical a pleasing coarseness, an earthiness, a sense that in spite of such flummery as a marriage 'in the sight of God' and a heroic sacrifice, we are in touch with human beings. His sacrifice at the end, so that the lovers may escape, arises of course from that curious fixed managerial idea that the public, which has always, from *East Lynne* to *The Constant Nymph*, enjoyed its good cry, demands a happy ending. As for Miss Constance Bennett it would be unfair to say much. I suspect that her blurred blonde performance can be laid to the account of our maleficent Board of Censors, who have imposed on Miss Bennett the complicated task of acting a prostitute without ever mentioning her profession. Innuendos, hints, little embarrassed flights from the truth, clients who may after all be just friends: the central situation is heavily obscured. The descriptive letter A – 'for adults' – can never under the present dispensation be taken literally.

But the film is very good entertainment of a kind, the kind that deals with disguises and pursuits and incredible resourcefulness, with policemen on the stairs and hunted men in bathrooms. Captain Hardy's book, from which the film is drawn, was better than that. In a novel he was able vividly to represent the mental background of his professional escaper, a man who was regarded by the other officers with a mixture of disapproval and contempt, someone who was getting the whole school, as it were, into trouble with his silly tricks, someone who couldn't settle down with prisoners of his own age and play the right recognized games. It was Captain Hardy's interesting achievement to show that the wartime escaper is born, not made, that a man who breaks prison three times and tries again is a mental case. But this kind of psychological theme film directors seem unwilling to tackle. There is an admirably exciting sequence at a Berlin railway station when the police close the exit and examine every male passenger: no novel could represent the danger and terror of the trap more vividly, but to authenticate McGrath's sudden love for the Berlin prostitute who takes him home, something less purely visual is needed, it is necessary to go further into the escapist mind than the film takes us. The book was not sentimental: the film is. Here was an occasion for soliloquy, for the voices from the air Clair used in comedy, for all the resources too of wild-track sound, to get the escapist *mind* upon the screen.

The dismal continental cavalcade goes on. 'The first Dutch comedy' – so the Academy advertise their film – is very badly photographed and very badly directed. The story proceeds with dreadful inevitability. A rich man's son marries a typist and is disowned by his father, a household tyrant. The typist introduces herself into the castle as a housekeeper and wins the heart of this male shrew. That is really the whole story, though there was one very funny scene – at the end of an hour. It was a long time to wait, when all the time you could see the conclusion ahead, like a church spire visible for ten miles to the tired walker across the Flemish flats. The direction was of that grim slow kind which never shows you a car without following it to the horizon or lets a character leave one room for another without a prolonged study of opening and closing, and then reopening and re-closing, doors, with a glimpse of the passage perhaps as well, lest the imagination should bear too heavy a burden.   *The Spectator,* 21 August 1936

Everything is Thunder (GB, Gaumont British, 1936). Director: Milton Rosmer. Constance Bennett, Douglass Montgomery, Oscar Homolka.
Die Kribbebijter (Holland, 1935). Directors: Herman Kosterlitz, Ernst Winer. Cor Ruys, Louis de Bree, Louis Borel.

Mr Deeds Goes to Town

Mr Deeds is Capra's finest film (it is on quite a different intellectual level from the spirited and delightful *It Happened One Night*), and that means it is a comedy quite unmatched on the screen. For Capra has what Lubitsch, the witty playboy, has not: a sense of responsibility, and what Clair, whimsical, poetic, a little precious and *à la mode*, has not, a kinship with his audience, a sense of common life, a morality: he has what even Chaplin has not, complete mastery of his medium, and that medium the sound-film, not the film with sound attached to it. Like Lang, he hears all the time just as clearly as he sees and just as selectively. I do not think anyone can watch *Mr Deeds* for long without being aware of a technician as great as Lang employed on a theme which profoundly moves him: the theme of goodness and simplicity manhandled in a deeply selfish and brutal world. That was the theme of *Fury*, too, but Capra is more fortunate than Lang. Lang expresses the theme in terms of terror, and terror on the screen has always, alas! to be tempered to the shorn lamb; Capra expresses it in terms of pity and ironic tenderness, and no magnate feels the need to cramp his style or alter his conclusion.

Mr Deeds is a young provincial who inherits twenty million dollars from an uncle he has never seen. An ardent tuba-player in the local band, he makes his living by writing verses which are printed on postcards on such occasions as Mothers' Day. The uncle's solicitors, who have absorbed, with the help of a Power of Attorney, half a million dollars of his money, hope to continue the process with his unsophisticated nephew who is quite unexcited by his fortune and only wants to do good with it. They bring Deeds up to town. Wealth educates Deeds, he learns the shabby side not only of business but of art, with the help of the opera directors and the fashionable poets; he learns, too, the deceit which may exist in ordinary human affection (the girl he loves, and who loves him, is all the time writing newspaper articles which make front-page fun of the activities of the Cinderella Man). A revolver and a would-be assassin's nerveless hand educate him socially, and he is arranging to use the whole of his fortune in providing ruined farmers with free land and free seed when society – controlled by racketeers – strikes its last blow at the elements it cannot absorb, goodness, simplicity, disinterestedness. Claimants are found to dispute his sanity and to try to remove the management of the estate from his hands.

It sounds as grim a theme as *Fury*; innocence lynched as effectively at a judicial inquiry as in a burning courthouse, but there is this difference between Lang and Capra: Lang's happy ending was imposed on him, we did not believe in it; Capra's is natural and unforced. He *believes* in the possibility of happiness; he believes, in spite of the controlling racketeers, in human nature. Goodness, simplicity, disinterestedness: these in his hands become fighting qualities. Deeds sees through opera directors, fashionable intellectuals, solicitors, psychologists who prove that he is insane merely because he likes playing the tuba and isn't greedy for money. Only for a few minutes in the courtroom does he lose heart and refuse to defend himself: he is never a helpless victim, like the garage-man behind the bars watching the woman lift her baby up to see the fun, and he comes back into the ring with folk humour and folk shrewdness to rout his enemies for the sake of the men they have ruined. The picture glows with that humour and shrewdness, just as Lang's curdles with his horror and disgust; it is as funny, most of the time, as *Fury* was terrifying. It is not a question of truth or falsehood: two directors of genius have made pictures with curiously similar themes which present a conviction, a settled attitude towards life as it is lived. The pessimist makes a tragedy, the optimist (but how far from sweetness and complacency is Capra's optimism) makes a comedy. And Capra, as well as Lang, is supported by a perfect cast. Every minor part, however few the lines, is completely rendered, and Mr Gary Cooper's subtle and pliable performance must be something of which other directors have only dreamed.   *The Spectator,* 28 August 1936

Mr Deeds Goes to Town (USA, Columbia, 1936). Director: Frank Capra. Gary Cooper, Jean Arthur, George Bancroft, Lionel Stander, Douglas Dumbrille, Raymond Walburn, H. B. Warner.

The Man Who Could Work Miracles

A dark handsome colossus broods obscurely through a starry sky, broods, rather like Mr Wells himself, histrionically. From the remark of two equally enormous, even more handsome, but this time indubitably Aryan giants, we learn in the authentic late-Wells dialogue his name. 'Our Brother, the Giver of Power, is yonder.' We remember the Dictator and the Airman in Mr Wells's previous film: 'Who are you?' 'I am Wings over the World', and arm ourselves against a sea of abstractions, couched in Mr Wells's embarrassing poetic diction. But, fortunately, after an interchange of rather wilting remarks about this obscure planet, we come to earth, to a Kentish inn and Mr Fotheringay, floor-walker in the local drapery, whom the Giver of Power has decided to endow with miraculous gifts, so that he may learn what really lies in the heart of a small mortal creature. The late Wells, we realize, has decided that the early Wells, the author of some of the finest comedies in English fiction, was not significant enough. A few immortals and great conspiracies are tacked, like news-cuttings in a Surrealist picture, to the early short story. The result is pretentious and mildly entertaining, with no moments as good as the war sequences of *Things to Come*, nor as bad as what followed them.

The direction and the production are shocking. That is not Mr Wells's fault. And it may not be altogether the fault of Mr Lothar Mendes, the director, for the slowness, vulgarity, over-emphasis are typical of Mr Korda's productions. Take for example an early sequence. The Giver of Power leans through the sky with outstretched finger. 'I will choose anyone,' he says, 'this little man for instance', and the film cuts to the stagy pasteboard (why not a proper exterior?) country inn and Mr Fotheringay hesitating at the door. You would think an audience could be trusted to catch the idea, you would think the spotlight which then shines down on the little man was the very limit of emphasis, but no! an enormous hand and wrist, a celestial signpost, is projected from the sky to point Mr Fotheringay out to dullards. For all this, and for the deplorable miscasting, Mr Wells is not responsible. Mr Korda, a publicity man of genius, who has not yet revealed a talent for the films, casts his pictures with little regard for anything but gossip paragraphs. Mr Roland Young is quite the wrong type for Fotheringay, with his intermittent accent and his eyes which twinkle merrily with lack of conviction: Mr Ralph Richardson's Tory colonel might have been entertaining in a stage farce, but there is no room on the screen for 'wigs by Clarkson' and false whiskers. The only performance of real character is Mr Lawrence Hanray's as the scared bird-like bank manager. As for trick photography, of which this film is naturally an orgy, and like orgies of another kind grimly repetitive, it is always to my mind dull and unconvincing and destroys illusion.

There remain Mr Wells's ideas. What *does* the Giver of Power find at the heart of his ordinary mortal? The answer is muddle, a rather too Wellsian muddle. The little man, badgered by business, by conservatism, by religion to make *their* world, rebels, and, announcing that he will make his own, summons before him all the great men, soldiers, politicians and lawyers, and gives them till day to form a plan for a peaceful society. Yet when the Reverend Mr Maydig protests that the time is too short, that the sun is already setting, Mr Fotheringay, for no reason at all, chooses to abolish his time-limit and stop the sun. The result is chaos, and Mr Fotheringay wheeled round by the ferocious elements puts everything back as it was before. Add to this Mr Wells's childish love of fancy-dress (the little man as dictator of the world goes, most improbably, Tudor) and a touch of sexual vulgarity (a beauty chorus of Kentish concubines suspiciously reminiscent of Mr Korda's idea of Henry VIII's wives) and you have the whole entertainment, sometimes fake poetry, sometimes unsuccessful comedy, sometimes farce, sometimes sociological discussion, without a spark of creative talent or a trace of film ability.

The Spectator, 4 September 1936

The Man Who Could Work Miracles (GB, London Films, 1936). Director: Lothar Mendes. Roland Young, Ralph Richardson, George Sanders.

As You Like It/Cover to Cover

As You Like It is a respectful film: that is to say there is far more Shakespeare in it than there was in Reinhardt's *Dream*, and I dare say it is a better production than you will often see on the stage. In Miss Bergner's Rosalind freedom may have become elvishness and poetry sometimes whimsicality, her tear-smudged, bewildered features may be more easily associated with a constant nymph than with the reckless-tongued Rosalind, but certainly in her private version she is, like white witches, 'mischievously good'; while Mr Laurence Olivier's Orlando, sullen, brooding, a little oafish, is even more satisfying. The only jarring notes in the acting were Mr Henry Ainley's Duke and Mr Leon Quartermaine's Jacques. Mr Ainley's false fruity enunciation carries us back to the Edwardian stage, when every Shakespearean actor ranted like a little Irving, and as for Jacques, his sting has been quite drawn. The great public may well wonder why this hearty good fellow was known to his companions as 'melancholy'. Horns and cuckolds have been heavily censored, the streak of poison which runs through the comedy has been squeezed carefully out between hygienic finger-tips, and what is left, apart from Arden and absurd delightful artificial love, is Shakespeare at his falsest, Adam and church bells and good men's feasts and sermons in stone, all the dull didactic unconvincing images. That, I think, is the chief objection to Shakespeare on the screen: the British Board of Film Censors will see to it that only the school versions of his plays are produced.

Regarded as a film, *As You Like It* is less satisfactory. There are far too many dull middle-length shots from a fixed camera, so that we might just as well be seated in the circle above the deep wide stage at Drury Lane. The special possibilities soliloquy gives are ignored: the 'Seven Ages of Man' is as falsely italicized as it

As You Like It: Elisabeth Bergner

usually is on the stage: we watch Jacques taking deep breath for the too famous passage, we watch his audience intently and unaccountably absorbed in the rather banal recital. How much more effectively this speech could have been expressed on the screen: say, through the ears and eyes of a *bored* listener who wanders off from the prosy cynic out of earshot but turns suddenly back to hear the better when a finer, more truthful line happens to reach his ear: 'even in the cannon's mouth', 'sans teeth, sans eyes, sans taste, sans everything.' Dr Czinner has been too respectful towards stage tradition. He seems to have concluded that all the cinema can offer is more space: more elaborate palace sets and a real wood with room for real animals. How the ubiquitous livestock (sheep and cows and hens and rabbits) weary us before the end, and how disastrously the genuine English woodland is spoilt by too much fancy, for when did English trees, in what is apparently late autumn, bear clusters of white flowers? Freedom of movement, too, is often misused, and why should poetry be cut merely to leave time for girlish games of touch-wood through the trees? On only one occasion is the camera a definite gain. The lyrical repetitions between Sylvius and Phebe, Orlando and Rosalind: 'It is to be all made of sighs and tears: And so am I for Phebe.' 'And I for Ganymede.' 'And I for Rosalind.' 'And I for no woman,' with the help of the rhythmically panning camera move beautifully into the memory.

Cover to Cover, Mr Paul Rotha's short film made for the National Book Council, is a far more interesting picture, for this director uses the counterpoint of sound and image with subtlety. Among the distinguished authors who take part, Miss Rebecca West has the best lines, and Mr T. S. Eliot, I was grieved to notice, has not so good a screen face or manner as Sapper. Verse is skilfully used in the commentary, though it has less simplicity, is less 'seeable' than Mr Auden's in *Night Mail*, and all the stages of a book from MS. to library and counter are dramatized with real imagination. From the documentary point of view I have one serious criticism. Did there ever exist such a heaven-born publisher as this who consults an author in the choice of his type and paper?   *The Spectator*, 11 September 1936

SAYING OF THE WEEK
'The whole of *As You Like It* is really an intimate memoir of a girl's first love-affair.'
(C. A. Lejeune.)

As You Like It (GB, Inter Allied, 1936). Director: Paul Czinner. Elisabeth Bergner, Laurence Olivier, Leon Quartermaine, Henry Ainley.
Cover to Cover (GB, National Book Council, 1936). Director: Paul Rotha. T. S. Eliot, Rebecca West.

The Great Ziegfeld/It's Love Again/Marchand d'Amour/East Meets West

The Great Ziegfeld is another of those films which belongs to the history of publicity rather than to the history of the cinema. This huge inflated gas-blown object bobs into the critical view as irrelevantly as an airship advertising someone's toothpaste over a South Coast 'resort'. It lasts three hours: that is its only claim to special attention. Like a man sitting hour after hour on top of a pole, it does excite a kind of wonder; wonder at how it manages to go on. It justifies its length as little as do the *Faraways*, the *Anthony Adverses*, the Severn novels which wind their dim protracted course through the realm of fiction. The padding is only too obvious. Instead of one love-affair, we have two; instead of one big musical set-piece, we have half a dozen. There is really no reason, except the patience of the public, why such a picture should ever stop. 'Long enough to bore, but not yet big enough to boost', I can imagine one of the great executives remarking, when the picture had not yet passed far beyond the second hour, 'throw in another grand passion and three more super-spectacles, and draw out for another thousand feet that death scene.' So Ziegfeld, for a quite unconscionable time, passes out to dim music, while the sky-signs of his latest shows flicker beyond the window-panes. This New World hero, who has 'glorified the American girl', in other words the dumber carnalities, the great glittering bogus blondes, is heard questioning for a moment the eternal values of his career, but his valet reassures him, 'You have done the most beautiful things that have ever been done on any stage.' Alas! we have watched them for the last three hours, and now for several minutes more they crowd back to their dying creator's memory. The glorified girls push him up towards Paradise, like the cherubs which throng round the topboots of William of Orange in Rubens's apotheosis. Mr William Powell does his best, Miss Myrna Loy rather less than her best, and Miss Luise Rainer brings a few moments of real distinction and of human feeling to this, the longest and, if superlatives have got to be used, the silliest, vulgarest, dullest novelty of the season.

For once it is possible to praise an English 'musical' above an American. Mr Victor Saville has directed *It's Love Again* with speed, efficiency, and a real sense of the absurd. Nor has the long tubular form of Miss Jessie Matthews, the curious charm of her ungainly adolescent carriage, ever been better exploited. The story is agreeably silly, a long way from the grand, the showman's, passions, the huge misplaced seriousness of the American film which weighs on the spirits like a visit to the Royal Academy. It is the story of a talented young singer and dancer who cannot get an audition until she has gate-crashed into the gossip columns with a bogus career of Eastern exploration and tiger-shooting behind her. Her encounter in a shower of superb double meanings and enormous gallantries, at an Oriental party given in her honour, with a genuine old tiger-shooting colonel, whom she believes to be her friend, a former gossip-writer, in disguise, is memorable indeed.

Apart from this picture and Mr Edmond Gréville's *Marchand d'Amour*, a melodramatic and rather silly tale of another showman's great, but more frankly carnal, love, directed with immense *panache* and a secret sense of amusement, the most enjoyable film I have seen this week has been *The Gift of the Gab*, an item in Gaumont-British News which I hope will not disappear altogether when the week is over. A carefully arranged anthology of modern oratory, it ranges maliciously from Mr Lloyd George's mechanic passion to the mumbled, almost inaudible, 'Awfully nice', of the too British winner of a King's Cup Air Race. And finally a warning – to avoid like the plague *East Meets West*, in which Mr George Arliss appears in one of his most kindly parts to date. This time he is an Eastern Rajah, but who can change the sly soft episcopal speech, the long upper-lip, like that of a well-bred horse, the general tone of a good club?

The Spectator, 18 September 1936

The Great Ziegfeld (USA, M-G-M, 1936). Director: Robert Z. Leonard. William Powell, Myrna Loy, Luise Rainer, Frank Morgan, Virginia Bruce, Fanny Brice, Harriet Hoctor.
It's Love Again (GB, Gaumont British, 1936). Director: Victor Saville. Jessie Matthews, Robert Young.
Marchand d'Amour (France, S.H.O. Films, 1935). Director: Edmond Gréville. Jean Galland, Rosine Deréan.
East Meets West (GB, Gaumont British, 1936). Director: Herbert Mason. George Arliss, Lucie Mannheim, Godfrey Tearle, Romney Brent.

It's Love Again: Jessie Matthews

The Song of Freedom/Anthony Adverse

The Song of Freedom is the story of Zinga, a black London dockhand, who, unknown to himself, is the descendant of a seventeenth-century 'Queen' of Cassanga, an island off the West Coast. All he has inherited is a crude medallion and a few bars of a song, handed down from father to son. Born in London he remains an exile at heart, passionately longing for some knowledge of his home. A distinguished musical impresario hears him singing in a public house, trains him and makes him a famous singer, but on the first night of an opera founded on *The Emperor Jones*, he meets an anthropologist who recognizes 'the king song' of Cassanga and the medallion. Cassanga, he tells Zinga, is a poor impoverished place. White men have not been allowed to land, and the island is ruled by witch-doctors. Zinga and his wife set out immediately with the idea of helping the people and – alas! for the inconsistencies of this tale – bringing them the blessings of white civilization. At first the witch-doctor's influence is too strong. Zinga's wife, who has watched a forbidden rite – the shadow of Hollywood has fallen across the screen – is condemned to death, and only at the last moment does Zinga remember 'the king's song' and establish his authority, for luckily these curious islanders seem to have as strong an instinct for hereditary rule as members of the White Rose League. Apart from the profound beauty of Miss Elisabeth Welch and Mr Robeson's magnificent singing of inferior songs, I find it hard to say in what the charm of this imperfect picture lies. The direction is distinguished but not above reproach, the story is sentimental and absurd, and yet a sense stays in the memory of an unsophisticated mind fumbling on the edge of simple and popular poetry. The best scenes are the dockland scenes, the men returning from work, black and white in an easy companionship free from any colour bar, the public house interiors, dark faces pausing at tenement windows to listen to Zinga's songs, a sense of nostalgia. There are plenty of faults even here, sentiment too close to sentimentality, a touch of 'quaintness' and patronage, but one is made aware all the time of what Mann calls 'the gnawing surreptitious hankering for the bliss of the commonplace', the general exile of our class as well as the particular exile of the African.

But everything goes badly wrong when Zinga reaches Africa, the fabulous island where the witch-doctors speak Biblical English ('The heart of Mandingo is heavy because you come'). That is not an authentic situation, for the part of Africa untouched by white influence is minute. If we were to take the film seriously, it should have been to a white colony that Zinga returned, a colony of the half-educated like Sierra Leone where the teaching must be stopped at a point not governed by the pupil's capacity but by the Government's policy. There, rather than in a fairy-tale primitive island, lies the real dramatic situation, but I doubt whether it could have been resolved as happily and easily. A few bars of a 'king's song' would not abolish the bounce and the subservience, the contempt and the laughter.

Anthony Adverse goes on too long, otherwise it might have been the funniest film since *The Crusades*, with its lyrical captions taken over from old silent days: 'Thus an unwanted child was given a name, and for ten years heard it spoken only by the good sisters and his kindly teacher, Father Xavier.' The sexual chronology is curious. I am still puzzled by the dreadful child in an Eton jacket who was waiting unexpectedly to call Anthony 'father' at the end of his wanderings, for Anthony, who married his wife secretly one morning, mislaid her before noon and only saw her again after seven years: a fishy situation which perhaps our film censors have unduly obscured. But most I welcomed our old friend Pedro de Cordoba, with his weaving tortoise head, who crops up in odd unexplained ways in Havana and West Africa wearing a cowl, and who dies at last on his back in the mud, his flippers feebly waving, his odd receding mouth opening and shutting, a masterly interpretation of Miss Potter's Ptolemy Tortoise.

The Spectator, 25 September 1936

The Song of Freedom (GB, Hammer, 1936). Director: J. Elder Wills. Paul Robeson, Elisabeth Welch. *Anthony Adverse* (USA, Warner Bros, 1936). Director: Mervyn LeRoy. Fredric March, Olivia de Havilland, Claude Rains, Pedro de Cordoba.

Maria Bashkirtseff/My Man Godfrey

It is little more than fifty years since Maria Bashkirtseff died; if her lungs had not failed, she might have been alive today, but already the film magnates are re-arranging her life in what they consider a better film pattern. No historical novelist would dare to take such liberties, to invent for the eighteen-year-old Maria Bashkirtseff, who as far as anyone can tell from her journal had no experience of sexual passion (the nearest she came to it was for the sick Bastien-Lepage), a reciprocated love for Maupassant. This melancholy, introspective and ambitious girl with the broad shoulders, big breasts and Spanish hips, becomes a blithe and bony blonde of mature years, who holds hands with Maupassant in moonlight and dreams of country cottages. The same evening she overhears her family doctor telling Maupassant's rival that she has only a few weeks to live, and so she dismisses Maupassant, feigning that she cares less for him than for the gold medal of the forthcoming exhibition. But the film imagination rises even higher into the great inane, the rival lover himself wins the medal, takes it to Maupassant and asks that he, as one of the judges, shall present it to Maria, so that she may die happy. And to Maupassant, at her bedside, Maria reveals that she cares nothing for the medal and had dismissed him only because she loved him. Who, after all this, could believe that there is not a single mention of Maupassant in Maria Bash-kirtseff's journal? 'A free adaptation of historical facts', the programme calls it, and one wonders that the adapters lost such an opportunity for Oriental passion, Disraeli and desert sands as Maria's meeting with De Lesseps at an Embassy reception gave them, where he told her 'a long story of nurses and babies and Suez canal shares', a story on which much might have been founded to convince the great public that real lives are as banal and melodramatic as those of the screen. It is difficult, repelled by the dishonesty and the vulgarity of this 'free adaptation', to be quite fair to the merits of the picture: the careful and discreet period setting and Herr Hans Jaray's performance as Maupassant, which gives the right impression of dapper despair, of spiritual nihilism in a well-cut coat, against the plush, the Baroque mirrors, the ornate decorations of private rooms.

My Man Godfrey, for three-quarters of its way, is acutely funny. The adventure of a sane man among the witless wealthy, the story opens with a 'scavenging party' at the Waldorf-Ritz to which competitors are expected to bring, besides such assorted objects as bowls of goldfish, goats and mangles, 'a forgotten man'. Mr William Powell, unshaven and for once more bitter than bright, is secured by a

My Man Godfrey: Carole Lombard, William Powell

lovely nitwit from a rubbish-dump under Brooklyn Bridge. The chaotic scene of
the shrieking alcoholic rich, leading goats and waving mangles through the great
chromium halls, is perhaps the wittiest, as well as the noisiest, sequence of the year,
but the film does not maintain quite so high a standard. Mr William Powell,
adopted in place of a dead Pomeranian by the lovely brainless competitor, Miss
Carole Lombard, whose voice unwinds in an endless enchanting ribbon of inani-
ties, becomes the family butler, but alas! before the end he proves to be of even
better blood, and Boston blood at that, than his employers, nor does 'the social
conscience' remain agreeably implicit. Mr Powell is made to preach a sermon to
the assembled family on social reform after saving them from bankruptcy by his
knowledge of the stock markets and – curious moral – a huge luxury club rises
on the site of the rubbish-dump in which his old down-and-out friends are given
employment in elegant uniforms. But though 'the social conscience' is a little
confused, the film, in the earlier sequences, well conveys the atmosphere of an
American Cherry Orchard, of a class with little of the grace and all the futility and
some of the innocence of its Russian counterpart. Unfortunately, to these Americans prosperity returns, there is no dignified exit while the axes thud in the orchard,
only the great glossy club rising over the wilderness of empty tins, and, last muddle
and bewilderment, the marriage of the reformer and the brainless 'lovely'.

The Spectator, 2 October 1936

Maria Bashkirtseff (Austria, Tobis-Sascha, 1935). Director: Hermann Kosterlitz. Olga Tschechowa,
Leo Slezak, Paul Heidemann.
My Man Godfrey (USA, Universal, 1936). Director: Gregory La Cava. William Powell, Carole Lombard,
Mischa Auer.

The Texas Rangers/Savoy Hotel 217/The King Steps Out

The Big Parade, The Crowd, Hallelujah; these are some of Mr King Vidor's
previous films, and *The Texas Rangers* is in the same tradition. Mr Vidor is one
of the best of the popular directors; D. W. Griffith, a much finer artist, is his master.
No one who had not learnt a great deal from Griffith could have directed the battle
between the Indians and a handful of Rangers with so sure a sense of old-time
suspense: will help come in time? And the Indians swarm up the rocks, revolvers
jam, the rescuers come galloping between the hills. A more sophisticated age has
dealt in this case kindly with Vidor, for in a Griffith film it was unthinkable that
help should ever *not* arrive, while now we are allowed a doubt.

In another way, too, Vidor is Griffith's successor: he does his best to give his
pictures epic value. At the beginning of this film a voice describes the circumstances,
the Indian wars and the bushranging, which brought the Texas Rangers into
existence, and in the last sequence the commanding officer, played by that fine
actor, Mr Edward Ellis, with his thin, twisted farmer's face, speaks over a Ranger's
grave an oration, pompous and political in its resounding abstractions, yet
curiously moving in Mr Ellis's plain, honest enunciation, on the 'guardians of the
frontier, makers of the peace'.

But in Vidor's 'epics', just as in Cruze's somewhat overpraised picture, *The
Covered Wagon*, the story gets in the way: they bear about as much relation to
epic drama as do the huge, artless, historical novels which have been so popular
recently in the United States. The story of *The Texas Rangers*, I should add, is a
great deal better than that of *The Covered Wagon*. It is the story of two bandits,

Savoy Hotel 217: Hans Albers, Gusti Huber

acted by Mr Fred MacMurray and Mr Jack Oakie, who join the Rangers in order to send useful tips to a bushranging friend. They are converted to law and order, and when one has been murdered in an attempt to trap his former friend, the other goes out and gets his man. The morality of their actions is all the more convincing for its curiously twisted nature: one does, at moments, feel a little way lowered into the unplumbed complex caverns of the simple soul.

Savoy Hotel 217, directed by Gustav Ucicky (who made that excellent melo-drama of the submarine war, *Morgenrot*), and photographed by Fritz Lang's old cameraman, takes us agreeably back to the old classical Ufa days of *Dr Mabuse* and *The Spy*. A philandering waiter (Hans Albers), an old-fashioned vamp who has had one husband put out of the way and ruined and divorced another and who meets a violent and expected end, a lover from Siberia, a little chambermaid and a jealous housekeeper: the fates of all these are agreeably crossed in a slow, good-humoured murder-story set in pre-war St Petersburg. The most vivid character is that of the murderer, the vamp's husband, a little bankrupt merchant with popping eyes and tiny moustache and breaking voice, who gives the impression of a small, soft, tormented animal, of a mouse-like tragedy. Love on the servants' twisting iron stairway, jealousy round the linen-cupboard; the melodramatic passions are given a pleasantly realistic setting by a very competent director and a first-class cameraman.

Miss Grace Moore as a Bavarian princess who pretends to be a dressmaker and wins the heart of a young Austrian Emperor to save her sister from a loveless marriage: a plot like that can hardly fail to have its painful moments. Miss Moore acts with the exaggerated vivacity of a games-mistress letting herself noisily go on the last night of term, but unexpectedly the film has some light and amusing sequences, a Lubitsch touch, while Mr Herman Bing's innkeeper holds the stage. Mr Bing's rolling eyeballs, his enormous splutter, his huge lack of understanding, have never before been given such generous room. He bears the whole film on his wildly expressive shoulders.   *The Spectator*, 9 October 1936

The Texas Rangers (USA, Paramount, 1936). Director: King Vidor. Fred MacMurray, Jack Oakie, Jean Parker.
Savoy Hotel 217 (Germany, Ufa, 1936). Director: Gustav Ucicky. Hans Albers, Käthe Dorsch, Brigitte Horney.
The King Steps Out (USA, Columbia, 1936). Director: Josef von Sternberg. Grace Moore, Franchot Tone, Herman Bing.

Nutrition

We are apt to forget, among the gangsters and the grand passions, that the cinema has other uses than fiction, and yet it is the Gas Light and Coke Company which is responsible for the most interesting film I have seen for a long time. This Company deserves the highest praise. For the second time it has undertaken a work which should have been the responsibility of the Ministry of Health. There is no gas propaganda in *Nutrition*, any more than there was in *Housing Problems*. Both pictures are the work of Mr Edgar Anstey, who is contributing something new to the documentary film. The documentary film has sometimes hovered too uneasily on the edge of art and story-telling. The GPO Film Unit in *Song of Ceylon* produced the most aesthetically satisfying film ever made in this country, but there have been times – in *Night Mail*, for example – when the demands of instruction and the instinct to create a work of art have conflicted. The final sequences in *Night Mail* were aesthetically satisfying, but earlier in the film one was aware of hesitation: we were shown too many technicalities for atmospheric purposes, we were shown too few for understanding.

In *Housing Problems* Mr Anstey was superbly untroubled by the aesthetic craving: he used the camera as a first-class reporter, and a reporter too truthful, too vivid, to find a place on any modern newspaper. He produced a poignant and convincing document simply by taking his camera and his microphone into the slums, the terrible tiny peeling rooms, up the broken stairways, into the airless courts and letting the women talk in their own way about the dirt and rats and bugs. The method was simple, certainly, but it cannot have been easy; it must have needed human qualities more common among Russian than English directors. (Compare the characters in *Housing Problems* with the frightened ironed-out personalities with censored scripts whom the BBC present as 'documentary'.)

Nutrition has everything which *Housing Problems* had (the same human interest, handled with the finest, self-effacing sympathy) and a great deal more beside. It goes deeper and speaks with more authority. It takes the statistics, the categories of food (energy, body-building, protective), and presents the problem at different dramatic levels: the chemist in his laboratory examining his rats (the small, under-sized, piebald creature, who scrambles in a scared way beneath his plump capitalist companion, has been fed on a typical working-class diet), Sir John Orr on his experimental farm, the Medical Officers of Bethnal Green and Stockton-on-Tees in conference, the street markets, the Bluecoat boys on their playing-fields, the working-class boys in their back streets. Professor Julian Huxley speaks the admirable, quite unpolitical commentary, which is interrupted occasionally for Mr Herbert Morrison to describe what the London County Council is doing for elementary schoolchildren, for medical officers to discuss the proper balancing of diets, for working women themselves to speak with a sad courage of their house-keeping, of cabbages at sixpence a pound, of the inevitable hungry Thursdays. It is the foods which build and the foods which protect that are most expensive: the energy foods, which the children need least, are cheapest, and who can blame the parents if they choose to give their children the foods which will at least prevent their *feeling* their starvation? And a long parade goes past the camera of cheerful child faces above under-developed bodies.

Mr Anstey has had no aesthetic end in view: he has wanted to explain the problem clearly and to make the fight for better diets personal by means of showing the actual sufferers, the actual investigators, but there is always an aesthetic delight in complete competence. Conrad once wrote an essay in praise of the literary merits of the official Notices to Mariners, and as the film reaches its end, the summing-up of the commentator coinciding with a quick repetition of images, one is aware of having attended not only a vivid and authoritative lecture but a contribution to Cinema.   *The Spectator,* 16 October 1936

Nutrition (GB, Gas Light & Coke Co., 1936). Director: Edgar Anstey

Romeo and Juliet

'Boy Meets Girl, 1436' – so the programme heads the story of *Romeo and Juliet,* which it tells with some inaccuracy; but this fourth attempt to screen Shakespeare is not as bad as that. Unimaginative, certainly, coarse-grained, a little banal, it is frequently saved – by Shakespeare – from being a bad film. The late Irving Thalberg, the producer, has had a funeral success second only to Rudolph Valentino's, but there is nothing in this film to show that he was a producer of uncommon talent. He has made a big film, as Hollywood recognizes that adjective: all is on the characteristic Metro-Goldwyn scale: a Friar Laurence's cell with the appearance, as another critic has put it, of a modern luxury flat, with a laboratory of retorts and test-tubes worthy of a Wells superman (no 'osier cage' of a few flowers and weeds); a balcony so high that Juliet should really have conversed with Romeo in shouts like a sailor from the crow's-nest sighting land; a spectacular beginning with the Montagues and Capulets parading through pasteboard streets to the same church, rather late, it appears from the vague Popish singing off, for Benediction; Verona seen from the air, too palpably a childish model; an audible lark proclaiming in sparrow accents that it is not the nightingale; night skies sparkling with improbable

Romeo and Juliet: Leslie Howard, Norma Shearer

tinsel stars; and lighting so oddly timed that when Juliet remarks that the mask of
night is on her face, 'else would a maiden blush bepaint my cheek', not Verona's
high moon could have lit her more plainly.

But on the credit side are more of Shakespeare's words than we have grown to
expect, a few more indeed than he ever wrote, if little of the subtlety of his dramatic
sense which let the storm begin slowly with the muttering of a few servants, rather
than with this full-dress riot. The picture has been given a Universal Certificate,
and one was pleasantly surprised to find how safely our film censors had slumbered
through many a doubtful passage: even 'the bawdy hand of the dial' had not
disturbed the merry gentlemen's rest. The nurse's part has suffered, but more from
Miss Edna May Oliver's clowning than from a censor. This part and Mercutio's
suffer most from overacting. Mr John Barrymore's middle-aged Mercutio is
haggard with the grease-paint of a thousand Broadway nights. Mr Basil Rathbone
is a fine vicious Tybalt, and Mr Leslie Howard and Miss Norma Shearer spoke
verse as verse should be spoken and were very satisfying in the conventional and
romantic and dreamy mode (one still waits to see lovers hot with lust and youth
and Verona fevers, as reckless as their duelling families, 'like fire and powder which
as they kiss consume').

It is the duels and violence which come off well, Mercutio's death and Tybalt's,
and, more convincing than on the stage, the final fight with Paris in the tomb, but

I am less than ever convinced that there is an aesthetic justification for filming Shakespeare at all. The effect of even the best scenes is to distract, much in the same way as the old Tree productions distracted: we cannot look and listen simultaneously with equal vigilance. But that there may be a social justification I do not dispute; by all means let Shakespeare, even robbed of half his drama and three-quarters of his poetry, be mass-produced. One found oneself surrounded in the theatre by prosperous middle-aged ladies anxiously learning the story in the programme for the first time; urgent whispers came from the knowing ones, as Romeo went down into the Capulet tomb, preparing their timorous companions for an unexpected and unhappy ending. It may very well be a social duty to teach the great middle class a little about Shakespeare's plays. But the poetry – shall we ever get the poetry upon the screen except in fits and starts (the small scene between Romeo and the ruined apothecary he bribes to sell him poison was exquisitely played and finely directed), unless we abjure all the liberties the huge sets and the extras condemn us to? Something like Dreyer's *Passion of Jeanne d'Arc*, the white-washed wall and the slow stream of faces, might preserve a little more of the poetry than this commercial splendour.   *The Spectator*, 23 October 1936

Romeo and Juliet (USA, M-G-M, 1936). Director: George Cukor. Norma Shearer, Leslie Howard, John Barrymore, Edna May Oliver, Basil Rathbone.

La Kermesse Héroïque/The General Died at Dawn

La Kermesse Héroïque is the rarest thing in the cinema, a really adult film. M. Jacques Feyder, who made one of the most memorable of all silent films, *Thérèse Raquin*, has produced a comedy which should appeal to the public which is now discovering *The Country Wife*. Like Restoration prose, his photography moves with a fine strut to the music of horns. The period is the sixteenth century, the place the town of Boom in Flanders during the rising against Spanish domination. But virility in Boom is low, though male conceit is as blown as the breeches. The Burgo-master, the butcher, the baker, the fishmonger, in their black balloon trousers and ribbons and chains of local office, are being painted at the council table for the municipal gallery when two dusty professional soldiers spur in to announce the Spaniards' approach. Action is quick and prudent: the volunteers disband: their arms are hidden in the bowels of fish, and the Burgomaster poses upon his bed, a stout and pompous corpse lit by candles and guarded by councillors with halberds. He will sacrifice himself, he announces through the town-crier, for the safety of the town: the Spaniards will respect the dead.

But his wife is of another mettle. She summons the women to a mass meeting: she lays her ambush, and when the weary Spanish troops arrive, ready for another night of street fights, flames, and the exaggerated pleasures of rapine, they find the women, dressed in mourning for their dead Burgomaster, waiting with refreshments and offers of hospitality. The husbands cannot resist: their weapons, even if they had the courage to use them, are in the bellies of tomorrow's fish course; nor can the Burgomaster protest at the courtesy of the Spanish Duke towards his wife, for officially he is dead. The Spaniards leave next day, their halberds wreathed in flowers, while his wife fingers her new pearl necklace. Boom is saved, the Burgo-master takes the credit, and the little town has as many horns as a hunting-lodge.

It is an admirable film, a little obscene like most good comedies, and beautifully

The General Died at Dawn: Gary Cooper, Akim Tamiroff, Porter Hall

acted. I admired particularly the Dominican chaplain with his mannered austerity and his concealed humour, the unctuousness which slips aside to disclose a pleasing natural frailty: the screen seldom allows one the pleasure of seeing more than a single layer of the human mind. M. Feyder's camera picks out with vividness and invention absurdities in costume and character and almost as skilfully as a Restoration dramatist he lightly works into his ribald story a touch of the genuine, the simple emotion. Even Mrs Pinchwife has her moments, and so has this war-weary Duke and this woman of character married to a Flemish clod, and a touch of lyrical poetry breaks charmingly and unexpectedly through the close of the bawdy comedy: the first grey watery Lowland light behind the shuttered houses and the solitary drummer strutting out into the small deserted square.

The first few silent sequences of Mr Lewis Milestone's *The General Died at Dawn* are as good as anything to be seen on the screen in London: the dead Chinese village with the kites circling down towards the corpses, the long pale grasses shivering aside as the troops trample through, the General with the scarred satisfied face riding away along the rough road in the slick American car. After that it becomes a melodrama, though a melodrama of more than usual skill, about an American with a social conscience (Mr Clifford Odets has written the dialogue) who tries to run a beltful of gold through to Shanghai with which arms may be bought to overthrow the local war-lord. He gets mixed up with a girl, of course, who's on the wrong side and shoots her father, and is pursued, even into the chromium Shanghai suite, by the sinister General. Mr Akim Tamiroff as the war-lord and Mr Porter Hall as his 'poor white' agent give vivid support to Mr Gary Cooper's tough laconic friend-of-the-underdog. If it were not for a rather ludicrous ending, this would be one of the best 'thrillers' for some years.

The Spectator, 30 October 1936

La Kermesse Héroïque (France, Films Sonores Tobis, 1935). Director: Jacques Feyder. Françoise Rosay, Louis Jouvet, Jean Murat, Alerme. [US title: *Carnival in Flanders.*]
The General Died at Dawn (USA, Paramount, 1936). Director: Lewis Milestone. Gary Cooper, Akim Tamiroff, Madeleine Carroll, Porter Hall.

Dodsworth/Mayerling/Fox Hunt

Dodsworth is a very well-made and well-acted film, with an essentially trivial subject. Dodsworth, a retired American magnate, urged by his wife, takes his first trip to Europe in the *Queen Mary* (the film has a breathless topicality about its inessentials). Mrs Dodsworth is a priggish, conceited woman, her thin mundane shell is stretched above a deep abyss of unsophistication. She feels the approach of old age and grand-maternity, and is determined to get in her fling first irrespective of her hus-band's feelings. She begins in the ship disastrously and ignominiously with a young Englishman of half her age and ten times her experience, but she graduates slowly at the various European capitals towards a degree in well-mannered adultery. Mr Walter Huston is admirable as the devoted and uncultured husband who is ready to stand almost anything once, even adultery, and who cannot rid himself of the deep sense of responsibility he has accumulated in twenty years of marriage, and Miss Ruth Chatterton presents grimly the fake worldliness, embittered egotism, meanness intense enough to verge on real evil, of his wife. Like *These Three*, another realistic film produced by Mr Goldwyn, *Dodsworth* is a little marred by almost incessant music, a relic of the small orchestras which used to accompany silent films. Music may be occasionally justified in a fictional film, but certainly not in *Dodsworth* or *These Three*, where the music sentimentally underlines emotional situations which have been carefully played down by the actors and the dialogue-writers.

No one, I think, will fail to enjoy *Dodsworth*, in spite of its too limited and per-sonal plot, the sense it leaves behind of a very expensive, very contemporary, Bond Street vacuum flask. Naturalness is so rare on the screen that it is difficult not to overpraise any picture which possesses it, but more than naturalness is needed for deep enjoyment. 'The best of them', Chekhov wrote of a few of his fellow novelists, 'are realistic and paint life as it is, but because every line is permeated, as with a juice, by awareness of a purpose, you feel, besides life as it is, also life as it ought to be, and this captivates you.' Life as it ought to be – the nearest *Dodsworth* comes to that is a quaint Italian villa on the Bay of Naples and the company of a too gentle, too flower-like widow. The subject of *Mayerling*, the love-story of the Archduke Rudolph and Marie Vetsera which ended with the discovery of their two bodies in a hunting-lodge, is equally purposeless – in the romantic manner this time, a too romantic manner for my taste. The shot which ends Marie's life leaves her in a lovely waxen pose upon her bed, with one becoming streak of blood and the eyes tactfully closed. Duncan's body may be 'laced with its golden blood', because we are not concerned with Duncan's death so much as with Macbeth's

Dodsworth: Paul Lukas, Ruth Chatterton

crime, but if we romanticize the horrible end of the Archduke and his mistress, we lose all sense of tragedy. The smashed cartilage, the face so disfigured that it was unrecognizable, the fear of mortal sin and damnation which must have accompanied the two shots, all this makes the tragedy, the contrast with what was young and happy. We are left with a Vienna 'musical' without the music: a pathetic ending. Granted the romantic manner the film is well made, M. Charles Boyer acts with distinction, and Mlle Danielle Darrieux is lovely and lost and childlike.

Undoubtedly the best film of many weeks is the coloured cartoon, *Fox Hunt*. The artists, Mr Hector Hoppin and Mr Antony Gross, use Technicolor with a freedom and beauty quite outside Mr Disney's picture-book range. A hunt which turns into a mechanized chase, a motor bus playing an agile part; swollen, narcissine, decadent horses preening before gilt mirrors: both theme and drawings have unusual wit, but what remains in the memory is the lyrical use of colour: the white ringletted horse ballooning over the dark box hedges of the little enclosed garden with its classical statue, the rich autumn ruin under hoof, the by-pass road lined with gay sublimated posters.   *The Spectator,* 6 November 1936

Dodsworth (USA, Samuel Goldwyn, 1936). Director: William Wyler. Walter Huston, Ruth Chatterton, Mary Astor, Paul Lukas, David Niven, Marie Ouspenskaya.
Mayerling (France, Nero Film, 1935). Director: Anatole Litvak. Charles Boyer, Danielle Darrieux.
Fox Hunt (GB, London Films, 1936). Directors: Hector Hoppin, Antony Gross (animated film).

Fredlös/The Gay Desperado

There are moods when one almost believes, remembering the great Westerns, from *The Virginian* to *The Texas Rangers*, and the classical Russian films, from *October* to *Storm Over Asia*, that the cinema is only about its proper business if it is in the open air, in natural surroundings, whether the open air be that of the American or Siberian plains or a stony Petrograd square. These scenes, at any rate, the theatre cannot reproduce. *Fredlös* gives us long sledge-rides across plains of snow, herds of reindeer moving north, Lapp encampments among frozen thorn trees: it is a Finnish Western, with a fine villain in the person of a despotic Russian Governor who, when he fails to rape the hero's Lapp wife, outlaws them both. The knife flung promptly across the snow at fifty paces takes the place of the quick shot from the hip; the pack of wolves breaking into the hut where the Lapp wife lies sick is a Nordic substitute for Red Indians and scalping-knives. There is even a moment of Griffith suspense when a Cossack soldier, under the orders of the wicked Governor, begins to saw through the piles supporting a bridge which the hero is about to cross as he journeys home.

A small wooden bridge, one reindeer, a single Cossack: there is something agreeably small scale about the familiar melodramatic formula: the elements of this Nordic film are closer to us than the crowded heroics on the Western plains, just as nature here seems more intimately part of our inheritance. The Redskins go back to Fenimore Cooper, but the wolves go back to Little Red Riding Hood and Grimm, and the reindeer to Hans Andersen. They are images from our racial memory, as the Texas plains will never be, and I found *Fredlös*, slower and more serious-minded though it is than a good Western, curiously moving. The melodramatic bones may have long lost their flesh, a threatened rape may no longer rouse our excited interest, but the lovely dark Lapp faces convey a nostalgia, as when we see a village or a house for the first time which somehow we seem to recognize.

Fredlös: Sten Lindgren

The Gay Desperado, made by Mr Rouben Mamoulian, is one of the best light comedies of the year. Set in Mexico it opens with the performance of an American gangster film, *Give 'em the Works*, to which a notorious Mexican bandit (acted with immense high spirits by Mr Leo Carillo) has brought his band so that they may profit by a lesson in American methods. His joyous and noisy comments provoke a free fight in the cinema, just as on the screen the police and the gangsters meet in battle. The desperate manager sends Mr Nino Martini on to the stage to sing, while the tough picture is quickly removed and a travelogue substituted: *A Glimpse of Sunny Mexico*. The fight subsides, but the bandit has been so charmed by the singer's voice that he has him kidnapped after the performance. He offers him, casually punctuating his sentence with a bullet for another prisoner, any rank in his band from lieutenant to general, and when he understands that the singer's ambition is confined to radio, he holds up a station for his benefit and puts him on the air. The scene in which Mr Martini sings extracts from *Aïda* before the bristling guns and beards of the bandits, in the neat glass cage of the radio station, is beautifully directed. There are many such moments, and a certain edge is given to the comedy by the implicit satire on two literary conventions, that of the free romantic

116

bandit, killing according to traditional rules, and that of the American racketeer, quick and cold and reptilian. When the Mexican joins the kidnapping racket and calls on Butch from across the border for help and advice, the contrast comes comically into the open. Mr Mamoulian's camera is very persuasive: Eisenstein's Mexico was no more sensuous than this. In a serious film the effect of the careful compositions might have seemed precious and unconvincing, but in artificial comedy these lovely shots of cacti like cathedral pillars, of galloping horses before old Spanish churches, of sombreros against skyscapes, are like a framework of fine and mannered prose.   *The Spectator,* 13 November 1936

Fredlös (Finland, Nordisk, 1935). Director: George Schneevoigt. John Ekman, Sten Lindgren, Gull-maj Norin.
The Gay Desperado (USA, Pickford-Lasky, 1936). Director: Rouben Mamoulian. Nino Martini, Ida Lupino, Leo Carillo, Mischa Auer.

Rembrandt

Reverence and a good cameraman are not enough. Mr Alexander Korda in his latest film has chosen the most difficult of all subjects, the life of an artist, and though he is indubitably on the side of Art with a capital A against the *bourgeoisie*, represented by the steeple-hatted Dutchmen who somehow always seem to remain film extras, literary and not realistic types, like the benevolent Doctor Manasseh, that Jew with the long white beard we have seen on so many screens, he has not himself produced a film which one can treat as a work of art. There are some good scenes: I remember a small dark figure making his way across a waste of snow, and Rembrandt, who has returned ruined to his father's mill, sitting down with the words, 'Black bread, peasant's bread, I am home': there are other scenes of melodramatic sentiment in an agreeable tradition, the scene when Rembrandt paints the beloved mistress whom he knows is dying, the scene when he softens the heart of the beggar posing for him as the King of Israel by telling him the story of Saul and David: these may be false, but they are false in a pleasant familiar way, like robins on Christmas cards, and they give Mr Charles Laughton a chance to show his remarkable powers as a 'ham' actor – the very best 'ham' – and they will undoubtedly be popular.

But the film is ruined by lack of story and continuity: it has no drive. Like *The Private Life of Henry the Eighth*, it is a series of unrelated tableaux. Tableau One (a far too emotional beginning): wife of famous painter dies while he is being feasted by the burghers. Tableau Two: famous painter loses, by his artistic experiments, his bourgeois clients. Tableau Three: but already I begin to forget how these unrelated scenes follow one another. From the dramatic point of view the first might just as well be the last and the last first. Nothing is led up to, nothing is led away from. In one tableau the painter, sold up by his creditors, goes back to his father's mill, but in a tableau a little further on we see him back in an apparently well-furnished home, only to be sold up for a second time in a later scene. The death of his first wife is duplicated by the death of his mistress, but I doubt if the tear-ducts will work a second time for the same cause. Odd scraps of biography litter the film like shavings in a carpenter's shop. When Rembrandt wants to marry his mistress, we learn for the first time of an impediment in the shape of a son by the first wife, and his inheritance. At the end of the film we are casually informed that there is a child by his mistress.

November 1936

The Gay Desperado

I have called the film reverent, but pompous, I fear, would be nearer the mark. Emotions are too obviously forced on us, like a card in the hands of an inexpert sharper. When Rembrandt, in Mr Laughton's beautiful voice, expresses at the burghers' dinner-table his views on marital love, the camera takes us from one whiskered face to another, each one baring his emotions with the dreadful intimacy of a peeress recommending a cream for oily skins (incidentally these are the same insensitive burghers who mock his later pictures). When Rembrandt reads the Bible at his father's table, you would think, from their expressions of amazement and rapture, that these pious peasants had never heard the Bible read before. Their faces are like warnings to us that these are solemn words beautifully uttered and that though they may have nothing to do with the story, we, too, ought to be, nay, must be, moved. But our cynical hearts, I am afraid, react in wicked amusement.

'Scenes From the Life of . . .' – that is how this picture should be described, and, in spite of Mr Charles Laughton's amazing virtuosity and Miss Elsa Lanchester's attractive Flemish impersonation (her refined voice, alas! betrays the charming ungainliness of her appearance), it is chiefly remarkable for the lesson it teaches: that no amount of money spent on expensive sets, no careful photography, will atone for the lack of a story 'line', the continuity and drive of a well-constructed plot.   *The Spectator,* 20 November 1936

Rembrandt (GB, London Films, 1936). Director: Alexander Korda. Charles Laughton, Gertrude Lawrence, Elsa Lanchester, John Clements, Roger Livesey.

The New Gulliver/Bullets or Ballots/The White Angel

The new, the Soviet Gulliver is a long way after Swift. The inventor of the Yahoos would have been bitterly amused by the blithe Bolshevik optimism of Mr Roshal and Mr Ptushko, the inevitable victory of the Lilliputian proletariat, the Victorian sense of Progress. But even if the theme seems to us a little dusty, like the sermons of Charles Kingsley, the execution and invention awake our admiration.

The New Gulliver begins like *Alice in Wonderland,* as an idyll of a summer day. The best workers in a corps of Soviet children have the honour of being the first to sail the little yacht they have built. They land on a small island off the shore, and the boy leader reads Gulliver aloud, a bowdlerized Gulliver, I feel sure, in this brave new world where virtue is always victorious. With the sound of the waves in his ears the boy falls asleep and dreams. . . . Only in dreams (but I doubt if the authors intended to point this moral) can he escape – unhappy Gulliver – from triumphant virtue to a world where evil can still put up a sporting fight. After a battle and a shipwreck ('Save my box. It has all my schoolwork in it'), he is cast ashore on Lilliput. Lilliput is oppressed by a King, a Parliament and at least one priest, and there are numerous police spies and armaments manufacturers. An exciting old world, but one already on the point of learning dialectical materialism. The workers plan the Revolution in a cave on the sea-shore, and there they find Gulliver's exercise-book washed up by the sea and on the first page a Soviet slogan. The rest of the film shows the triumph of the workers assisted by Gulliver. There are moments of delightful satire: the Chancellor putting a small gramophone under the robe of the King who cannot make a speech ('my people are muddled, are muddled, are muddled . . .' creaks the record as the needle sticks in a crack); the tiny Queen hastily packing her hats at the news of the workers' seizure of the arsenal.

The invention is often delightful (one wonders how such humour in detail can exist with so humourless a philosophy), and the marvellous ingenuity of the puppets is beyond praise. One soon begins to regard them as real people and to give critical applause to the performers who amuse Gulliver at dinner: the ballad-singer (an exquisite parody), the elderly mezzo-soprano, and the troupe of ballet-girls with their black gloves and transparent fans. This doll world is pure pleasure, a child's dream with its inconsequence: the tiny tanks manœuvring on the shore with frigates attacking from the sea, the periwigged ladies listening to the radio, the cameraman in check plus-fours filming the royal procession; sometimes a child's nightmare: the gross idiot faces, the evil King with his loopy laugh, the arsenal with its white-hot furnaces and pounding machines in the caves underground. But Gulliver wakes, that is the profound difference, wakes into the bright, happy, virtuous Soviet day; he has not to live on, like his poor ancestor, among his native Yahoos.

Bullets or Ballots is a good gangster film of the second class. Mr Edward G. Robinson (his mouth more than ever like the long flat slit in a pillar-box) gives a reliable performance as a tough detective who stages a dismissal from the police force in order to work from inside a racket. Third degree is curiously idealized, and the detective dies on the field of honour with a bullet in the guts. All the old chivalrous situations of *Chums* and the *B.O.P.* are agreeably translated into sub-machine-gun terms.

The White Angel is not another Pasteur. Miss Kay Francis, handicapped by her beauty, does her best to sober down this sentimental version of Florence Nightingale's character, but she is defeated by the scenario-writers. There is one dreadful sequence when Miss Nightingale is made to visit a Crimean cemetery at night in order to read above a soldier's grave a letter from his mother, and another, less agreeable to English than to American ears, when she patrols the wards, lamp in hand, to the accompaniment of voices repeating Longfellow's too famous poem.

The Spectator, 27 November 1936

The New Gulliver (USSR, Mosfilm, 1935). Directors: Grigori Roshal, Alexander Ptushko. V. Konstantinov, puppets.
Bullets or Ballots (USA, Warner Bros, 1936). Director: William Keighley. Edward G. Robinson, Joan Blondell.
The White Angel (USA, Warner Bros, 1936). Director: William Dieterle. Kay Francis, Ian Hunter.

The Green Pastures

Mr Marc Connelly's black Biblical pageant has come to us with the best possible advertisement: the Lord Chamberlain's ban. It has lost nothing by being transferred to the screen, not so much as a line of dialogue, and the rather jerky succession of short stage scenes is given smoothness and continuity in the cinema. The author, too, in this version is able to emphasize the point of his narrative by bringing us back again and again to the Sunday school, where the black minister, Mr Deshee, is explaining the Old Testament to the children, telling how the Lord (a black minister with a string tie) created man at a fish-fry in heaven; how the Lord banished Cain and preserved Noah; how He brought a chosen people out of Egypt; how He saw his prophet murdered in Babylon. Hollywood must be praised for the simplicity of the settings. Pharaoh's throne-room, the King of Babylon's Court must have offered enormous temptations which have been admirably resisted. Moses performs his miracles under the dusty guild flags of a small church hall, and the Prophet in Babylon is shot down by a smirking waiter at a scene of dingy revelry, based, in the mind of the preacher, on a long-ago visit to a cheap cabaret.

December 1936

Most people, I think, will find the film continuously entertaining, if only intermittently moving. But it is a little absurd to class it, as some critics have done, with the medieval mystery plays. It is not only that pathos has taken the place of poetry, that the anonymous and popular playwrights had better words at their command than Mr Connelly's, and that 'the five cent seegar, Lawd?' humour cannot take the place of 'Wode and wynde and watters wane', but that those plays, like the cathedrals, were spontaneous expressions of popular belief. Mr Connelly is a sophisticated writer trying to see through the eyes of a negro preacher. He is on the outside looking in. The result is occasionally patronising, too often quaint, and at the close of the film definitely false. For at the end Mr Connelly deserts the Bible story and indulges in a little personal Protestant mysticism, and I do not think the author of *Dulcy, To the Ladies* and *Helen of Troy, N.Y.* is naturally a mystic. He invents a character, Hezdrel, a soldier fighting to preserve Jerusalem from the Romans, whose prayers penetrate disturbingly to the ears of God after He has long given up the world in despair. God comes down among the smashed artillery and the dead and dying, and in the light of a camp-fire encounters Hezdrel. 'He looks like the first man I made, but he ain't in no garden now.' It is an excellent melodramatic scene, but Mr Connelly has quite forgotten the negro preacher and the Sunday-school class. Hezdrel begins to teach God the quality of mercy and to explain to his Creator that He can only learn mercy through suffering, and so we proceed to the sentimental end when Gabriel, peering over Heaven's wall, reports to the Lord a man's weary progress under a cross to Golgotha and God with His arms outstretched shares the suffering. The author of *Dulcy* has neatly, smartly and unsatisfactorily by-passed Christianity.

But Mr Connelly deserves praise for his ingenious pathos (though the theme of pity poor God might, perhaps, have a sentimental ring even to a black preacher) and his great technical dexterity. The Noah sequence is admirably dramatic when it is not too easily comic; the dingy sexual drama played out beside the Ark under the rain-clouds, the jealous gangster with his razor-blade and his cheap girl, the sudden heartless, passionless knifing, occupies only a very few feet of film, but it conveys the right snake-like air of incurable corruption. One may feel uneasy at Mr Connelly's humour and wonder whether the negro mind is quite so material, but he is extraordinarily successful with the two extremes of good and evil. Mr Rex Ingram's performance as De Lawd (he also plays Adam and Hezdrel) is very moving, whether he is presiding at a Paradisiacal fish-fry or walking disillusioned through the evil world. Indeed this is as good a religious play as one is likely to get in this age from a practised New York writer.   *The Spectator,* 4 December 1936

The Green Pastures (USA, Warner Bros, 1936). Directors: Marc Connelly, William Keighley. Rex Ingram, Eddie Anderson, Oscar Polk, Frank Wilson.

Sabotage/The Tenth Man

I have sometimes doubted Mr Hitchcock's talent. As a director he has always known exactly the right place to put his camera (and there is only one right place in any scene), he has been pleasantly inventive with his sound, but as a producer and as a writer of his own scripts he has been appallingly careless: he has cared more for an ingenious melodramatic situation than for the construction and continuity of his story. In *Sabotage* for the first time he has really 'come off'.

Sabotage is not, of course, Conrad's *Secret Agent*. That dark drab passionate tale of Edwardian London could never find a place in the popular cinema, and only M. Jacques Feyder, I think, the director of *Thérèse Raquin*, could transfer its peculiar qualities – of madness and despair in four-wheelers and backstreets – to the screen. But Mr Hitchcock's 'variations on a theme' are on a different level from his deplorable adaptation of Mr Maugham's *Ashenden*. This melodrama is convincingly realistic, perhaps because Mr Hitchcock has left the screenplay to other hands.

The story retains some of the ruthlessness of the original. Mr Verloc, no longer an *agent provocateur* but a straightforward destructive agent of a foreign Power, keeps a tiny independent cinema in the East End, and the film opens with his secret return home one night during a sudden black-out. (Mr Hitchcock has not overcome in these sequences the difficulty of lighting a black-out. How far a little candle throws its beams!) Mr Verloc has succeeded in getting sand into the Battersea generators, but his employers are dissatisfied: he is told to lay a bomb in the cloakroom at Piccadilly Circus on Lord Mayor's Day. Mr Verloc's friends fail him, he is himself closely watched by the police, and he has to entrust the bomb to his wife's small brother, who, delayed by the procession, is blown to fragments with a busload of people. Mrs Verloc, after hearing the news, passes through the little cinema hall to her living-room. A children's matinée is in progress and Walt Disney's *Cock Robin* is on the screen. She is pursued by the children's laughter and the diminishing repetitions of the song, 'Who killed Cock Robin? Who killed Cock Robin?' This ingenious and pathetic twist is stamped as Mr Hitchcock's own, but unlike so many of his ideas in the past it is an integral part of the story: it leads on to the admirably directed scene when Mrs Verloc, serving dinner to her husband, finds herself against her own will continually picking up the carving-knife – to serve the potatoes, to scoop up the cabbage, to kill Mr Verloc. The happy ending of course, has to be contrived: Mr Verloc's body is plausibly disposed of: a young detective is there to marry her: but this is all managed with the minimum of offence.

Mr Hitchcock has been helped by admirable dialogue, written by Mr Ian Hay and Miss Helen Simpson, and a fine cast, a cast with only two weak members. Mr John Loder as the detective is unconvincing, and for Master Desmond Tester's prep. school accent I feel an invincible distaste (it glares out at you, like a first-fifteen muffler, from every disguise). Mr Oscar Homolka, a slow, kindly, desperate Mr Verloc, and Miss Sylvia Sidney, as his innocent wife, raise the melodrama at times to the tragic level, and Mr William Dewhurst gives a superb performance as the Professor, a soapy old scoundrel who supports his shrewish daughter and her bastard child with a bird business, concocting his explosives in the one living-room, among the child's dolls and the mother's washing.

Another English director, Mr Brian Desmond Hurst, has upset prophecies this week with a well-directed film: *The Tenth Man*, the story of an English Kreuger written by Mr Maugham. There was nothing in Mr Hurst's two previous films, *Riders to the Sea* and *Ourselves Alone*, to show him capable of these humorous and satirical political sequences, and the very fine melodramatic close. The credit is all Mr Hurst's, for the dialogue is stagy, and the principal actor, Mr John Lodge, continues to suffer from a kind of lockjaw, an inability to move the tight muscles of his mouth, to do anything but glare with the dumbness and glossiness of an injured seal.

The Spectator, 11 December 1936

Sabotage (GB, Gaumont British, 1936). Director: Alfred Hitchcock. Oscar Homolka, Sylvia Sidney, John Loder. [US title: *The Woman Alone*].
The Tenth Man (GB, British International, 1936). Director: Brian Desmond Hurst. John Lodge, Antoinette Cellier, Athole Stewart, Clifford Evans.

Girls' Dormitory/Go West, Young Man/Hortobagy

This week we have run the gamut of sex, from the incredible virginities of *Girls'
Dormitory* by way of Miss Mae West to the leaping stallions in *Hortobagy*. For
dignity and decency the horses have it. Was there ever quite so virginal a finishing
school as that in the Tyrolean Alps presided over by Dr Stefan Dominik, acted by
Mr Herbert Marshall in his Old English sheep-dog manner? This film of adolescence
is the more curious coming as it does from America. We are accustomed to the
difficult adolescence of Teutons; Americans, one has always understood, have
solved their problems characteristically. There has never been any hint of shy pent
passions on the campus among the co-eds.

Mr Marshall is loved by one of his pupils, Marie Claudel, acted with staggering
conviction and charm by Mlle Simone Simon. He is also loved by Professor Anna
Mathe (Miss Ruth Chatterton), who has been assisting him in compiling an Ancient
History for Advanced Classes. 'I wish you to share in any glory there may be,' he
tells her, but he does not realize the worm that feeds on her cheek. Nor does he
realize Marie Claudel's love even when a compromising letter in her writing is
found in a waste-paper basket. Marie is nearly expelled for a quite imaginary meeting with her dream-lover, but when she runs away in a nocturnal thunderstorm
pursued by her headmaster (it is difficult not to recall the less virginal chase through
the rain in *Lady Chatterley's Lover*), he learns the truth. Complications, of course,
have still to be devised before the happy ending, for Mr Marshall must be allowed
to put on his characteristic act: dumb suffering. This picture, dewy as it is, has
merit even apart from Mlle Simon (it is well directed and the performance of Mr
Edward Bromberg as a cruel, warped pedagogic type is admirable), but I am afraid
its concentrated atmosphere of young innocence (even the bathing-costumes are
white like the nightdresses) defeats its own purpose. Mr Marshall, of course, has
the damp muzzle of a healthy British dog, but the film itself is undoubtedly sexy.

Not quite in the manner of Miss West: the Edwardian bust, the piled peroxided
hair, the seductive and reeling motions reminiscent of an overfed python. Miss
West, for once, has not written her own script, and this story of a film star, forbidden
by contract to marry for five years and closely watched for that reason by her agent,
is quite incredibly tedious, as slow and wobbling in its pace as Miss West's famous
walk. The wisecracks lack the old impudence, and seldom have so many feet of
film been expended on a mere dirty look.

Undoubtedly the horses have it. *Hortobagy*, a film of the Hungarian plains, acted
by peasants and shepherds, is one of the most satisfying films I have seen: it belongs
to the order of Dovjenko's *Earth* without the taint of propaganda. The photography
is extraordinarily beautiful, the cutting superb. The thin thread of story, of a
shepherd's young son drawn away from horse-breeding to agriculture, is unimportant: we need no story to enjoy the sight of these wild herds tossing across the
enormous plain, against the flat sky, the shepherds in their old traditional cloaks,
with the heavy buckles and the embroidery, galloping like Tartar cavalry between
the whitewashed cabins. The leaping of the stallions, the foaling of the mares are
shown with a frankness devoid of offence and add to the impression that here we
are seeing, as far as is humanly possible, the whole of a way of life. But we are not
asked to admire one way more than another, the horse more than the tractor. We
see the mounted shepherd deliberately smash his small son's bicycle with the hooves

Girls' Dormitory: Herbert Marshall, Simone Simon

of his horse, and the act is as ugly and as natural as the mare's foaling. Alas, one has little hope that this film will be passed by the British Board of Film Censors, who are not quick to distinguish between a Yahoo and a Houyhnhnm. In their eyes, I am afraid, it is Miss Mae West who wins.

The Spectator, 18 December 1936

Girls' Dormitory (USA, 20th Century-Fox, 1936). Director: Irving Cummings. Herbert Marshall, Simone Simon, Ruth Chatterton.
Go West, Young Man (USA, Paramount, 1936). Director: Henry Hathaway. Mae West, Warren William, Randolph Scott, Alice Brady.
Hortobagy (Hungary, Hoellering Film, 1935). Director: George Hoellering. Istvan Kamyasi, Janos Cinege.

The Garden of Allah

Mr Charles Boyer, a renegade monk from a Trappist monastery in North Africa, Miss Marlene Dietrich, a lovely orphan heiress suffering from world weariness

('Go to the desert', she is told at the convent school to which she returns for advice and prayer. 'In the face of the infinite your grief will lessen') meet in a Moroccan dance-hall. A desert soothsayer does his best to warn the woman against her doom ('I see a camel by a church door, and then a tent in the far desert', as he describes it with Surrealist fervour), and so does the local Catholic priest, who distrusts this man who is apt to stagger uneasily back at the sight of a crucifix. 'This is the land of fire,' he says, 'and you are a woman of fire.' Nobody talks less apocalyptically than that: the great abstractions come whistling hoarsely out in Miss Dietrich's stylized, weary, and monotonous whisper, among the hideous Technicolor flowers, the yellow cratered desert like Gruyère cheese, the beige faces. Startling sunsets bloom behind silhouetted camels very much as in the gaudy little pictures which used to be on sale on the pavements of Trafalgar Square. Needless to say – but many thousand feet of film are expended in saying it – the pair are married by the Catholic priest (according to the Church of England service), and there, waiting for them outside the church door, is The Camel, the foredoomed camel, ready to carry them, with an escort of twenty-five armed Arabs, on their honeymoon – to that Tent in the Far Desert. There Fate has a coincidence in store for them in the person of a French officer lost in the Sahara with his men. 'We are a lost patrol,' he succinctly explains to the lady in a low-backed evening dress who is waving a lighted torch from the top of a ruined tower (the Surrealism of this film is really magnificent). He recognizes the former monk (he had been a guest in the monastery), and sitting together on the Gruyère cheese, silhouetted like camels, the lovers make the great decision to renounce all. The Catholic priest (Mr Aubrey Smith, who has kept a straight county bat to the bodyline bowling) shakes hands all round at the railway station, the monk slowly wends his way up an avenue of cypresses, a grey glove flaps from the window of a four-wheeler. Alas! my poor Church, so picturesque, so noble, so superhumanly pious, so intensely dramatic. I really prefer the *New Statesman* view, shabby priests counting pesetas on their fingers in dingy cafés before blessing tanks. Even the liqueur made at this Trappist monastery is Mysterious. Only one monk at a time knows the secret of its making, and when Mr Charles Boyer disappears from the monastery the secret is irrecoverably lost. The thought that this sweet and potent drink will be once again obtainable during licensed hours mitigates for us the agony of the parting.

The Spectator, 25 December 1936

The Garden of Allah (USA, Selznick International, 1936). Director: Richard Boleslavsky. Marlene Dietrich, Charles Boyer, C. Aubrey Smith.

The Jungle Princess/Windbag the Sailor

A laughing tiger puts fear into the hearts of the Malayan natives; but we, of course, who have borne the white man's burden of sunny Southsea and the picture page, as soon as we hear that silvery and self-conscious tinkle, recognize its source. This particular holiday girl is the daughter of a dead American, and has been brought up by an old Malayan until a stampede of elephants wrecks the village and a tiger kills her foster-father. Aged about six, and accompanied by a tiger cub, she goes alone into the jungle; and from that time on she is seen by no human being until an American expedition arrives in the island: a retired Colonel and his daughter, her fiancé (a travel-writer), and poor Mr Lynne Overman, who is expected to lend humorous relief to a film already richly comic. The Colonel and his daughter go to Shanghai for the rains, but the other two stay to investigate the native superstitions.

Needless to say, the hero is attacked in the jungle by the pet tiger, now as mature as his mistress, and Lemo (its name is Lemo) is called off only just in time. The girl assists the wounded travel-writer to her lair (a scurry in the tree-tops overhead, and we recognize the simian features of one of Hollywood's most famous comedians), and the rains opportunely catch him there with Bogo, the baboon, and Lemo and the girl. Mysterious white women whom explorers discover in the world's jungles always have an embarrassing directness towards the male. The horror of triumphant possessiveness, the snaking of well-covered limbs along the floor, the animal flash of strong female teeth in a confined space, is vividly conveyed:

> When you hold me tight
> In a jungle night,
> My sweet,

as an old Malayan ballad, translated by our hero, puts it. But the possessiveness is not immediately triumphant: he remembers his betrothed in Shanghai firmly all through the rainy season, and at its close we see him still manfully resisting the temptation to kiss his companion. Her directness while sun-bathing scares him, and he departs ('You won't mind really. You have Bogo and Lemo') to rejoin his companions who have given him up as dead. 'It's time for you to shave, dear, and change for dinner,' his fiancée remarks (she has returned with the Colonel from Shanghai) to her lover resurrected a bare half-hour. The girl has followed him, and the Colonel's daughter cannot, petty-minded creature, believe in a chastity maintained all through the rainy season in a cave. She plans to make her rival ridiculous and we have one of those scenes, so common in pictures from the great democracy, of exaggerated social consciousness. Will this jungle-bred girl use a spoon with her grape-fruit? Heavens, she has taken a fork: her rival will conquer. But no! Mr Lynne Overman in the nick of time has conveyed with a wink and a whisper the correct information; the hero hasn't noticed.

The climax is magnificent. The natives, who think the girl is a witch, trap the party, tie them to trees and begin to bury the girl alive. Who is to save her? Lemo, you think, but you are wrong. He charges and they kill him. The overseer frees himself – but he, too, dies heroically (the girl by this time is buried up to the neck). The hero gets free – but what is one travel-writer among a horde of natives without a rook-rifle? No, it is Bogo who saves them all, who spies their plight from the tree-tops and summons every baboon in the jungle to a magnificent charge.

The censors have given this lively picture an 'A' Certificate in spite of the hero's heroic chastity. To those under sixteen debarred from these adult delights by Lord Tyrrell, I recommend *Windbag the Sailor*, a farce with Mr Will Hay admirably directed by Mr William Beaudine. Mr Hay, since his Narkover days, has progressively improved, and he has never had a better part than that of Captain Ben Cutlett, the skipper of a canal barge given to boasting of experiences on the seas he has never sailed, who finds himself in command of a cargo steamer, with a villainous crew under secret orders to scuttle the ship.

The Spectator, 1 January 1937

The Jungle Princess (USA, Paramount, 1936). Director: William Thiele. Dorothy Lamour, Ray Milland, Lynne Overman.
Windbag the Sailor (GB, Gainsborough, 1936). Director: William Beaudine. Will Hay, Moore Marriott, Graham Moffatt.

The Garden of Allah: Charles Boyer, Marlene Dietrich

Sensation/Mazurka

A curious air of unreality pervades *Sensation*, the story of a murder in a country village and the mob of crime reporters from Fleet Street who settle down at the local pub and unscrupulously manufacture good copy. Nothing, a novice might think, could be easier than to catch reality with a camera, and yet this shy bird evades almost every English director. There is a moment in *Mazurka* when an experienced womanizer kisses an awkward adolescent girl. The director cuts up from her bewildered eyes, as the mouth presses home, to the electric globes hanging from the ceiling: they mist, disappear, come back to view again, and the uneven mixture of passion and practice has been vividly conveyed. Mr Desmond Hurst's *Sensation* never comes so close to life, and as its failure is typical of English films, perhaps I may be forgiven for discussing its unrealities in some detail.

It is never easy for a film critic, who has no sight of the script, to apportion responsibility between actors, writers and director. Mr Desmond Hurst has obviously been handicapped by his cast. Mr John Lodge, who plays the smart crime reporter, remains dumbly dependent on a stony and protuberant jaw, and there is a persistent Oxford and BBC undertone to the synthetic accents in the local bar. The only players who help illusion are Mr Anthony Holles as a reporter, Miss Athene Seyler as a fortune-teller, and Miss Joan Marion as the murderer's wife.

Now for the screenplay. A cowardly 'commercial' murders one of his many girl-friends, a reporter robs a bedroom, finds a clue to the crime and bullies the murderer's wife into supplying his paper with her love-letters, the details of her private life, her small son's picture, in return for money to defend her husband who stands no chance of acquittal. A promising plot, which could be handled with pity and anger, but the genuine situation is lost in false trails, in an absurd love-story, in humour based on American films, and in the complete unreality of the 'murder gang'.

There remains the director, and I am afraid he has contributed little to illusion. The lovers drive down Fleet Street before one of the worst false backgrounds I have ever seen. The Yard detective picks up a hammer, which he believes the murderer used, with his bare fingers and carries it with him into a crowded café. Worst weakness of all, two independent situations which depend for their effect on accumulating excitement – the fortune-teller in a fake trance describing the crime in the presence of the murderer, the crime reporter questioning the murderer's wife – are run concurrently, the director cutting from one to another, so that the excitement of each scene drops like a stone at every cut. Bad casting, bad story construction, uncertain editing: these are the three main faults of English films.

Mazurka leaves a rather sinister impression. The first twenty minutes – the scared duel between the adolescent girl (beautifully acted by Ingeborg Theek) and the middle-aged expert in sexuality – are admirable. With the appearance of Miss Pola Negri Herr Willi Forst seems deliberately to guy not only the melodramatic tale of an unknown mother and a good woman's ruin, but the star herself. Miss Negri's technique belongs to the war years and the silent film. Forst makes her run across rooms, bound along streets, a crazy corsetted Cassandra in 1917 draperies. In a scene of drunken seduction which is like an ancient still from Mr Rotha's album, the villain (with long Svengali hair and the manner of a lion-tamer) props tipsy Miss Negri against the doorpost while he takes down his top hat.

Miss Negri may be unwise to return to the films, but it is a cruel idea of fun to guy this stout, glossy, gesticulating woman for the pleasure of audiences who have forgotten the star of Lubitsch's *Forbidden Paradise*.

The Spectator, 5 February 1937

SECOND OPINION

'Every pert little miss who fancies herself an embryo star should, in a spirit of awed humility, take this opportunity of studying the methods of an artiste whose passions come from the heart, whose voice is vibrant with feeling and whose emotions are expressed with every fibre of her being.' – Sydney Carroll on Miss Negri.

Sensation (GB, British International, 1937). Director: Brian Desmond Hurst. John Lodge, Athene Seyler, Anthony Holles.
Mazurka (Germany, Cine-Allianz, 1935). Director: Willi Forst. Pola Negri, Ingeborg Theek, Paul Hartmann.

The Plainsman/The Great Barrier

Mr Cecil B. de Mille: there has always been a touch of genius as well as absurdity in this warm-hearted sentimental salvationist. *The Crusades, The Ten Commandments* were comic and naïve, but no director since Griffith has handled crowds so convincingly. Now – startlingly – Mr de Mille seems to have grown up. *The Plainsman* is certainly the finest Western since *The Virginian*: perhaps it is the finest Western in the history of the film.

The story is of the Indian rising after the Civil War when General Custer's forces were annihilated, with Mr Gary Cooper as a famous Scout, Wild Bill Hickok, the lover of Calamity Jane. Mr de Mille has never before handled stars of Mr Cooper's and Miss Jean Arthur's quality, and another unexpected trace of sophistication, the music is by George Antheil. Indeed, one might wonder whether Mr de Mille's name had been taken in vain if it were not for the magnificent handling of the extras in the big sets: the brilliant detail, depth and solidity of the dockside scenes at St Louis, the charge of the Indian cavalry. A few great spectacular moments in the history of the film remain as a permanent encouragement to those who believe that an art may yet emerge from a popular industry: the long shots of the Battle of Bull Run in *The Birth of a Nation*, the French attack in *All Quiet*. Some of the scenes in *The Plainsman* belong to that order.

That might have been expected, and the excellent dialogue may be a fortunate accident; what takes one by surprise in a de Mille film is the firm handling of the individual drama: the silent moments in the cleared street of the shabby frontier town when Hickok crosses the road to meet his would-be murderers: the final poker-game he plays in the barred saloon with the white prisoners he is keeping for the military to hang, the air of doom while we wait for the inevitable shot in the back from the little treacherous bowler-hatted comic behind the bar: and most surprising of all the brilliant satirical sequence when the armament directors, whose new repeating rifle has been put on the market too late for the Civil War, discuss how to dispose of their unwanted stocks and the cynical old Pickwickian chairman persuades them to sell to the Indians 'for hunting purposes'. This actor's performance, when the news of Lincoln's murder comes roaring down the street, is superb: the conventional shocked regrets, the roaming, faintly speculative eye. It is a pleasure too to see Mr Charles Bickford back in one of his rough scoundrelly parts as the trader who smuggles the rifles to the Indians. Only in the character and treatment of Buffalo Bill Cody does the dreaded softness of the traditional de Mille intrude.

The Plainsman takes the wind out of Gaumont British sails. *The Great Barrier* is a sporting and fairly successful attempt to make a film of *The Iron Horse* type with the smaller resources of an English company. It deals with the building of the Canadian Pacific Railway at the moment when the work was held up by the muskeg, the swamps deep enough to swallow whole trains. The men are in revolt for want of pay, no more money will be invested in the company unless a new way to the coast is discovered past the great barrier of the Rockies, and an expedition sets out. . . . It is one of those films which are sometimes called 'epic', though their intellectual and poetic quality is hardly higher than that of the interminable historical novels which reach us from America. It should appeal enormously to CPR shareholders, it is a thoroughly worthy picture, with an excellent saloon shindy, an exciting race on horseback to save the Montreal express, and an attractive new English star, Miss Lilli Palmer. Well acted, well produced (a little less than well written: 'Hell's bells, boys, we are in luck. We've struck the Old Trail'; 'Is that – all you've got to say?') it shrinks into insignificance, with its conventional love-story and the impression it leaves that the building of a railway depends on the heroic efforts of two or three men and a girl, beside *Turksib* or the dash and drama of *The Plainsman*.   *The Spectator,* 12 February 1937

The Plainsman (USA, Paramount, 1936). Director: Cecil B. de Mille. Gary Cooper, Jean Arthur, Charles Bickford.
The Great Barrier (GB, Gaumont British, 1937). Director: Milton Rosmer. Lilli Palmer, Richard Arlen, Antoinette Cellier. [US title: *Silent Barriers.*]

The Deserter/Dreaming Lips

The Deserter is Pudovkin's first talkie, the story of a Hamburg strike put down by machine-guns, of the German strike delegate to the USSR who settles down as an engineer in the country where the revolution is already won, until his conscience tells him that he is a deserter and should go back. Though the picture is only three years old it would be unfair to forget that, as far as Pudovkin himself is concerned, it belongs to the stage of *The Singing Fool*.

It is a bad film with some superb moments. Technically it cannot be compared with the older Soviet film *Men and Jobs*, which the Forum will soon be showing. We are aware all the time of the theorist who has written many articles on the new medium of sound, who has produced on paper in the *avant-garde* Press a number of ideas for its unrealistic use, faced by the picture itself, by the so many weeks of production, by a job which has got to be done. And to a great extent the ideas have vanished: they are left as isolated tricks, like the suicide in slow motion, outside the context of the picture. A curious feature of the studio world is the number of old *avant-garde* directors who spend their energies in avoiding production. Pudovkin at any rate comes into the open, with his stale caricatures (how much better Lang can work on our feelings with his sense of real evil), his shocking continuity, his Boy Scout idealism, his misuse of fast cutting, and a few sequences which remind us that after all this is the director who eleven years ago shot *Mother*.

The opening is admirable. Pudovkin establishes at once the documentary scene for the fictional story, which few directors trouble to do: the ships and tugs in Hamburg harbour, the great docks and tunnels, the unemployed sleeping on benches, the crowded proletarian trams; he works inwards towards the centre of the city, to the uniformed street-sweepers in the flowery boulevards and the smart cars and the gross and obsequious police on point duty. But there he throws away his hand, throws away all the value of the documentary approach for the sake of caricature, very good caricature sometimes as in the restaurant ritual with tiny bottles over the salad. There may be ideological value in the contrast between the capitalist automatons and the real, the suffering, thinking workers, but there isn't dramatic value. The awful Victorian shadow of inevitable Progress falls across the screen.

But the film should be seen: there are moments magnificent as well as naïve, and again one notices the curious fact that Pudovkin is never a better movie director than in his still-lifes, never worse than in his fast movements. One will go on remembering these static scenes: the body of the dying picket, shot diagonally from far above, sprawled and motionless on the grey cobbles, the whimper of pain that carries on, a mournful chorus, through the following scenes: the view-point of the pickets down the empty industrial road to the huge grit-blackened tunnel, the silence, waiting and emptiness, and then the first hardly detectable movements of the strike-breakers coming out at the edge of the tunnel.

Unsatisfactory picture it may be, but it takes the heart out of any praise one might have given to *Dreaming Lips*, a sumptuous glossy rendering of *Der Trau-mende Mund*, which at least avoided the falsity of these luxurious English sets. Anyway it doesn't need a critic's praise, although one critic has been so moved by its discreet sentimentality that she has bared her heart embarrassingly to her large newspaper public. The theatre is packed with just such ecstatic women who squeal with admiration as Miss Bergner's mechanical sure-fire performance proceeds: the bemused and avaricious eyes, the swinging arms, prehensile cooing lips: an elfin charm maybe, but how sex-conscious an elf. And how the handkerchiefs flutter at the close, when the policeman reads aloud the last letter of the drowned wife unable to choose between the lover-genius and the boy-husband. The story, of course, is neat and plausible, the acting refined, the photography expensive, it is a shapely piece of sentiment. But there is nothing to remember when the night's over: it is not the Constant Nymph but the constant corpse on the cobbles which has imaginative truth.   *The Spectator,* 19 February 1937

The Deserter (USSR, Mezhrabpomfilm, 1933). Director: Vsevolod Pudovkin. Boris Livanov, Tamara Makarova, Vasili Kovrigin, Judith Glizer.
Dreaming Lips (GB, Trafalgar Film Productions, 1937). Director: Paul Czinner. Elisabeth Bergner, Raymond Massey.

We from Kronstadt

From the moment when the elderly Commissar with a sad and unprofessional face, dressed in a shabby macintosh and a soft hat which has known better days, takes his seat in the naval motor-boat which chugs softly out in the last evening light, under the bridges of Petrograd towards the lamps of the naval port, *We from Kronstadt* takes a firm hold on the imagination, and it will be a thousand pities if the British Board of Film Censors prevents this unusual mixture of poetry and heroics from enjoying a success in London equal to that which it has met in Paris and New York.

This story of 1919, the year of foreign intervention, up to the last shot of Bala-shov, the marine, standing on the cliff where his companions had been flung to death, shaking his fist towards the sea – 'And now does anybody else want Petrograd?' – this very simple story of rivalry between the marines and the workers' battalions is in the tradition of boys' stories, full of last charges and fights to the death, heroic sacrifices and narrow escapes, all superbly directed: the single soldier crawling, grenade in hand, towards the monstrous tank which has terrified the marines; the ragged band in the last trench between the enemy and the capital striking up the cheerful rallying tune which calls the wounded from the dressing-station to stagger back into a last desperate action; the voice whispering 'Kron-stadt, Kronstadt, Kronstadt' into the dumb phone as the camera tracks along the wire, the birds peacefully preening, to the ragged ends, the fallen post, and silence.

But magnificently as all this is done, what makes the picture remarkable is less the heroics than the lyrical, the poetic, the critical sense. This is what the poetic cinema should mean: not plays by Shakespeare adapted to a medium even less suitable than the modern stage; but poetry expressed in images, which let in a little more of common life than is in the story. This the stage can only crudely do (it has its words), but the cinema is closer to the novel, and *We from Kronstadt* was written and directed by the countrymen of Chekhov and Turgenev. In Pudov-kin's early pictures of course we had our glimpses of nature, but nature strictly harnessed to the revolutionary idea; the hurrying clouds, dust-storms over the Asiatic plains, the Baltic ice breaking in the spring, had small lyrical value, they were used metaphorically to reinforce the one-sided plot. *We from Kronstadt*, on the other hand, from the first shot to the last, is as impregnated with the poetic sense (poetic as defined by Mr Ford Madox Ford: 'not the power melodiously to arrange words but the power to suggest human values') as *A Nest of Gentlefolk*, and, curiously enough, among the gunshots, the flag-waving, the last stands, it is of the same gentle and reflective and melancholy kind. There is a scene here of humorous and pathetic irony which might have been drawn directly from one of the great classic novelists. The hall and stairs of a one-time palace on the Baltic shore is packed nearly to suffocation with soldiers and marines; they lie massed together like swine: at dawn a door opens at the stair-head and a little knot of children, lodged for safety in the palace, emerges, climbs softly down, ready to start like mice at any movement. They finger the revolvers, the rifles, the machine-guns, climb quickly away when a man moves, percolate down again among the sleepers persistently, to finger a butt, a holster, the barrel of a Lewis gun.

There are many other examples of the poetic use of imagery and incident: the gulls sweeping and coursing above the cliffs where the Red prisoners are lined up for their death by drowning, the camera moving from the heavy rocks round their necks to the movement of the light white wings: one sooty tree drooping on the huge rocky Kronstadt walls above a bench where a sailor and a woman embrace, against the dark tide, the riding lights of the battleships, the shape of the great guns, the singing of a band of sailors going home in the dark to their iron home. Life as it is: life as it ought to be: Chekhov's definition of a novelist's purpose comes to mind. Every poetic image is chosen for its contrasting value, to represent peace and normal human values under the heroics and the wartime patriotism.

The Spectator, 26 February 1937

We from Kronstadt (USSR, Mosfilm, 1936). Director: Yefim Dzigan. Vasili Zaichikov, Grigori Bushuyev, Oleg Zhakov, Raisa Yesipova.

We from Kronstadt

Fire Over England/Maid of Salem/Theodora Goes Wild

Herr Pommer, the German producer, and Mr William K. Howard, the American
director, of Mr Korda's great national Coronation-year picture of Elizabethan
England have done one remarkable thing: they have caught the very spirit of
an English public-schoolmistress's vision of history. *Fire Over England* should be
enormously popular at Roedean and Cheltenham, and Miss Robson catches the
very accent and manner of an adored headmistress, that blend of refined authority
(alas! for great Harry's daughter), of familiar crotchets to set common-rooms
buzzing, and a hidden histrionic tenderness towards the younger worshippers. I
know I find myself in a tiresome minority (there are always a few sour disloyal
spirits in every common-room). It is not, I am sure, Miss Robson's fault: she has
only too faithfully carried out the suggestions of the script, and it must be remembered that the screenplay is by the author of *Will Shakespeare* and the novel
by the author of *The Four Feathers*.

From neither of these authors do we expect a very penetrating or realistic study
of the Queen, but at least they might have avoided a few of the absurdities which
mar this well-directed and lavish picture. No headmistress, leave alone Elizabeth
Tudor, would have allowed quite so much cuddling and kissing in her presence,
and a little study of Court etiquette might have assisted the actors in deciding

135

Theodora Goes Wild: Irene Dunne, Melvyn Douglas

when they had to kneel and on what occasions they could sprawl negligently at Her Majesty's feet. The occasional suggestions that all is not quite straightforward in the Queen's character are only embarrassing; they don't belong, they have strayed out of history; one doesn't want this sex stuff in common-room. As for the story of a young spy sent to Madrid to discover the names of English plotters, it belongs to the good old horsehair tradition of Charles Kingsley and the Low Church romancers: the distinction is between Papists who burn their prisoners in the name of religion and the honest Protestants who sail round the world and singe Philip's beard, sportsmen all. No stench from Campion's quarters offends the nostrils here.

Nevertheless, this is the best production to come from Denham yet. The sets are magnificent (in the case of the English Court too magnificent, if we are to accept the dramatic theme, presented in the opening lines by Burleigh, of a small poor island rashly threatening the wealth and power of a great empire), the direction, until the closing scenes which are spoilt by the absurdity of the story, spirited, and the acting is far better than we are accustomed to in English films. Mr Laurence Olivier can do the hysterical type of young romantic hero with ease, Mr Leslie Banks is a Leicester who might have been on the board of governors of any school, and Mr Raymond Massey presents a fine and plausible portrait of King Philip. Mr Massey is the only memorable thing about the film.

Maid of Salem is historical romance in the American manner, a story of the witch-hunts in New England. *Fire Over England* has the easier dialogue (*Maid of Salem* is pompously period) and is more pleasing to the eye, but as a story the American picture derives from Hawthorne not Kingsley, and a little authentic horror is allowed to creep in. Miss Bonita Granville, as the child who pretends for her own mean motives that she has been bewitched, gives a performance equal to her earlier study of evil adolescence in *These Three*. Miss Claudette Colbert and Mr Fred MacMurray as the Puritan girl and her rebel lover are a little out of place: but not so that magnificent actor Mr Edward Ellis, a fierce and austere player who strides through this picture with a terrifying conviction.

I have it on my conscience that I have not yet recommended *Theodora Goes Wild*. Miss Irene Dunne will be remembered for many patient, womanly and rather smug performances (*Roberta* and *Magnificent Obsession* are the worst cases on record); now she has been regroomed and appears as one of the best comedians on the screen in the best light comedy since *Mr Deeds*.

The Spectator, 5 March 1937

Fire Over England (GB, London Films, 1937). Director: William K. Howard. Flora Robson, Laurence Olivier, Leslie Banks, Raymond Massey.
Maid of Salem (USA, Paramount, 1936). Director: Frank Lloyd. Claudette Colbert, Fred MacMurray, Bonita Granville, Edward Ellis.
Theodora Goes Wild (USA, Columbia, 1937). Director: Richard Boleslavsky. Irene Dunne, Melvyn Douglas.

Pluck of the Irish/The Sequel to Second Bureau/Thunder in the City/ Head Over Heels

Weighing machines which can be made to record any weight at the touch of a finger; chickens filled with lead sausages which fall quietly into a drawer of saw-dust after the chicken has been weighed: the racket which cheats housewives of a few cents every time they make a purchase is the subject of Mr James Cagney's new film. *The Sequel to Second Bureau* deals with the theft of a new French cart-ridge by German agents and the successful attempt of two French spies, posing as an art critic and his sister, to recover the cartridge before it has been analysed by the head of the German Secret Service. The issue, compared with that of the American picture, seems oddly theoretical. The imagination, however Francophil, refuses to be really stirred. 'You carry the best wishes of four million Frenchmen,' an officer remarks loudly outside the Paris-Berlin wagon lit (after reading Mr Compton Mackenzie's reminiscences we can swallow any amount of military indiscretions), but the imagination refuses to forget entirely the bad wishes of the four million Germans. The cartridge is treated with immense pomposity by the heads of the rival Secret Services, but one knows quite well that very soon some-one else will invent a better one. It is all an amusing game to keep the Army Estimates up. It hasn't the immediate importance of the weighing-machines in the grocery stores. But as a military variation on the Tale of the Three Bears – 'Who's been eating up my porridge?' – this French melodrama has charm. The story is told with a great deal of malicious humour, especially in the Haus Vaterland scenes – the bogus Tyrolean singers, the huge tankards, the absurd painted mountains under an artificial storm, the Horst Wessel song booming from the loud-speaker, the outstretched arms and the heartfelt *Heils*.

Mr Cagney as the Deputy Chief of the Weights and Measures Department of a big American city: one knows what to expect and Mr Cagney seldom disappoints: the lightweight hands held a little away from the body ready for someone else's punch: the quick nervous steps of a man whose footwork is good: the extreme virtuosity of the muted sentiment. In his latest picture it is all there, with perhaps a more sophisticated humour than usual: the scenes with the ward politicians, the Mayor, the philanthropist, crooks all, are pleasantly phosphorescent with corruption, and so is the admirable climax at an evening party (given by a retiring boxer) where all is tuxedos and gentility, but a little uppercut in a corner passes unnoticed among pals.

Head Over Heels: Jessie Matthews, Robert Flemyng

Thunder in the City, with the American star Mr Edward G. Robinson, and *Head Over Heels*, with Miss Jessie Matthews, compete for the position of worst English film of the quarter. I think the former has it, with its tricky self-conscious continuity, its horde of Hollywood stars on holiday, Mr Ned Mann's worst 'special effect' to date, and its complete ignorance – in spite of its national studio – of English life and behaviour. It is a fantasy (an American publicity man dismissed from his New York firm because they want English dignity comes over to England and puts over a big business flotation by what are supposed to be American methods), a fantasy by an elephantine disciple of M. Clair (astonishingly his name is Robert E. Sherwood) but even a fantasy needs some relation to life. Perhaps the only really English thing about the picture is its humour: an awful vista of old bound *Punch*'s dwindling down the dark shelves of a country-house library.

As for Miss Jessie Matthews, she has been ill served in her latest film, a moribund tale of poor young people with ambitions in Parisian garrets. The dialogue has a moral earnestness for which it would be hard to find a parallel even in the Victorian Age. 'You do – trust me?' the hero asks the heroine after she has accepted an invitation to lunch in his garret. Only one song:

> Why must I weep on
> The pillow I sleep on?

possesses a kind of awful charm.   *The Spectator,* 19 March 1937

Pluck of the Irish (*Great Guy*) (USA, Grant National, 1936). Director: John Blystone. James Cagney, Mae Clarke.
The Sequel to Second Bureau (*Les Loups entre eux*) (France, Compagnie Française Cinématographique, 1936). Director: Léon Mathot. Renée Saint-Cyr, Jules Berry.
Thunder in the City (USA, Columbia, 1937). Director: Marion Gering. Edward G. Robinson, Ralph Richardson.
Head Over Heels (GB, Gaumont British, 1937). Director: Sonnie Hale. Jessie Matthews, Sonnie Hale. [US title: *Head Over Heels in Love.*]

Three Smart Girls/For Valour

Since Henry James wrote *What Maisie Knew* a good many writers have been attracted to the subject of divorce as it affects the child – one remembers Mrs Wharton's *The Children* and the novel and film *Little Friend*. It is a *real* subject as James described it, and as these other writers to the best of their ability dealt with it: 'To live with all intensity and perplexity and felicity in its terribly mixed little world would thus be the part of my interesting small mortal; . . . really keeping the torch of virtue alive in an air tending infinitely to smother it; really, in short, making confusion worse confounded by drawing some stray fragrance of an ideal across the scent of selfishness, by sowing on barren strands, through the mere fact of presence, the seed of the moral life.' It has needed Hollywood to make of this subject, which of its nature contains all the possible darknesses of corruption, a story almost as dewy as *Girls' Dormitory*, when it is not relieved by passages of quite amusing farce. As for the fragrance of an ideal – one's nose detects at once the vapid and virginal and inexpensive odour of lavender water.

That scent lies most heavily over the first half-hour: the new young star, Deanna Durbin, singing sentimental and precocious lyrics while her sisters manœuvre a boat on a Swiss lake surrounded by over-romantic woods; squeals and tussles, a chalet in a garden full of smudged and bogus blossoms, the old family servant, a mother's tears, and as much as possible of that unnaturally mature soprano voice. (As usual we become acquainted only too intimately with the hideous cavern of the human mouth.) The three children – so consciously girlish that they might all be budding Bergners – learn from their mother's tears that their father, ten years divorced, is about to marry a blonde gold-digger, and with an old servant they sail for New York to stop the marriage at all costs and reconcile their parents. Only then with the tardy entrance of 'Precious' (Miss Binnie Barnes), her scheming mother (Miss Alice Brady), a bogus Hungarian Count (Mr Mischa Auer) and a real English nobleman (Mr Ray Milland) does some welcome humour of an adult kind creep tardily into the sentimental film. It is these actors who make the picture, rather than the much-advertised Miss Durbin (Mr Mischa Auer confirms the fine impression left by *The Gay Desperado* and *My Man Godfrey*).

It may seem unfair to complain that this picture does not do something more serious and more worth while: I would be the last to complain if the note had been set in the farcical passages: it is hopeless to expect an American to remain unmoved by mother love, and the tears with which the picture begins fall again with happiness at the close. Father and mother clasp hands, while Miss Durbin's face appears between them in place of the traditional horse.

For Valour is a very pleasant antidote to the Coronation, though it is a little marred by an inability to remain wholly flippant. Mr Tom Walls as an old convict and also as his son, a crooked financier: Mr Ralph Lynn as an ancient Boer War veteran and also as his thieving and incompetent grandson, play most of the parts themselves. The burlesque on wartime patriotism – recruiting meetings in the Victorian and in the Georgian manner with the appropriate songs strummed out in church halls under the painted stare of Roberts and Kitchener – may prove puzzling to audiences properly conditioned by the patriotic Press, and our more earnest visitors from the Dominions may be a trifle put out by the elaborate and almost universal roguery (even the Boer War veteran becomes a kleptomaniac at the close). But those of us who are tired of the sturdy, sober and imperial virtues of the new reign will welcome this return to the tradition of *The English Rogue* and *Moll Flanders*. It is not, of course, quite as good as all that; Mr Tom Walls is better as an actor than he is as a director, and the shadow of schoolmaster *Punch* – 'so much cause for mirth and so little for harm' – has to be placated with an honest character and a few good resolutions.   *The Spectator,* 26 March 1937

Three Smart Girls (USA, Universal, 1937). Director: Henry Koster. Deanna Durbin, Binnie Barnes, Alice Brady, Ray Milland, Charles Winninger.
For Valour (GB, Capitol, 1937). Director: Tom Walls. Tom Walls, Ralph Lynn, Robertson Hare.

The Good Earth/Dark Journey

The way is less long from China to Stockholm than is the imaginative distance between these two pictures. One is about life and the other is about – what? I find it hard to say, but certainly not life. One is simple and direct and true: it catches successfully that legendary quality Mr Flaherty failed to put into *Man of Aran*: the characters are shown in incidents common to their class and race, a marriage, a famine, a revolution; the other is composed (unwise policy even for a thriller) of incidents which never happened to anybody yet: a kind of collage of old Lyceum dramas and Drury Lane dialogue.

The Good Earth is the story of a Chinese peasant-farmer, how he marries a wife, who is a slave in the Great House, has children, adds field to field; how drought comes and kills his crops and cattle, how he refuses to sell his land, though his family starves, how they trek south to the city. A revolution quite meaningless to them sweeps through the town, his wife is caught up in a mob and flung through a looted palace, luck saves her incomprehensibly from a firing-squad, luck leaves in her hands a bag of jewels. Understanding nothing of what it is all about they can go back to their land, and Miss Luise Rainer's beautiful performance, the stupid stuck-out lips, the scared, uncalculating and humble gaze, convey all the peasant's fear of hope, of the envious gods, the Oriental equivalent of the touched wood, the salt over the shoulder. 'My daughter is of no account' (and a hand shields the *son's* face from the dangerous heavens) 'and ugly with smallpox.' Mr Muni's performance is not of the same quality, he exaggerates his Chinoiserie, it is Miss Rainer and the character she presents who carries the film: the awful pathos of the wedding walk from the Great House at the heels of the bridegroom she has never seen, the scrabbling in the ditch for the peach stone he has spat out (from it a tree may grow); toiling heavy with child in the fields to save the harvest from the hurricane; her proud and ceremonial return to the Great House to show her son to the Ancient One; in the long drought taking the knife to the ox her husband fears to kill ('Infirm of purpose, give me the dagger', in acting like Miss Rainer's we become aware of the greatest of all echoes). The drought marks the highest point of the film. Like clear exact epithets the images stab home: the plough jammed in the rocky soil, the vultures on the kid's carcase, the dark sullen stare of the starved child.

Afterwards the picture becomes a little less than life. Something goes wrong with story and direction when the farmer has returned to his land with the loot and bought the Great House: too much plot-making, too many cinematic themes (father against son, love against lust): not even the big set-piece of the locust plague saves the last hour from banality and ennui. The peasant is no longer legendary: he is no longer any peasant who marries and suffers and endures: he is a character called so-and-so who becomes astoundingly rich and loves a dancing-girl, who loves his son whom he turns out of his home, and so on and so on, plot running away with subject, life left behind in those magnificent earlier reels.

'Abandon life all ye who enter here': the pedestrian unreality of most Denham pictures lies over this spy drama directed by Mr Victor Saville, about a fashionable dressmaker in Stockholm who works for the German Secret Service when all the time she is in French pay. Mr Saville directed *The W. Plan*, a good thriller, but he is defeated by the incredible naïvety of this script. 'Fig leaves were good enough for Eve and she was the first lady in the land.' So runs the wicked cosmopolitan dialogue. 'You love me – why are you trying to resist? I want to take you away from here,' and the Count's monocle glitters. There is one superb moment of anti-climax when the Germans accuse the heroine of bringing false information about French movements at Verdun. She pleads nervously: 'But wasn't there an attack?' to receive the stern reply, 'Yes, but our troops stopped the wrong one.' The heroine is rescued by a Q-ship in the nick of time from a German submarine, and the final shot is of two small and dubious ships on a waste of water. One of them hoots derisively, and to that maritime 'raspberry' the film fittingly fades out.

The Spectator, 2 April 1937

The Good Earth (USA, M-G-M, 1937). Director: Sidney Franklin. Paul Muni, Luise Rainer, Walter Connolly, Tilly Losch.
Dark Journey (GB, London Films, 1937). Director: Victor Saville. Vivien Leigh, Conrad Veidt.

Winterset

Winterset belongs to the same kind as *The Petrified Forest*. Adapted from a romantic play, in which poetry and gangmen are curiously linked, it still bears about it on the screen some of the unreality of the stage: almost as desperate a pursuit of the unities as you will find in Corneille lands all the characters, during

Winterset: Margo, Burgess Meredith

the course of a few night hours, on one bleak rain-drenched square under the arches of Brooklyn Bridge. The hero, too, has some likeness to Mr Sherwood's Sparkenbrokish tramp, and there are occasions when Art is rather embarrassingly wooed, but the resemblances end there: this play (in the original it was in blank verse) has far more solid merits.

The film begins with a prologue, a rather obvious echo of the Sacco-Vanzetti case. Romagna, a Radical, is electrocuted for a murder of which he is innocent, committed by gangsters in his car. Sixteen years later he is not forgotten: a Professor of Jurisprudence throws doubt on the whole case: why was Garth Esdras, an important witness connected with the gang that did the killing, not called? The Judge who tried the case has gone out of his mind, he is wandering from State to State trying to prove to everyone he meets that Romagna was really guilty (even acted by Mr Edward Ellis he remains the stock mad figure of Georgian poetic drama and is more unconvincing than ever upon the screen). Esdras is hiding away with his father and sister in a basement under Brooklyn Bridge, Romagna's son Mio is on the hunt to prove his father innocent, and Trock, the man who did the killing, is on parole from the gaol where he has served a sentence for dope traffic, carrying the prison doctor's verdict in his brain that he has less than six months to live. We have had plenty of Scarfaces, of men whose trigger-fingers act like the conditioned reflexes of dogs who dribble when a bell sounds: Trock has more interest: the sick man who hates the healthy, who kills from envy because he has to die himself. In this character, acted with evil magnificence by Eduardo Ciannelli, there is some of the poetry of a Renaissance tyrant, with basilisks in the eyes and the everlasting cold pinching the heart.

And there are situations, too, which have more intensity than mere 'thriller' stuff: Mio's dance with Esdras's sister to the barrel-organ in the square: the return of Shadow, Trock's chief gunman, from the East River into which he has been pitched with two bullets in his body: the whole wintry scene in the drenching sleet under the sooty arches of people 'passionately met in this sad world'. It would be almost as easy to burlesque this film (love at first sight, the scraps of not quite good enough poetry, the mad Ophelian judge) as *The Petrified Forest*, but the latter film depended almost entirely for its effect on philosophic ideas of more than Emersonian solemnity and emptiness. Here, as in all good plays, it is in the acts themselves, as much as in the dialogue, that the poetic idea is expressed. And in the cinema it is only right that the symbols should be popular ones: a disappearing body, a sentimental barrel-organ tune, silencers and sub-machine guns. We may have our doubts about the literary dialogue; the physical images at any rate convey a general and poetic idea. Watching Trock dragging others to the grave along with him, one remembers Webster's line: 'Security some men call the suburbs of hell, Only a dead wall between', for it is the merit of *Winterset* that when we are not reminded of Mr Masefield at his vaguest we are reminded of the Jacobeans at their most bloody and exact.   *The Spectator,* 9 April 1937

Winterset (USA, RKO, 1936). Director: Alfred Santell. Burgess Meredith, Eduardo Ciannelli, Margo.

Elephant Boy

Mr Robert Flaherty is said to have spent more than a year in India gathering material for this picture: a scene of elephants washed in a river, a few shots of markets and idols and forest, that is all. It cannot be compared in quantity or quality with what Mr Basil Wright brought back from Ceylon after a stay of a few weeks. *Elephant Boy* has gone the same way as *Man of Aran*: enormous advance publicity, director out of touch with the Press for months, rumours of great epics sealed in tins, and then the disappointing diminutive achievement. In *Man of Aran*, a so-called 'documentary', Mr Flaherty had the islanders taught to hunt sharks for the sake of an exciting climax: there is nothing quite so flagrantly bogus in the new picture, but in all other respects it is inferior, even in the inevitable Flaherty skylines, against which the elephants in single file tactlessly take up the graduated positions of those little ebony and ivory toys Indian administrators bring back to their female relatives at Cheltenham. With this exception Mr Flaherty's faults are negative: the more positive crimes, the bad cutting, the dreadful studio work, the pedestrian adaptation so unfair to Kipling's story, must be laid at Denham's door.

The climax of Kipling's story of an elephant-drive is the dance of the wild elephants which little Toomai, the Mahout's son, watched from the back of Kala Nag. The story is quite legitimately padded out up to this point with incident: Toomai's father is killed by a tiger, Toomai is ordered home by the great white hunter, Petersen, Kala Nag infuriated by the brutality of his new mahout runs amok, and Toomai returns only just in time to quieten the elephant as the hunter prepares to shoot it down. Kala Nag has broken the mahout's leg and the man claims that its life is forfeit; Toomai, not knowing that Petersen has made the man forgo his claim, slips out with the elephant at night from the camp and is carried at dawn by Kala Nag to the secret dance. This is all reasonable and necessary embroidery on Kipling's story, but Mr Zoltan Korda, who is associated as director with Mr Flaherty, has made nothing of these incidents. The episodes are not led up to, they just happen and are over before you have time to feel excitement or even interest.

Kala Nag's attack on the camp should have been the first great climax of the picture, but through lack of preparation and rhythm in the cutting, the scene is thrown away. As for the elephant dance – I suppose the fault rests with the Indian elephants who will not dance as Kipling describes them, stamping steady as trip-hammers, rocking the ground, though a little could have been done with music and we might have been spared the models. But what has no excuse at this point is the story construction. To use the gathering of the wild elephants on their jungle dance-floor merely to resolve the problem of Petersen Sahib who has got to trap a certain number of elephants for labour if he is to retain his job – this is to throw away the whole poetic value of the original.

Anyone who has had experience of British studios will know how they are governed by one word – suspense – and here is a case where the most childish form of suspense is preferred to any other value, human or poetic. No attempt has been made to interest us in Petersen (Mr Walter Hudd acts with a tiring over-emphasis), and yet the whole story is made to turn on whether or not his hunt will be successful, and we are expected to feel satisfaction at the thought of the wild dancers driven into the stockade to be tamed. Kipling's mind, heaven knows, had its chasms; he was capable of crudities and cruelties, but not of that, and it is noticeable in this faltering and repetitive picture that it is only when Kipling speaks – in his own dialogue when Machua Appa apostrophizes Toomai – that the ear is caught and the attention held. 'He shall take no harm in the Keddah when he runs under their bellies to rope the wild tuskers; and if he slips before the feet of the charging bull-elephant, that bull-elephant shall know who he is and shall not crush him.' Unwise, unwise to let those weighted and authoritative syllables fall among the cheap china values, the 'Presents from Mysore'.   *The Spectator,* 16 April 1937

Elephant Boy (GB, London Films, 1937). Directors: Robert Flaherty, Zoltan Korda. Sabu, Walter Hudd.

Pépé le Moko/The Golem

A thief wanted by the French police who has found a safe, but terribly constricted, asylum in the Casbah, the native quarter of Algiers, from which he cannot move without arrest: a native Police Inspector, allowed, in return for a certain licence, the contemptuous liberty of the quarter: the mistress of a millionaire, drawn by curiosity to the Casbah and used without her knowledge by the inspector to lure Pépé into the European town: on these three simple and well-realized characters, the first generous, natty and common, his pockets chock-a-block with fags and revolvers, the second sly, patient, obsequious, the third, the woman acquisitive, prehensile, risen from the ranks, and groomed for chromium concubinage, on these three is based one of the most exciting and moving films I can remember seeing.

It is rarely, very rarely, that a picture is produced so unhampered as this by plot-making, where theme dominates incident in so masterly a manner. In this film we do not forget the real subject in a mass of detail: the freedom-loving human spirit trapped and pulling at the chain. A simple subject, but fiction does not demand complex themes, and the story of a man at liberty to move only in one shabby, alien quarter when his heart is in another place widens out to touch the experience of exile common to everyone. One of the subtlest and most moving scenes is that in which the thief and the mistress count over their memories of Paris, starting a world and class apart, her Bois du Boulogne capped by his Porte d'Orleans, until they meet on common ground with the Place Blanche on both their lips at once. In the love scenes we are a whole continent away from the usual studio banalities, and when some gesture of the beloved woman calls up the fish-and-chip shops on the boulevards, her scent the Métro, we are aware (rare and unexpected delight) of a film which is really trying to translate into dramatic terms the irrelevances, the grotesque wit, the absurd, passionate tangle of associations which make up the mind.

Perhaps there have been pictures as exciting on the 'thriller' level as this before (though it would be hard to equal the shooting of Regis, the informer, with its comic horror: the little fat eunuch sweating and squealing in the corner between the aspidistra and the mechanical piano, the clash and clatter of the potted music as his dying victim is helped across the room to finish him at point-blank range, friends steadying the revolver on its mark), but I cannot remember one which has succeeded so admirably in raising the thriller to a poetic level. *Winterset* seems a little jejune and obvious and literary beside it. *Fury*, perhaps, is its equal, but in *Fury* Fritz Lang was not allowed to follow his subject to the right, the grim conclusion. *His* hero couldn't burn; but Pépé cuts his throat with a penknife in his handcuffed hands outside the dock gates as the steamer leaves for France. The theme of no freedom anywhere is not lost in a happy ending.

Acting and direction are both superb. No tricky montage here, but a beautiful smooth flow of images which results from the frank use of panning and trucking shots. It is as if the camera were handled like a brush in broad sweeps as distinct from the restless *pointilliste* effect given by many cuts. Particularly successful is Pépé's last walk in his glossy shoes and his best muffler down the steep steps to the European town where the Inspector awaits him, the camera trucking down ahead of him registering the happy, crazy stride, the rash, nostalgic impulse.

The Golem is very Jewish, very traditional: if it were not for sound and dialogue, it might belong to the classic Ufa days: synagogues and sacred music, pale, dark Rebeccas, a monarch who wines and wenches in the *Jew Süss* manner. There is a curious, almost Surrealist, acceptance of the most fantastic situations, so that no one seems in the least surprised by the presence in an enormous, raftered attic above the synagogue of a human statue which may at any moment come alive at the right incantation and rescue the downtrodden and chosen race. M. Harry Baur as the Emperor gives one of his most brilliant performances, and the film, I suppose, is quite worth seeing as a kind of survival – a Semitic survival – of the old, romantic Caligari cinema.   *The Spectator*, 23 April 1937

Pépé le Moko (France, Paris Film, 1936). Director: Julien Duvivier. Jean Gabin, Mireille Balin, Line Noro, Lucas Gridoux.
The Golem (*Der Golem*) (Czechoslovakia, AB-Film, 1935). Director: Julien Duvivier. Harry Baur, Roger Karl, Germaine Aussey, Jany Holt.

Lost Horizon

Nothing reveals men's characters more than their Utopias: the scientific senti-mentality of Mr Wells, the art-and-craftiness of William Morris, Mr Shaw's eternal sewing-machine, Samuel Butler's dusty alpaca. Shangri-La must be counted among the less fortunate flights of the imagination, the lamaserai in Thibet ruled by a Grand Llama, a Belgian priest who discovered the rich valley among the

April 1937

Pépé le Moko

mountains in the eighteenth century and who was still alive when Robert Conway, explorer, diplomat and – rather improbably – Foreign Secretary elect was kidnapped from a Chinese town and brought there by aeroplane. This Utopia closely resembles a film star's luxurious estate on Beverly Hills: flirtatious pursuits through grape arbours, splashings and divings in blossomy pools under improbable waterfalls, and rich and enormous meals. 'Every man carries in his heart a Shangri-La': but I prefer myself the harps and golden crowns and glassy seas of an older mythology. Shangri-La is intended to represent a haven of moderation, beauty and peace in the middle of an uncompromising and greedy world, but what Conway finds there, what he loses in a weak moment of disbelief, and struggles across the Himalayas to find again, is something incurably American: a kind of aerated idealism ('We have one simple rule, Kindness') and, of course, a girl (Miss Jane Wyatt, one of the dumber stars), who has read all the best books (his own included) and has the coy comradely manner of a not too advanced schoolmistress.

It is a very long picture, this disappointing successor to *Mr Deeds*, and a very dull one as soon as the opening scenes are over. These are brilliantly written and directed, and show Conway (Mr Ronald Colman) organizing the aerial evacuation of the white inhabitants from a Chinese town in the middle of a revolution before he takes the last plane himself in company with a crooked financier wanted by the police, a prostitute (sentimental variety), a scientist (comic), and a younger brother. Here the Capra-Riskin partnership is at its best, and we are unprepared for the disappointments which follow: the flavourless uplifting dialogue, the crude humour, the pedestrian direction, and the slack makeshift construction. 'You shouldn't look at the bottom of the mountains. Try looking at the top.' So Chang, the suave philosophical second-in-command of Shangri-La, addresses the prostitute who believes that she is dying of consumption (one of the virtues of this mysterious valley is health, the body beautiful, and a life which goes on and on and on). It might be Wilhelmina Stitch translated into American prose, and one can hardly believe that this script is from the same hands as *Mr Deeds*, though perhaps Mr James Hilton, the author of the novel and of *Goodbye, Mr Chips*, may be responsible for the sentimentality of these sequences.

Of course, the picture isn't quite as bad as that. It does attempt, however clumsily and sentimentally, more than the average film; a social conscience is obscurely at work, but at work far less effectively than in *Mr Deeds*, and as for the humour – it consists only of Mr Edward Everett Horton wearing Eastern clothes. The conscious humour that is to say, for the glimpses of English political life give a little much needed relief. 'The Far Eastern Conference must be postponed. We cannot meet these nations without Conway': the Prime Minister's measured utterances to his Cabinet gathered Gladstonianly round him fall with an odd sound on ears accustomed to more dispensable Foreign Secretaries. But it is in the last sequence that the Capra-Riskin collaboration fails most disastrously. Conway, persuaded by his younger brother that the Grand Llama has lied to him, that there is misery and injustice in this seeming Utopia, makes his way back to China across the mountains. A few newspaper headlines tell us that Conway has reached safety, and it is only at second-hand in a long uncinematic scene in a London club that we learn what we should have seen with our own eyes: Conway's reaction to 'civilization'. If the long dull ethical sequences had been cut to the bone there would have been plenty of room for the real story: the shock of Western crudity and injustice on a man returned from a more gentle and beautiful way of life.

The Spectator, 30 April 1937

Lost Horizon (USA, Columbia, 1937). Director: Frank Capra. Ronald Colman, Jane Wyatt, Margo, Edward Everett Horton, Sam Jaffe.

Generation of Conquerors/Lloyds of London/The Gap/Glamorous Night

The pictures I have had to see this week have been terribly voluble: voluble about patriotism, voluble about romance, most voluble of all about the class war. Oh, how that Generation of Conquerors seems to have talked: little wonder that the Revolution was drawn out from 1905 to 1917. I fell asleep on the hot Sunday Film Society afternoon and when I woke five minutes later everything was just the same, the same Siberian hut, the same serious faces arguing in Russian the same point: whether the Bolsheviks and Mensheviks were right to split the Party Congress in 1903. For it was a period film, the women wore wildfowl in their hats and high celluloid collars and sometimes smoked a cigarette with awkward emphasis, and everyone talked and talked, earnest, fanatical, oddly domestic revolutionaries. One remembered how Lenin in his Siberian exile presented his wife with a little ornamental brooch made in the shape of a book labelled *Das Kapital*.

Generation of Conquerors is hardly likely to be seen in London again: the poor entertainment-loving flesh is weak, and for those who do not understand Russian there is little to recommend it. Its presentation was chiefly interesting for the new method the Film Society used to translate the picture. Between the sequences, between the fade-out and the fade-in of the images, a voice, dubiously BBC in accent, gave a short synopsis of how the plot was going to progress (this synopsis did not quite agree with that in the programme; perhaps the film was too much even for the Society's Council, and we were left in doubt whether the gentleman in black waxed moustaches and a bowler who dogged Sophia – celluloid collar, feather hat – through the park was really a secret police officer or, as the programme stated, a *roué*).

Lloyds of London is a fairly astute piece of sentimentality which occasionally overreaches itself when the stage becomes a little too packed with historical figures rather oddly juxtaposed like the waxworks at Madame Tussaud's, so that it is almost a miracle that Lord Nelson doesn't actually meet Benjamin Franklin or Dr Johnson the Prince Regent. The name of England is so frequently on the characters' lips that we recognize at once an American picture. These people live, make love, bear children from the most patriotic motives: and it is all rather like London in Coronation Week. Like a colonial visitor, Miss Madeleine Carroll falls heavily about the screen, large and lost and oddly dressed.

The Gap at the same cinema is more worth seeing, an appeal for Territorial recruits to fill the gap in London's air defences. The actors who play the parts of staff officers behave with unmilitary enthusiasm, but the imaginary air raid on London is very ably directed and the special effects, not by Mr Ned Mann, are finely managed. War without a declaration, a fleet of bombers from the East zooming out of the evening mist over a British trawler in the North Sea, civilian observers grouped round their metal tripods as they report the strange planes crossing the coast in the late evening light, the bomb-proof control-room where wireless-operators sit round an enormous map moving model aeroplanes while lights flash on as the patrolling squadrons take off over Kent and Sussex and the Eastern counties: zero hour modern style is impressively conveyed.

Glamorous Night is about a Ruritanian King who loves a gipsy, and a scheming Prime Minister, who exiles the royal mistress, makes himself dictator and is about to murder the King when the gipsy enters the capital at the head of her people.

The plot belongs to the age of *The Bing Boys* and *The Maid of the Mountains*; one waits for jokes about Blighty, although Mr Novello has tried to bring it up to date with arch references to coloured shirts. It is about as bogus as a film could be, but it is well photographed by Wagner, Lang's ace cameraman in the old Ufa days, and quite well directed by Mr Brian Desmond Hurst. It has the advantage of Miss Mary Ellis's daemonic good looks, and Mr Hurst deserves some credit for never once taking Miss Ellis's mouth in a close-up as she sings Mr Novello's peculiarly flat songs.   *The Spectator*, 7 May 1937

Generation of Conquerors (USSR, Mosfilm, 1936). Director: Vera Stroyeva. Boris Shchukin, Nikolai Khmelyov, Xenia Tarasova, Vera Maretskaya.
Lloyds of London (USA, 20th Century-Fox, 1936). Director: Henry King. Tyrone Power, Madeleine Carroll, Freddie Bartholomew.
The Gap (GB, G.B. Instructional, 1937). Director: Donald Carter.
Glamorous Night (GB, British International, 1937). Director: Brian Desmond Hurst. Mary Ellis, Otto Kruger.

We from Kronstadt/The Frog/Make Way for Tomorrow/Der Herrscher

No need to stop and think about which is the best film to be seen in London. It's undoubtedly *We from Kronstadt*. Russian, full of absurd heroics, noble deaths, last-minute rescues, wounded men played up to the trenches by a scarecrow band, it is no more propagandist than Henty. In a sense all writing for schoolboys is propaganda for the established order, and in this film, just as much as in *Tom Brown's Schooldays*, the people who don't stick to the old school code end by having a thin time. What makes the film immeasurably superior to its rivals is the strain of adult poetry, the sense of human beings longing for peace, grasping moments out of the turmoil for ordinary human relations, and the most cynical Conservative will cheer at the defiant closing line: 'Who else wants Petrograd?'

The best line to cheer on in *The Frog*, an English thriller, is 'I must get John Bennett's gramophone record if I am to save his son's life.' The dialogue otherwise goes rather like this: 'My name is Bennett. Stella Bennett.' 'No, not really? Stella Bennett? What a charming name! I very much hope we shall meet again one day soon.' 'Must you really go? Good-bye then.' 'What Stella! Are these gentlemen still here?' 'We were on the point of leaving, Sir.' 'This is my father, Inspector. May I introduce Inspector Elk of Scotland Yard?' 'Good-bye, Miss Bennett. Please don't trouble to see us out. Good-bye, Sir. Haven't we met somewhere before?' 'No. Good-bye.' While the well-mannered dialogue drones on, a bomb is touched off in Scotland Yard, the voice of the master criminal is trapped on a gramophone disc by a bird-watcher, the factory containing the matrix is burnt to the ground, an innocent man is sentenced to death, and the public executioner entering the condemned cell finds his own son there. Badly directed, badly acted, it is like one of those plays produced in country towns by stranded actors: it has an old-world charm: Scotland Yard is laid up in lavender.

Make Way for Tomorrow is a depressing picture about an old couple driven by hard times to live on their children. No one wants them, no one can put them both up at the same time. After months of separation they meet for a few hours in New York before the old man goes off to a daughter in California and the old woman into a home, with no hope of seeing each other again. The Pullman slides out, the aged tortoise in fact runs away, the tight thin bun of hair drearily fades out, and a sense of misery and inhumanity is left vibrating in the nerves. Anyhow that was how the story appeared to me, though Paramount describe it in these terms. 'One of the Three Smart Girls goes a lot faster. She wants to taste the Thrills of Life itself. *What Happens?*'

Der Herrscher, except for a pleasantly savage opening, a funeral frieze of dripping umbrellas and heartless faces, is a wordy picture about an elderly ironmaster who wants to marry his secretary and is almost driven insane by his children's opposition. Herr Jannings has the meaningless gaze of a sea-lion with huge sloping shoulders and watery whiskers, to whose emotions we apply, for want of anything better, such human terms as pity, anger, terror, though we cannot tell, on the evidence of those small marine eyes, whether he is really registering anything more than a dim expectation of fish.

Night and Day, 1 July 1937

We from Kronstadt (USSR, Mosfilm, 1936). Director: Yefim Dzigan. Vasili Zaichikov, Grigori Bushuyev, Oleg Zhakov, Raisa Yesipova.
The Frog (GB, Herbert Wilcox Productions, 1937). Director: Jack Raymond. Gordon Harker, Jack Hawkins.
Make Way for Tomorrow (USA, Paramount, 1937). Director: Leo McCarey. Victor Moore, Beulah Bondi.
Der Herrscher (Germany, Tobis-Magna-Film, 1937). Director: Veit Harlan. Emil Jannings, Marianne Hoppe, Käthe Haack, Rudolf Klein-Rogge, Hilde Körber.

Black Legion/Night Must Fall/Top of the Town/The Last Train from Madrid

Black Legion, an intelligent and exciting, if rather earnest film, is intended to expose the secret society of that name and the financial racket behind it. The Black Legion, with its policy of America for Americans, its melodramatic black hoods, must have had an appeal as wide as humanity: to the natural bully, to the envious and the unsuccessful, the man with a grievance, the romantic. Frank Taylor (admirably acted by Humphrey Bogart), a factory-hand who finds himself passed over for the post of foreman in favour of a Pole, attends a meeting at the local chemist's, a little rabbity man with defective eyesight who resents the cut-price drugstore further down the street. We hear the long pompous literary oath full of words too difficult for Taylor to pronounce; then the playboy hoods are raised to disclose the familiar faces, the chemist's, the bully's from the works, the organizer's, who informs the new recruit that he can now get 'a regular thirty-dollar revolver for fourteen dollars fifty cents', and afterwards the drinks all round, the hearty good fellowship.

It is an intelligent film because the director and script-writer know where the real horror lies: the real horror is not in the black robes and skull emblems, but in the knowledge that these hide the weak and commonplace faces you have met over the counter and minding the next machine. The horror is not in the climax when Taylor shoots his friend dead, but in the earlier moment before the glass when he poses romantically with his first gun; not in the floggings and burnings but in the immature question at the inaugural meeting, 'If we join up don't we get a uniform or something?', in the secret accounts read to the Managing Director, so much from the sale of uniforms and regalia, so much from officers' commissions, so much from revolvers at wholesale rates: total profits for the month, $221,049, 15 cents.

151

Black Legion: Humphrey Bogart

Comparisons can obviously be made with *Fury*, and at least one to the advantage of *Black Legion*: no factitious happy ending is tacked on (though the producer probably has one up his sleeve in case of need). But *Fury* with all its faults was the work of a very great director, *Black Legion* only of an intelligent one. The immediate impact of the horror has seeped away somewhere – perhaps in the camera positions – between the script and the 'take'.

There never was any genuine horror in *Night Must Fall*, and Emlyn Williams's pretentious little murder play has made a long dim film. Like an early talkie, it is no more than a photographed stage play and its psychological absurdities are mercilessly exposed. But there are worse pictures in town than this. *Top of the Town* may appeal to readers of *London Life* (the heroine wears very high heels, a kind of long Cossack coat and carries a little cane), but it is one of those distressingly carefree musicals (elderly people in evening dress romping up and down a restaurant for ten whole minutes at a stretch) when the only ungay faces are among the audience.

As for *The Last Train from Madrid*, it is probably the worst film of the decade and should have been the funniest. Emotional and uplifting dialogue ('I don't want to die, Senorita. I'm young, I want to live. My father kept a farm . . .'). Mr Lionel Atwill ('a grand old trooper', as Miss Lejeune would say) playing the Madrid Commandant, full of sternness and duty and tenderness ('You will be tried by court martial tomorrow', and his warm encouraging paw falls like a headmaster's on the prisoner's shoulder): all we still need for a really good laugh are the presence of the Dean of Canterbury and the absence of actual war. For there is something a little shocking about these noble self-sacrifices and heroic deaths – the eyes close always of their own accord – in front of a back-projection of ruined Madrid itself, about the facetiousness of the screen journalist in a screen air raid mingled with news-shots of the genuine terror. *Night and Day,* 8 July 1937

Black Legion (USA, Warner Bros, 1936). Director: Archie Mayo. Humphrey Bogart, Ann Sheridan, Dick Foran.
Night Must Fall (USA, M-G-M, 1936). Director: Richard Thorpe. Robert Montgomery, Rosalind Russell, Dame May Whitty.
Top of the Town (USA, Universal, 1937). Director: Ralph Murphy. Doris Nolan, George Murphy.
The Last Train from Madrid (USA, Paramount, 1937). Director: James Hogan. Lew Ayres, Dorothy Lamour, Lionel Atwill, Anthony Quinn, Gilbert Roland.

God's Country and the Woman/Michael Strogoff

The Technicolor expert, like Wordsworth, is most at home with Nature. In *God's Country and the Woman*, a tale of the timber forests, we see some pretty shots of trees cutting huge arcs against the sky as they fall, but no technical advance since *The Trail of the Lonesome Pine*. In the city sequences the lounge suits don't come out too badly, but there's an appalling orange taxi and the headlights of cars are curiously ugly. An attempt at fast cutting and quick dissolves confirms our belief that colour will put the film back technically twelve years.

The plot may roughly be described as a combination of *Romeo and Juliet* and *The Taming of the Shrew*. Katharina has become a Capulet, the Montagues and Capulets run rival timber companies, and Romeo has to do some taming as well as loving. But it is his loving which fascinated me. A wealthy young man fresh from Paris and the Riviera, he has earned a reputation as a wonderful quick worker with women, a breaker of hearts, an American Juan. His technique is interesting and perhaps national. We see a few flashes of it in a Paris lift and on the quayside at Cherbourg: he treads hard on a woman's foot and then apologizes or else he takes a crack at her ankle and catches her as she falls. The method never fails. When he meets Juliet-Katharina for the first time he remarks 'O boy, what a fuselage!' with his eye on her bust, and when he kisses her he says 'That went right down to the soles of my goloshes.' Irresistible in strong-toed shoes, he hacks his way to happiness.

It isn't a very good film, and Mr George Brent is hardly improved by blue-black Technicolor hair and a little Parisian moustache (next to the orange taxi he's the worst bit of colour in the picture). Far more interesting is the effect it has had on a veteran film critic. 'The thought of so much beauty of forest and mountain being ruthlessly destroyed,' Mr Sydney Carroll writes, 'almost broke my heart. These trees were treated so savagely. Their sufferings made me feel the need for a Society for the Prevention of Cruelty to Trees.' And Mr Carroll concludes his outburst, written on woodpulp which ought to account for a fair-sized sapling: 'I could not see this picture again. It would for this reason alone give me a heartache.'

'Captain Strogoff, the fate of Siberia is in your hands. Go for God, for Russia and the Tsar.' The words echo down the years from the caption of the early Mosjoukine film. Mosjoukine will be remembered as the player Pudovkin cites as an example to prove that acting was a matter of montage. Intercut Mosjoukine's face with a child's coffin and you got tragic acting. Intercut the same white turnip of countenance with charging cavalry and you had the heroic. Mr Anton Walbrook does a lot better than Mosjoukine in this new *Michael Strogoff*. As dashing and open-air as a good Western, this Jules Verne tale of a Tartar rising is motivated in the grand manner. A Grand Mission to save the Russian Empire; a Grand Sacrifice when the hero denies his mother; a Grand Courtesan who repents and dies grandly for love ('Do you not want to be a Quin?' the renegade Colonel – Mr Akim Tamiroff – whispers into her jewelled ear); even the Sensualities are Grand in a torture scene which begins with dancing-girls and ends with a white-hot sword. Simple, passionate and certainly sensuous, the whole thing is like a poem for boys, and not a bad poem either. If we cannot treat it quite seriously, it's because Russia, whether under Tsar or Stalin, remains incurably comic even in tragedy. 'To Omsk!' the renegade leader cries to his Tartars; 'I must get to Omsk,' the heroine piteously murmurs, and the hero, wounded and feverish in a peasant's hut, can find no better syllables to murmur than 'Irkutsk, Irkutsk.' How wise the Soviet policy of re-naming their cities – and how pathetically useless when 'Gorki' is the only substitute.   *Night and Day,* 15 July 1937

God's Country and the Woman (USA, Warner Bros, 1936). Director: William Keighley. George Brent, Beverley Roberts, Alan Hale.
Michael Strogoff (*The Soldier and the Lady*) (USA, RKO, 1937). Director: George Nicholls Jr. Anton Walbrook, Akim Tamiroff, Elizabeth Allen, Margot Grahame.

Parnell/Call it a Day

The fictional screen has never really got beyond wish-fulfilment dreams, and the only interest this week is in seeing the kind of wish-fulfilment the big film executives enjoy. In that light *Parnell* becomes almost interesting. At any rate it isn't shocking like *Call It a Day*, the close adaptation of Miss Dodie Smith's popular play, the day-dream of a good woman.

July 1937

Of course the first thing one notices about the Metro-Goldwyn-Mayer dream of how history should have happened is the absence of Parnell's beard. Pigott is allowed a beard (a magnificent spade-shaped affair in which there is ample room for two owls and a wren, five larks and a hen), but he's a villain. How exactly this beard-neurosis has arisen one cannot say. I think it may have something to do with the astrakhan coats film financiers wear: a kind of whisker-weariness.

Then, too, anything secretive, anything middle-aged, anything a little bit lecherous in the story has been eliminated. No illegitimate children, no assignations in seaside hotels under assumed names, no furtive vigils at Waterloo Station. In the divorce suit O'Shea hasn't a leg to stand on (it's just his dirty mind): the suit is followed immediately by Parnell's political overthrow and his death the same night. Far from any adulterous meetings the lovers are not even allowed to marry, and never in this film hangs the engraving of Lord Leighton's *Wedding* above the legalized bed. But poor though the picture may be, it is pleasing to think how clean a film magnate's wish-fulfilments are, how virginal and high-minded the tawdry pathetic human past becomes when the Mayers and Goldwyns turn the magic ring.

I'm a lot less happy about *Call It a Day*. A picture of one spring day in the life of an ordinary prosperous English family, full of characteristic touches about bathrooms and the cat kittening and how women can't be trusted to read *The Times* tidily, crowded with dreadfully recognizable details ('My dear, that's just how Henry behaves'), it might have been compiled from the sly diaries of members of the PEN Club. Good aunts or wives all, we know, whatever we may think at literary parties of their long incisors and prominent shoulderblades, but who would imagine, before seeing this film, of what *their* wish-fulfilments consist?

In this picture the middle-aged husband, a chartered accountant, is 'tempted' by an actress with whose income-tax he is dealing. She is the sort of vicious woman only a really unsullied female could invent, and sets to work on the traditional pair of steps as soon as she is alone with her man. Then it's no time at all before she's playing hot music to him after a little dinner in her flat. Follows the dirty look, the well-known phrase, 'Do you mind if I slip into something more comfortable?', the strategic retirement. But at this point the authoress's imagination wavered, or perhaps fear of being blackballed from the PEN checked her exuberant fancy, for to our astonishment the temptress reappeared in just another evening dress. Meanwhile, the wife, middle-aged but handsome in an aunt-like way, understanding and healthy minded, is ardently besieged at home by a man she only met at tea-time. Nobody, of course, gives way: but what agreeable titillations and temptations, what a Dodie dream of a world where all the heavy labour and the missed cues of infidelity are eliminated and the two-backed beast is trotted out quaintly, gaily and whimsically like a character in *Winnie the Pooh*.
Night and Day, 22 July 1937

Parnell (USA, M-G-M, 1936). Director: John M. Stahl. Clark Gable, Myrna Loy.
Call It a Day (USA, Warner Bros, 1937). Director: Archie Mayo. Olivia de Havilland, Ian Hunter, Bonita Granville.

The High Command/On the Avenue/Yiddle with his Fiddle

It isn't so often that the English cinema throws up a new director of promise – Mr Edmond Greville, whose *Secret Living* is being shown this week at the Paramount, had to go to France for his opportunity – and when a new face does appear among the old gang, it is often greeted with rotten vegetables. That the critic of so distinguished a paper as the *Sunday Times* should dismiss Mr Thorold Dickinson's *The High Command* in two glib sentences is rather shocking. 'As for *The High Command*, this is a picture made by Fanfare, a new British film company. Its avoidance of reality and its slowness make it a first-class soporific in this sultry weather.'

No one will deny that *The High Command* is full of faults. The story is wildly improbable: of an English officer who murders a man for chivalrous reasons in an Irish ambush, of how years later, as a Major-General in command of a West African fort, he finds his crime discovered and allows himself to be murdered in his turn so as to save his daughter from the disgrace. The first half of the film suffers from a slow, jerky and obscure script, and there is one unfortunate scene of unconscious humour when a villainous trader about to placate his wife with a pearl necklace is interrupted by an unexplained woman in a similar pearl necklace who pops silently through a window, gives a dirty smile and pops out again, like the horse in Mr James Thurber's story which was always putting its head through the drawing-room curtains. Then the sets sometimes reveal too obviously the strict economy with which the film was made (£30,000, including the cost of sending a unit to West Africa, is a remarkable bill to put beside the enormous expenditures of Denham). The devil's advocate indeed has plenty to play with in this picture, but a film critic should be capable of distinguishing, from the faults due to a poor story, an uncertain script and mere poverty, the very high promise of the direction.

Taking a tip perhaps from Duvivier and *Pépé le Moko*, Mr Dickinson establishes the West African scene at the start in a series of beautifully cut documentary shots, though I would have preferred a rather different choice of image from the picturesque market and the native hospital to represent the white civilization of the Coast. Tin roofs, maybe, and broken windows, long dreary bars and ants on the floor, vultures pecking like turkeys in arid back gardens.

What will remain longest in my memory is the little scene in the Club when the band breaks into 'God Save The King' for the Governor, just as the evening wind begins to blow: the black servants start towards the flapping shutters and banging doors and then, seeing the rigidity of their masters, leap to attention while the tune penetrates fitfully through the din of the Hammatan: 'happy and glorious', the potted palms bend towards the floor, the great green lights swing above the billiard-table, 'long to reign over us', the wind smashes through the clubroom and British West Africa comes alive as it never did in Mr Korda's lavish and unimaginative *Sanders of the River*.

There are other moments of direction one might expect a critic, however irritated by a stumbling script, to notice. The human crisis worked out in whispers as the native village dance reaches its climax, flames on the bystanders' faces, shaken spears, the polite accusation, and then the General's harsh order as he learns his secret is known, 'Put out those fires', the slow withdrawal of the two Africans behind the rising smoke after they have drenched the flames; the whole scene has a touch of lyric imagination one seeks in vain in most English films.

No musicals could be less alike than *On the Avenue* and *Yiddle with his Fiddle*. *On the Avenue* is a magnificently efficient, very entertaining piece of American routine work, only a little marred by Miss Madeleine Carroll's performance as the heroine. She has what must be, to all but the most blindly devoted keepers, the less endearing traits of a young elephant. We expect to see the sets rock a little beneath her stupendous coquetry, and we cannot help wondering whether

The High Command: Lucie Mannheim

Mr Dick Powell, with his little moustache and his laving hands, has the stamina to withstand her more-than-lifesize embrace. Handsome in a big way, given to intense proboscine whispers, she lends an impression of weight to every action, of awful fidelities to the lightest love ('an elephant never forgets'), but we don't want weight or fidelity in a musical comedy.

Nevertheless, it is a good film with some charming songs – 'I saw the girl I can never forget, on the cover of the Police Gazette', 'I can't remember a worse December', and a delightfully dreary and nostalgic piece about last year's kisses which the director, Roy del Ruth, astutely and with excellent effect throws away on a routine rehearsal, with men chewing gum and the hero busy revising a scene and no one paying the least attention to the deep belly-ache of the torch-song.

There are no torch-songs in *Yiddle with his Fiddle*, a Polish film made in Yiddish, a story as old as the hills about vagrant musicians and a girl who is dressed as a boy, with all the ancient situations – the bathe in the river, the bed in the barn – guyed with a lightness, a charm, a sense of poetry, a story in which even the music seems to have the dignity and patina of age and race. An odd feeling of freedom pervades the film full of ugly people in bowler-hats strumming in courtyards, walking through cornfields, dancing at weddings, freedom even from the close tyranny of a well-made script, as if the whole picture were an impromptu performance, like the stories in the *Decameron*, people of incredible accomplishment happy for a while among themselves on a hill-top while the world dies.

Night and Day, 29 July 1937

The High Command (GB, Fanfare, 1937). Director: Thorold Dickinson. James Mason, Lionel Atwill, Lucie Mannheim.
On the Avenue (USA, 20th Century-Fox, 1937). Director: Roy del Ruth. Dick Powell, Alice Faye, Madeleine Carroll, The Ritz Brothers.
Yiddle with his Fiddle (Poland, 1936). Directors: Joseph Green, Jan Nowina Przybylski. Mollie Picon, S. Fostel, M. Bozyk.

A Day at the Races/King Solomon's Mines

Of course the long vulpine stride of Groucho is still there, *ventre à terre* with a suitcase and an umbrella, Chico's piano-playing and Harpo's dumb pagan beauty – but there is so much else these days as well. The money is fairly splashed about; the capitalists have recognized the Marx Brothers; ballet sequences, sentimental songs ('Your eyes will tell me secrets your lips cannot say'), amber fountains, young lovers. *A Day at the Races* is a lot better than *A Night at the Opera*, it is easily the best film to be seen in London, but all the same I feel a nostalgia for the old cheap rickety sets, those titles as meaningless and undifferentiated as Kipling's, *Duck Soup* and *Horse Feathers*. I confess to a kind of perverse passion for Miss Maureen O'Sullivan (she satisfies a primeval instinct for a really nice girl), but what business has she in a wild Lear world where a veterinary doctor is in charge of a sanatorium, with Chico as handyman and Harpo – no room to tell why – as a jockey? Miss O'Sullivan is a *real* person – at least I have a dim idea that one met girls like her when one was adolescent; she is the archetype of 'a friend's sister'; but real people do more than retard, they smash the Marx fantasy. When Groucho lopes into the inane, they smile at him incredulously (being real people they cannot take him for granted), and there was one dreadful moment when Miss O'Sullivan murmured the word 'Silly.' Silly – good God, we cannot help exclaiming since we are real people too, have we been deceived all along? Are Groucho and Chico just silly and not poets of Edward Lear's stature?

> Sun-Up's the worst horse on the course.
> I've noticed he wins every race.
> That's only because he comes in first.

Silly? How horribly possible it sounds when we watch Miss O'Sullivan, and how thankful I felt that I was not in her company at the Surrealist Exhibition. Those charming, dewy and hygienic eyes would have taken all amusement out of an exhibit like the '*Virginal Slipper*' – the white dance-shoe, the piece of fungus and the contraceptive.

No, these revellers of the higher idiocy should not mingle with real people nor play before lavish scenery and an arty camera. Like the Elizabethans, they need only a chair, a painted tree. There *are* moments in this picture as good as there have ever been, and it is Harpo who shines the brightest, with his carved curls, his lunatic goodness, his air of having strayed out of Greek woods in his battered topper. I shall remember the short miming scene at night in the hedged garden where Harpo tries to convey to Chico that Groucho (Dr Hackenbush) has fallen for a woman and is about to be framed (it takes Chico a long time to understand the ritual of whistle and gesture – 'Dr Hackenbush has got an apple-dumpling?'), a scene oddly young and Shakespearian in its lunacy. And the scene when Harpo takes his pipe and leads a rabble of negro children from hut to hut, interrupting this black man tying his best tie, that black woman at her cooking, to the musical refrain, as the faun face peers in, 'Who dat man?', has an emotional effect he has never previously secured.

King Solomon's Mines must be a disappointment to anyone who like myself values Haggard's book a good deal higher than *Treasure Island*. Many of the famous characters are sadly translated. It remains a period tale, but where is Sir Henry Curtis's great golden beard (into which, it will be remembered, he muttered mysteriously 'fortunate' when he first met Allan Quartermain)? Mr Loder's desert stubble is a poor substitute. Umbopa has become a stout professional singer (Mr Robeson in fact) with a repertoire of sentimental lyrics, as un-African as his figure, written by Mr Eric Maschwitz. Worst crime of all to those who remember Quartermain's boast – 'I can safely say there is not a petticoat in the whole history' – is the introduction of an Irish blonde who has somehow become the cause of the whole expedition and will finish as Lady Curtis (poor Ayesha). Miss Anna Lee's performance is rather like one of Miss Carroll's seen through the wrong end of a telescope, with the large tortuous mouth, the intense whispers and the weighty coquetry.

Yet it is a 'seeable' picture. Sir Cedric Hardwicke gives us the genuine Quartermain, and Mr Roland Young, as far as the monocle and the white legs are concerned, is Captain Good to the life, though I missed the false teeth, 'of which he had two beautiful sets that, my own being none of the best, have often caused me to break the tenth commandment' (what a good writer Haggard was). The one-eyed black king Twala is admirable, the direction by Robert Stevenson well above the English average, the dovetailing of Mr Barkas's African exteriors with the studio sets better than usual, but I look back with regret to the old silent picture which was faithful to Haggard's story: I even seem to remember the golden beard.

Night and Day, 12 August 1937

A Day at the Races (USA, M-G-M, 1937). Director: Sam Wood. The Marx Brothers, Allan Jones, Maureen O'Sullivan.
King Solomon's Mines (GB, Gaumont British, 1937). Director: Robert Stevenson. John Loder, Cedric Hardwicke, Anna Lee, Roland Young, Paul Robeson.

Slave-Ship/Stradivarius/Woman Chases Man

This is the season of slow-motion emotions: Warner Baxter in *Slave-Ship* staring from his boat at back-cloth Africa (we still read in little books on the cinema: 'The film as compared with the play has the advantage of real backgrounds') registers his conscience coming on, and come on it does, reel after reel of it, as he flaps his heavy insomniac eyelids at Elizabeth Allen, saying, 'I tried to tell you, but I couldn't. . . . Will you ever find it possible to forgive?'; at the cabin-boy, remembering he slapped his face; at his friend and first officer whom he has just shot in the stomach: 'I didn't want to do it, Thomson. . . .'; flapping them stubbornly at the English court martial.

It isn't a bad film, it has excellent moments – seamen flinging knives from top-gallants and Wallace Beery as the soapy and mutinous mate, less soft-hearted than he has been for years, giving his finest performance since *Treasure Island*. The film story is by William Faulkner, the direction by Tay Garnett, the course seems set for distinction, but it remains a hot-weather picture: human relationships converge with the slowness and inevitability of pawns, though a film should consist of knight's moves only: the oblique jump, the unexpected encounter.

In *Stradivarius*, the worst film to be seen in London, we are so much ahead of the picture that we can come out, thank God, half-way through. A violin, which brings bad luck to all who own it, is left to a young Austrian army officer who takes it for valuation to a Professor. In his house he meets an Italian pupil-teacher (the year, of course, is 1914), and we watch an infinitely slow-motion love registering on Pierre Richard Willm's foxy features. The violin is an unsigned Stradivarius (dreadful hark-back to seventeenth-century Cremona and Stradivarius, in a little white sailor's cap, lifting a pointed nose and remarking pansily 'What does the reward matter? My dream is to liberate the voice that dwells within'). Then the Great War breaks out, and the rest of the picture is just hearsay to me. *Stradivarius* is full of sublimated sexuality and artistic abandon. 'I adore it', the heroine says, stroking the violin. 'It has such a tender note. . . .' People are always hearing violins played on the other side of doors and going into rapt attitudes in passages. It is packed with the awful gusto of the balletomane: the sweet Haskell-trained tooth, nourished on nougat and Nijinski, moistening at the sound of music.

Woman Chases Man is a blessed relief. Sex isn't sublimated, and the knights do move, jumping obliquely, landing the rich man and the out-of-work female architect drunk in a tree at midnight, and instead of gipsy orchestras, classical music, back projections of Budapest, Miriam Hopkins's sad volubility and her predatory and rewarding eyes. This picture is what *Easy Living* sets out to be, though *Easy Living* has the better subject: the huge importance in a moneyed world of the rich man's eccentric act. But *Easy Living* is too strenuously gay: people drop plates and fall cheerily downstairs on every foot of film. And it is the cheeriness which is wrong. As Chaplin learnt long ago, the man who falls downstairs must suffer if we are to laugh; the waiter who breaks a plate must be in danger of dismissal. Human nature demands humiliation, the ignoble pain and the grotesque tear: the madhouse for Malvolio.   *Night and Day,* 19 August 1937

Slave-Ship (USA, 20th Century-Fox, 1937). Director: Tay Garnett. Warner Baxter, Elizabeth Allen, Wallace Beery.

Stradivarius (*Stradivari*) (Germany, Boston-Film, 1935). Director: Geza von Bolvary. Pierre Richard Willm, Edwige Feuillère (French version); German version with Gustav Fröhlich, Sybille Schmitz.
Woman Chases Man (USA, Samuel Goldwyn, 1937). Director: John Blystone. Miriam Hopkins, Joel McCrea, Charles Winninger.

Saratoga/High, Wide and Handsome/His Affair

There is more than curiosity value in *Saratoga*, Miss Jean Harlow's last film which she didn't live to finish. A comedy of the race-tracks with Mr Clark Gable as a bookie, it has points of odd documentary interest: a yearling sale attended by Miss Harlow in a silver lamé evening dress, an amusement car in the Racing Special noisy with the innocent songs of men who in this country would be busy in the third-class carriages with packs of cards. At first one may be a little repelled by the unlikelihood of such enormous good-fellowship. The broad poster smile of 'The Old Firm' on a racing-card doesn't seem quite plausible in private life. But wait awhile and you'll find it's only the Rotarian smile after all. The bookie at the start may refuse payment of a fifty thousand dollar debt because it means foreclosing on a stud-farm which is the sole joy of somebody else's 'grandpop' (Mr Lionel Barrymore makes his usual blot on a not so virgin film), but his morality isn't as strict as that for long; he's quite crooked enough before the film's through to satisfy our passion for probability, wringing the dollars out of Miss Harlow's rich and unoffending fiancé, helped by Miss Harlow who double-crosses her fiancé by tipping the wrong horses. Later she has a quarrel with the bookie and double-crosses him, but that cross doesn't come off, the millionaire retires baffled by these bewildering moralities, and Mr Gable and Miss Harlow are left together in the happy expectation of a lifetime of false tips and bought jockeys. Tough and conscienceless, containing one admirable scene of carnal comedy with a nerve specialist, *Saratoga* is one of Miss Harlow's better films, though there is no sign that her acting would ever have progressed beyond the scope of the restless shoulders and the protuberant breasts: her technique was the gangster's technique – she toted a breast like a man totes a gun. The film has been skilfully sewn-up, and the missing scenes and shots lend it an air of originality which the correctly canned product mightn't have had: the story proceeds faster, less obviously: the heroine is less unduly plugged. The psychological transitions have a surface obscurity similar to those of living people, and not the steady movie progression from love to jealousy to reconciliation.

The old Irene Dunne, not the new groomed Dunne of *Theodora Goes Wild*, appears in *High, Wide and Handsome*. She plays a showgirl, oh so generous and unspoilt, in the 1850s who loves and marries a Pennsylvanian farmer. He discovers oil, gets too busy fighting the wicked railroad trusts, neglects her; so she goes back to the road and returns only in the nick of time with the elephants and trick-riders of her circus to defeat the hired toughs who are breaking up his pipe-lines. There are two hours of this long, dumb and dreary picture ('so good that it might have been inspired' – Mr Carroll); the story doesn't really get under way for an hour; and one is left with a few dim distressing memories: Miss Dunne splashing and kerning away in her bathtub while Mr Mamoulian's camera pans coyly round the kitchen, carefully avoiding her till it fetches up for climax on the glossy face and the shiny knees and the discreet soapsuds: Miss Dunne singing beside the farm horse (Miss Dunne is the one without the white patch on her forehead): a song by Mr Kern about 'Darby and Joan who used to be Jack and Jill', and masses of

His Affair: Brian Donlevy, Robert Taylor, Victor McLaglen

irrelevant Mamoulian blooms flowering at the right, the sentimental, time: nature panting to keep abreast with studio passions, flowering for first love and falling for separation.

His Affair, on the other hand, is exactly what a melodrama should be: the best American melodrama of the year, a tough story of bank-robbers set in Edwardian times to give it a light and spurious romance. The boater and the belted waist take the too-sweetness off the love, and we don't mind suspending the disbelief we should normally feel when the President of the United States personally sets a young naval officer to track down men his whole Secret Service has failed to catch, because we get so much in return: admirable acting by Mr Robert Taylor and Mr Victor McLaglen and quick and cunning direction which gives us from the first shot an expectation of the worst, so that this shocker does – however fallaciously – carry about it a sense of doom, of almost classic suspense in the skittle-alley and the music-hall.   *Night and Day,* 26 August 1937

Saratoga (USA, M-G-M, 1937). Director: Jack Conway. Jean Harlow, Clark Gable, Lionel Barrymore, Frank Morgan, Walter Pidgeon, Una Merkel.
High, Wide and Handsome (USA, Paramount, 1937). Director: Rouben Mamoulian. Irene Dunne, Randolph Scott, Dorothy Lamour, Alan Hale.
His Affair (*This Is My Affair*) (USA, 20th Century-Fox, 1937). Director: William A. Seiter. Robert Taylor, Victor McLaglen.

A Castle in Flanders/For You Alone

English films often enough have their scenes laid abroad, but the compliment is
infrequently returned. At the moment I can recall only that delightful picture
Sans Famille, in which a troop of London police, small men with sloping shoulders
wearing curious helmets which fell low over the eyes, drew their truncheons to
pursue juvenile offenders through the London fog. The German director of *A
Castle in Flanders* has really returned good for evil. For all the ruthless militarists
in monocles, the sentimental inn-keepers, the student princes and the Schuberts
in lilac time, he offers us a romantic and aristocratic England where a man falls in
love (a love of Nordic depth and fidelity) with a singer called Gloria Delamarre
merely from hearing her voice on a gramophone record; an England where a
gentleman must take the blame – and go to Australia – for a forgery he hasn't
committed, to save a woman's name. It isn't *our* England, and yet we are haunted
by an odd sense that somehow we know this fairy-tale place, that we've been
here before. It isn't only that the officers in the prologue, listening to the gramophone while the shells burst over Ypres, smoke pipes to the English manner born
(the sturdy word while the thumb prods the bowl, the pat-pat on the pocket
feeling for the pouch); nor can we be misled by the oddly wrong taxis with huge
luggage-racks like howdahs, nor by the sight of Tower Bridge through the window
of an aristocratic study. This *is* a place we know, and at last when the hero is
vindicated, when Gloria Delamarre has got her man, we realize this is the England
of the early tattered Tauchnitzes on continental bookstalls (2271. Rita: *Introduced
to Society*; 3243. Alexander, Mrs: *Barbara, Lady's Maid and Peeress*; 3617.
Norris, W. E.: *Lord Leonard the Luckless*). Writers have often been called their
country's ambassadors abroad; but from what a curious diplomatic service they
are usually recruited.

Yet this picture has merits: there are excellent scenes in dark wet post-war
Ypres: the little stuffy hotel where every room is booked when Gloria Delamarre
arrives; the leering porter who directs her to a neighbouring castle; and by the
fireplace, where the pipes were prodded years ago and the gramophone ground,
what we believe to be the ghost of the English officer last seen at zero hour. The
ambiguous atmosphere is admirably maintained; it is when the hero turns out
not to be a ghost at all that we lose interest and the film reality. There remain some
songs of the Ho-ho-ho-Ha type only too adequately sung by Miss Marta Eggerth,
who has been well groomed this time – a very necessary grooming to prevent
confusion, for Miss Eggerth used to look a ghost herself, her pale blonde features
shading off into her background, so that you could never be quite certain where
her face ended and the tallboy began.

I prefer her to Miss Grace Moore. Miss Moore, even in trousers singing 'Minnie
the Moocher', can make the craziest comedy sensible and hygienic. In *For You
Alone*, the story of an Australian singer who buys an American husband in Mexico
so that she may re-enter the States where her permit has expired, Mr Riskin, the
author of *Mr Deeds* and (let's forget it) *Lost Horizon*, has tried his best to write
crazily, but he comes up all the time against Miss Moore. That friendly, genteel
and frolicsome personality would be more at home among blackboards and the
smell of chalk and dusters and the dear children. If you want to escape from a

cinema where Miss Moore is playing – I always do – before the end, you feel impelled to raise a hand and wait for permission to leave the room.

Night and Day, 2 September 1937

A Castle in Flanders (*Das Schloss in Flandern*) (Germany, Tobis-Magna-Film, 1936). Director: Geza von Bolvary. Marta Eggerth, Paul Hartmann, Georg Alexander, Otto Wernicke.
For You Alone (*When You're in Love*) (USA, Columbia, 1937). Director: Robert Riskin. Grace Moore, Cary Grant.

Marked Woman

'It's feudal,' a character remarks with resignation in *Marked Woman,* and there are moments of creative imagination (vivid enough to have suffered British censorship) in this picture of the night-club racket and the night-club baron which do convey some of the horror and pathos the Anglo-Saxon chronicler recorded of Stephen's reign: the exactions, the beatings and murders, and above all the hopelessness. We remember Faustus' questions and Mephistopheles' replies.

> Where are you damned?
> In Hell.
> How comes it then that thou art out of Hell?
> Why, this is Hell, nor am I out of it.

The time is 3.30 in the morning and the cars drawn up outside the Club Intime; the new boss with the lined scorched face of Eduardo Ciannelli taking a look round while his henchman gives his pekinese an airing (the air's too stale inside for a dog), issuing his orders to the dancing partners (he owns every club in town: there's no escape); the trailing of the long evening gowns down the pavement to the shabby digs as the milkman goes his rounds; the routine murder of a young man who has paid with a phoney cheque; the impregnability of the baron in his tenth-floor flat with his seedy lawyers. It's been done before, of course, this picture of the feudal hell, but it has never been done better than in some of these scenes: the awful contrast between the Rotarians' liquored cheerfulness in the early hours with the bad champagne and the sentimental songs, and the next morning, when one of them has been found dead in the river, and the little sober shamefaced group drifts into the police-station to identify their dance companions; the spirituous poetics of the middle-aged lecher in the roof-garden – 'Those stars . . . they remind me . . . that moon, you've only to ask me for that. . . .' between the nuzzlings of the big grey moustache. Ciannelli lends distinction to any film: he can convey not only corruption but the sadness of corruption: the mind in – unpolitical – chains. But it is unfortunate so many of us said once that Miss Bette Davis was potentially a great actress, for now she plugs the emotions with dreadful abandonment. Only once does she really get across: in the horrifying scene of her beating up by the pervert henchman Charlie (her sister has been murdered and the worm tries to turn).

Night and Day, 9 September 1937

Marked Woman (USA, Warner Bros, 1937). Director: Lloyd Bacon. Bette Davis, Humphrey Bogart, Eduardo Ciannelli.

Action for Slander/Brief Ecstasy

Mr Victor Saville is one of the few directors who bring something of value out of Denham, and *Action for Slander* is a picture of which we needn't feel ashamed if it reaches the United States, even though the story is novelettish in the extreme. Mr Clive Brook, falsely accused of cheating at cards by a brother officer whose wife he has pursued, suffers as only Mr Brook can suffer: the routine of suffering, suffering in *Cavalcade*, suffering in *Shanghai Express*, suffering in a hundred feature films, has indelibly lined his not very expressive face. In *Action for Slander* he suffers all the time with immense virtuosity, smelling a little of tweeds and pipe-smoke. His wife leaves him, he is slandered at a house-party, the rumour gets about and he suffers in the club, in the mess, in a four-shilling bed-and-breakfast hotel (last degradation for an officer and a gentleman and quite sufficient to bring his wife hurrying back); he brings an action and suffers in the law-courts (the legal procedure here is very odd, and Mr Morton Selton is badly miscast as the Judge – why not Billy Bennett while they are about it?); then the film snaps quickly to a close before he can be asked to do anything else but suffer. Yet Mr Saville has made something out of this unpromising material: people on the whole behave naturally – and shabbily – in rather Galsworthian circumstances: the wife leaves her husband without fuss: the tactical moves in adultery are played between shots at pheasants. The Denham love scene for once is not written in.

We need not feel ashamed of *Action for Slander*, but we can feel proud of *Brief Ecstasy*, directed by Mr Edmond Greville for a small English company, Phoenix Films. It must have cost only about a third as much as *Action for Slander*, but the producer Mr Hugh Perceval, has learnt to wring twenty shillings' worth out of every pound. The subject is sexual passion, a rarer subject than you would think on the screen, and the treatment is adult: there isn't, thank God, any love in it. In *Action for Slander*, of course, there's a hint of adultery, but the characters have really little more sex-life than amoebas. They haven't time, poor things, mixed up all the while in elaborate plots: card-games, false accusations, law-courts. Mr Greville's story is the simplest possible – a young man picks up a girl, sleeps with her, goes to India: she marries a middle-aged scientist and four years later the young man turns up; the story is of the struggle between tenderness and sexual desire. With so bare a plot Mr Greville has time to dwell on everything other directors cut: the 'still-lifes': the husband's trousers laid pedantically in the press, while the wife beautifies herself in the bathroom for nothing at all. Other directors have to 'get on with the story'. Mr Greville knows that the story doesn't matter; it's the atmosphere which counts, and the atmosphere – of starved sexuality – is wantonly and vividly conveyed. Mr Greville learnt in France how to photograph a woman's body – uncompromisingly: every close-up of Miss Linden Travers drives the sexuality home: a leg in the library, buttocks over the billiard-table. We can leave 'characters' to the stage (the jealous housekeeper in this picture would be more at home there): the film at its finest – in the acting of Garbo and Chaplin or in the direction of Pudovkin – generalizes, and Miss Linden Travers sprawling across the bed behind her locked door, sobbing with passion while the man she wants hammers to come in, represents any human being under the ugly drive of undifferentiated desire.   *Night and Day,* 16 September 1937

Marked Woman: Mayo Methot, Bette Davis, Carlos San Martin

Action for Slander: Ann Todd, Clive Brook

Action for Slander (GB, London Films, 1937). Director: Victor Saville. Clive Brook, Enid Stamp-Taylor, Percy Marmont.
Brief Ecstasy (GB, I.F.P., 1937). Director: Edmond T. Greville. Linden Travers, Hugh Williams.

Knight Without Armour/Café Metropole

One had thought it was good-bye to M. Feyder when he entered the gates of the Denham studios: one began to write the obituary of the director of *Thérèse Raquin* and *La Kermesse Héroïque*. The news that Mr ('Hungarian') Biro and Mr ('Naughty') Wimperis were responsible for the scenario and dialogue: the sight of Miss Dietrich floodlit before well-advertised crowds at first nights: a New York première – followed by months of silence: rumours of gigantic expenditure – some put it at over £300,000: all prepared us for the traditional Denham mouse.

But – astonishingly – a first-class thriller has emerged, beautifully directed, with spare and convincing dialogue and a nearly watertight scenario (only marred by a bath and a bathe in the Naughty Wimperis vein). The story, of course, is melodrama, but melodrama of the most engaging kind, the heroic wish-fulfilment dream of adolescence all the world over – rescues, escapes, discarnate embraces. A young Englishman, who translates novels for a Russian publisher in pre-war St Petersburg, is ordered by the police to leave the country because of an indiscreet magazine-article. Instead he joins the British Secret Service, takes on with beard and passport a Revolutionary personality and is condemned to Siberia after a bomb outrage of which, naturally, he is innocent. From this point his second personality has complete control: as an Englishman he is dead. War is followed by Revolution and he becomes automatically and will-lessly a hero of the new Russia, a Commissar. He is entrusted with the job of taking an important prisoner, a Countess, to Petrograd. He lets her escape, she is recaptured, he saves her again: White prisoners fall to Red machine-guns and Red prisoners to White and White to Red again, a kaleidoscope of murder: we get the impression, so difficult to convey on the screen, of almost interminable time and almost illimitable distance, of an escape along the huge corridors of a prison an Asiatic empire wide. Mr Robert Donat as the stubbornly chivalrous Englishman deserves more than the passing tribute we accord to a director's dummy. Mr Donat is the best film actor – at any rate in star parts – we possess: he is convincing, his voice has a pleasant roughness, and his range is far greater than that of his chief rival for film honours, Mr Laurence Olivier. Mr Olivier's burnt-out features, his breaking voice require the emotional situation all the time; he wants all Blackfriars to rant in: he must have his drowned Ophelia, his skull and sword-play. Mr Donat is sensible, authentic, slow; emotion when it comes has the effect of surprise, like plebeian poetry.

There is one sequence in *Knight Without Armour* which should take its place among the classic moments of the screen – the student of Prague in the old silent days running down from the wood to the duelling-place and meeting his second self coming up with dripping sword between the trees; the perambulator bouncing down Odessa steps: the lovers in Von Stroheim's *Greed* walking down the long breakwater between the grey seas under the drenching rain. The English Commissar with his prisoner has reached a small wayside station: the station-master tells him a train is due, and presently his repeated call 'Train No. 671. All aboard for Petrograd' brings the Englishman from the waiting-room to an avenue of empty line and the station-master striding beside an imaginary express repeating his mad parrot cry, while the soundtrack grinds with his proud and gleeful dream. Beautifully shot, adeptly written and finely acted by Mr Hay Petrie as the station-master (Mr Petrie enriches every picture in which he appears) the scene owes a great deal of its authenticity to Mr Donat's quiet stocky personality. And how Mr Olivier would have torn into haunted neurotic tatters a later scene in the waiting-room when the Commissar recites to his prisoner a poem of Browning's ('Fear Death? To feel the fog in my throat. . . .') and the Red soldiers pass across the window come to rape and murder. Mr Olivier's acting is of the nerves: it demands an audience and a partner: Mr Donat's acting is so calculated that no tape-measure from nose to lens, no studio rabble of make-up men and continuity girls, no fourth 'repeat' from the director affects it. And as to a partner – he has in this picture to do without, for Miss Dietrich never acts. She lends her too beautiful body: she consents to pose: she is the marble motive for heroisms and sacrifices: as for acting – that is merely the word for what goes on all round her: she leaves it to her servants.

But the measure of Feyder's achievement cannot really be judged from this film: one must take into account the failure of his predecessors at Denham after who knows what internecine conflicts with a producer who can pick men but cannot delegate responsibility – M. Clair, Mr William K. Howard, the lost adventurers, his peers. No Denham stamp has obliterated his private signature – the very rare use of long shots – long shots used like close-ups to punch an effect home, not as by most directors to get through the duller parts of a narrative. To me the most aesthetically satisfying of all cinematic shots is – in rough script terms – the medium close shot, and this is the distance at which Feyder remains consistently from his characters: close enough for intimacy and far enough for art.

It is instructive, after Feyder's picture, to visit *Café Metropole*. Here is a very amusing script, admirable acting by Mr Menjou, Miss Loretta Young and Mr Tyrone Power, all thrown away by inferior direction: the wrong angle, the ugly shot, the cluttered set, so that the faces of the characters have to be distinguished from a fog of furnishing (a nose disentangled from a picture-frame, a dowager's hair from the window curtains), and the camera is planked down four-square before the characters like a plain, honest, inexpressibly dull guest at a light and loony party. *Night and Day,* 30 September 1937

Knight Without Armour (GB, London Films, 1937). Director: Jacques Feyder. Marlene Dietrich, Robert Donat, John Clements.
Café Metropole (USA, 20th Century-Fox, 1937). Director: Edward H. Griffith. Loretta Young, Tyrone Power, Adolphe Menjou.

The Road Back/Gangway

The Road Back, adapted from a novel by Herr Remarque, is meant to be a grim picture of the kind of life to which the German soldier returned from the trenches in 1918: starvation, revolution and the family tragedies of infidelity. It opens in the trenches, with the one imaginative scene in the whole film when the wild geese pass over no-man's-land and their drumming is taken for a gas warning and the old soldier (Slim Summerville, hopelessly miscast) remarks 'They'll be in Egypt for the week-end.' Apart from this minute in the hundred minutes it's an awful film, one big Mother's Day, celebrated by American youth, plump, adolescent faces with breaking sissy voices. Voices which began to break in the trenches – remembering the kid sister or watching a companion die – are still breaking an hour and a quarter later and the film's not over yet. We've lived through a lot in that time, but not through war, revolution, starvation – but through 'Can you turn me a little so I can see you go down the road?' and the young fleshy face is turned away from the dying friend to hide the drip of tears; French girls dancing in a barn and crying 'O-la-la'; the sudden and puzzling inability of the whole cast of so-called Germans to speak their native American to a company of Yankee soldiers they meet on the road (even Slim Summerville is rendered speechless); love scenes in Teutonic beer-houses – 'You are just as I've been dreaming of you all these years.' Like Buchman boys starved of confession they break out on the moral front – 'There's one more battle to be fought. I must find myself.' And always all the time the breaking voices, the unformed unlined faces and the well-fed bodies of American youth, clean-limbed prize-cattle mooing into the microphone. They call it an all-star cast and that always means there isn't a single player of any distinction to be picked out of the herd.

It might be funny if it wasn't horrifying. This is America seeing the world in its own image. There is a scene in which the returned soldiers all go back to their school. Sitting in uniform on the benches they are addressed by the Headmaster; they start their lessons again where they left off – it may be meant as irony (I'm not sure), but what it really emphasizes is the eternal adolescence of the American mind, to which literature means the poetry of Longfellow and morality means keeping Mother's Day and looking after the kid sister's purity. One came daunted out of the cinema and there, strolling up the Haymarket, dressed up in blue uniforms with little forage-caps and medals clinking, were the American Legionaries, arm in arm with women dressed just the same – all guide-books, glasses, and military salutes: caps marked Santa Anna and Minnesota: hair – what there was of it – grey, but the same adolescent features, plump, smug, sentimental, ready for the easy tear and the hearty laugh and the fraternity yell. What use in pretending that with these allies it was ever possible to fight for civilization? For Mother's Day, yes, for anti-vivisection and humanitarianism, the pet dog and the home fire, for the co-ed college and the campus. Civilization would shock them: eyes on the guide-book for safety, they pass it quickly as if it were a nude in a national collection.

Miss Jessie Matthews has only once been properly directed – by Mr Victor Saville. Mr Sonnie Hale, whatever his qualities as a comedian, is a pitiably amateurish director and as a writer hardly distinguished. The best one can say of *Gangway* is that it is better than his previous picture. It is a comedy about a Scotland Yard detective (acted with repulsive boyishness by Mr Barry Mackay – he should have been in *The Road Back*) and a newspaper reporter (Miss Matthews) and it develops, about three-quarters of the way through, into a passable shocker when American gangsters mistake the reporter for one of the old school, an international jewel thief. It is Mr Alastair Sim, however, as an insurance detective who really saves the film. Horrifying passions pent in his twisting secretive body, Mr Sim always shatters illusion right and left. His acting, unctuous with Nonconformity, demands other characters too that are larger than life, or else ones like these so dim they don't disturb the dreadful and comic dream. As for Miss Matthews she isn't given a chance. Her figure like an exaggerated and Voguish advertisement is oddly asexual: coquetry – much less love – should never be demanded of her. When she dances – attractive and ungainly – it should be by herself; no dance of hers should end in the sentimental lyric and the labial embrace.

Night and Day, 7 October 1937

The Road Back (USA, Universal, 1937). Director: James Whale. John King, Slim Summerville, Andy Devine.
Gangway (GB, Gaumont British, 1937). Director: Sonnie Hale. Jessie Matthews, Barry Mackay, Alastair Sim.

Big City/Tales from the Vienna Woods/Children at School

It has been a bad week in the commercial cinema – *Big City* and *Tales from the Vienna Woods*. I think it is just possible to sit through the first, thanks to Borzage, the sentimental but competent director who made *Seventh Heaven*. Spencer Tracy plays a taxi-driver, Luise Rainer his foreign wife. In a war between a taxi combine and the independent owners a bomb is thrown, a man killed, the woman framed. Though she is the wife of an American, by United States law the woman can be deported because she hasn't been in the country three years. If the drivers can hide her another six weeks from the police she'll be safe. Pathos accumulates. She is going to have a baby, she gives herself up when her friends are arrested for sheltering her, harrowing farewell in a steerage cabin, last-minute release. Domesticity and tenderness are heavily laid on: people in this film are *too* happy before disaster: no one is as happy as all that, no one so little prepared for what life is bound to do sooner or later. One remembers with how few shots Lang in *Fury* established the deep affection between his characters: the shop-window gazing in the rain, the torn macintosh sewn up on the platform. This good-bye while the detectives wait in the corridor and the drabs watch from the other bunks is moving, of course, but one resents being moved by so exorbitant an agony – the eight-berth metal cabin, the imminent labour, the permanence of the separation – the woman bound for some central European village, the husband without the money to follow her.

173

October 1937

Tales from the Vienna Woods is an Austrian film and you know what that means: it means Magda Schneider's deep-sunk eyes and porcine coquetry; courtyards where everyone in turn picks up a song as they mend cars, clean windows, wash clothes; a festival in a beer-garden with old Viennese costumes, balloons, slides, laughter, and driving home at dawn in a fiacre; Magda Schneider's trim buttocks and battered girlishness; a musical tour of Vienna – no sign, of course, of the Karl Marx Hof, only palaces and big Baroque dictatorial buildings; Magda Schneider's mouth wide open – rather too much gum like a set of false teeth hung up outside a cheap dentist's. Leo Slezak with his magnificent buffoonery tries to save the film, but Austrian films are born dead: horrible bright fakes from a ruined country, libellous laughter.

The Gas Light and Coke Company – uncompromising and gritty name – provide the only relief from these gay and gloomy fictions. They have followed up their excellent nutrition film of last year with an even better documentary, *Children at School*, directed by Mr Basil Wright with a commentary by the Editor of *The Spectator*. It begins a little untidily with the Parthenon (only because the commentary refers to Plato), it reverts too often to Mr Wilson Harris's modulated and Liberal features, his discreet tie-pin, and Lady Astor tries to storm Hollywood with untimely histrionics, but these are the only serious criticisms to be made against a film with the exciting lyrical quality one admired in Mr Wright's *Song of Ceylon*. The picture starts with a comparison between State education in England and that of the Dictatorship countries ('Drill the children, school them into believing that the Dictator is always right'). It presents first the new type of Infant and Nursery Schools – romantically in terms of sunlight, of absorbed and brooding infant faces, of a child by a blackboard telling an obscure Surrealist tale to his class about a policeman, a man with a sword. . . . The romantic movement reaches a lovely and nostalgic climax as the camera sweeps a huge grass plain, children exercising, playing games, a sense of freedom in the bright wide air, while high immature voices are overlaid in a traditional hymn, overlaid across open windows, gymnasium, changing-room. ('O les voix d'enfants chantant dans la coupole.') Then the realistic movement, the reminder that hell too lies about us in our infancy. A small child hurries down a dreary concrete passage, while from behind a door comes a voice reciting the rich false lines – 'And softly through the silence beat the bells along the Golden Road. . . .' Cracks in the ceilings and the beams, damp on the walls, hideous Gothic exteriors of out-of-date schools, spiked railings, narrow windows, scarred cracked playgrounds of ancient concrete: AD 1875 in ecclesiastical numerals on a corner-stone: the wire dustbin, the chipped basin, the hideous lavatory-seat and the grinding of trains behind the school-yard. Teachers with drawn neurotic faces flinching at the din: two classes to a room: conferences of despairing masters – the thin-lipped face, the malformed intellectual night-school skull, the shrewish voice of the cornered idealist as he reports progress to his colleagues – a new set of desks.

For the second time this commercial company has done the Health Ministry's work. It is just as well: a politician is professionally an optimist: he has the cheery complacency of the salesman (listen to Mr Chamberlain in a week or two); and in spite of its romantic first movement this is not an optimistic or a complacent picture.   *Night and Day*, 14 October 1937

Big City (USA, M-G-M, 1937). Director: Frank Borzage. Spencer Tracy, Luise Rainer.
Tales from the Vienna Woods (*G'schichten aus dem Wiener wald*) (Austria, Mondial International, 1934). Director: Georg Jacoby. Magda Schneider, Leo Slezak, Georg Alexander.
Children at School (GB, Realist Film Unit, 1937). Director: Basil Wright. Commentary spoken by Wilson Harris.

174

Les Perles de la Couronne/Exclusive

It is not easy to review M. Guitry's films – so much depends on the effect of M. Guitry's personality. To me it is always, at the beginning of a picture, before the charm works, a little repulsive: the rather fleshy figure seems to have been ripened by so many Riviera suns; so many years of popular applause have contributed to the flat arrogance of the voice: he seems the image of that superb Gallic complacency which drove Henry James from Paris. There is more than a touch of astrakhan. . . . Late in life he has taken light-heartedly to the cinema, breaking every rule, using – in *Bonne Chance* – the most outrageous wipes successfully. Successfully: there's the rub. There is some jealousy in our distaste. Everything seems to have come to him so easily. He behaves outrageously, accepting none of the dogmas we have chosen as guides through the awful un-Aristotelean waste of this Semitic and commercial craft. But he is no revolutionary. The rules remain rules for all of us but M. Guitry. The impertinence of it!

So I find myself driven back to the personal statement – that I was delighted by *Bonne Chance* (but how far as an aphrodisiac?); that *Le Roman d'un Tricheur*, with its silent miming and continuous Guitry, rather bored me; that *Les Perles de la Couronne*, callous, impudent, disregarding all continuity, entertained me even more than it irritated me. One can generalize about M. Guitry's personality, not about his films or his ideas. He is quite without integrity.

Perhaps the experiment in his latest film has more general value than usual: ingeniously he attempts to give a wider circulation to a French picture by working the story out in three languages – French, English and Italian according to the characters, with the essential clues to understanding expressed in every language (I suppose to a really accomplished linguist the tale would seem unbearably repetitive). Unfortunately, others have not taken the opportunity M. Guitry gives them for eliminating the tiresome sub-title. Even when M. Guitry has cunningly and quite naturally arranged that an English telephone-girl, listening in at a switch-board, should translate to a friend a conversation which is being carried on in French, we are not spared sub-titles to make the conversation clearer still.

The story – a fantastic tale constructed round the four pearls in the English crown and three missing pearls which once formed part of the same necklace – starts in the reign of Henry VIII, Clement VII and Francis I, and ends in the *Normandie* at Southampton, with the last of the missing pearls slipping from M. Guitry's grasp and falling through the water, nuzzled by curious fishes, until it sinks appropriately into the open shell of an oyster. M. Guitry plays Francis, Napoleon III, and a writer of our own day, and Mlle Delubac is consistently beautiful as Marie Stuart, Josephine Beauharnais and the writer's wife.

Exclusive is a routine film of American newspaper life. Charlie Ruggles – it has been looming on us for a long time – acts a tragic part, that of an old-style journalist whose daughter rats on him and joins a rival paper owned by a racketeer. It should be tough enough – an honest politician commits suicide in front of the girl after she has dug up his past record for her scandal sheet, a lift at a department store crashes with a load of women and children (a good scene this), and Ruggles bleeds to death across his typewriter after saving his daughter from the gangster – but curiously enough the general impression is one of slow old-fashioned sentiment. In the tough race it falls behind – it can't make the 1937 speed in murder, and the result, like lavender, is not unagreeable. I liked the dying lines of the old journalist to his daughter: 'Just state the facts in the simplest words you can find. Make your paragraphs short.' But the smell of lavender became rather too overpowering at the curtain: 'There's a heaven somewhere for old used-up newspapermen, and Pop's up there looking down, thinking we've done a good job.'

In the same programme there was a little film in technihorror of a Schubert symphony: it revealed, so we were told, the pictures which must have passed through the composer's brain. They were odd pictures under the circumstances: an Alsatian dog, a mountain in the Rockies, a sunset, the sea, and, most puzzling of all, a blond American youth wearing an open-necked shirt and carrying his sports coat over his arm. He never dropped the coat, though most of the time he was singing to a girl in evening dress in a garden. It hung there, over the left arm, carefully folded while he kissed her. Then the mountain again, the sunset, the sea, but not the dog. There seems to have been some Freudian censorship in Schubert's mind over the dog: it only slipped through once. *Night and Day*, 21 October 1937

Les Perles de la Couronne (France, Cinéas, 1937). Director: Sacha Guitry. Sacha Guitry, Jaqueline Delubac. [US title: *Pearls of the Crown.*]
Exclusive (USA, Paramount, 1937). Director: Alexander Hall. Charles Ruggles, Fred MacMurray, Frances Farmer.

Wee Willie Winkie/The Life of Emile Zola

See Appendix, page 276.

Wee Willie Winkie: C. Aubrey Smith, Shirley Temple

More pompous than *Pasteur* and far more false, the theme of *The Life of Emile Zola* is supposed to be truth – but truth to the film mind is the word you see on news-posters. We begin in 1862 with Zola starving in a garret with Cézanne who keeps on popping up irrelevantly from then on. Zola meets Nana, and soon she is giving him her diaries and her letters, but not – what apparently Zola particularly wants – a baby's vest. ('Take all, all but this.') Then Cézanne pokes his head round the door, and Zola writes *Nana* which is an enormous success. (He had really, of course, been a successful writer for about eighteen years before he wrote *Nana*.) Then suddenly – everything in this picture happens suddenly including Cézanne – comes war. Soldiers in the street; a woman says 'Where are they all going?' and a man says 'Haven't you heard? War's been declared.' Zola says 'Never did I think I should live to see France grovelling in the dust under the German heel.' Cézanne pokes his head round the door – or doesn't he? Anyway the war's over. Zola's middle aged at Meudon, though his wife's not changed at all. Cézanne looks round the door again. 'The old struggling carefree days.' He takes an ugly look at the majolica and starts away. 'Paul, will you write?' 'No, but I will remember.' Then the Dreyfus case, and on the night before Dreyfus's rehabilitation Zola – he's an old man now – dies (it's more than un-studio, it's un-American to live another two years). Paul Muni acts Zola – quaintly, and lots of old friends turn up in fancy-dress but quite themselves as the Governor of Paris, Clemenceau, Colonel Piquart, Count Esterhazy.   *Night and Day*, 28 October 1937

Wee Willie Winkie (USA, 20th Century-Fox, 1937). Director: John Ford. Shirley Temple, C. Aubrey Smith, Victor McLaglen, Cesar Romero.
The Life of Emile Zola (USA, Warner Bros, 1937). Director: William Dieterle. Paul Muni, Joseph Schildkraut, Donald Crisp.

The Life of Emile Zola: Paul Muni, Erin O'Brien-Moore

They Won't Forget/Nitchevo

Occasionally a film of truth and tragic value gets somehow out of Hollywood on to the screen. Nobody can explain it – perhaps a stage needs using, all the big executives are in conference over the latest Mamoulian 'masterpiece' – Jehovah is asleep, and when he wakes he finds he's got a *Fury* on his hands, worse still *They Won't Forget*. Worse because Lang is a showman as well as a great director: he knows how to get his mixture down: he gives the melodramatic close, the happy ending, and the executives, after the first shock, discover a success. But I doubt whether *They Won't Forget* will have the same success – it hasn't in this country. It's a better, less compromising story than *Fury* – taken as a whole a better picture, though Mervyn LeRoy isn't in Lang's class.

It is the story of a murder trial run by an ambitious District Attorney for political reasons (Mr Claude Rains gives his finest performance to date). It takes place in the South and the South has banned the picture. A girl in a business college is found murdered on Commemoration Day – again the picture is uncompromising, she isn't a lay figure, the audience see enough of her before her death, young, quiet and vital, to feel the shock of her murder. The police at first settle on the negro janitor of the building, but the District Attorney isn't satisfied. Beat a negro up enough and, innocent or guilty, he'll confess – it's too easy, it's unspectacular. The Attorney's a stranger and he has the Governorship in mind, and so a young teacher in the school – who has come down with his wife from the North – is charged. He was in the building, there is a spot of blood on the jacket he sent to the cleaners, the girl was in love with him – but above all, of course, he's a Northerner. 'Sell prejudice angle,' the tape-machines of the newspapers tap out continually: the trial becomes a sensational sporting event: a detective is sent by a Northern newspaper and is beaten up by a Southern mob: a well-known New York counsel arrives and conducts the defence with cynical and heartless efficiency to get the spotlight on the prejudice and hang his client: the rival mothers are flung into the arena. The Attorney, tie off, sweating in braces down the ranks of the jury while electric fans hum and the Judge smokes a pipe and the audience applaud, wins all along the line; the man is – inevitably – found guilty; the Governor, an honest man, commutes the sentence to life imprisonment and ruins his career; a mob take the young man from the train which is carrying him to the State prison and lynch him; the Attorney's well on his way to the Senate. In the last shot the Attorney and the newsman who has supported him watch the widow go down the street – 'I wonder if he was guilty?' The doubt is valuable – we are not sold the usual story of the innocent man. The evidence was heavy against the teacher, the Attorney was not completely unscrupulous – we are dealing with human beings. The direction of the picture is brilliant, the cameraman agilely snapping the wife as she falls in a faint at the news of her husband's arrest; the last scene of the lynching with the down-line express sweeping by and extinguishing the screams, snatching from the gallows-shaped erection by the line the small bundle of the mail-bag. If it makes a little less impression than Lang's more melodramatic story it is because Lang has a finer talent for expressing human relationships; we are never so close to the married pair as we were to the garage-man and his girl; relationships give the last twist to the agony – and we are spared that here.

Nitchevo has a bad story – and a very obscure one; it boils down in the end to the usual situation of French naval films – elderly officer with young wife; arrival of junior officer who once – platonically – served her in a sensational but not discreditable past; unreasonable mystifications; arrival of gunrunner and blackmail; 'Bring me the news of your husband's consent at the Pacha ball'; 'Your wife can at this moment be found at the house of Lieutenant. . . .' But the picture is worth a visit for the final situation in a sunk submarine and for the acting of M. Harry Baur. Those features – of an old reptile which has learnt all the secrets the jungle can offer – can adapt themselves with perfect naturalness to any profession. A submarine commander, a police officer, a Kulak – M. Baur always seems about his proper unsensational business.   *Night and Day*, 4 November 1937

They Won't Forget (USA, Warner Bros, 1937). Director: Mervyn LeRoy. Claude Rains, Allan Joslyn. *Nitchevo* (France, Méga Film, 1937). Director: Jacques de Baroncelli. Harry Baur, Marcelle Chantal, Georges Rignaud.

Land Without Bread/Personality Parade

'First will I question with thee about Hell. . . .' Two films shown last Sunday by the Film Society were enough to shake anyone's complacency or self-pity: they followed each other in the programme with horrifying force: *Land Without Bread*, a five-year-old documentary study of the Hurdanos, a Spanish people inbred, diseased, forgotten, the adjective 'poor' a mockery of their complete destitution, and *Personality Parade*, a deft little dramatization of one day in the life of Mr Godfrey Winn.

Land Without Bread is the picture of a pocket of misery in the mountains within a few miles of Burgos – life petering out in the stone crevices; images of awful inertia and more awful patience: a man shaking with fever: the goitred antique face of a woman of thirty-two: a child left in the road three days to die: the little edge of cultivation, a foot or two across, beside the river which will wash it out in the rains: the men trudging to Castile for work and returning without it, bony wrists and hollow chests, incredible rags: dwarf morons cackling at the camera, bobbing empty turnip faces above the rocks: the look of a mother whose baby has just died, shaken by human feeling into something you might take for the shadow of happiness after all those blank faces: the small body carried along stony tracks, up rocks from which we have seen even the goats tumble, pushed across a shallow river on its platter – like a tiny ferry-boat on an ignoble Lethe – until it reaches their only cemetery miles away – a few wood sticks stuck in long grass and weeds: at night between the stone cells, up a street like a crack in parched ground, an old woman walks clapping a death-bell. An honest and hideous picture, it is free from propaganda, except for a single shot of a church interior – a couple of cheap statues and a little cheap carving – with some glib sentence about clerical wealth. . . . Wealth! one smiles at the word in face of that twopenny interior and wonders whether five years of Republican politics have done so much for these people that one can afford to stop up this one hole they have to creep to for cleanness and comfort.

It's a grotesque world: the morons touching each other with private incommunicable meanings among the rocks, the dying child showing her throat to the cameraman ('We couldn't do anything about it. A few days later we heard she was dead'), and Mr Winn waking prettily to order, kissing his dog upon the pillow – 'the famous Mr Sponge'. 'He really lives his page,' the commentator remarks, and we watch him, at his country cottage, get into his car ('some flowers and a kiss from his mother'), start for the office. Next he is at work with his secretary, opening letters from readers. A mother writes: will he come and see her new-born baby? 'Other things must wait. He will not disappoint her,' the commentator tells us, and Mr Winn kneels by the bed and the baby is introduced to 'Uncle Godfrey'. After that we are shown Mr Winn entering a neo-Gothic doorway ('He finds time from his engagements to pause at church'), and while the organ peals a voluntary we see in close-up Mr Winn's adoring face lifted in prayer, sun falling through stained glass on the soft, unformed, First-Communion features. Lunch at Quaglino's ('his genius for friendship'), a swim in the Serpentine, tea with a reader in Regent's Park, back to the office for his article, a game of tennis, behind the scenes at the ballet, and so home to mother – 'sometimes after twelve o'clock'. The commentator sums Mr Winn up: 'At ease with the great and happy with the humble.' We have seen him with the great – with M. Quaglino and Mr Nelson Keys – and we are tempted to imagine him for a moment with the humble. (After all his commentator describes him as a 'traveller' – mother waving over the horizon and Mr Sponge chaperoning him in his berth.) Suppose that among those rocks a correspondent should summon him to see *her* new-born, or new-dead, baby. 'He will not disappoint her', and we picture him among those goitred and moron and hunger-tortured faces – the set boyishness, fifth-form diffidence and thinning hair. What message for these from 'Uncle Godfrey'? and Mr Winn's own voice recalls us to the actual screen: 'Friendship is the one thing that matters in the end', and the eyes look out at us so innocently, so candidly, so doggily they might really be the eyes of 'the famous Mr Sponge'. *Night and Day*, 18 November 1937

Land Without Bread (*Las Hurdes*) (Spain, Ramón Acín, 1932). Director: Luis Buñuel.
Personality Parade (GB, 1937). Produced by the *Daily Mirror*.

Dead End

The slum street comes to a dead end on the river-bank: luxury flats have gone up where the slum frontage has been cleared, so that two extremes of the social scale are within catcall: the Judge's brother's son has breakfast with his governess on a balcony in sight of the juvenile gang on the waterside. For some reason the front entrance of the flats cannot be used and – too conveniently – the tenants must take their way by the service door past the children's ribald gibes. In this coincidence alone do we get a whiff of the cramped stage. Several plots interwind – a house-painter (Joel McCrea) has a transitory affair with a rich man's mistress from the flats; a girl (Sylvia Sidney) hides her kid brother from the police – he is the leader of the children's gang who beat up the Judge's brother's son. And all the time, looking on at the game, is Baby-Face Martin (Humphrey Bogart), a gangster on the run with eight deaths to his credit. He is the future as far as these children are concerned – they carry his baton in their pockets. He was brought up in the same dead end and like a friendly Old Boy he gives them tips – how to catch another gang unawares, how to fling a knife. Only the housepainter recognizes him and warns him off. I'm doubtful whether this interweaving of plots, which end in the kid brother giving himself up, in the housepainter realizing he loves the sister, in the gangster's death from the housepainter's bullet, is wise. It gives too melodramatic a tone to the dead end: some emotion of grief, fear, passion happens to everybody, when surely the truth is nothing ever really happens at all. It remains one of the best pictures of the year – but what we remember is the gangster, the man who in a sentimental moment returns to the old home. He wants to see his mother and his girl: sentiment is mixed with pride – he's travelled places; he shows his shirtsleeve – 'Look – silk, twenty bucks.' And in two memorable scenes sentimentality turns savage on him. His mother slaps his face ('Just stay away and leave us alone and die'), his girl is diseased and on the streets. This is the finest performance Bogart has ever given – the ruthless sentimentalist who has melodramatized himself from the start (the start is there before your eyes in the juvenile gangsters) up against the truth, and the fine flexible direction supplies a background of beetle-ridden staircases and mud and mist. He and the children drive virtue into a rather dim corner, and only Sylvia Sidney with her Brooklyn voice and her driven childish face is visible there.   *Night and Day*, 25 November 1937

Dead End (USA, Samuel Goldwyn, 1937). Director: William Wyler. Humphrey Bogart, Sylvia Sidney, Joel McCrea, Claire Trevor.

Lo Squadrone Bianco

It is a change to hear Italian spoken on the screen – an ugly language which spits like a quick-firer, and though this story of passion, disappointed love and forgetting-a-woman-in-the-Libyan-desert may sound as conventional as *Beau Geste*, it has odd and refreshing differences – it isn't, for one thing, a bit tight-lipped ('What!' exclaims a Commander, showing a Subaltern orders to pursue marauders, 'such news doesn't excite you at all?'), and the morality is totalitarianly changed. Mr Ronald Colman, of course, might quite well quarrel with a woman and join a Foreign Legion, but to romantic Nordics such an action is meritorious, like shooting lions. We cannot imagine his Commander – who would obviously be played, with heavy moustaches and a straight bat, by Mr C. Aubrey Smith – being anything but sympathetic – what else can a fellow do but join the Legion or a Buchman house-party? But Captain Santelia complains on meeting the new Subaltern, 'another of those who come here simply to forget', and the Subaltern himself, when his Commander has been killed and he has led the squadron back to safety, politely dismisses his mistress who has hunted him down with a tourist-party. He isn't a bit high-minded about it. He has simply learned to prefer the military kind of service. Indeed, there is something pleasantly reasonable and un-dignified about this superficially melodramatic film: the lover making a hellish din outside his mistress's door, wailing 'Why do you tease me so, Christiana?' – heroics are left to the set military orations over dead heroes which have the right tombstone serenity and are moving in their marble way. It is a very slow picture – but at the end we realize slowness is a value. The long desert chase of the marauding Arabs – first the delay at an oasis waiting for overdue spies, then the fever, the forced march over waterless sands, the guide losing the way, the storm, the nearly drained wells on the other side, the pause for rest, pursuit again, the protracted and confusing fight – we do get the impression of time passing, of immense privation which would be lost in the smartly cut Hollywood scramble. *This* squadron behaves with unheroic common sense: when they are too tired they stop. The photography is at the same time unsensational and memorable: the curious crosses on the camels' saddles coming up in a long line over the dunes like a pilgrimage of friars; the bounce and dip, the riders' bare soles kneading at the necks. The names of the players, all

Dead End

December 1937

excellent, will convey nothing, but we cannot help noting Fulvia Lanzi who brings to the screen a thin Renaissance beauty, a Florentine arrogance.

Night and Day, 2 December 1937

Lo Squadrone Bianco (Italy, Roma, 1937). Director: Augusto Genina. Antonio Centa, Fulvia Lanzi, Fosco Giacetti. [US title: *White Squadrons*.]

Un Carnet de Bal/Underworld

A rich widow looks back on her first ball with melancholy nostalgia, she wonders what fate has done to the men who said they loved her when she was sixteen. Their names are there on an old dance-programme.... The mood is meant to be autumnal – memories dance through empty *salons*, woo her at her bedside. But Duvivier is not the director for so intangible a mood (we remember what Kirsanov did ten years ago in *Brumes d'Automne* with a few dripping boughs). A great director – *Pépé le Moko* his masterpiece – his mood is realistic, violent, belongs to the under-side of the stone. This widow's nostalgia is too corseted; some other device than her prosaic ringing of doorbells and presenting of cards was needed to introduce the story of the men's lives – the provincial Mayor marrying his cook, the mad mother pretending her son had never killed himself, the night-club keeper and gang leader quoting Verlaine with deft sentiment ·as the detectives arrive at 4 a.m., the middle-aged monk teaching choirboys to sing. Each episode is beautifully acted and directed, whether comic, melodramatic, sentimental, but whenever the widow appears upon the scene illusion rocks like stage scenery under her heavy and soprano tread. Nevertheless, it is a film which must be seen – Harry Baur, Françoise Rosay, Raimu, Fernandel, it contains the finest French acting, and in one episode we have Duvivier's real greatness – the seedy doctor at Marseille so used to furtive visitors and illegal operations that he doesn't wait for questions before he lights the spirit flame: the dreadful cataracted eye: the ingrained dirt upon his hands: the shrewish wife picked up in God knows what low music-hall railing behind bead curtains: the continuous shriek and grind of winch and crane. Nostalgia, sentiment, regret: the padded and opulent emotions wither before the evil detail: the camera shoots at a slant so that the dingy flat rears like a sinking ship. You have to struggle to the door, but you can run downhill to the medical couch and the bead curtains. There has been nothing to equal this episode on the screen since *Pépé*. It makes Renoir's *Underworld*, a slow agreeable undistinguished picture based on Gorki's novel, about a thief and a bankrupt Baron and a doss-house keeper and innocent love, oddly stagy and unconvincing. The doss-house squalor is laid Dickensianly on, but you never believe in its aspiring thief, its poetic madman, its old philosopher, its virginal affection. This isn't what poverty does – tatter the clothes and leave the mind unimpaired. The genuine poverty is in Duvivier's Marseille flat – the tin surgical basin, the antiseptic soap, the mechani-cal illegality and the complete degradation. *Night and Day*, 9 December 1937

Un Carnet de Bal (France, Sigma Films, 1937). Director: Julien Duvivier. Marie Bell, Françoise Rosay, Louis Jouvet, Pierre Richard Willm, Harry Baur, Pierre Blanchar, Sylvie, Raimu, Fernandel. [US title: *Life Dances On*.]
Underworld (*Les Bas-Fonds*) (France, Albatros, 1936). Director: Jean Renoir. Jean Gabin, Louis Jouvet, Wladimir Sokolov, Jany Holt, Suzy Prim. [US title: *Lower Depths*.]

Un Carnet de Bal: Pierre Blanchar

Les Bas-Fonds: Vladimir Sokoloff, Jean Gabin, Suzy Prim, Junie Astor

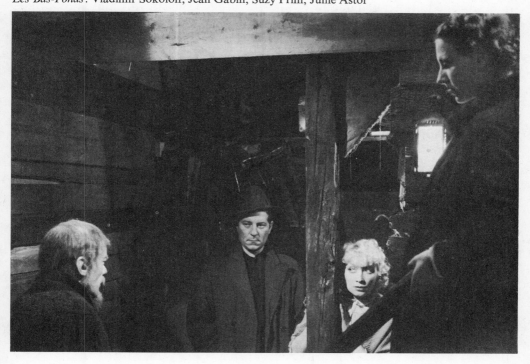

Monica and Martin/Mademoiselle Docteur/Eastern Valley

An artist who doesn't trouble about money, who isn't interested in selling his pictures, who lives in domestic bliss with his wife (she is his model too) – it's the old Bohemian fairy-tale which once, I suppose, represented a nostalgic dream of the successful bourgeois making money to satiety in the industrial age. But it was already a bit unconvincing by the time of du Maurier, and *Monica and Martin* has the added disadvantage of being Teutonic – Germans are congenitally unfitted for irrational behaviour. We sigh with relief when the plot emerges from the garret (Monica sells Martin's pictures as her own and complications arise when she is commissioned to paint a mural in a new sports stadium and is awarded the Cranach Prize), away from the playful hunger and the humorous poverty which is like a cruel insult to genuine destitution. There *is* one point of interest: Consul Brenckow, a stupid, self-important would-be patron, insulted, mocked, led up the garden. That absurd poster dignity and preposterous moustache: where have we seen them before? We are haunted by the memory of an upraised arm and a fast car and lines of Storm Troops facing inwards with hands on their revolvers towards a loyal populace.

Mr Ford Madox Ford has divided fiction into novels and nuvvels. So one may divide films into movie and cinema. *Monica and Martin* is movie: so, too, I'm afraid, is Mr Edmond Greville's spy film *Mademoiselle Docteur*. Mr Greville has an impeccable cinematic eye, but he has been badly served by a really shocking script, with childish continuity. Even a thriller cannot thrill unless the characters are established in our imaginations, and the packed plot of this film allows them no chance. Things are happening all the time: there's no opportunity to establish anything. Once the ghost of a theme did seem about to emerge when the medical student turned spy (played by Miss Dita Parlo with a charming spherical vacancy) protests to her employer 'My ambition was to save lives.' But the idea is never developed: it is swept away on a torrent of secret plans, villainous agents, dancing-girls, passwords. As for the dialogue, it ambles flatly along, like conversation between strangers at the beginning of a cocktail-party before anyone's had a drink. The general idea seems to be that people must talk all the time even if they've got nothing relevant to say. Erich von Stroheim makes his come-back in this film – one recognizes the uniform and the monocle. The uniform is as tight but a good deal less shapely than it used to be in the old silent days of *Foolish Wives*. 'The man you will love to hate' – so they used to advertise him (climbing a ladder in his skin-tight Prussian breeches towards an innocent bed). No one will hate him now. Inclined to stoutness, with a rough friendly American accent, he looks dressed up for a party. I shall prefer to remember him as the great realistic director of *Greed* (1923) – the dentist's chair, the hideous servant's bedroom, the lovers walking in the rain down the long grey breakwater.

Finally, one example of cinema. *Eastern Valley* has been made by the Strand Film Company to describe the activity of a society called the 'order of friends' in a distressed Welsh area. The older men have been given a chance to work on the land without losing their unemployment pay. The object is a psychological one – they receive no pay; but the whole community of unemployed families benefit by the cheaper goods. The film has been directed by a newcomer, Donald Alexander. He has learnt from Anstey the value of direct reporting: the appalling cottages held up by struts from falling, dwarfed by the slagheaps; the trout stream turned in-to a drain, one empty fag packet floating down between the old tins; the direct interview with the wife of an unemployed man; but he has learnt too from Basil Wright how to express poetically a moral judgment. Life as it once was before industry scarred and mutilated the valley; life as it is; life as it should be.

Night and Day, 16 December 1937

Monica and Martin (*Versprich mir Nichts*) (Germany, Meteor-Film, 1937). Director: Wolfgang Liebeneiner. Viktor de Kowa, Luise Ullrich, Heinrich George.
Mademoiselle Docteur (GB, Grafton, 1937). Director: Edmond T. Greville. Dita Parlo, Erich von Stroheim, John Loder (G. W. Pabst directed the French version, with Pierre Blanchar, Pierre Fresnay, Dita Parlo). [US title: *Street of Shadows*.]
Eastern Valley (GB, Strand Films, 1937). Director: Donald Alexander.

Marie Walewska/True Confession

She is, of course, the finest filly of them all. . . . And yet a dreadful inertia always falls on me before a new Garbo film. It is rather like reading *Sartor Resartus* – Carlyle's a great writer, but need one – now – this week . . . he's waited half a century: he can afford to wait a little longer: he'll still be on the public library shelves when one is old. And so too, I expect, will Garbo be: she will figure like Duse and Rachel in the reminiscences of bores; that magnificent mare's head of hers will puzzle our descendants, seeking a more obvious beauty, as it stares dumbly from the printed page, caught in a still in Napoleon's embrace, in Armand's embrace, in – the fictional names fail us – Fredric March's embrace, John Gilbert's embrace. A great actress – oh, undoubtedly, one wearily assents, but what dull pompous films they make for her, hardly movies at all so retarded are they by her haggard equine renunciations, the slow consummation of her noble adulteries. She is a Houyhnhnm in a world of Yahoos, but, being Yahoos ourselves, we some-times yearn for less exalted passions, for people who sin for recognizable reasons, because it's pleasurable. 'It's a bawdy planet.'

She has been badly served, of course, by writers and producers. They seem to feel uneasily that the films are unworthy of so superb an actress, and in compen-sation they treat her with deathly reverence: she is like a Tudor mansion set up again brick by numbered brick near Philadelphia. *She Married Her Boss*, *True Confession*, films like these – contemporary, carefree – are good enough for Claudette Colbert, Carole Lombard, but for Garbo you've got to have Great Scenarios (supplied lavishly and rotundly to order by S. N. Behrman). So we are given *Queen Christina*, *Marie Walewska*: fake history, masquerades in fancy-dress, dialogue written in the conventional rhetoric of the middlebrow historical novelist. But there's no satisfactory half-way house between poetic and realistic drama: if you can't give Garbo poetry to speak, you ought to give her prose. 'I kiss the hand which refused to sign away our country's independence' – that isn't prose.

Marie Walewska is one of the dullest films of the year. O, it has its moments when the Frenchman Boyer and the Swede Garbo are together alone, but the awful ocean of American vulgarity and good taste (they are the same thing) laps them round – soon Marie's brother will bounce in like a great Buchmanite Blue troubled about sex, or her husband (Henry Stephenson) will slip through the lath and plaster, honeyed and Harvard and humane, behaving as America thinks the Polish aristocracy behaved – with New World courtesy. There are moments too of un-conscious comedy – when Prince Poniatowski (one of our old gangster friends,

True Confession: John Barrymore, Carole Lombard

uneasy, speechless and pouter-breasted in his Hussar uniform) and one or two unidentifiable Polish leaders call on Marie Walewska and in her aged husband's presence suggest gently and avuncularly that she sleep with Napoleon for the sake of her country. An awkward situation for romantic drama, and one which attains a fine height of crazy comedy when they embrace Count Walewska – 'Good-bye, old friend' – and retire reverently on tiptoe from the awkward domestic impasse they have created. There is another scene too which is dangerously close to laughter when Napoleon's bastard child prays by the bed in Elba – 'Bless my father whom I have never seen and help him to be good' – and Napoleon lurks and listens round the night-nursery door. There's 'Old Stephan', too, the faithful retainer; a Revolutionary whom you recognize at once by his tousled straw-coloured wig, who cries 'Liberty' in front of a firing-squad; and printed captions – 'Two Months Later. The Castle of Finkenstein.' And all the while the great fake emotions booming out – Love, Country, Ambition – like a *Times* leader-writer taking a serious view of the Abdication crisis.

You aren't like me – you don't *have* to see Garbo. Go to *True Confession* instead – this is that rare thing, cinema, and the best comedy of the year. Do not be put off by the stock phrase – 'crazy comedy': this picture is constructed firmly and satisfactorily on human nature. It is – more or less – about the murder of a lecherous businessman who goes in for private secretaries; the heroine – an inveterate and charming liar played by Carole Lombard – pleads guilty to a murder she didn't commit because it seems easier to get off that way, the trial scene is a magnificent parody of all American trial scenes, and the picture succeeds in being funny from beginning to end – never more funny than when the corpse is disclosed under the carpet, or the heroine is warned that she will 'fry'. If it appears crazy it is only because we are not accustomed on the screen to people behaving naturally and logically. An inexperienced young barrister defends his wife on the charge of murder: we expect heroics and we get comic incompetence: that isn't crazy – it's an old melodramatic situation presented for once in terms of how people really behave. This is one of those comedies – Capra made them before he read James Hilton – in which the small parts are perfectly cast and played. I advise a quick visit: the public, I think, found it oddly shocking, for the middlebrow screen is more and more dictating how people ought to behave – even at a deathbed. I remember lying in bed a few years ago in a public ward listening with fascinated horror to a mother crying over her child who had died suddenly and unexpectedly after a minor operation. You couldn't question the appalling grief, but the words she used . . . they were the cheapest, the most improbable, the most untrue . . . one had heard them on a dozen British screens. Even the father felt embarrassment standing there beside her in the open ward, avoiding every eye.

Night and Day, 23 December 1937

Marie Walewska (*Conquest*) (USA, M-G-M, 1937). Director: Clarence Brown. Greta Garbo, Charles Boyer, Reginald Owen, Alan Marshal, Henry Stephenson, Leif Erickson, May Whitty.
True Confession (USA, Paramount, 1937). Director: Wesley Ruggles. Carole Lombard, Fred MacMurray, John Barrymore.

Orage

Robert Browning, you remember, wrote a poem called 'A Light Woman' – about 'my friend and the mistress of my friend with her wanton eyes and me'. An old story even in those days, it hasn't worn well with the years – but it is better in its latest French disguise than it has ever been in an Anglo-Saxon.

An engineer in a French naval dockyard (the dockyard doesn't matter: it's only an excuse for a good opening documentary shot) goes to Paris on business and promises to intercede for his young brother-in-law with a girl who has led him to the verge of suicide – or so he passionately protests as he runs beside the Paris express panting out his grief with Gallic irreticence. The engineer persuades the girl to come back with him, they miss the train, go for a ride in the country, and you know the rest, know it even to the tinkling sheep-bells which waken them, the secluded inn:

> . . . see – my friend goes shaking and white:
> He eyes me as the basilisk.

You would say it was a very Anglo-Saxon story in its muddled morality and irrational sentiment, with its Constant Nymph and Constant Wife confronting each other in the traditional great scene, before the Nymph, with poison in her tooth-mug, performs the traditional sacrifice; but admirably acted as it is by M. Charles Boyer and Mlle Michèle Morgan, and superbly directed by M. Marc Allegret, it does possess an odd and unexpected reality. All of us at one time or another must have found ourselves in some deplorable and banal situation haunted by literary parallels and have discovered how actual life provides the untraditional twist: the untimely hiccups; the laugh in the wrong place. So in this film it is the twists (very Latin twists) which make the story look like truth.

The French, of course, in a tale of this kind have an immense advantage over us. An English or American director would regard this quadrilateral story as 'a love interest': it would be affixed, like part of a Surrealist collage, to some odd plot of Bengal Lancers on the North-West Frontier or gangsters in Chicago – a kiss stuck in a corner next a sub-machine gun, a night of love obscured by an overlapping Afghan attack. But to the French director passion is the whole plot – the camera is focused all the time upon the bed; and we can believe in this untidy desperate affair as we have no time to believe in a Lancer's love – because it is a whole-time job: the little hot bedroom in the country inn with the girl asking for the fly-swatter and the man too lazy to stir from his chair and the clothes flung untidily about, the sense that they haven't been downstairs for days and the bed hasn't been made: the listening at doors: the opening of other people's letters: the sudden appearance of the former lover with his scarecrow face, his hysterical impudence, his too short sleeves and bony wrists and immature jumper: all the ignobility of a besetting pleasure. Only compare that inn room with the one Garbo and Gilbert occupied in *Queen Christina* and you have the difference between literary and living passion – Garbo dangling the grapes and fumbling whimsically along the walls, and these two, lazy and hot and happy among the cigarette ash and the too many flies.

Admirable, too, are the backgrounds – the concierge's lodge, palms and hideous china and overcrowding; the small French restaurant with its '8 francs 50 table d'hôte' which ends with assorted cheese. 'What is the assorted cheese tonight?' 'Camembert.' 'Ah, he never recommends the Camembert.' And there are flashes of symbolism which take us back in memory to the old classic silent days when people thought about such things – the lover attempting to analyse the girl's character while the lights of a passing train break up the simple outline of her face. It is only when M. Bernstein's story begins its noble sacrificial drift that reality seeps away – gondolas and evening dress and trying to forget in Venice: the wife saying 'When you're tired of her, I shall still be there' – and then the train pounding back to Paris: scraps of sentimental morality: 'You're doing right as long as you don't cause suffering': and the girl saying 'It's you he really loves' as wife and mistress both try with broken hearts to pass the male like a marked card.

The Spectator, 10 June 1938

Orage (France, Lauer Films, 1937). Director: Marc Allégret. Charles Boyer, Michèle Morgan, Jean-Louis Barrault. [US title: *The Storm*.]

L'Alibi/A Slight Case of Murder

Murder, if you are going to take it seriously at all, is a religious subject; the interest of a detective-story is the pursuit of exact truth, and if we are at times impatient with the fingerprints, the time-tables and the butler's evasions, it is because the writer, like some early theologians, is getting bogged in academic detail. How many angels can stand on the point of a needle?

L'Alibi begins very promisingly because very simply. A professional fortune-teller (Mr von Stroheim) shoots an old enemy and arranges an alibi with one of the dance-partners attached to the night-club at which he performs. She doesn't know he has committed a murder, she thinks he has something to do with the drug traffic. Then when the Detective-Inspector has got the hollow, deceiving-no-one statement from her, he lets her learn the truth – suddenly, and there is an admirable cinematic moment as she stands horror-struck and hesitating in the hygienic corridor: shot of M. Louis Jouvet's astute sad reptile face watching the handle of his door: shot of the handle beginning to turn: shot of M. Jouvet's face, hopeful and incredulous (he knows from long experience how seldom human nature gives way at the first attack): the handle ceases to turn. The whole plot now should be psychological: a female Raskolnikov resisting the urge to confession: a French Porphyrius waiting like a priest in the confessional-box: and life putting on its pressure – the *peine forte et dure*.

Alas, *l'Alibi* doesn't work out that way. It explodes, as it were, at the edges into thriller terms – Professor Winkler's absurd consulting-room where he sits, surrounded by plaster hands, dressed in monkish robes and cowl, like one of those waxwork figures you see in little dirty Mexican booths beating naked nuns; a sinister manservant, slavishly devoted, who will do anything for his master, and a Chinese girl who manicures Winkler in his bath. Mr Stroheim in a dinner-jacket and a boater acts very well, loosened from the constriction of those tight Prussian uniforms he used to wear: his slow uncertain French is effectively evil; but there is something about Mr Stroheim which apparently calls for dressing-up – like a wooden torso behind plate-glass he mutely demands a costume, and so we have the monkish robe, and an odd creation in tight white silk – court breeches and a rapier.

But the picture remains worth seeing if only for Mr Jouvet's acting. He represents all that Mr Conrad Veidt did in the old Ufa days: he has only to turn from a window and disclose that ugly, humorous and tragic face to exercise the charm of something real – as in *Un Carnet de Bal* he steps out of a bogus story into life. Listen to him soliloquizing in the morgue as he turns the sheet back over the murdered man's face: 'Ex-convict, ex-gangster and now ex-Gordon': the nutmeg-grater voice, a rasp capable of extraordinary expression, like those musical instruments made out of old metal which street performers play.

Murder is certainly not taken seriously at the Odeon. There was one corpse, you will remember, in *True Confession*, last year's funniest film: there are four

L'Alibi: Roger Blin, Erich von Stroheim

corpses in *A Slight Case of Murder* and the picture is nearly four times funnier. Where will this mathematical progression end? Mr Edward G. Robinson, admirably supported by Mr Allen Jenkins and various Damon Runyon boys, plays an ex-gangster and unsuccessful brewer of post-Prohibition beer who drives out one evening with his wife and daughter to spend a week-end in the country and finds the bodies of Little Dutch and his three associates sitting dead and murdered round a table in the spare bedroom. Mr Robinson, a bit uneasy about the police but exhilarated by a breath of the old life, decides to leave the bodies on the neighbours: there are wild discussions – 'Old so-and-so, what about leaving one on *his* doorstep?' 'Say, boss, can't I just keep one in the kitchen for later on?' Afterwards his henchmen read there's a reward offered for the gangsters dead or alive (ten grand apiece) and they fetch the bodies back in the middle of a party and stow them in a clothes-cupboard, on coat-hangers – the complications crazily mount, sentiment never raises its ugly head, a long nose is made at violence and death.

The Spectator, 17 June 1938

L'Alibi (France, Tellus, 1936). Director: Pierre Chenal. Erich von Stroheim, Louis Jouvet, Jany Holt. *A Slight Case of Murder* (USA, Warner Bros, 1938). Director: Lloyd Bacon. Edward G. Robinson, Ruth Donnelly, Allen Jenkins, Edward Brophy, Harold Huber, Jane Bryan, Willard Parker.

From the Manger to the Cross/Swing, Sister, Swing/Sally, Irene and Mary/ Sinners in Paradise/The Devil's Party

From the Manger to the Cross was made in 1913, and shown at the Albert Hall. As it runs for an hour and a quarter, it must have been a 'super-production' in those days – it is a rousing picture even in these. The exteriors – and the film is very nearly all exterior – were taken in Palestine and Egypt, and the unobtrusive backgrounds give the film an authenticity no studio could get from technique alone. How often in the most lavish Hollywood spectacle, when the sets have cost half a million and the heroine weighs 128 pounds, the illusion of life is broken by the use of back projections or unconvincing models: in this old faded picture the Holy Family rest before the genuine Sphinx and Judas comes with torchbearers to the real Garden of Olives. You have only to accept certain period conventions of film acting and no further demand is made on your credulity.

The Rev. Brian Hession has inserted a few close-ups (in 1913 Griffith was only just introducing them to the screen): he has added a commentary from the Authorized Version: those are the only human changes, but time too has done its work well. Perhaps when the picture was first shown, all glossy in the Albert Hall, the audience was aware of 'art' doing its self-conscious and destructive work, but art has been successfully faded out – twenty-five years in film history is equal to five centuries of painting. This is a primitive: the producer has no cunning; he hasn't learned the modern tricks of angle and close-up, panning and trucking – he can't move his camera about, and we seldom come closer to the characters than what some scenarists call 'a medium close shot'. They stand there in the middle distance, emotion stamped like a humour on the face, expressing themselves with the minimum of movement. That is Herod – you recognize him by the attitude, head sunk on arms, and by the expression of broody hate. He is like the Herod you sometimes see in cribs at Christmas-time, leaning down from his battlements towards the miniature Bethlehem – the plaster sheep and Wise Men and cows. The contrast with modern methods becomes vivid in one sentimental, melodramatic and symbolic shot of the empty tomb, inserted by Mr Hession – a white slab and the black shadow of a moving door, and in the final fancy cuts of skyscrapers and Chinese churches and Rome, culminating rather parochially with St Paul's and Canterbury and a flickery cross like an electric sign. The only false notes in fact are the modern notes.

Granted that *From the Manger to the Cross* is well made, was it worth making? The film critic of *The Times* who didn't like it at all – 'sincerity is not enough' – noted 'a tendency towards gross materialism', and certainly, as in Spanish churches, you are allowed no escape at all from physical suffering; Christ is a man beaten up, like a Nazi prisoner in the Brown House. The physical horror is never far away and always well conveyed – whether it is the Massacre of the Innocents, dark passages and patches of brilliant sunlight and the sudden intrusion of spears in the old city, or the raising of Lazarus from the tomb – the awful wait after the stone has been rolled back until out of the cave the grub-like figure emerges, the tight cerements and the face all eyes. With all due respect to the *Times* critic, I find the value of the film in what he dislikes – the unsentimental reminder of the material horror, the link between the raising of Lazarus and *The Monkey's Paw*.

Of the other films this week – *Swing, Sister, Swing*; *Sally, Irene and Mary*;

Sinners in Paradise; *The Devil's Party* – I retain a confused impression of carnality on the campus ('U' certificate), a night-club, a showboat, a coral island, a lot of people making good – a casino proprietor and ex-reformatory boy dying nobly, his pal in a clerical collar kneeling beside him, and a plaque unveiled at a boys' club in his memory; a manicurist becoming a star; a murderer giving himself up ('unless we face our responsibilities' – Madge Evans's sunken eyes and whimsy teacher's voice – 'we can't respect ourselves'); and Miss Gracie Allen* passing an examination: the horrifying inanity of human entertainment.

The Spectator, 24 June 1938

From the Manger to the Cross (GB, Kalem, 1937). Director: Brian Hession.
Swing, Sister, Swing (USA, Universal, 1937). Director: Joseph Santley. Ken Murray, Johnny Downs, Kathryn Kane.
Sally, Irene and Mary (USA, 20th Century-Fox, 1938). Director: William A. Seiter. Alice Faye, Tony Martin, Fred Allen, Joan Davis.
Sinners in Paradise (USA, Universal, 1938). Director: James Whale. John Boles, Madge Evans, Gene Lockhart.
The Devil's Party (USA, Universal, 1938). Director: Ray McCarey. Victor McLaglen, Beatrice Roberts, William Gargan.

* Confused impression indeed: presumably Joan Davis is the actress meant.

L'Homme du Jour/You and Me

Now that the great Russians have shot their bolt and belong to history – the age of early *Close Ups* and the old Windmill Theatre, of earnest lectures (which have come to so little) in tea-shops on how to use sound 'constructively' – one would name, I think, Julien Duvivier and Fritz Lang as the two greatest fiction directors still at work. Duvivier has gone to Hollywood, where Lang has been now for some years – I hope Hollywood doesn't treat Duvivier as it has treated Lang.

For it is impossible not to believe that Lang – surrounded by the Virginia van Upps and the Paul Weatherwaxes, by the odd names of Hollywood credit titles – has been sabotaged. Given proper control over story and scenario, Lang couldn't have made so bad a film as *You and Me*: the whole picture is like an elegant and expensive gesture of despair. The advertised subject is '50,000 Girls Forbidden by Law to Marry', which merely refers to the reasonable regulation that convicts mustn't marry while they are still on parole. This surely is to go through the code-book with a fine-toothed comb in search of an injustice, a hard case, a little social significance. In fact, the inability of Sylvia Sidney to marry George Raft (I don't remember what they are called in the picture: it doesn't matter: they are only a couple of capable actors registering the regulation heartbreak) isn't an important part of the story at all. The real plot is concerned with an incredible philanthropist who makes a point of employing paroled convicts in his mammoth store as shop-assistants. Raft, who has worked off his parole, marries Sylvia Sidney, who hasn't finished hers – he tells her his past, but she's afraid to tell him hers. He learns the truth, takes a high moral line about deception, and joins with the other convicts in robbing the store. They are caught by the obstinate philanthropist and a couple of private guards, and as the price of their forgiveness have to sit through a talk by Miss Sidney, who demonstrates on a blackboard that crime doesn't pay. She then disappears into the night without telling Raft that she's going to have a baby, and has it – apparently next day. Physiological tact could hardly be carried further.

You and Me: Jack Pennick, Robert Cummings

Everyone has heard of the Hollywood 'doghouse' – the practice of ruining a star by providing bad parts. No star has been treated worse than Lang is here by his scenario-writers. The continuity is quickie in its naïvety. 'How do we get to the information bureau?' Miss Sidney asks. 'By subway,' Raft says, and there, of course, they are – in the subway. A few experiments are made with verse and chanted speech (how unhappy Roscoe Karns looks about it all), but they are only the desperate contortions of a director caught in the Laocoön coils of an impossible script.

L'Homme du Jour – a charming comedy, with Maurice Chevalier, about an electrician who becomes famous for a day after he has given blood to save the life of a tragic actress, who is taken heavily up by the great interpreter of Racine and then, when he sleeps through a bedroom date, heavily dropped again – may not be vintage Duvivier, but it is admirable *vin ordinaire*. It is the kind of story Clair might have directed in the old days; the Pressmen cynical over the champagne, the enthusiastic straphangers in the Métro, are Clair characters, inhabitants of a whimsical fairyland where Providence strikes blindly and luck never lasts long and the lottery-ticket gets lost among the top-hats, yet no one really cares. But Duvivier's pictures have a stronger sense of human life – even in a comedy the shadow is there, and somewhere in the shadow the abortionist throws a fit at Marseille and Pépé cuts his throat with an inadequate knife. Strangers in the

Métro may be carried away by a wave of altruistic sentiment, but in the electrician's boarding-house – among his *friends* – there is only jealousy, the mean middle-aged passion to take him down a peg. And so we get, in this airy ridiculous comedy, one of Duvivier's saddest episodes – bogus letters that arrange an assignation between the electrician and a flower-girl who secretly and hopelessly loves him, while the hideous inhabitants of the boarding-house sit in the evening light sniggering over their cruel joke.   *The Spectator,* 1 July 1938

L'Homme du Jour (France, Films Maurice, 1936). Director: Julien Duvivier. Maurice Chevalier, Elvire Popesco, Josette Day, Alerme.
You and Me (USA, Paramount, 1938). Director: Fritz Lang. Sylvia Sidney, George Raft, Robert Cummings, Barton Maclane.

Kidnapped/I Cover the Waterfront

They call it *Kidnapped*: that is what I resent most as Mr Warner Baxter, with a gleam of those too prominent and even teeth of his, waves a sword among the sepia-tinted Highlanders and shouts – in an American accent – 'On to Edinburgh', and Master Freddie Bartholomew, with his Fauntleroy features and Never-Never-Land voice, makes winsome remarks – to Jennie Macdonald. And who in Tusitala's name is she? She is the girl who loves Alan Breck (that is what they call Warner Baxter), and Breck is trying to restore her to her betrothed, James Stewart, whom he wants to ship out of the country because he has killed the Red Fox. . . . Do you catch strange echoes of a story you once read? There *was* a Red Fox, and a James Stewart, though neither killed the other, and as for Alan trying to get anyone but himself out of the country or loving a girl. . . .

I doubt if the summer will show a worse film than *Kidnapped*; the only fun you are likely to get from it is speculation, speculation on the astonishing ignorance of film-makers who claim to know what the public wants. The public will certainly not want this *Kidnapped*, where all the adventures which made them read the book have been omitted. Is it even honest to bring in Stevenson's name? (There should be a society for protecting authors who may be out of copyright.) Apart from the title and the circumstances of David Balfour's kidnapping, there is practically nothing of the original story here – you will find no trace of the magnificent battle in the round house or of the flight in the heather. Alan Breck's character, with its cunning and vanity, is not so much altered as lost – he is only an American voice shouting over and over again, 'To Edinburgh' or 'The Redcoats': he is only a set of teeth like those exhibited in the windows of cheap dentists. A little of David's priggishness is left (it comes easily to the actor), but none of that 'darkness of despair and a sort of anger against all the world' which when we were young dragged us with him through the heather. All that remains is an odd echo – familiar names misused, lines out of the book misplaced, trivial incidents, which any competent scenarist would have cut, dragged in to take the place of – everything. All the great filmic scenes of battle and flight are eliminated, and a tiny incident without bearing on the story, like that of the minister who asked David for snuff, is retained. As for the girl with her great dewy eyes, her dimples and her tartan and her kissing mouth, she represents, I suppose, the love interest – as if there wasn't love enough in the original story to wither these wistful caresses and misunderstandings and virginal pursuits, the love of an exile for a particular scene and of a sick man for a life of action he couldn't lead.

I Cover the Waterfront is a revival from a period before the Hays dictatorship – when it was still just possible that the films might become an adult art. It dates a little with its hard-drinking newspapermen and its boisterous badinage, but it does achieve something of value and maturity in the character of Eli Kirk, played by the late Ernest Torrence, an illiterate sea-captain who smuggles Chinamen into a Pacific seaport and throws them overboard, tied to an anchor chain, when he's in danger from the Revenue officers. Watch the stubble face sweat as the Chink drops, the rudimentary conscience at work in the old starry eyes: listen to the rough, deep, melancholy voice like something heavy and phosphorescent dragged out of a well: see him scared and huddled in a corner while his Mate dies from a shark's bite, breaking out at his men, 'Don't you men know enough to take off your hats,' while he forgets his own: watch him drunk in a brothel – the awful paralytic happiness caged in the huge body. There are scenes in this film which Hays now would never pass – they are the scenes which give the picture veracity – the daughter (Miss Claudette Colbert) waiting in the cheap brothel to take her tipsy father home, quite naturally, exchanging friendly words with the big blonde madame; the Chinaman's body fished out of the water by the harbour scavenger, the death casually dated ('Not more'n a day. Crabs aint got 'im yet'). A bit raw and a bit sentimental and a bit routine, the film does let life in through the cracks.

The Spectator, 5 August 1938

Kidnapped (USA, 20th Century-Fox, 1938). Director: Alfred Werker. Warner Baxter, James Stewart, Freddie Bartholomew, Arleen Whelan.
I Cover the Waterfront (USA, Reliance, 1933). Director: James Cruze. Claudette Colbert, Ben Lyon, Ernest Torrence.

Little Tough Guy

Don't be put off by the absurd title. *Little Tough Guy* is one of the best melodramas in recent years – very nearly as good as *Dead End*, and with the same cast of boys. The theme too is roughly the same: the natural adolescent virtues decaying on the East Side under the iron ladder of the Elevated, courage becoming toughness, the love of justice a hatred of the whole possessing world. Billy Halop, in appearance a younger Robert Taylor but with twice the acting ability, takes the part of Johnny Boylan, whose father is sent unjustly to the chair. The whole family – the lower-middle, keeping-up-appearances class – have to move away from home into the slums: the daughter drops from shop-girl to burlesque-girl, the son from schoolboy to newsboy, the leader of a tough gang. It isn't a gang which usually would get further than an occasional petty theft for bravado's sake or a stone flung through a window – an impotent protest against Justice in a luxury car, Justice keeping a luncheon appointment – without the assistance of a leader with more imagination and more cruelty; and an original feature of this melodrama is the way it keeps an adolescent unity in the character of the Big Shot. The Big Shot (admirably acted by Jackie Searle) is a rich youth who wants excitement. We see him first under pious posters and ugly banners, the honoured guest of the Young America Onward and Upward League, listening to the Chairman's speech ('I've seen this movement grow – from the teeniest idea . . .') with well-bred patience: a long cynical eyelid and a nervous nihilist humour. He takes the gang up, organizes their petty thefts, and then, when the police pressure grows too great, betrays them. Boylan and his henchman Pig (a pale weedy bully with strangled loyalties cleverly hinted at) escape and are brought finally to bay in a small grocer's shop, with guns in their immature hands and an armed police cordon across the road. That scene in its psychological horror atones for much false sentiment, for naïve sociology and a truly appalling happy end – the tough gang with busbies and bugles at a State school, and Johnny Boylan twirling a baton on prize-day. Day-dream violence is confronted appallingly with actuality – the guns they had played with must be either used or surrendered. There is a long spell of inaction, while the old grocer prays to God under the counter, 'Let me get safe home . . . let me get safe home', the antique whisper eating at the boys' nerves, and then the squeal of the ambulance – 'I guess that's what they're waiting for' – the noise of the brakes going on, and all the cramped loneliness between the counter and the wall with the lights turned out and the police guns pointed and death really about to happen.

The Spectator, 12 August 1938

Little Tough Guy (USA, Universal, 1938). Director: Harold Young. Billy Halop, Jackie Searle, Robert Wilcox, Helen Parrish.

Son of Mongolia

Trauberg, the director of *New Babylon*, that magnificent, ludicrous and savage version of the Paris of 1871, has made *Son of Mongolia*. This Trauberg has a genius for legend; one is sometimes still haunted on evenings of rain and despair by the midinette of *New Babylon* with her rain-soaked face and her gawky body, her expression of dumb simplicity and surprise, as she plods painfully in her own person through the stages of evolution and dies with the first glimmer of human intelligence. The son of Mongolia, too, is a simple and stupid creature whom we watch evolve an intelligence, but with his physical strength and his rich half-conscious humour he is the hero of a happier legend – though one we find more difficult to accept than goodness dying in the rain against a wall.

This son of Mongolia loves a shepherdess (the Trianon title could hardly be less applicable than to this girl astride her stocky pony – small, rough and almond-eyed). A rival bribes a fortune-teller in a caravanserai (full of bicycles and old priests telling beads, spittoons, and ancient melancholy traditional songs) to get rid of him, and the fortune-teller reads the Mongolian's palm: 'Many days journey to the East you find an enchanted garden. Taste of one of its fruits and you will become a hero. If you encounter any obstacles simply call out "I am Tseven of Shorot".' And so poor simplicity starts out in the usual manner of a youngest son, slipping in a sandstorm past the border-posts into Manchuria, into a world of feudal injustice, of astute Japanese spies, of the casual execution, where human suffering goes on and on like breathing and sleeping. He befriends a shepherd who has been flogged for saying that Mongolia will one day be free; he listens to a Japanese officer plotting a secret assault with a wrestler in a circus, and when he denounces the spy, he finds himself shut in a cage in the enchanted garden of his imagination, condemned to death by the local Chinese Prince who is preparing to betray his country.

There is a rescue and a flight – little fairy-tale ponies pursued by a tank across the long Mongolian plain; there is last-minute salvation by means of a Biblical subterfuge; Tseven and the shepherd lie on the ground hidden by a friendly chewing unfrightened flock while the soldiers sweep the horizon in vain with their Leitz

199

lenses. Let us forget the crude propaganda close, and remember the curious mixture of the very old and the very new, of melodrama and fairy-tale. Inside a Daimler decorated with flower-pots on the hood and quilted with satin the Chinese Prince makes desultory and lubricious love; the spy swings in a hammock dressed in long Oriental merchant's robes and discusses troop movements with a half-naked wrestler; a clown in a long white beard packs an army revolver; and while the executioner stands by with naked blade, the Prince's secretary, in a lounge suit and horn-rimmed glasses, reads the *Arabian Nights* sentence: 'Tseven of Shorot is to be made shorter by a head.' There is one magnificent panoramic shot when the camera sweeps down a whole long Chinese street: camels and bicycles: criminals squatting on a little platform with their heads stuck through great square wooden collars: butchers' stalls and tea-drinkers: soldiers on an unexplained hunt through the crowd: rows of sewing-machines: a gabled gateway through the ancient walls and the dusty plain outside.   *The Spectator*, 19 August 1938

Son of Mongolia (USSR, Lenfilm, 1936). Director: Ilya Trauberg. Tseven, Itchin-Horlo.

Fools for Scandal/Booloo/Five Faces

They say you cannot hear a bat squeak . . . and certainly Miss Carole Lombard's high enchanting fatuous voice has risen in this latest film of hers beyond the capacity of the microphone – or so it seemed at the Press show. It rises, breaks, is lost . . . and that's a pity for all of us. But it is more of a pity that her directors should have given her so humourless, so hopeless a story (perhaps that's why she has to scream so loud). Even Mr Allen Jenkins, sure-fire Jenkins, can make nothing of this picture. A penniless French Marquis (acted with a plump repulsive confidence by Mr Fernand Gravet) pursues a film actress (Miss Carole Lombard of course) to London, and after dining at her house takes advantage of a joke to install himself there as her cook and butler, answers telephone calls – compromisingly, so that soon a pack of reporters are waiting at the door trying to glean a paragraph about the 'love chef', and the actress finally succumbs. . . . Perhaps it is meant to be a crazy comedy, but the secret of the crazy comedy is that people do behave with the irrelevance of human beings and break out through the Hollywood frame into life. Here they proceed with daunting high spirits and dreadful inevitability between the pasteboard walls towards – what an end! The only character for which the script-writer does deserve some praise is Miss Lombard's cavalier, an insurance agent, the parody of a familiar type: the big boyish lover with his sulks and his enormous optimism and his gawky abandonment to joy and grief. As for Miss Lombard . . . it is always a pleasure to watch those hollow Garbo features, those neurotic elbows and bewildered hands, and her voice has the same odd beauty a street musician discovers in old iron, scraping out heart-breaking and nostalgic melodies. But you will be well advised to wait another occasion of serving at her shrine.

Jungle pictures are always great fun, and the *Booloo* expedition led by Captain Rogers to discover in the Wilds of Malaya a white tiger and a maiden sacrifice deserves to rank with the epic exploits of the Marquis de la Falaise and the heroes of *The Jungle Princess*. Captain Rogers had produced a volume from the hunting reminiscences of his father, a famous explorer, and some of these, which concerned the tiger and the sacrifice, so shocked the Imperial Geographical Society that they removed the old man's portrait from their walls ceremoniously in the presence of the son. So Captain Rogers left his sweetheart in Aldershot and penetrated into the territory of 'the Sakai savages' to prove his father's tales were true. How familiar we are by now with that jungle: 'stir but a stone and start' – not a mere wing, but whole tribes of monkeys, tigers, herds of elephant. Laboriously, the expedition hacks its way along a little path with machetes, studiously averting their faces from the wide easy clearing a foot away; faces peer out of the shrubbery; poisoned arrows flick into tree-trunks ('One scratch, you must know, means death. Do you still want to go on?' 'Yes, Sir.' 'Stout fellow' – it's that kind of dialogue), and a girl dressed like a South Sea islander from *Hurricane* waits in a trap for the tiger.

Those who see Mr Alexander Shaw's picture, *Five Faces*, at the Academy in a few weeks will wonder – 'Why the Sakai of all people?' In *Five Faces*, a documentary study of Malaya, we have genuine pictures of these gentle persecuted people. We watch them use their poisoned arrows – against small rodents, the poison just strong enough to kill but not to taint the meat. And we see, too, the real Sakai women – decorative creatures, certainly, with sticks poked through the nostrils and uncovered breasts, but hardly to be compared for shampooed beauty with the maiden sacrifice of *Booloo*, the long combed raven hair, the Dorothy Lamour eyes, the elegant and refined sarong.

Five Faces is good workmanlike documentary, and it has more important values than the exposure of jungle absurdities. Most interesting is its treatment of history – the use of old prints to illustrate the commentary, the alternation on the screen of the seventeenth-century engraving and the ruins as they stand today. The effect is exciting and reassuring – to see how little Time can really do: to recognize the face so easily from the skull.   *The Spectator,* 26 August 1938

Fools for Scandal (USA, Warner Bros, 1938). Director: Allen Jenkins. Carole Lombard, Fernand Gravet, Ralph Bellamy.
Booloo (USA, Paramount, 1938). Director: Clyde Elliott. Colin Tapley, Jayne Regan.
Five Faces [*of Malaya*] (GB, Strand Films, 1938). Director: Alexander Shaw.

Katia/Sixty Glorious Years

Perhaps it is as well that Mlle Darrieux has gone to Hollywood to be groomed for crazy comedy. Her type demands too much of the scenario-writer: the innocence she conveys has nothing to do with life: it must be poetry or nothing. The sense of extreme youth, death and eternity and love-for-ever glib upon the tongue – it doesn't signify whether it's fine acting or fine camerawork or just a trick of carriage, the head so precariously poised on the long slender immature neck. Whatever the cause, the effect she makes demands poetic tragedy: innocence like that has got to be legendary, doomed, a scapegoat.

She succeeded in *Mayerling* because her partner Charles Boyer could carry the right atmosphere of predestination. She was sentenced to death by the world as soon as she appeared in the pleasure-garden, lost in the boisterous darkness. In *Katia* the French have tried to repeat *Mayerling* – a meeting in a pleasure-garden, royalty incognito, the girl's secret visit to the palace interrupted by a wife this time instead of a mother. We can see now that if she had stayed she would have been used over and over again to play the child-mistress of nineteenth-century royalties, until the time came when she couldn't make-up quite. so young, and innocence would have been turned on like a tap. In *Katia* she is first the mistress and then the wife of the Tsar Alexander. The story is conventional, naïve, loosely constructed: the assassination of the Tsar is followed by an interminable deathbed – 'This is

201

Katia: Danielle Darrieux

your little Katia. Speak to me.' A story could have been made out of the constant threat of the terrorists, private life broken all the time by the need of protection, and the end inevitable. But no such story is attempted. There is nothing doomed about this Tsar, played by Mr John Loder, who even on our shores is hardly known as a pliant actor and who, under the added handicap of the French language, becomes no more than a dummy for full-dress uniforms. The story too, is absurdly speeded up. 'Free the serfs,' the child implores Alexander on their first meeting, and freed the serfs are – in the next shot. There is one good scene, when the Tsar drives with Napoleon III through the Paris streets and the two Emperors salute the loyal people with bows and smiles, as they talk about boots and caviare, illicitly like chorus-girls.

And so to another royal romance, heavy this time with lavender and right feelings, Elgar and quotations from Kipling. Sweet Nell of Old Drury, Nell Gwyn, Queen Victoria – Miss Neagle seems to be attempting all our great national figures, and though it is sometimes a little difficult to distinguish between them, I think I prefer her in breeches as sweet Nell: her dimpled aseptic coquetry is a bit out of place under a crown, just as the straining naked naiads trailing golden bath-towels who leap towards the Odeon screen are not well suited to this rather absurd picture of royal domesticities, all loyalty, sentiment and Technicolor. The dialogue by Mr Miles Malleson and Sir Robert Vansittart is undistinguished, and the casting which begins grotesquely with Miss Neagle remains – to say the least of it – odd. What strange whim induced Mr Wilcox to cast one of our youngest actors in the part of Disraeli? If there is one thing as bad as age imitating youth, it is youth imitating age. And that, I fear, goes for Miss Neagle, too. Both the director and the star seem to labour under the impression that they are producing something important, and this gives what is really an inoffensive picture a kind of humourless pomp. Incidentally, the Indian Mutiny and the Boer War, not to mention other rather inglorious campaigns in Africa and Afghanistan, are omitted: the Crimea and the Sudan alone disturb this love-life of a queen.

The Spectator, 4 November 1938

Katia (France, E. Alcazy, 1938). Director: Maurice Tourneur. Danielle Darrieux, John Loder.
Sixty Glorious Years (GB, Imperator, 1938). Director: Herbert Wilcox. Anna Neagle, Anton Walbrook, C. Aubrey Smith.

You Can't Take It With You

It is really what we should have expected from Frank Capra, whose portrait hangs outside the cinema: bushy eyebrows, big nose and the kind of battered face which looks barnacled with life, encrusted with ready sympathies and unexacting friendships, a good mixer. It is always dangerous, of course, to generalize about a director's subjects – he hasn't invented his own stories; but the Capra-Riskin combination is strong enough by now to dictate, and we can assume Capra is doing what he wants to do. What he wants is increasingly what the public wants. It will adore the new picture which contains what it treasures most – a good laugh and a good cry.

As for the reviewer, he can only raise his hands in a kind of despair. The new picture is the *Christmas Carol* over again – with its sentimentality and its gusto and its touches of genius: no technical mistakes this time as there were in *Lost Horizon*. The director emerges as a rather muddled and sentimental idealist who feels – vaguely – that something is wrong with the social system. Mr Deeds started distributing his money, and the hero of *Lost Horizon* settled down in a Tibetan monastery – equipped with all the luxury devices of the best American hotels – and Grandpa Vanderhof persuades, in this new picture, the Wall Street magnate who has made the *coup* of his career and cornered the armaments industry to throw everything up and play the harmonica. This presumably means a crash in Wall Street and the ruin of thousands of small investors, but it is useless trying to analyse the idea behind the Capra films: there *is* no idea that you'd notice, only a sense of dissatisfaction, an urge to escape – on to the open road with the daughter of a millionaire, back to small-town simplicity on a safe income, away to remote, secure Shangri-La, into the basement where Mr Vanderhof's son-in-law makes fireworks with the iceman who came seven years ago with a delivery-van and stayed on. A belief, too, in bad rich men and good poor men – though Mr Vanderhof doesn't, when you come to think of it, seem to lack money. Like the British Empire, he has retired from competition with a full purse.

That is really all there is to the film – a contrast between life on Wall Street and life in the Vanderhof home, where everybody is supposed to lead the life he likes and like the life the others lead. A granddaughter practises ballet-dancing while she lays the table, a boy-friend plays on the marimba, a daughter writes novels which will never be published, just for fun – what an extraordinary idea of fun! It is very noisy with the fireworks going off, and good-hearted and Christian in the *Christmas Carol* tradition. The most embarrassing moments in a film which is frequently embarrassing occur at meal-times when Grandpa Vanderhof (Mr Lionel Barrymore) talks to God in a man-to-man way instead of saying Grace. 'Well, sir, here we are again. We been getting on pretty well for a long time now....' This whimsical household is meant, I think, to be symbolic of life as it should be lived (one prefers Wall Street), and mixed up in the whole thing is the routine love-story of Vanderhof's granddaughter and the magnate's son, played sensitively by Miss Jean Arthur and Mr James Stewart.

It sounds awful, but it isn't as awful as all that, for Capra has a touch of genius with a camera: his screen always seems twice as big as other people's, and he cuts as brilliantly as Eisenstein (the climax when the big bad magnate takes up his harmonica is so exhilarating in its movement that you forget its absurdity). Humour and not wit is his line, a humour which shades off into whimsicality, and a kind of popular poetry which is apt to turn wistful. We may groan and blush as he cuts his way remorselessly through all finer values to the fallible human heart, but infallibly he makes his appeal – to that great soft organ with its unreliable goodness and easy melancholy and baseless optimism. The cinema, a popular craft, can hardly be expected to do more.   *The Spectator,* 11 November 1938

You Can't Take It With You (USA, Columbia, 1938). Director: Frank Capra. James Stewart, Jean Arthur, Lionel Barrymore.

Alerte en Méditerranée/Men With Wings

This latest French film is a routine melodrama of naval life in the Mediterranean. It enables us better than more unusual films to judge the quality of the French industry, for it is hard to remember that usually we are shown nothing but the best. In this picture there is no originality; its theme of international comradeship between men of the same trade recalls the far finer German picture *Kameradschaft* (how the world has altered! It was France in those days which had to be reminded that there were other values than that of war).

A tramp steamer puts into Tangier, where German, English and French men-of-war ride at anchor: there is said to be yellow fever on board, so the Customs officer neglects his duty. Then the ship's drunken doctor slips on shore with a tongue ready to blab and is murdered during a brawl. French, English and German sailors are arrested; they each blame the other nationalities, and their officers who have made friends over a child's toy destroyer quarrel now like their Governments over death-guilt. Then the Captain of the tramp escapes from his own ship (an exciting scene, handled very quietly); he brings news that the sailors are innocent; the murderer is the man who chartered the steamer – a mysterious Mr Martin who is smuggling a dye called 424 through the Mediterranean. The French torpedo-boat leaves in pursuit, bearing the English and German officers with her to keep liaison with their Admiralties. They must not sink the steamer, for if the dye mixes with salt water it throws off poison gas, capable of killing all life within two hundred miles. So they run alongside and bluff with blank charges. The crew surrender, and Mr Martin scuttles the ship. The poisonous fog moves at 20 knots across the sea, and a liner from Tangier to Marseille lies with engine trouble helpless in its path – on board the French Commander's wife and son. Seaplanes are sent to rescue the children, but for the adult passengers and crew the only chance is for the torpedo-boat to break through the gas. The attempt succeeds with ten minutes to spare, and the German officer – who had been gassed in the War – dies protractedly on the bridge with a message for the French child. There are moments when internationalism becomes as sentimental as some forms of patriotism, but on the whole the film succeeds – not as a peace tract but as a naval thriller.

It succeeds mainly in the accuracy of its details – which is where English films so often fail – in the dying seagull scrabbling against the glass: the top of the masts moving into obscurity through the black clouds of gas: the unnautical fountain-pen in Mr Martin's breastpocket and his sad drooping outcast mouth. It may be the function of the French cinema to teach us how to handle realism, as they taught it in the novel years ago – realism on a more imaginative level than our facile and whimsical use of national types. The Anglo-Saxon – whether English or American – always tempers the direct impact of life sooner or later with a laugh or a good cry.

Men With Wings is also routine melodrama – on the Anglo-Saxon level. One of those clean stories which call for Freudian analysis, it is about two men who have loved one woman from childhood. One marries her and is always leaving her; the other stays around, doglike. Eventually, the husband gets killed flying in China – and I suppose the dog has his day. This story is said to be about 'man's conquest of the air from the first flight of the Wright Brothers in 1903 to the making of super-speed bombers in 1938' (the last a family affair of the woman, the child, and the dog – Mr Ray Milland). But we saw no Wright Brothers, and what we heard ran on these lines: the heroine asking in the maternity ward, 'How can I be this happy?' frail under Technicolor sunburn, and the nurse saying 'That's why there's so many mothers.' The director has dedicated his prize egg 'To all women who love and admire the fearless heroes of the air, and who, with brave hearts, encourage them, hope, and pray for them.' The new star, Miss Louise Campbell, was formerly a dental assistant, but none of the painful scenes at which she then assisted ever lasted two hours.   *The Spectator*, 18 November 1938

Alerte en Méditerranée (France, Véga Films, 1937). Director: Léo Joannon. Pierre Fresnay, Rolf Wanka, Kim Peacock. [US title: *SOS Mediterranean.*]
Men With Wings (USA, Paramount, 1938). Director: William A. Wellman. Fred MacMurray, Ray Milland, Louise Campbell.

Lenin in October

Lenin in October is one of the best entertainments we have seen in a cinema for a long while, and I hope for everyone's sake that it will soon be shown publicly. Hardly less entertaining are the programme notes put out by the Film Society in that curious gritty hyphenated prose which seems to go with ideological convictions:

By contrast with *October, Lenin in October*, covering the same ground, concentrates upon a particular figure and deals with the part he played therein. This concentration is obtained at the expense of what, in comparison with certain identical mass scenes in *October*, will be seen as a considerable relative neglect of the compositional qualities of the image. This falling-off is characteristic of Soviet films of the period, and apparently a concomitant of the effort at reorientation of interest around personality on the part of the creative group. In later films, those recently completed and still in production, it is apparent that already usage is affording sufficient facility to enable a high compositional level to be retained together with depiction of personality.

From this lumpy gruel of inexact and abstract words, you may or may not get the idea: that we have reached the end of the Communist film. It is to be all 'Heroes and Hero-Worship' now: the old films are to be remade for the new leaders: no more anonymous mothers will run in the van of the workers against the Winter Palace. The USSR is to produce Fascist films from now on.

History, of course, has to be rewritten in the process, and it would be absurd to expect from *Lenin* the old excitement of conviction (which used to drive the very bourgeois members of the Society to sing the 'Red Flag'). What is left is the excitement of melodrama handled with the right shabby realism, the interest of seeing an actor reconstruct the mannerisms of Lenin (his widow believes them to be over-emphasized), most agreeable of all the unconscious humour of the rearrangement – the elimination of Trotsky and the way in which Stalin slides into all the important close-ups.

'Before anything else,' Lenin commands his bodyguard as soon as he has set foot in Petrograd (he has been smuggled in by train from Finland in the driver's cabin), 'before anything else arrange a meeting with Stalin.' And at that meeting he tells the Central Committee: 'Comrade Stalin is absolutely right. The proposals of Kamenev and Zinoviev and Trotsky are either complete idiocy or a betrayal' (more names, it is to be supposed, will be added to the soundtrack after every trial). Then we have the kind of shadowgraph upon a window once popular in love-stories – Stalin statuesque with his pipe and Lenin, little and nervous, gesticulating up at him. Throughout Lenin is played on humorous lines, a little Robin Goodfellow of a man, full of elfish tricks, who has to be controlled and looked after and lent macintoshes by Stalin and the Central Committee, while his big sound brother-in-arms is played on Worcestershire lines: you feel he reads Mary Webb. In the final close-up of Lenin addressing the first Soviet, he sidles up behind Lenin's shoulder, pipe in hand, wearing an approving and patronizing smile – a headmaster on founder's day glad to welcome an old boy who has made good. You expect a sly comment about canes.

There is the usual fine assortment of unreliable old liberal faces among the Mensheviks and of simple tow-haired workers who wear cartridge-belts, with the

Lenin in October

gawky charm of Bottom and his flowers. But everybody, even Lenin, is acted off
the set by whichever Honoured Artist of the Republic it is who plays the police
agent set by the Mensheviks to trace Lenin. This is a magnificent portrait – in the
Cruikshank manner – of seedy and unscrupulous gentility; the wet loose hand and
the battered bowler, the mole and the lank lock and the stringy tie and the calculated
impudence.   *The Spectator*, 25 November 1938

Lenin in October (USSR, Mosfilm, 1937). Director: Mikhail Romm. Boris Shchukin, Nikolai Olchlopkov,
Vasili Vanin, I. Golshtab.

The Dawn Patrol/Persons in Hiding/Kentucky/Never Say Die

There has been such a chorus of praise for *The Dawn Patrol* that to let the little
worm of doubt creep in on this heroic occasion seems like a breach of taste. Never
have the critics been so unanimous since those *Glorious Years* – and perhaps
psychologically the two pictures have something in common. They both flatter
our national pride by emphasizing what are known as the 'masculine virtues'. The
theme of this flying picture is that of *The Light Brigade*: somebody at headquarters
has blundered, and day after day the Light Brigade, as it were, rides forth against

March 1939

Persons in Hiding: Patricia Morison

208

the guns – 'Their's not to make reply, Their's but to do and die.' The officers who in turn command the flight, condemned to a desk and a whisky bottle, unwillingly send out batch after batch of replacements – schoolboys with less than ten hours' solo flying – to be shot down by the German ace and his squadron, and their nerves rather histrionically collapse. As a protest against war, it is insincere: the emphasis is on the heroic and the patriotic – Von Richter, it will be noted, always wears an ugly sneer behind his machine-gun.

It *is* quite a good picture, well directed and in some cases well acted, but I don't believe it's true – a great deal of self-pity and romanticism have gone to the making of this excellent ham-sandwich. The critics have made great play with the fact that there isn't a woman in the cast, but personally I found myself regretting the old intruder in her abbreviated skirt and her WAAC hat – the film wouldn't have been any less like life, and in her stead we get an even more romantic love. The young blond officer with the Frohlich face weeps over the dead school-friend, and the kid brother arrives full of morning glory to join his brother's squadron – the last war seems to have been littered with younger brothers. Mr Basil Rathbone adds to the general effect of melodrama: he can't – whatever his part – do much else with that dark knife-blade face and snapping mouth.

Persons in Hiding is a gangster picture, a little on the tame side, distinguished by the presence of a crooked and merciless heroine, acted by a newcomer, Miss Patricia Morison. Miss Morison is lovely to look at, but never persuades us she is more. She has small chance, since the story opens, as it were, in the middle, with her first theft as a hairdresser's assistant – and after that it's all speeding cars and montage: we are given no background, and there is nothing in her acting to suggest the past which launched her on this anarchic storm. That is exactly what Mr Lynne Overman as the G-man supplies: with every intonation and weary cock of the head we get the whole contented bourgeois home, the comradely wife and the furniture from a plain van, the melancholy crack over the breakfast-table, the law-abiding background to the dangerous life.

Kentucky is the first film I have seen which has been made by its colour. A banal story of an old Kentucky feud, dating from the Civil War, with Montague and Capulet owning rival race-studs, it wouldn't amount to much without colour – as it is, there is continuous pleasure in watching the horses and Miss Loretta Young – I am not sure which are the most beautiful; and there are one or two fine touches of direction – when the child, whose father has been shot by the Federal troops come to seize his horses, runs frantically beside the dusty blue breeches and the chestnut flanks babbling incoherently of brood mares, and again when a commentator reads out the names of old Kentucky winners – Diamond, Rocksand, Gallant Fox and Galahad the Second – while the mares stream by across the wide pastures.

But the most enjoyable film for weeks has slipped by unnoticed among the heroic and romantic. *Never Say Die* is consistently absurd – it has no dignity, no passion, and a magnificent cast, headed by Mr Bob Hope as Kidley, a multi-millionaire who is supposed to be suffering from quite abnormal acidity (the chemist has mixed up his test with that of a dog called Kipper) and to be slowly digesting himself. 'Side by side,' his physician proudly announces, 'we will live down eternity – Schmidt and his disease.'   *The Spectator*, 3 March 1939

The Dawn Patrol (USA, Warner Bros, 1938). Director: Edmund Goulding. Errol Flynn, David Niven, Basil Rathbone.
Persons in Hiding (USA, Paramount, 1938). Director: Louis King. Lynne Overman, Patricia Morison.
Kentucky (USA, 20th Century-Fox, 1938). Director: David Butler. Loretta Young, Richard Greene, Walter Brennan, Moroni Olsen.
Never Say Die (USA, Paramount, 1938). Director: Elliott Nugent. Bob Hope, Martha Raye.

Three Smart Girls Grow Up/Black Eyes/Inspector Hornleigh

Innocence is a tricky subject: its appeal is not always quite so clean as a whistle, and in *Black Eyes* the Edwardian dresses, the droshkies and chandeliers of pre-war Russia do not altogether disguise the brutality of the plot – which is simply will the roué get the innocent? Innocence is just the turn of the screw, to make the suspense more breathless.

Miss Deanna Durbin's film, needless to say, is not a bit like that. She is not the innocent centre of a sly story; everything is innocent all round her: youth is laid on with a trowel. The white feminine room which the three sisters share, the quilted beds, the little furry jackets over the pyjamas – the whole upholstery is so virginal that it awakes little twitters of nostalgia from the stalls. Pillow-fights and first love and being sent to bed without any dinner – the awkward age has never been so laundered and lavendered and laid away. And it is all charming, very charming. There is no doubt any longer of Miss Durbin's immense talents as an actress; any undertones that there are in this amusing, astute and sentimental tale are supplied by her. Singing 'The Last Rose of Summer' to her preoccupied Wall Street father, blundering into her sisters' love-affairs and rearranging them with crude, unscrupulous success, she swings the picture along in her gauche and graceful stride. The competence of the director, Mr Henry Koster, matches hers: a kind of national value emerges from the *schwarmerei* – it is all Fifth Avenue and girlish freedom – tea at the Waldorf and cold, clear New York spring.

Black Eyes is slower, dingier, really more sentimental. Hollywood has tampered with Mlle Simone Simon's acting, and even her appearance: she gives the impression of having been smudged. It is on M. Harry Baur that we depend – of course, not in vain – for our pleasure, on M. Baur and the odd, outmoded plot which takes us back in memory nearly twenty years. Seduction in the early cinema was always a serious and nearly always an unsuccessful business – a matter of galloping horses, lariats and pistol-shots, or else of gipsy singers and champagne. *Black Eyes* belongs to the champagne school. The climax is reached when the young girl, Mlle Simon, is shut in a restaurant's private room with a lustful banker and a buffet large enough for a battalion, while her father – he has kept from her all these years the knowledge that he is a head waiter – palpitates outside the door. First the gipsies emerge, jingling with spangles and tips, then one by one the waiters – has she taken wine? are they still safely at table? – at last the anxious parent can contain himself no longer and breaks in. . . . I enjoyed this picture. The cinema has lost some of its charm since those naïve days, and I could not help feeling a little wistful watching the elaborate surgical preparations for a seduction – the practised movements of waiters like nurses round an operating-table, everybody and everything assigned an exact part from the insinuating musical harridans to the chosen vintage, until the climax – the dirty look and the turning of the key. M. Baur, too, is a great enough actor to lend what might otherwise seem a somewhat grotesque situation genuine suspense. No mockery can survive those heavy pouched eyes set in the antique turtle face: they convey an abysmal experience of human nature: and we are reminded as we watch that turtles are said to survive for many hundred years.

How the financial crisis has improved English films! They have lost their tasteless Semitic opulence and are becoming – English. *Inspector Hornleigh* is a routine

Inspector Hornleigh: Gordon Harker, Alastair Sim

picture, the first of a series, starring Mr Gordon Harker as the Inspector and Mr Alastair Sim as his incapable subordinate, and it nearly deserves to be classed with the Chans and the Motos. The opening shots – the murder in the squalid lodging and the stamp auction with the row of poker faces and the elaborately mute bids – are not only good cinema, they are good English cinema, as national as a shot, say, from a Feyder, a de Mille or a Pommer. But the picture doesn't quite maintain that realistic level: there are too many bogus exteriors and menacing shadows, talk, and the murderer's motives remain hopelessly obscure at the end.

The Spectator, 7 April 1939

Three Smart Girls Grow Up (USA, Universal, 1938). Director: Henry Koster. Deanna Durbin, Nan Grey, Charles Winninger.
Black Eyes (*Les Yeux Noirs*) (France, Milo Films, 1935). Director: Victor Tourjansky. Simone Simon, Harry Baur, Jean-Pierre Aumont. [US title: *Dark Eyes.*]
Inspector Hornleigh (GB, 20th Century-Fox, 1939). Director: Eugene Ford. Gordon Harker, Alastair Sim, Hugh Williams.

Hotel Imperial

Perhaps it is because I associate the name Miranda with an old family donkey which used to take the washing to the laundry on Saturdays that I cannot enter whole-heartedly into Paramount's enthusiasm for their new imported star. The most glamorous woman in the world comes to the screen at last! Beautiful .. exciting ... Isa Miranda ... Men drank to her loveliness and marched off to die! Her love sealed the fate of armies! . . . Generals moved armies to be near her!' We are told that D'Annunzio rushed home to write poems after he had seen her on the screen, and that Mascagni held up the rehearsal of an opera to lead the orchestra impromptu through a piece she loved: it seems horribly flat after all that to write for this sober and reliable journal one's little prosaic piece describing the long, gaunt face, the husky Marlene accent, and the slinky feathery dress. And the acting? Oh, well, I don't think it can have been the acting which sent D'Annunzio to his poetry. Miranda (forgive me if I smile, remembering that other long, awkward, friendly face) is not a Duse.

As for the picture, it is a very competent rehash by Robert Florey of the story Pommer directed so brilliantly in 1926 with Pola Negri: you may remember Sucha, the small Galician town, captured four times by the Russians, three times by the Austrians: the faded elegance of the hotel which caters alternately for the staff of the two armies – the portrait of Franz Josef is quickly changed to the portrait of Nicholas, the order for cutlets is cancelled in favour of beef. An Austrian officer who has been on patrol returns to find the town fallen again; he is hidden in the hotel by the porter and the chambermaid and dressed as a waiter: a traitor from the Austrian Staff arrives with the plans for the counter-attack, is killed in his room by the fugitive, who escapes to the Austrian lines, and the girl is about to face a Russian firing-squad when – tanks go over the top, cavalry charge, bombing squadrons take off, and all the old hocus-pocus of the last-minute rescue is set going with a grotesque mechanized elaboration which must make Griffith turn in his retirement. I miss the old finale when the chambermaid was decorated before the troops and kissed on the cheek by the Commander-in-Chief – we have grown a little more wary in these days of heroics. And there are other alterations – this chambermaid is not a real chambermaid, but an actress who is trying to discover an officer who betrayed her sister: have we grown more snobbish? And I seem to remember that the old film was full of charming central European humiliations, and there was no Don Cossack choir (the first time on any screen), and it was economical and shoddy and convincing, and Negri scrubbed the steps to the manner born instead of slinking around, like Miranda, singing huskily and drinking champagne.

All the same, the picture has merits – Mr Gene Lockhart, for instance, as the timid and heroic hotel porter; Mr Ray Milland, until he has to speak, looks just right, muddy and tired and desperate – it is the waiter's uniform and love which spoils all; Mr Carroll Naish is excellent as the vulgar, cynical, amusing spy, and the whole heroic picture warms into first-class comedy, with Mr Reginald Owen as the Russian General who paints. Even the dialogue comes to life as when he phones headquarters, after recapturing Sucha, 'How dare you bombard the civilian population when it lives in such picturesque houses?' or rebukes the spy on his last spectacular entrance for 'an increasing tendency towards melodrama in your

Hotel Imperial: Isa Miranda, Ray Milland, J. Carroll Naish

opening lines'. And for one glorious moment the hearts of all old lovers of the cinema are elated at the sight of Von Seyffertitz's narrow white photogenic features bobbing speechlessly up like memory out of a black cloak. Yes, for the unexacting the picture has its moments.   *The Spectator*, 14 April 1939

Hotel Imperial (USA, Paramount, 1939). Director: Robert Florey. Isa Miranda, Ray Milland, J. Carroll Naish, Reginald Owen, Gene Lockhart, Gustav von Seyffertitz.

Idiot's Delight/Beach Picnic/They Drive By Night

It is possible that Mr Sherwood as a film-writer does small credit to Mr Sherwood as a dramatist; I have not seen his plays, but *Idiot's Delight* has exactly the same pseudo-qualities as *The Petrified Forest*, a moral pretentiousness, a kind of cellophaned intellectuality. They are all supposed to make one think, these windy abstractions, the literary quotations, the little scraps of popular philosophy. The introduction in one film of a realistic killer and in the other of a rather less realistic air raid does not alter the fact that we are in a Sparkenbroke world in which literature, passed through the filter of a naïve mind, is a substitute for character. Mr Eliot once remarked that the metaphysical poets experienced thought as directly as the scent of a rose, but Mr Sherwood and his kind seem to experience a rose as dimly and indirectly as a thought.

The plot of *Idiot's Delight* is by now well known. Padded out for the screen with a long, rambling, not unamusing prologue, it loses all grip at the very point where the play started, in the winter-sports hotel perched over a military aerodrome at the start of a European war. We have the usual set of representative characters, a munition-maker, a cancer expert, a sentimental lefty, a hoofer with his chorus-girls, young English honeymooners. 'Jimmy feels he must do his bit,' the child-wife remarks as they leave for England, and the dialogue is all on that level – it either reads like a war poster or a peace poster ('Wings of Death' is what the feverish, all-for-love Communist calls a bomber), or else like a passage from Dr Hiram Q. Entwhistle's *World's Great Philosophers for Everyman.* In the end everybody escapes, except the Communist, whom we gather has been obscurely shot off-stage, the hoofer, and the girl he had met years ago in variety and who is now uncon-vincingly in back projection all around while they swing a tune. Why? Nobody knows: the play has no theme – except the widely held notion that war is unpleasant, and no character is given any personal life against the too important background – if one can refer to the bad models and worse back projections as important. Mr Clark Gable does his best, but Miss Norma Shearer adds to the heavy saturated ennui the weight of a far too powerful personality. Over-acting could hardly go further. The programme is saved by one of the best Disneys for years – the adventures of Pluto with a rubber sea-horse, coy, flippant and aerated.

The resurrection of the English film continues. In another twelve months we may find ourselves pursuing English films into obscure cinemas in the Edgware Road. *They Drive by Night* is a murder-story set against an authentic background of dance palaces, public houses, seedy Soho clubs, and the huge wet expanse of the Great North Road, with its bungaloid cafés, the grinding gears, and the monstrous six-wheeled lorries plunging through the rain. Well acted by Mr Emlyn Williams as a young gaol-bird wanted for a murder he hasn't committed, and superbly acted by Mr Ernest Thesiger as Mr Hoover, the sedate, pedantic sex-maniac with the sloping, humble walk, the grasshopper head, and the abominable pride, it gets the realistic twist out of every situation. One remembers Mr Hoover expatiating on the crime in the public house – the most authentic pub conversation I have heard on the screen: Mr Hoover saluting the stray cat, 'Ah, you pretty thing! Ah, my subtle one!': the absurd formalities of the dance palace. Dialogue, acting and direction put this picture on a level with the French cinema – the settings for the first time in an English low-life story are not romanticized, and for once we are not conscious of the brooding auntie-like presence in Carlisle House – perhaps they didn't know what some of the words meant. Set beside this picture, Mr Sherwood's picture can be seen for the sham it is. *Idiot's Delight* begins vaguely with an idea, an idea that it is treating an important subject – war and peace; but war is only important in the sense that an elephant or a dowager is important, by size. The author of the English film has taken characters in a simple melodramatic situation and given them a chance to show with some intensity their private battlefields.

The Spectator, 21 April 1939

Idiot's Delight (USA, M-G-M, 1938). Director: Clarence Brown. Norma Shearer, Clark Gable, Edward Arnold, Burgess Meredith, Joseph Schildkraut.
Beach Picnic (USA, 1939). Disney cartoon.
They Drive By Night (GB, Warner Bros, 1939). Director: Arthur Woods. Emlyn Williams, William Hartnell, Ernest Thesiger.

They Drive By Night: Ernest Thesiger

The Four Feathers/The Sisters/Thanks for Everything

The story of *The Four Feathers* must be known by this time to everyone – four films have now been made of this ham-heroic tale, which describes how Lieutenant Harry Faversham, the Coward who resigned his commission at the start of the Sudanese War, disguised himself as a dumb Sangali and forced his brother officers to take back the white feathers they had sent him. What is new is the drive – and in the Sudanese sequences the conviction – of this new version. Far better than the American, it cannot fail to be one of the best films of the year. Even the thickest of the ham – the old veterans discussing the Crimea in the Faversham home, among the portraits of military ancestors – goes smoothly down, savoured with humour and satire. For almost the first time the huge ambitious Denham studios have produced something better than a mouse.

On the screen a ham story doesn't matter: *The Sisters*, too, is ham, and even more conventional – the girl who marries a hard-drinking journalist who loves her, but loves his freedom more. The pathos is very familiar – the husband returns drunk on the evening when his wife intends to tell him she is pregnant: they quarrel on Christmas Day beside the Christmas-tree. The San Francisco earthquake is thrown effectively in as makeweight, there is a tiny, timid sketch of a brothel which probably passed our universal aunts as a happy picture of family life, but the main situation is as old as the cinema – you remember it in *Cimarron* – the husband who rides away and goes on loving all the time. But, as I say, ham doesn't matter: *The Sisters* is worth seeing for the sake of the adroit period direction and the fragile, pop-eyed acting of Miss Bette Davis.

So in *The Four Feathers* the plot hardly matters: what is important is the colour, which is almost invariably pleasant and sometimes gives a shock of pleasure such as we have not experienced since the moment in *Becky Sharp* when the scarlet-cloaked cavalry poured out by the dark Brussels streets on the road to Waterloo. What is important is nocturnal London smoking up through Faversham's grey windows: the close-up of mulberry bodies straining at the ropes along the Nile: the cracked umber waste round the dried-up wells: the vultures with their grimy serrated Lisle-street wings dropping like weighted parachutes. It is impossible to divide the credit between Mr Zoltan Korda, the director, who has wiped out the disgrace of *Sanders of the River*, and Mr R. C. Sherriff, author of the film-play. They seem to have perfectly fulfilled each other's intentions – as Riskin and Capra did in the old days. We forget the silly plot when the voice repeats monotonously, 'Load, present, fire', behind the black smoke of the burning zariba: when the blinded man, the only survivor of his company, cries for his brother officer, and at every cry the vultures rise squawking from their meal and settle again. The picture is finely acted by Mr John Clements and Mr Ralph Richardson, and Miss June Duprez not only looks lovely, but also holds her own with these first-class actors.

This is, I fear, a week of monotonous praise. *Thanks for Everything* is the funniest film I can remember seeing for many months, with something of the old Kauffman touch. It is a great deal in these days to be made to laugh at the sight of a man in a gas-mask. An advertising agency through a competition discover a 100 per cent average American (whom they bilk of the prize so as to keep even his income average). By watching his reactions they are able to predict with uncanny accuracy movements of public taste. The representative of a European Power asks

The Four Feathers

them to discover what would induce the American public to fight: the wretched man is quarantined with an imaginary disease, supplied through specially printed papers with imaginary news, but remains unstirred by attacks on Embassies, tourists, trade. Only when an imaginary air raid is ingeniously staged for his benefit does he react – embarrassingly. Adolphe Menjou walks through this ingenious and witty film with a kind of brazen efficiency, followed dubiously and protestingly by Jack Oakie as his henchman.   *The Spectator*, 28 April 1939

The Four Feathers (GB, London Films, 1939). Director: Zoltan Korda. John Clements, Ralph Richardson, June Duprez.
The Sisters (USA, Warner Bros, 1938). Director: Anatole Litvak. Bette Davis, Errol Flynn, Anita Louise, Ian Hunter, Donald Crisp, Beulah Bondi.
Thanks For Everything (USA, 20th Century-Fox, 1939). Director: William A. Seiter. Jack Oakie, Adolphe Menjou, Arleen Whelan, Jack Haley.

Wuthering Heights/La Bête Humaine

How much better they would have made *Wuthering Heights* in France. They know there how to shoot sexual passion; but in this Californian-constructed Yorkshire, among the sensitive neurotic English voices, sex is cellophaned; there is no egotism, no obsession. This Heathcliff would never have married for revenge (Mr Olivier's nervous, breaking voice belongs to balconies and Verona and romantic love), and one cannot imagine the ghost of this Cathy weeping with balked passion outside the broken window: Miss Merle Oberon cannot help making her a very normal girl. The plot has been simplified (quite reasonably) to cover only one generation: the minor characters have been tidied up or away: and darkness, darkness most of the time, takes the place of the original's disquieting passion. Candle-flames flicker, windows blow in draughts, monstrous shadows lie across the indifferent faces of the actors, all to lend significance to a rather dim story which would not have taxed the talents of Mr Ben Hecht to have invented himself. Perhaps Mr Goldwyn, who has a bold mind, realized what was needed, for he chose the admirable director of *Dead End*, and the fault may not be altogether Wyler's. There is Hecht's script to be considered – and the cast of sensitive and distinguished Britons. So a lot of reverence has gone into a picture which should have been as coarse as a sewer. Some readers may remember *Orage*, a not very distinguished French film: the lovers in the stifling inn room beating off flies, lying about among the soiled clothes without the will or wish to go down for meals. Something of that carnality was needed here: the sentimental rendezvous under a crag where Heathcliff and Cathy used to play as children is not a substitute. The whole picture is *Keepsake* stuff.

La Bête Humaine is a very different matter: Zola's story of a sadistic maniac may not be much more plausible, but Renoir aided by a magnificent cast gets right underneath the plot – so that again and again we hear the ghost in the cellarage: as when Jean Gabin, as the maniac, questions Simone Simon about the murder to which she had been an unwilling accomplice (the murder of a former lover by her jealous husband), the very gentle twitching of the eyebrows as the stifled excitement begins to work, the uneasy movements of the mouth, the strained, too casual, voice seeking details: 'And how many times did he strike?' Gabin gives an impeccable performance. Watch him after the murder of the girl as he pauses by the mirror on the bourgeois sideboard – the relaxed muscles, the unobtrusive weakening of the mouth, the appalling sense of melancholy satiety. And Mlle Simon, too, acts with intensity the little, sensual, treacherous wife. Pitiably ineffective in *Les Yeux Noirs*, she is helped here by a cameraman who knows how to deal with the coarse black electric hair, the snub nose, the rather African features. But *La Bête Humaine* is more a director's than an actor's picture – a director who knows how to get the most out of the everyday life of his characters, the routine of their work – in this case the immediate surroundings of a great railway station: all the small incidents which English directors cut out of a script because they are not 'on the story line' and do not advance the plot. As if a plot mattered at all except as a dramatized illustration of a character and a way of life. The picture opens with Gabin and his taciturn, anxious fireman (a lovely piece of acting) on the footplate of the Paris–Havre express, and closes in the reverse direction – sidings flowing back into fields. That is easy: it has been done before, though not so well: what is most deft is the way in which Renoir works the depot and a man's job into every scene – conversations on platforms, in washrooms and canteens, views from the station master's window over the steaming metal waste: the short, sharp lust worked out in a wooden platelayer's shed among shunted trucks under the steaming rain.

The Spectator, 5 May 1939

Wuthering Heights (USA, Samuel Goldwyn, 1939). Director: William Wyler. Merle Oberon, Laurence Olivier, David Niven.
La Bête Humaine (France, Paris Films, 1938). Director: Jean Renoir. Jean Gabin, Simone Simon, Carette, Fernand Ledoux, Jean Renoir. [US title: *The Human Beast*.]

The Oklahoma Kid/The Lone Ranger

I open the only Western I have at hand, and come immediately on one of those classic sentences (Hardy's phrase about the President of the Immortals is a familiar example) in which an author's whole way of writing and thinking is crystallized. '"There's certainly a pile of hell being raised around Cougar," Blaze commented thoughtfully.' That expresses about everything – the heavy decorative gun-holsters and the ten-gallon hats, the wooden sidewalks and the saloons, the double-crossing sheriff, the corrupt judge, the fine old man with white whiskers and the girl in gingham, and the final 'slug feast' – to borrow a Western phrase – among the toppling gas-lamps.

The Oklahoma Kid is a good specimen of new-style Western, more refined than the old silent ones with their rapes and hair-breadth escapes (it is typical of a certain intellectuality nowadays that the only rescuers here arrive too late): it hasn't the expensive finish of *The Virginian* or *The Plainsman*, and Mr James Cagney, the gunman with a social conscience, takes perhaps a little less kindly to the big hat and the tight breeches and the intense sexual purity than Mr Humphrey Bogart as the bad man in black. But Mr Cagney can do nothing which is not worth watching. On his light hoofer's feet, with his quick nervous hands and his magnificent unconsciousness of the camera, he can pluck distinction out of the least promising part – and this part has plenty of meat. A pile of hell is certainly being raised around Cougar – or, rather, the new Tulsa city, built by pioneers in the Cherokee strip of Oklahoma, where the bad man has established by trickery his monopoly of vice centres, and has corrupted the law with bought juries. There's a lot of gun-play around the sinister Mr Bogart before he frames the fine old man with white whiskers and has him lynched by saloon loungers. That's when the Oklahoma Kid begins to make good – the dead man's worthless son with a price on his head takes the law into his own hands and disposes of his father's murderers one after another. His brother is the new reforming Sheriff, who, at the end of the last magnificent slug feast with Mr Bogart, dies with a bullet in his stomach after telling the Kid that he has procured his pardon. So the Kid is free to marry his brother's girl, the dumb plain pure creature in gingham with little filly ways – you expect her to whinny whenever she opens her mouth. (In the old days it would have been the no-good who died nobly, ginghams then were more careful of the stock they raised.) Apart from one scene in which Mr Cagney sings *Rock-a-bye Baby* rather unconvincingly to an Indian papoose, this is a direct and competent picture.

The Lone Ranger is a serial which has swept the States. Before it finishes there will be a bigger pile of hell raised than in any other known Western – there are big twenty-minute gobbets of riding and gunning every week. The first instalment, called *Hi-yo, Silver*, introduces the now-famous call of the masked ranger to his white steed – a cry uttered, often in the most unsuitable circumstances, in an odd and congested, rather Harvard voice. Who is the Lone Ranger, sworn to avenge his comrades, who are ambushed by the villain in the first instalment? We shall not know until the last. Meanwhile the first chapter lines up the characters of this immense saga: the chief villain, a snakey hound who is posing with false papers as the Federal Commissioner of a new territory; his henchman, small, treacherous and dirty, who betrays first the rangers and then the farmers who have risen against the tyranny of the false Commissioner; the hero, his horse, a few assorted Texans, and the girl in gingham – or so I suppose, for she has not yet had a word to say. There has been no time; events have moved with such rapidity. The hero has escaped a massacre and a firing-squad already, and we leave him with his guns empty, the farmers' stockade blown up by gunpowder, falling under the charging hooves of the villain's cavalry.   *The Spectator*, 12 May 1939

The Oklahoma Kid (USA, Warner Bros, 1939). Director: Lloyd Bacon. James Cagney, Humphrey Bogart, Rosemary Lane, Donald Crisp.
The Lone Ranger (USA, Republic, 1939). Directors: William Witney, John English. Lee Powell.

Jamaica Inn

This passionate, full-blooded yarn could only have been conceived by a young authoress of considerable refinement. The drinking, leching, blaspheming, Cornish wreckers are reminiscent of the noisier characters in Shakespeare acted at a girls' school – the well-cushioned Falstaff with the voice of beloved Miss Peridew, the games-mistress, and tight-laced Pistol from the sixth form. But, after all, we are not concerned with the story: a bad story is a small handicap to a good director or a good actor, and there must have been something in Miss Du Maurier's novel which caught the attention of Mr Laughton and Mr Hitchcock. Mr Laughton may have seen in one character the germ of his own magnificent and vinous portrait of a Regency buck, Sir Humphrey Pengallan, the secret leader of the wreckers. With his nose adeptly reconstructed into a little cocky beak and his too familiar manner-isms sternly checked, he gives a superb performance, though I am reminded uneasily when I write this of those too perceptive dramatic critics who are able to recognize genius even when it speaks Yiddish, for, owing presumably to the acoustics of the cinema, no one where I was seated was able to hear more than scattered words of the dialogue.

It is more difficult to know why Mr Hitchcock embarked on this bogus costume-piece and submitted himself to a producer. There is only one Hitchcock incident here in embryo, when the pseudo-wrecker, saved by the heroine from his comrades who are hanging him, takes refuge with her in the house of the nearest magistrate, and he, of course, is Pengallan, the wreckers' leader. This situation translated into contemporary terms might well have been the high-spot of a Hitchcock chase, with rather more care taken over the realistic details; but costume has so confused Mr Hitchcock that he allows the hero, wet through by a long swim, to borrow a tight-fitting officer's uniform from Pengallan which fits him like a glove. This is only one example of frequent failures in imagination which sometimes caused untimely laughter from the audience – laughter which swelled as the film dragged on to the absurd rape and the cavalry to the rescue, and stout booted Pengallan climbing backwards up the shrouds for his suicidal jump. Mr Hitchcock's talent has always been for the surprise situation, but here, perhaps because he had to stick closely to a conventional and sentimental tale, perhaps because the presence of a producer cramped him, there are no surprises – and no suspense: we can see everything that will happen half an hour away.

The unsatisfactory picture has been most lavishly produced, though the whole set of the sinister inn creaks like its own signboard. No expense has been spared, and I was irresistibly reminded of an all-star charity matinée. A face looks round a door – and it is Horace Hodges, or Stephen Haggard, Hay Petrie, Clare Greet, George Curzon, Jeanne de Casalis (so good of them, we feel, to give their services for the Fresh-Air Fund). Mr Emlyn Williams has a rather longer part as a wrecker, but that plump Celtic face lamentably failed to make my flesh creep; Mr Robert Newton is the hero, the naval officer who is playing spy, but I find this young actor with his gasps and glittering eyes peculiarly unsympathetic; and there is a brand-new heroine, Miss Maureen O'Hara, who leaves (it is really not her fault) a rather comic impression: she, too, finds a perfectly fitting costume in the Squire's house, and the smart Regency dress doesn't look well at midnight on the Cornish coast. Only Mr Leslie Banks matches Mr Laughton as an actor and introduces some sense of real evil into a girl's dream of violent manhood.   *The Spectator*, 19 May 1939

Jamaïca Inn (GB, Mayflower, 1939). Director: Alfred Hitchcock. Maureen O'Hara, Charles Laughton, Robert Newton, Emlyn Williams, Leslie Banks.

Men in Danger/Spare Time/Health of a Nation/An Elephant Never Forgets

I am getting a little tired of that word 'documentary'. It has a dry-as-dust sound: we think of incomprehensible machinery revolving before the camera eye: earnest 'expert' faces mouthing abstractions behind very polished and very empty desks: it carries a false air of impartiality, as much as to say 'this is what is – not what we think or feel'. But the best documentaries have never been like that: as long ago as Rotha's *Shipyard* they took political sides, and to call *The River* – or Wright's *Children at School* – documentary is about as meaningless as to call a sonnet documentary: they document the creator's mind, that is all.

So the personal element – the lyrical and the ironic – is the important thing in the documentaries which the GPO are sending to the World Fair. Only one of them might easily have belonged to the dry-as-dust order – Cavalcanti's *Men In Danger*, which begins as a factual record of occupational diseases and the methods used to minimise the danger. It is, at the start, frankly dull: information is being pains-takingly conveyed. Then the horror begins to grip – the director as well as the audi-ence. What will America think of these children working barefooted at the looms, in danger of cancer-creating oils? 'It is hoped,' we hear, 'to find a safer oil', and the laboratory assistant holds up his tentative test-tube, and the child pads back and forth. It is the atmosphere – and, alas, the country – of 'The Song of the Shirt'. Perhaps more horrifying still are the shots of monotony – and of the means taken to alleviate it: interminable trays of potted-meat jars passing before stooping, spotty girls: the information that in a biscuit factory the girls can sing to relieve the boredom and 'are allowed to choose their own songs'. *Allowed* – a word to make the angels weep. We see psychological researchers at work – the unimaginative theoretical faces, that can judge a worker's nervousness so much better by watching him knot string than by any human contact. We hear the lectures to miners' children on the safety-lamp: they wear already the steel shock-helmets and the grime of the future.

Next *Spare Time* by Humphrey Jennings, a study of how the industrial worker spends his off-hours: greyhounds, pigeons, bicycles and bands: we see the Victoria Prize Band – Morris Troop – hoisting a gauche Britannia up among the twirling brass and batons in the withered, hemmed-in recreation-ground: zoos and toy boats, cinemas and wrestling: we watch the miner's leisure dying out with daylight: the casual, friendly choir gathering round the pianist, trying the first notes as they take off overcoats, settling in to the oratorio – and the sad sedate singing is carried on over long sweeping shots of small confectioners and window-gazing lovers, the high tea, the darkening windows and the pubs closing, and the night-shift going on. Simply and without self-consciousness this film catches a mood of pity.

Cavalcanti's *Health of a Nation* is more ambitious and perhaps not quite so successful. The commentary, spoken by Mr Ralph Richardson, is far too reminiscent of *The River*. A pity, because the visual and sound effects are magnificent. The picture shows the industrialization of England, and the measures taken to clean up afterwards: a lyrical counterpart of *Men In Danger*, and a contradiction. In the latter we saw the latest mechanical safety devices, but here they seem oddly lacking. Where are the robot men in their heavy boots and gas-masks and protective spectacles? The most effective feature is the soundtrack: for the first time a director has allowed his sound really to rip: the roar of a furnace, the terrific crack of a pick underground, the blast of sparking steel – they explode in the ear.

An Elephant Never Forgets, with Oliver Hardy. Mr Hardy thought he could bring it off alone – he even tries to be dignified and pathetic, reading the Declaration of Independence – but it won't work. When his hat is flattened under an enormous hoof and he lifts it with the old expression of patient stifled fury, we look sadly round for blinking twisting Laurel, and Zenobia, the elephant, is no substitute.

The Spectator, 26 May 1939

Men in Danger (GB, GPO Film Unit, 1939). Director: Pat Jackson. (Produced by Alberto Cavalcanti.)
Spare Time (GB, GPO Film Unit, 1939). Director: Humphrey Jennings.
Health of a Nation (GB, GPO Film Unit, 1939). Director: Alberto Cavalcanti.
An Elephant Never Forgets (*Zenobia*) (USA, Hal Roach, 1939). Director: Gordon Douglas. Oliver Hardy, Harry Langdon, Billie Burke.

Union Pacific/The Lone Ranger

'The guns which Gary Cooper carried as Wild Bill Hickok in *The Plainsman* bark again in *Union Pacific*. Owned by de Mille, they were taken down from the peg in his office, where they had been hanging for two years, and buckled on Joel McCrea.' So runs the publicity sheet, and the little reverent anecdote will be believed by anyone who has had any personal contact with film-makers. They have an inexhaustible fund of admiration, and when they encounter a big story – full of history and high-mindedness like the Crusades or the Ten Commandments or the construction of a railroad – their reverence falls with the adhesive effect of a tin of treacle. This latest de Mille epic contains all the Excelsior qualities we expect in his work – that sense of a Salvationist drum beating round the next corner – but it is never as funny as *The Crusades* and he has lost his touch with crowds, the stamp of a broad, popular genius who used to remind us a little of Frith.

Apparently the Union Pacific was constructed in a race against the Central Pacific. The motives are extraordinarily obscure, but a bad businessman apparently stood to gain by delaying the UP and helping the CP. As both railways were going, eventually, to join, with the rival directors amicably knocking in a golden sleeper, it doesn't seem to the ordinary spectator to matter a great deal where they meet. This casts rather a damper over the suspense, over the murders and the Indian massacre and the wrecking of a train and the robbery of a pay-roll – all laboriously engineered by the bad man with the idea that the complimentary speeches shall be made at one obscure siding rather than another. Mr Joel McCrea plays a 'troubleshooter' – a kind of Western G-man, whose job it is to see that law and order are kept all down the line. One of his old army friends is a gambler employed to delay the construction, and we can recognize him at once as a mortality type, one of the gay reckless kind who prepare for a far, far better thing all through a long film. This one can hardly fail to die, since he marries the railway girl Mr McCrea loves, who is acted – for want of a better word – by Miss Barbara Stanwyck. Paramount supply us with a sketch of this actress's career, which could hardly be bettered by the sourest critic. 'Beauty opened doors for her and talent got her jobs. By fifteen she was in the Ziegfeld Follies. In such vehicles as *A Night in Spain* and *A Night in Venice* she was seen hanging from chandeliers composed of herself and other beauties.' The trouble is that there are no chandeliers in *Union Pacific*, and Miss Stanwyck has no chance of displaying her curious talent or her beauty. She does display the most bogus brogue I have heard on the screen. Lines like 'You have turned the night to fear and the wind from warm to cold' sound a bit spiritual to a girl used to hanging upside-down. The cast is enormous, with a little real acting from Mr Akim Tamiroff as a Mexican bodyguard; Mr Lynne Overman peeps oddly out of a thicket of pioneering whiskers, and all sorts of funny elfish little men with black beards and top hats, looking like Grumpy or Dopey, turn up inappositely at intervals and refer to each other as General Dodge or General Casement or General Grant.

I have missed three episodes of *The Lone Ranger* and the synopsis at the beginning of the fourth doesn't help much. I last saw the Ranger, his guns empty, falling under the charging hooves of the villain's cavalry at the entrance to the fort set up by the oppressed Texan farmers – there don't seem to be any Texan farmers any more, the Ranger is galloping – 'Hi-yo, Silver!' – in pursuit of Joan (who is Joan?), who is riding into a trap set by Keston (who is Keston?). It doesn't really matter: that trap's evaded in the first two minutes and another one is ready. 'Fetch me Black Taggart', and a little later 'Looks like they're torturing someone', one of the Ranger's troop comments behind a boulder; at the end of this episode the Ranger, knocked out by a stone and covered by guns, is unconscious at the feet of his enemies, and a hand is already stretched out to tear away the mask – 'Now we shall know who the Lone Ranger is.' I doubt it. This week: *The Steaming Cauldron*.

The Spectator, 2 June 1939

Union Pacific (USA, Paramount, 1939). Director: Cecil B. de Mille. Joel McCrea, Barbara Stanwyck, Akim Tamiroff, Lynne Overman.
The Lone Ranger (USA, Republic, 1939). Directors: William Witney, John English. Lee Powell.

The Story of Vernon and Irene Castle/La Femme du Boulanger

It's no use going to the new Astaire-Rogers film in a hard-boiled mood – it is all, as James said of *La Dame aux Camélias*, champagne, young love and tears. The scene is pre-war America and war-time France, but you won't find those countries on any map, any more than you will find in any stage history this particular Vernon and Irene Castle. It must have been an odd experience for Mrs Castle herself, who acted as technical adviser, to watch her own life lifted out of reality altogether – her first meeting with Vernon Castle at New Rochelle becoming a period piece with funny bathing-costumes and grotesque blazers; failure in America, ruin in Paris, sudden overwhelming success when they danced for their dinner at the Café de Paris, becoming light, sad, humorous and agile like the long black spider legs of Fred Astaire; the War, Vernon Castle snatching leave in Paris from the RFC, the instructor's appointment in Texas, the crash due to a novice's silly mistake – all the horror and finality of loss becoming something sentimental, pathetic, tear-jerking,

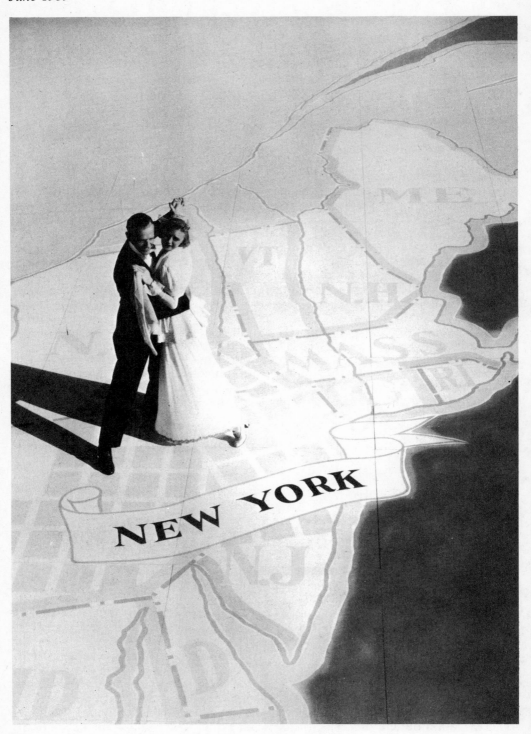

The Story of Vernon and Irene Castle: Fred Astaire and Ginger Rogers as the faithful retainer comforts Irene Castle: 'There's got to be something of him in every boy and girl who gets up to dance', and the dream figures move through the hotel garden in the Castle Walk. It must have been a bit creepy watching one's own life become so fictional.

This is not to say that it's a poor film – it's an admirable film, perhaps the best the marvellous couple have made since *Gay Divorce*. We can accept the sentimental convention because it is never broken: no other world than the film world of eternal fidelity, picturesque starvation and meteoric success is ever held up to it for comparison. The whole affair takes wings, and what do we care if it is through the inane? The tiny black and white figures dance over an immense map of the States (thirty-five cities in twenty-eight days) sowing a crop of dancers everywhere, shot from a lunar angle: or they are whirled in diminishing perspective down Broadway, or dance, with an effect of triviality and gaiety, against a background of spangles. Perhaps the picture is at its best when they are alone in this way, without people acting, an abstraction.

Nothing could be more different from the method of M. Pagnol, whose latest picture, *La Femme du Boulanger*, is the best entertainment to be seen at the moment in any cinema. He uses no pasteboard and as few professional actors as he can manage: he planks his camera down in a Provençal village and shoots in brick and stone. A new baker has come to the village, and the inhabitants gather for the first baking – even the silly old lecherous Marquis, with his plus-fours and his patronage. The oven-door creaks open and the baker takes a sniff – no, another two minutes. The suspense is terrific: again the heavy door creaks: perfect: the village has obtained a good baker at last. But the baker is an old man with a young and sensual wife, who already at that baking has marked down her man – the Marquis's shepherd. She elopes in the early morning while the baker sleeps and the loaves burn. There is no more bread for the village – the baker drinks to drown his sorrow, and the inhabitants, who have been split into warring groups by quarrels about politics, religion, untrimmed trees, unite to bring back the wife and save their bread. Even the Curé makes up his quarrel with the school-teacher, who has told the children that Joan of Arc *believed* she heard voices. It is a long film with a small subject, but the treatment is so authentic that it seems over far too soon, and the acting is superb – Raimu as the pathetic, good-hearted old cuckold: Ginette Leclerc as the young wife with the thirsty bivalve mouth, and Robert Vattier as the Curé – a man of thin, hard principles with a discreet respect for wealth. How often in a French country church has one heard the kind of sermon he gives us here, with the precise, melodramatic gestures and the too carefully modulated voice. But the human actors are only part of the general setting – the well and the olive trees and the crude, crowded church and the Cercle Republicain with the tin advertisements, and the hunter going out in the dawn with his dog and his gun while the baker sleeps in his trough beside the oven.   *The Spectator*, 9 June 1939

The Story of Vernon and Irene Castle (USA, RKO, 1939). Director: H. C. Potter. Fred Astaire, Ginger Rogers, Edna May Oliver.
La Femme du Boulanger (France, Charles Pons, 1938). Director: Marcel Pagnol. Raimu, Ginette Leclerc, Robert Vattier. [US title: *The Baker's Wife*.]

Goodbye Mr Chips/Louise

Some of us may feel unsympathetic to Mr Chips and the rosy sentimental view of an English public school, but there can be no doubt at all of the skill of this production.

The whole picture has an assurance, bears a glow of popularity like the face of a successful candidate on election day. And it is wrong to despise popularity in the cinema – popularity there is a *value*, as it isn't in a book; films have got to appeal to a large undiscriminating public: a film with a severely limited appeal must be – to that extent – a bad film.

Nor, even to those of us whose ideas of a public school can best be expressed in terms of discomfort, cracked bells, stone stairs, bad food and inadequate amenities, is *Mr Chips* often embarrassing. The picture, it is true, opens earnestly among the mouldering courts of Brookfield, where a new master is spelling reverently out the inscription beneath the statue of the founder; but, on the whole, sentimentality is ably balanced by humour, the direction and acting are almost everything to be desired, and the school-song by Mr Richard Addinsell has the right banality and the right grim swing. Miss Greer Garson as Mr Chips's short-lived wife lifts the whole picture temporarily into – we are tempted to call it reality: common sense and tenderness, a sense of happiness too good to last – this is an atmosphere more easily recognizable than the cleanness, the earnestness, the quaintness of Brookfield.

Mr Chips would have gained from quick reviewing – one enjoys it enough at the time to feel as ungrateful this creeping back of the critical faculty which asks whether there is really any continuity in the chief character – any common experience between the young Chips (Mr Donat mustn't overdo his popular wide-eyed stare) asserting his authority with difficulty, the stuffy middle-aged timid Chips who falls in love on a Tyrolean mountain, the quite normal and too rejuvenated married Chips, and the old quaint creature with the straggle of white hair and the senile voice who haunts the school precincts and is brought back during the War to act as temporary Headmaster. The portrait is half caricature, half straight – this is not Mr Donat's fault, but the author's, and the make-up man's. And why should the charming episode of Mr Chips's foreign walking tour be spoilt by a silly scene at a Vienna ball? Apparently he had carried tails in his rucksack, and Miss Garson an elaborate evening gown on her bicycle.

. *Louise* is a French film of Charpentier's opera with Miss Grace Moore. I know nothing about the music or the quality of the singing – but visually and dramatically it is one of the funniest films to be seen in London. It is all bacchanalia among the blossoms and situations whose grotesqueness is deliciously enhanced by the personality of the distinguished singer. Oh, the tiptoeings of Miss Moore, the sedate coquetry, the little trills and carollings, and the great stony teeth. And M. Georges Thill, the great tenor (is it?), with his plumpness and roguery and tiny moustache. Memories crowd back disjointedly of these artistic abandoned 'doings' in old Montmartre – Miss Moore's aged puritanical father turning over the little socks she wore when she was young, the magic phrases of the English captions – 'All around I see but laughter and light and joy', the scene in the garden – like one of those mauve amorous French postcards – when M. Thill kneels at her feet, pressing her hand against his cheek, among the dubious paper blossoms, while Miss Moore sings 'Ever since the day when unto thee I gave me', then floats away among the bowers, leaving him, plump and ecstatic, kissing her picture hat. Undoubtedly a film to be seen.   *The Spectator*, 16 June 1939

Goodbye Mr Chips (USA, M-G-M, 1939). Director: Sam Wood. Robert Donat, Greer Garson, John Mills.
Louise (France, Société Parisienne, 1939). Director: Abel Gance. Grace Moore, Georges Thill.

Confessions of a Nazi Spy/Hôtel du Nord

Confessions of a Nazi Spy is an impressive piece of propaganda. Based on the recent spy trials in the United States, it adopts the techniques of *The March of Time* – between the fictional scenes there are spoken commentaries, maps and extracts from newsreels to give the impression of a sober news record. The moral is drawn by the Judge who sentences the four prisoners that remain after Gestapo agents have removed the others, against their own will, to the country they served. 'You are fortunate,' he tells them. 'Here we spread no sawdust on the surface of our prison yards.' (Propaganda appeals to the emotions, not the reason – otherwise it would be hard for us to forget the overcrowding, the brutality, the tear-gas and machine-guns we have learnt to associate with American prison-yards in such films as *The Big House*.) Well, the war of nerves is on, and the Censor who refused last autumn to pass a *March of Time* issue criticizing the Munich Settlement now allows an actor made up as Dr Goebbels to refer to 'our glorious victory at Munich': he even gives the 'U' Certificate, which he refuses most Westerns, to this picture of methodical violence and treachery. Our children must be allowed to hate, and we can really feel, when the Board of British Film Censors abandons the policy of appeasement, that it is really dead at last. So – repressing a slight shudder – let us give as whole-hearted a welcome as we can to this magnificently constructed engine-of-war.

The picture opens in Scotland where a middle-aged spinster acts as a forwarding agent between certain leaders of the Nazi Bund in the United States and the Ministries in Berlin. We watch the activities of Gestapo agents on board German liners and in the Teutonic beer-houses of New York: we are present at Bund summer camps, where young American boys *heil* Hitler and young girls recite their maternal duties to the State. Nothing is too dramatic to be convincing: the kidnapping of unwanted German-Americans and their transfer to the Fatherland by way of Hoboken Pier is managed with little fuss. All is muted, and the more creepy for that. Mr Paul Lukas gives a fine performance as the fanatical doctor at the head of the Bund who breaks down under examination and is betrayed to the Gestapo by his wife, and Mr Francis Lederer bursts his bonds of central European charm to play the stupid egocentric failure who ruins the whole spy system by his absurd co-operation. This is a magnificent performance edged, one feels, by hatred, for Mr Lederer is a Czech. 'It is terrific, daring', so he describes his schemes – and in the end gives everything away to the Federal Investigator who plays on his vanity. There is one moment of the finest imaginative acting when this stupid man, who has been successful in a minor job of work, finds himself suddenly accepted – by an impatient and contemptuous agent – on a beggarly salary of fifty dollars a month and listens to a long list of dangerous demands rapped out to his trapped and shifty face.

The method of this picture does impose a kind of reality – the reality of 'news'. The trouble is – none of us believes very deeply in news, and news anyway is concerned only with the big events, the march of an army corps and the elimination of a people. French directors at their best have always known the trick of presenting a more intimate reality: the horrible or the comic situation – in the hands of Duvivier or Clair – is made convincing, by its careful background of ordinary life going on, just as Madame Bovary's furious passion was caught up in the dust and cries of the cattle auction. So in *Hôtel du Nord* we believe in the desperate lovers and the suicide pact on the brass bed in the shabby room, just because of the bicyclists on the quay, the pimp quarrelling with his woman in another room, and the First-Communion party on the ground floor with its irrelevant and unsuitable conversation. And the French novelist taught the French cinema too the immense importance of the careful accessory: the ugly iron bridge down which the lovers silently and sadly emerge into our lives: the tuft of cotton-wool in the young man's ear which seems to speak of a whole timid and untidy life.

The Spectator, 23 June 1939

Confessions of a Nazi Spy (USA, Warner Bros, 1939). Director: Anatole Litvak. Edward G. Robinson, Paul Lukas, Francis Lederer, George Sanders, Lya Lys.
Hôtel du Nord (France, SEDIF, 1938). Director: Marcel Carné. Annabella, Arletty, Louis Jouvet, Jean-Pierre Aumont.

Beethoven/Peter the Great/This Man in Paris

The echoes of the laughter at *Louise* have hardly died away when M. Abel Gance pops up again with another musical film, based on the last years of Beethoven's life. Pops up? No words could be less suitable to describe Mr Gance, a kind of Victor Hugo of the screen – terrific storms blow out his characters' cloaks, enormous chords bellow from the microphone: the actors gesture and moan and wring their hands in Gargantuan griefs, and the banal symbols of blossom and thunder and dawn, all shot with a fine pictorial sense, magnify still further the human emotions. Only once, I think, has M. Gance 'brought it off', and that was in his huge *Napoleon* (terrific, enormous, huge – one cannot avoid these adjectives). A vulgar and popular mind like M. Gance's can express itself best in tales of violent action, and Griffith, with whom M. Gance has much in common, never made the mistake of directing the lives and loves of intellectuals. In spite of M. Harry Baur's acting – that roughly carved monumental face never fails to convey a great reserve of power and when it drops into the hands it is as if a statue were to weep – this film never rises above the level of a cheap novelette – Beethoven's passion for Juliette Guicciardi and the fidelity of Teresa of Brunswick become words, two-penny-library words so that it is impossible not to laugh at the ubiquitous devotion of the suffering woman who is always cropping up in thunderstorms, in old mills, with rain-drenched clothes. There is a hideous vulgarity, indeed, about all these pictures based on composers' lives (we have already had Chopin, Mozart, Liszt); the human melodrama belittles the music all the time like programme notes, so that Beethoven's music becomes only a sentimental illustration to sentimental dialogue. 'That piece you have been playing – what is it?' 'The Moonlight Sonata.' Only once does M. Gance make his effect, and that is when Beethoven becomes deaf – the hideous grinding of atmospherics in the ear-drum followed by complete silence: the panorama of the silent smithy, the silent washerwomen, the silent birds, and then the jumble of selected sounds recalled by the imagination – one ring of steel, an isolated bird note, the slap of a wet cloth, a single laugh played over in the brain.

Peter the Great is the kind of picture Gance should be engaged in making – a boisterous, violent tale. There have been no better battle scenes since *The Birth of a Nation*, and the Marxist interpretation of history gives a kind of contemporary vividness to the costume-piece. The defence of foreign experts, the defence of violence for social ends, the contempt for religion – these have the interest of modern controversy: only the sentimentality of the last scene a little jars when Stalin-Peter fills his pipe and watches with paternal devotion the awkward movements of his naked baby feeding among the Boyars. What is most effective – apart from the admirable photography (how dusty and shabby and real the costumes look!) – is the dramatic contrast between the old and sad and the new and vigorous, between the grotesque Boyars, bearded and solemn and superstitious, and the pastry-cook aide-de-camp to the Tsar, with his cheerful eye for a woman, his irreverence, and his parvenu laugh which sweeps through the picture like the high wind in *Storm Over Asia.*

This Man in Paris is an extremely competent, and sometimes very exciting, sequel to *This Man is News*, with Mr Barry K. Barnes, of course, as the crime reporter, Miss Valerie Hobson as his rather too comradely wife, and Mr Alastair Sim again acting everybody else off the set as the Scottish news-editor. The picture ends with the hint of yet another sequel: I only wish that either Mr Barnes or Miss Hobson would this time stay at home. Five years have passed since *The Thin Man,* and this particular uxorious relationship of loving insults, hygienic sex, and raillery from twin-beds is period enough for *Punch.* If only the boyishness of Mr Barnes had got a little lined, and the bright breezy intelligence of Miss Hobson had become a little tarnished by these later thirties, how much more we should have enjoyed this care-free record of forgery and murder. *The Spectator,* 30 June 1939

Beethoven (Un Grand Amour de Beethoven) (France, Général Production, 1937). Director: Abel Gance. Harry Baur. [US title: *Beethoven's Great Love.*]
Peter the Great (USSR, Lenfilm, 1937). Director: Vladimir Petrov. Nikolai Simonov, Alla Tarasova, Nikolai Cherkassov.
This Man in Paris (GB, Pinebrook, 1939). Director: David MacDonald. Barry K. Barnes, Valerie Hobson, Alastair Sim.

The Hound of the Baskervilles

The cinema has never yet done justice to Sherlock Holmes. The latest attempt is by no means the worst – that palm must go to the early talkie with Mr Clive Brook, when the great detective shipped as passenger on the latest transatlantic liner in pursuit of a Professor Moriarty who used electricity, sub-machine guns, the radio, in eliminating his enemies, instead of a two-horse van and a broken slate. For the most grotesque, the prize undoubtedly goes to Germany. I happened to see the Ufa *Sherlock Holmes* in Mexico, and I still wonder what they made of it, those dubious *mestizos* in the cheap seats, made of the two crooks who, posing in a German spa as Holmes and Watson, were always encountering an enigmatic man in a deerstalker and a cape given to fits of hearty Teutonic laughter in hotel lounges whenever he caught sight of them – he finally testified in court, to the astonishment of Judge and police, that there were no such people as Holmes and Watson and that his name was Conan Doyle. An erudite and rather Pirandelloish plot.

In this new film Holmes is undoubtedly Holmes, and he hasn't to compete desperately with telephones and high-speed cars and 1939. ' "Your hat and boots, Watson, quick! Not a moment to lose!" He rushed into his room in his dressing-gown, and was back again in a few seconds in a frock-coat.' That atmosphere of unmechanized Edwardian flurry is well caught: the villain bowls recklessly along

Un Grand Amour de Beethoven: Jany Holt, Jean-Louis Barrault

Baker Street in a hansom and our hero discusses plans of action in a four-wheeler. The genuine Holmes London, too, is neatly touched in through the cab windows – the long trailing skirts and the Sargent hats; and if Dartmoor is a rather Gothick landscape, so it was in the original book. It is quite forgiveable, I think, to have transformed young Dr Mortimer into a formidable figure with thick glasses and a black beard and a terrified-terrifying wife with a little plump pastry face who dabbles in the occult: the film is better for an added suspect. Nor am I worried at all by the fact that the hound is no longer painted with phosphorus – such a monster sounds well in print, but he would be a little too bizarre upon the screen. Even the transformation of wronged revengeful Mrs Stapleton ('it is my mind and soul that he has tortured and defiled') into a Miss Stapleton, blonde and innocent and made for a baronet, may possibly pass. What is wrong, surely, is Mr Rathbone's reading of the great character: the good humour (Holmes very rarely laughed) and the general air of brisk good health (there is only one hushed reference to the depraved needle). And, of course, as always happens, the deductions are reduced to a minimum and the plot is swollen. So we have an absurd scene with Holmes following the hound's bloody spoor by the light of an electric torch and getting shut into an empty tomb by Stapleton at the end of the hunt. Producers of detective films are obsessed with action: there is no dramatic value in that tomb: Holmes immediately begins to cut his way out with a scout-knife, but something, they feel, is happening – nobody's standing around, just detecting. Yet what we really need in a Holmes picture is far more dialogue and much less action. Let us be presented in a series of close-ups, as poor Doctor Watson was, with all the materials for deduction, and let the toothmarks on a walking-stick, the mud on a pair of boots, the stained finger-nail be the chief characters in a Holmes film.

The Spectator, 14 July 1939

The Hound of the Baskervilles (USA, 20th Century-Fox, 1939). Director: Sidney Lanfield. Basil Rathbone, Richard Greene, Nigel Bruce, Wendy Barrie.

Hostages

Academic critics are apt to refer to the comedy of humours as an historical curiosity belonging to the time of Ben Jonson, as though it were not still the most common form of comedy – from Mr Coward upwards. *Hostages* is a very charming and intelligent example. This is not a realistic French village, the kind of village Pagnol cuts accurately in celluloid. The dispute between the Mayor and the landed aristocrat about a right of way – a dispute that survives war, foreign occupation and the danger of death – doesn't belong to human nature as we know it: it is human nature simplified and reconstructed and legendary. There is one big difference between these modern humours and Jonson's. Nowadays we want flattery, and these petty, quarrelsome, but, at the pinch, noble figures, make us feel that, after all, man is a fine creature: there's no harm in us really, and if we dispute one day over a parcel of land, we will die extravagantly the next for love of our village. It is a fairy-story, but it makes the most agreeable film to be seen in London.

It is the story of a village on the Marne, of the outbreak of war, and the sudden arrival of the German cavalry while the Mayor, the barber and the landowner quarrel about strategy in the café and stick little flags into a map – gloved fingers suddenly descend and alter their arrangement. A love-story goes dimly on in the background between the Mayor's daughter and the landowner's conscript son: a Uhlan is shot in a barn by the boy, who escapes to join his regiment, and the grotesque little Mayor drives the body out by night to bury it in the woods. But the Germans find it and threaten to destroy the village if the murderer is not found. The Mayor offers himself as a hostage instead, and is told there must be four others. In his astute provincial way he haggles over the number – but the German Commandant is not commercially minded. The Mayor and the landowner claim the privilege of being hostages, and the other villagers draw lots – the poacher gate-crashes by a ruse into the company of these respected men. The clerk, the policeman and the braggart draw the winning cards, and the braggart hangs himself: so the scared barber is invited with ceremony to take his place. Of course, at the last minute, the taxis of the Marne drive out of Paris, and the hostages are saved from the firing-squad. Then the quarrel begins again whimsically . . . I have said it was a fairy story. All the same, finely acted and magnificently shot, the picture does again and again strike the right legendary note: the little lay figure under the lamplight at the door of the Mairie raising his best bowler with depressed dignity to the German officer; the scene in the silent square at dawn when the hostages gather for their long walk to German Headquarters, and the walk itself, the finest piece of symphonic cutting on the screen since Pépé took *his* last walk – the early morning light over the flat French countryside, the Mayor in his sash of office and the landowner in his top hat, and human self-control failing – in the barber first – and the hasty embarrassed dodging behind the haystacks.

The Spectator, 21 July 1939

Hostages (*Les Otages*) (France, Helvetia Films, 1939). Director: Raymond Bernard. Charpin, Saturnin Fabre, Pierre Larquey. [US title: *The Mayor's Dilemma.*]

Le Drame de Shanghai/The Rebel Son

It would be funny, of course, if it wasn't Pabst: if we could forget *Kameradschaft, Jeanne Ney, Dreigroschenoper, Pandora's Box, The Joyless Street, Secrets of the Soul, Westfront 1918*, that long unsurpassed record of sombre German talent. The great Russians are nowhere beside the director who created Rasp in the hall of the shabby Parisian hotel-for-a-night, sent the rescuing miners tapping along the pipes, and showed Garbo to us in the shabby fur and the black stockings of her disreputable beat. It is possible to grasp the rise and fall of the post-war film by this man's work alone. Well, I suppose we must attribute this absurd Chinese thriller to the exigencies of exile and the stupidity of producers. Pabst isn't really here at all, except for a few seconds in a neat knifing, in a little squalid set in the studio corner with a forger of passports, and in the march of the workers at the climax, a beautifully cut movement, though one would have liked to be clear as to who they were and what exactly they were doing: the plot of this thriller is appallingly obscure.

I can't pretend to say what it's about and how all these people fit in. There's a young Chinese intellectual called Tcheng, whom the members of an organization called the Black Serpent want to liquidate. That's why – they couldn't get him any other way – war is arranged against Japan. That doesn't help, because then China is united and their men join Tcheng's men and Tcheng, who is a pacifist, puts on uniform, and after an orgy of news-shots of Japanese bombers, all the characters live happily ever afterwards – except Kay Murphy, who has been stabbed by a man in a sun-helmet and Ivan, whom Kay shot to save her little girl, who had arrived from an English High School in Hong-Kong (architecture Scotch Baronial) and didn't know her mother was a singer in a cabaret, where the tatty costumes – all spangles and ostrich feathers – and the debauchery – all champagne in ice-buckets – seem to date from 1925. 'Won't you kiss me?' Kay says, and the girl shrinks away. 'It's just the rouge, Mummie.'

Kay's name is not really Kay – they are all White Russians in the cabaret ('Hunger holds them prisoner'), and she has a photograph of Ivan in Guards uniform. He nearly repents before she shoots him to save her child from the Black Serpent, blowing out her bosom like a puff adder. With her big black eyes and her plump soulful features, she reminded me a little of Pola Negri caught in the coils. 'I am reborn!' she exclaims prematurely. 'O for pure air! wind!' – though she gets plenty of that. She toasts her lovers, presenting an immovable and melancholy profile: 'Here's to the night that passes'; and when she lures a man to death, she carries herself with sad self-pity. 'This hurts me more than it hurts you' is her daunting attitude towards a victim. O those pure maternal eyes peeking coyly above the ostrich fan, those slightly bandy legs in black silk, the rather prominent behind which swings in a thicket of plumage up towards the attic where the emissaries of the Black Serpent wait. One must mournfully add that M. Louis Jouvet is wasted on this film: that slow soporific voice, the heavy eyes with their pessimistic amusement, and the nihilist gait, are butchered in a minor part.

The Rebel Son is hardly less incredible. A bad French film about Tarass Boom-deay, with M. Harry Baur as the old Cossack leader, seems to have been bought by an English firm and some of the shots remade with our most refined young men and women – including Miss Joan Gardiner ('I can fight like a man'). M. Baur's voice has been unsuitably dubbed, and the dialogue has the prattling innocence of a play written by a Women's Institute. I liked particularly the scene when the young Cossack (played by Mr Anthony Bushell with his keen young Oxford accent) bursts into the bedroom of the girl he loves. 'I know it's very late to call, but . . . O, I'm glad you are not angry.' After half an hour the joke had gone on long enough and I left. A man in the audience was remarking slowly, with some of Dr Johnson's weight, 'I am still wondering what the reason for the existence of this film can be.'

The Spectator, 28 July 1939

Le Drame de Shanghai (France, Gladiator Films, 1938). Director: G. W. Pabst. Louis Jouvet, Raymond Rouleau, Dorville, Elina Labourdette, Suzanne Desprée.
The Rebel Son (France, Omnia Films, 1939). Director: Adrian Brunel. Harry Baur, Joan Gardiner, Anthony Bushell, Patricia Roc, Roger Livesey. (English version of *Tarass Boulba*, directed by Alexis Granowsky.)

The Rich Bride

So they still dream in Russia of going to Moscow; Revolution hasn't altered that; again and again in this bouncing boisterous musical comedy of a collective farm we are reminded of Chekhov – perhaps the difference is that these people, unlike the three sisters, will really get there: the tractor-driver because he is a shock-worker, the girl Marina because she has put in more working days than anyone else on the farm; they'll get their tenement and their Parks of Culture. As for the others, they get the next best thing – a brass bedstead or a trumpet or a radio set –

when the prizes are given out at Harvest Home: even the comic villain, the assistant book-keeper, gets the bicycle he has dreamed about; and they are all so noisy and delighted at their new toys that perhaps even Moscow may seem worth the bother to those who win it. The awful simplicity of these characters weighs on the spirits like a long summer afternoon at a school sports – the earnest competition, the unacceptable loyalties, and the odd-shaped cups of silver alloy handed out at the end.

It is an incredible and a pathetic picture. One begins to hope that it is just propaganda for internal use – to tell the Russian world of the happy time had by what the English caption-writer calls with coy, fairy-like, progressive joviality 'the lusty lads and bouncing lasses' – music and dancing, and even babies, if the prefects approve. One wouldn't like to feel that this Angela Brazil world really existed anywhere: the stout female shock brigadier giving a first-day-of-term speech to her girls (a chorus, to Western taste, of incomparable dumplings) – 'Save your strength to keep our banner': the stout male brigadier addressing his tractor-drivers – 'It's our task to attack along the whole front', warning them that the rival House is two hundred acres ahead and has economized six hundred gallons: the Ukrainian School Song. At midnight the old watchman stops the dancing – it is time for dormitory: 'Citizens, remember the harvest', and the girls break squealing through the underbrush before the heavy tread of their brigadier – 'Run girls, it's Pelaga.' The book-keeper wants to marry Marina for the sake of her working days (he'll go to Moscow as her husband, and even perhaps to the seaside), so he sows suspicion between her and a young tractor-driver who looks astonishingly like Laurence Olivier. The dreadful question which all lovers have to face is 'Is he – or she – a loafer? Or a real shock-worker?' There's a lot of dirty juggling with figures, but the two shock brigadiers put their heads together in the end for the sake of their favourite pupils, and two young Stakhanovites find happiness. If it's true, of course, it's awful – but as long as you can treat it as a fairy-story for simple Slavs it's fun, though one gets a little tired by the noise – the bellows of comradely laughter, the continuous sounds of animal satisfaction, which seems to be roused even by a simple shave, and by the sight of that awful acreage of stout female flesh in the Ukrainian sun, stirring sluggishly during the midday rest, scratching a little, satisfied under the team banner. Sometimes, as the film draws to an end, with the huge panorama of the rain-threatened harvest, an effect does get through – of air and sky and space and liberty: gets through, that is to say, to us, the tired inhabitants of a small industrial island: not to them who seek only smoky Moscow – or a prize bedstead and the honour of the side.   *The Spectator,* 4 August 1939

The Rich Bride (USSR, Ukrainfilm, 1938). Director: Ivan Pyriev. Maria Ladynina, Anna Dmokhovskaya, B. Bezgin, Ivan Lyubeznov.

Beau Geste/Un de la Légion

Thirteen years have passed since the first *Beau Geste* was produced with Ronald Colman, William Powell, Noah Beery, but not a set seems to have been altered. Of course, memory plays strange tricks, and Fort Zinderneuf, with the dead legionaries leaning from the baronial embrasures, can hardly have stood unchanged since 1926 in the Arizona deserts; yet I feel sure that the old English mansion of Brandon Abbas has been tucked away all those years on some abandoned stage in the great rambling lots, dust collecting on the stained glass, and the panelling, and the suit of armour in the hall, and on Lady Patricia too, her aristocratic suffering only bleaching a little with the years, and the birds beginning to roost in the high rooky hair. For why trouble to destroy what is certain to be needed sooner or later? Alas! we have not yet reached the end of *Beau Geste*; Technicolor and stereoscopy wait another decade. There is something in the brazen tale which appeals to the worst in human nature – the cowardly will always find satisfaction in the impossible heroisms they will never have to imitate, and the weak in the disgusting and irrational brutalities of Sergeant Markoff, the Tom Brown bully who kicks over a water-bucket in the presence of the deserters dying of thirst.

A morbid picture, but I doubt whether any morality council will take action, the whole story being so wrapped up in the school colours – in comradeship and loyalty and breeding, and the pure girl left behind; morbid because the brutality has no relation whatever to the real world; it is uncriticized day-dreaming. We do not criticize our dreams, or feel responsible for our Markoffs. Indeed, this particular product of the half-conscious mind is praised by one of the heroic characters as 'the best soldier we're ever likely to know', much as a bully is excused if he is a good centre-forward. Day-dreams, adolescence, the popular story go together, and out of the same nocturnal sub-region as the Sergeant emerges the little scene when the three Gestes as children play with toy boats and real gunpowder, and one gets hit in the leg, and another gouges out the bullet with a penknife – exquisite agonies! – and the third asks, 'Are you crying because you are proud or because you are wounded?' Only sentimentality? Then take the crucifixion of Rassilof on the mess-table. I am glad to note that our Censors, with a moral discrimination they do not always show, have given this unhealthy picture an 'A' Certificate.

What a relief to change from Beau's Legion to Fernandel's. This Legion, too, may not be the real thing (at least, we have correct uniforms, genuine exteriors, and a sense of routine – it isn't all hell and heroism; it is medical inspections and route-marches and meals and leaves); but if it's a little too good to be true, with the charming officers and the humorous companionships, and Miss Suzy Prim on a Sunday afternoon – a frankly recruiting picture – at any rate, there's nothing adolescent about it, and no apparent reason for its 'A' Certificate. Fernandel, the inspired clown with the medieval face made to peer through a horse-collar, plays the part of a hen-pecked husband, who is not allowed meat or wine because he suffers from aerophagie ('whenever I eat I swallow air I cannot digest'). He is robbed by a crook, stuck drunk on a boat with a recruit's papers in his pocket, and after a few indignant muddled days settles happily down in the Legion. When his wife traces him, he disowns her, goes south with his battalion, and wins the Legion of Honour with a good deal less fuss than the Geste family play boats.

Fernandel's laugh is the most memorable thing in any of his pictures; he can carry half a minute of film with a laugh alone, the camera fixed on the huge mouth and the great mulish teeth. Watch him in the café with the crook as he suddenly realizes that he doesn't love his wife; the sudden disconcerting bellow, then the splutter, the attempt to explain, the feeble flap-flap of one hand, the hopeless movements of the equine head, and laughter welling out, bursting between the big rocky teeth, unstemmable, like an oil-gusher running to waste over a whole countryside.   *The Spectator*, 11 August 1939

Beau Geste (USA, Paramount, 1939). Director: William A. Wellman. Gary Cooper, Ray Milland, Brian Donlevy.
Un de la Légion (France, Calamy, 1936). Director: Christian Jaque. Fernandel, Suzy Prim, Thérèse Dorny.

Shipyard Sally/Blind Alley

We come heavily to earth in 1939 with Miss Gracie Fields's new film – about a variety singer with an improvident father who saves Clydebank from ruin by forcing her way into the house of an old peer and presenting a petition from the workers; at the end a large close-up of Miss Fields singing 'Land of Hope and Glory' is transposed over the launching of a new liner by the Queen – values are confused: the liner is the background to the face. All Miss Fields's pictures seem designed to show a sympathy for the working class and an ability to appeal to the best circles: unemployment can always be wiped out by a sentimental song, industrial unrest is calmed by a Victorian ballad, and dividends are made safe for democracy. This picture has the embarrassment of a charade where you don't know the performers well. What is Mr Sydney Howard doing in this household?

   Blind Alley has crept rather silently into the West End. Survive a sticky ten minutes and you have a thriller of quite unusual merit. A killer (Mr Chester Morris) escapes from gaol, eliminates the warden and arrives with his girl and bodyguard at the lakeside house of a university psychiatrist. He expects to be picked up by a motor-boat which doesn't come; he is jittery, shoots down a young student of the Professor's who shows fight, tries to sleep. Time passes – a gunman watches from the nursery window among the juvenile junk – the killer tosses in nightmare. One bad dream has haunted him since childhood – a dream of rain dripping through an umbrella, bars all round; two fingers of his gun hand are paralysed: he fears insanity. The Professor, with the intention of destroying his motive power, offers to rid him of the dream. We watch the neurotic damned-to-violence creature struggle against the analysis. Everything, of course, is simplified and speeded up, but that's legitimate. There's nothing false about the analysis itself, and the camera is magnificently used to express the selected distorted facts of memory as it returns; the lens is transformed to a child's eye, seeing the hated father sitting far off at the bar-room table, swinging round to the group of police following across the street to the scene of betrayal, the underside of a table, the legs of policemen closing round, while blood drips through a crack. This is the old Ufa touch. The analysis is completed, the police arrive, the killer hesitates, and is shot down. The end, like the beginning, falters, but that doesn't harm the central situation and the superb acting of Mr Chester Morris, sweating, badgered, disintegrating.   *The Spectator,* 18 August 1939

Shipyard Sally (GB, 20th Century-Fox, 1939). Director: Monty Banks. Gracie Fields, Sydney Howard. *Blind Alley* (USA, Columbia, 1939). Director: Charles Vidor. Chester Morris, Ralph Bellamy, Ann Dvorak, Melville Cooper.

Les Disparus de St Agil

It would be possible, I suppose, to praise and dismiss the new French film at the Polytechnic as a skilful, exciting, rather absurd 'story for boys', similar to the innumerable tales which come out around Christmas – *The Boys of St Ethelburga's, For the Sake of the Side,* and their like. There is a Headmaster who commits murder, and is tracked down and denounced by one of his pupils; there is an art master who forges banknotes, a kidnapping, a secret passage behind a blackboard, but, strange though it may seem in such a plot, there is also a sense of reality; a child's dream of what Alain-Fournier called 'this wild life, full of risks, games and adventures', is expressed through an adult imagination. One is re- minded again and again, in the elusive poetry of the story of escape, of Fournier's great novel *Le Grand Meaulnes*: the small curtained dormitory cells, the school play with its daggers and doublets, the master padding by at night on insomniac feet, the classroom after dark by candlelight with the white phosphorescent chalk marks on the board, these are like vivid inexplicable symbols in a Surrealist painting. One remembers Fournier's remark: 'If I have been childish and weak and foolish, at least I have, at moments, had the strength in this infamous city to create my life like a marvellous fairy-tale.' One is apt to forget that the literature of escape is literature just because it is a real escape; it contains a recognition of life as much as the action of a deserter contains the recognition of an enemy; *For the Sake of the Side* is not an escape – it is hallucination. But the author and director of *Les Disparus* know all there is to know about 'the infamous city'. You can recognize escape by its unsuccess: the shadow is always there across the fantasy, just as it is in folk-tales, in the stories of Grimm.

Les Disparus has inevitably been compared with *Emil and the Detectives*: in both the criminals are brought to justice by a horde of children, and the infamous city casts much the same kind of shadow. We remember Rasp going to bed in his bowler in the horrible little hotel which belongs in a quarter nobody from St Ethelburga's has ever visited, and we shall remember a long while after the details of *Les Disparus* are forgotten M. Michel Simon as the forger and secret drinker, with his great loose squashy face and his unconvincing swagger, getting tiddly and malicious at the school play, furious with his class in an observation test because no one has noticed the engraver's signature on a banknote (they had all noticed the naked women), a grotesque and dangerous figure of fun who ends with a scream and a thud. (There are times when Simon reminds us of Laughton, but he is a less histrionic actor: we never notice the mechanics of his elastic voice.) Perhaps it is as well to add in these jittery days that the story is more humorous than sombre – the kidnapped child writing an account of his adventures in the old mill, badgering his admiring captors who read out the latest chapter every evening with pride and excitement; the little groups of quarrelling pedants; the pale porter who believes in the evil eye; the whole unfamiliar atmosphere of a French school where a drum takes the place of the cracked bell and the worst accusation you can bring against another master is harshness to his class. The acting of the children is magnificent.   *The Spectator,* 25 August 1939

Les Disparus de St Agil (France, Francinex, 1938). Director: Christian Jaque. Michel Simon, Erich von Stroheim, Armand Bernard, Marcel Mouloudji. [US title: *Boys' School*.]

Professor Mamlock

Professor Mamlock is a Soviet film which attacks the brutality of the Nazi revolu- tion. Played with sincerity by so many 'Honoured Artists of the Republic', breathing an honest indignation against the political racketeers who put Dimitrov in the dock, the picture would have seemed a fortnight ago rather more moving. History has travelled fast: we are reminded too often in the first half of the film that the ideo- logical argument is made more of wind than stone. But I think in any case the first half-hour would have proved disappointing: like so many worthy middlebrow novels, it has about it the air of a Foyle Luncheon; the characters are all caught at their most abstract, talking like Left Book Club speakers. The theme of a story should never be expressed so plainly; argument is valueless in fiction unless it is dramatic and individualized. For a long time we feel little interest in Professor Mamlock, the Jewish head of a Berlin hospital, who disapproves of politics. To discover in the blood of a patient the right germ is the important thing, and he urges his son, who is also his assistant and an ardent Communist, to take as his models Koch and Pasteur. But he isn't alive; he is just a martyr type, until argument ceases, and we watch him paraded through the streets in his rubber gloves and his surgical dress marked with the word Jew, the victim of his assistant, a vicious, jealous little figure in pince-nez, who has been appointed Commissar of the hospital.

The dead wood in this picture is divided from the live by the night of the Reichstag fire: enormously impressive the noisy radio followed by shots of rain-wet silent streets: hardly anybody about, except a few little groups of scared people scurrying home, and at intervals the squads of Brown Shirts marching heavily on unknown errands. This is real cinema; and so are the last-minute attempts to hide the evidence, the papers burned in stoves, the picture taken down from over the bed, while the lorry-loads of Brown Shirts draw up to the kerb below. All that is more or less silent in this film is first class; it is only when the characters talk too glibly of their ideals that we lose touch with the truth, and there is very little talk after the Reichstag fire, except in the final shots when Dr Mamlock arraigns the armed Gestapo guards from the balcony of the clinic in the name of humanity (but not, we know now, in the name of Communism), and is shot down by a machine-gun.

The Spectator, 1 September 1939

Professor Mamlock (USSR, Lenfilm, 1938). Director: Adolf Minkin. Herbert Rappoport, Sergei Mezhinsky, Oleg Zhakov, Nina Shaternikova, Vasili Merkuriev.

Young Mr Lincoln

At the best of times *Young Mr Lincoln* would be impressive, and entitle Mr John Ford, who made *The Informer* and *Stagecoach*, to be regarded as one of the best directors of the day, but now there seems an added value in this attempt to draw in the simplest and least rhetorical terms a man who cared passionately for justice.

We see Lincoln first as a storekeeper exchanging goods for a cask full of old books which include Blackstone: his love for Ann Rutledge is touched in with unexpected restraint – an inarticulate duologue on a river-bank and a monologue over a grave. We watch him begin his career as a lawyer, take part in the small-town celebrations of Independence Day, win a log-splitting contest, defeat an opposing team at tug-of-war by hitching the rope to a mule cart, judge with extreme deliberation in a pie contest between the merits of apple and peach. Mr Henry Fonda gives a fine performance; the grotesque slow wisecracks seem to emerge from a whole background of country breeding, and Mr Ford and his cameraman never let us forget the odd leggy appearance – an interesting example of what camera angles can do with a young actor as well made as Mr Fonda. Mr Fonda's performance has been compared with Muni's as Pasteur – certainly we never feel that the acting falls below the legendary nature of the subject, and he has none of the mannerisms which grate on us a little with Muni. But it must be remembered that the direction is far finer, and much of the credit we give to Fonda belongs to Ford. That flash of fanatical hatred in the eyes when a man pays him in bad coin is less a matter of acting than of cutting, and much of Mr Fonda's expressiveness is montage. But all the same it is not every actor who allows himself to be so cut and mounted into his part by a great director.

The main part of the plot is, I imagine, fictitious. That doesn't really matter: this is intended to be legend, not history, and it may have been impossible to discover in the events of the early life a single incident which could bear the weight of the whole future. So we have a story of two simple country boys who are suddenly on Independence Day caught up in the murder of a bully: they each for the other's sake admit guilt, and their mother, who thought she saw the stabbing, will not say which of her sons struck the blow – tortured by her appalling knowledge, she won't save one at the expense of the other. The scene of the fight, taken in the half-dark from a long way off, the little swaying group under the trees, the dull gunshot as the bully fires, then the bush of smoke standing still over the body, the two children (they are little more) running together to their mother's side, all obscurity and hurry and muffled sound, will remain in mind as a classic example of direction which does more than directly represent an action, direction which conveys a mood.

Lincoln saves them from lynching, undertakes their defence, and the opening stages of the trial are particularly well written: the direction of the little country judge, 'Now, you men, take off your hats and put down those jugs'; the choosing of the jury. The climax is the only weak point in the film. For Lincoln to discover that a witness for the prosecution is the real murderer (from a point in his evidence which would not have escaped any member of the audience) is banal. There have been so many court dramas and ingenious plots, and for a while the picture loses its legendary interest, and we find ourselves concerned with an exciting situation and not with a man who, loving justice and hating iniquity, was preparing himself for his last defeat at the hands of a violent world.

The Spectator, 22 September 1939

Young Mr Lincoln (USA, 20th Century-Fox, 1939). Director: John Ford. Henry Fonda, Alice Brady, Marjorie Weaver, Richard Cromwell, Ward Bond.

War always seems to surprise somebody; a year after Munich trenches which were begun that autumn are still being dug on the common outside; even the news-reel companies have been caught unprepared. They must have expected the temporary closing of the cinemas; they must have been prepared for censorship, and yet, like the newspapers, they have to rely on Germany as their chief source of supply – an admirable picture of the siege of the Westerplatte, and another of the war in Poland. What have they got ready for us from the home front, and how have their commentators risen to the great occasion? One remembers what Hemingway did for *Spanish Earth*, and one hopes . . . Even a war of nerves has its heroic angle.

As we fumble for our seats the too familiar voice, edgeless and French-polished, is announcing: 'The Queen has never looked prettier.' Royalty is inspecting something or other: 'Royal interest inspires them to redoubled efforts.' Women bus-conductors climb aboard: 'For men passengers it will make going to work almost a pleasure'; they wave holiday-girl hands. Mr and Mrs Chamberlain walk in the Park; complete strangers take off their hats – an odd custom. The Duchess of Kent, instead of going to Australia, makes splints: 'We never thought we would live to be grateful to Hitler.' Very slowly we approach the violent reality; the

Expeditionary Force marches to the coast, whippet tanks move through the woodlands, and the voice remarks something about 'shoulder to shoulder in this death struggle for liberty'. Surely by now we should realize that art has a place in propaganda; the flat and worthy sentiment will always sound hypocritical to neutral ears beside the sharp and vivid statement. There was much that Hemingway had to slur over in his commentary: his cause was far more dubious than ours, but the language was much more effective. Let us hope that Germany is not employing a commentator of his standard, for I cannot believe that neutral opinion – or home opinion if it comes to that – will be impressed by the kind of words we listen to – shoulder to shoulder, liberty, baby-killers. . . .

The siege of the Westerplatte provides the best few minutes in any news cinema. It would have been interesting to hear the German commentary, for the picture seems to make the same odd psychological mistake as the Italian film of the Abyssinian War. The emphasis is all on power directed towards an insignificant object – we cut from the belching guns of the Schleswig-Holstein to the huge bombers taking off, from the calm complacent face on the Captain's bridge to the pilot's face at the wheel, sweating, shadowy, intent: it is all smoke, flame, blast, inevitability. Nobody, we feel, can stand against this for an hour, and the mind answers quickly back that two hundred men stood it for a week. It was an astute move to show this film in England.

From Poland come some pathetic scenes of mob enthusiasm. Colonel Beck and the British Ambassador bow from a balcony: the faces of the crowd are excited, enthusiastic, happy. . . . The German film of the advance into Poland is beautifully shot and well staged – so well staged (the cavalry cantering in broken sunlight through the woods, the machine-guns rushed to the edge of the meadow grass) that one suspects old sequences of manœuvres turned and mounted at leisure. Only the huge smashed bridges – like back-broken worms writhing in water – carry the stamp of real war. The same effect is given by the French films cleverly cut in with shots from the pre-war German film of the Siegfried Line: the balloon falling in flames is too tidy.

None the less, fake or not, these war pictures from the East and West are impressive, well directed, and edited with imagination, and there is no reason why pictures from the defence front should not be equally effective. A different conception of news is needed – shadows of gold keys and cut ribbons and beauty queens linger. But news no longer means leading figures; we want the technique Anstey used in *Housing Problems*; America is more likely to listen with sympathy to the rough unprepared words of a Mrs Jarvis, of Penge, faced with evacuation, blackouts, a broken home, than to the smooth-handled phrases of personalities. Above all, we don't want the old commentators, with their timid patronizing jokes; this is a people's war.

The Spectator, 29 September 1939

An Englishman's Home/The Face at the Window

It has already become a war-time habit for reviewers to iron out their criticism. The poor old British film industry has had another knock: better not say anything to do it further harm. The result, one supposes, will be the survival of the worst. Art in England after three years of war may, if we are not careful, resemble art in Germany after three years of Nazi dictatorship. Far better to sharpen our pencils and stab the poor thing to death. No art is better than bad art, for somewhere in some ruined barn an ignorant peasant may begin to whittle at a stick.

The Face at the Window: Tod Slaughter (in beard)

An Englishman's Home, written before the last war, was brought up to date with radio, bombing fleets and ARP, just too late to anticipate this one. New dialogue has been written by Ian Hay, Edward Knoblock and Rodney Ackland – I don't know why, for Guy du Maurier's dialogue could hardly have been more absurd. Mr Edmund Gwenn acts the Brown father with his too well-trained pawkiness – the sob in the throat perfected by ten thousand performances; he is the only star. He lives in an awful house, all fake beams and leather-seated lounges, in a garden the size of a small park, and has the oddest friends – a retired sailor, a little piece, and the German owner of a radio-shop: his daughter is loved by a Territorial officer, who wears curious cad breeches, and loves the German – who is, of course, a spy. This is meant to be a typical English home. A radio-set in the attic guides the German air fleet, and their attack coincides with an old English custom, Mr Brown's birthday-party – an enormous candled cake and a dance and a lot of aircraft officers and the Territorial who snoops around, reading inscriptions in his girl's books. The radio suddenly goes dead: all stations closed down – most improbable as we know now: the BBC would certainly have put on gramophone records. The Germans arrive by parachute, clanking up the garden-path, and Mr Brown is shot and the house is bombed and Betty loves the Territorial after all and England goes to war rather tardily in montage. There is nothing to be said for this film – though it might prove useful propaganda in enemy countries, purporting to illustrate the decadence of English architecture and taste.

The Face at the Window is a much older melodrama about Victorian Paris with a wicked Count who commits murders under the name of Le Loup, helped by the awful appearance at windows of his moron foster-brother whom he keeps between whiles in a cage in a cellar. He is hunted down by a bank clerk who loves his banker's daughter: the Count, of course, covets her and lures her to a disreputable tavern and a private room. It doesn't sound very promising, but it is one of the best English pictures I have seen and leaves the American horror films far behind. You go to laugh, but find yourself immediately – from the ingenious titling on – in the grip of the fine firm traditional dialogue, the magnificent casting, sets and camerawork which plank you surely back into that vague Victorian period when anything might happen – when Jekyll was shrinking into Hyde and the ape committed its murders in the Rue Morgue. Mr Tod Slaughter is certainly one of our finest living actors: we see in this picture at whose feet Mr Laughton must have sat – that dancing sinister step, the raised shoulder and the flickering eyelid. What makes this kind of melodrama so much more convincing than the Du Maurier brand? Perhaps it is that the author really believes – however fantastic his illustrations – in good and evil, in a morality which has the tradition of a thousand years behind it; the characters are at least as distinguishable as black is from white, while the characters in *An Englishman's Home* are all of the same piece, just fine chaps doing their duty according to their lights and putting up a good show.   *The Spectator*, 6 October 1939

An Englishman's Home (GB, Aldwych Productions, 1939). Director: George Dewhurst. Edmund Gwenn.
The Face at the Window (GB, Pennant, 1939). Director: George King. Tod Slaughter.

Ignace

There are people, I gather from other reviews, who do not like Fernandel. They must on no account go to this film, for there is very little else in the picture to please. It is certainly not a good picture: it begins as fair comedy and ends as fair farce, with a heavy slab in the middle of bad musical comedy: and it is oddly confusing in its details – why, for instance, should a troop of lovelies be rehearsing a charity performance in a colonel's house, the commander of the local barracks to which Fernandel has been sent as a conscript? And why should the superbly heavy and foolish Baron des Orfrais be drinking the waters there? And why should he send a bottle of champagne across to a fellow guest as if he were dining in a hotel? Is it, after all, a hotel? But, if so, why is all the service done by the Colonel's batman (Fernandel) and his very piquant maid? Why? . . . But let us leave it to the enemies of Fernandel to clean out all the holes in this sieve.

There remains Fernandel: Fernandel of the huge teeth, the heavy soprano eyelids, the mulish face and the long ape-like arms: an animal that laughs – it sounds like somebody's definition of Man: Fernandel with the celluloid collar that always creaks and the long greasy lock of hair. Nobody has ever laughed so infectiously as Fernandel: it is like an epidemic, and yet a prim colleague has found him in close-up disgusting. Fernandel in this film is a conscript and the most intractable material any army has to deal with – a human being. It is, with all its faults, a better picture than *Un de la Légion* because there is no propaganda: it doesn't pretend, as the other film did, that the military mind can deal with human beings – in no time at all Fernandel has been sentenced to thirty days – the good-humoured innocent creature impervious to discipline because it doesn't make sense. There comedy ends and farce begins, for the thirty days must be worked off as batman to the Colonel and slave to the Colonel's wife, a great brawny woman with hips like the horses she rides who is absurdly pursued by the shifty and romantic Baron. The Colonel himself (acted with his usual lovely suavity by Charpin) is as human as Fernandel: he doesn't like wearing uniform and he prefers a bicycle to a horse. This trait, when the bicycle breaks down on the day that the Inspector-General makes a surprise visit, provides the climax, for Fernandel rising hurriedly from the maid's bed puts on the Colonel's uniform she had been given to mend, and is mistaken . . . Before he knows where he is, he is presiding at luncheon and addressing the Colonel's wife by her Christian name (he has learnt too much of who loves whom in the household for anyone to betray him). A humanity which is not permitted to a private is charming in a Colonel, and he earns his commanding officer promotion.

Told like that the story seems to go quite smoothly: I cannot understand why the middle of the film should be filled with lovelies and a stage show and Fernandel dressed as a Mexican blundering on to the stage with a note for the wrong person and pursuits up and down stairs and a cast-off mistress of the Baron – only real lovers of Fernandel will put up with all that. There is one delightful piece of direction, the high-spirited pairing off of Fernandel and the maid – and then the silent scurry up the stairs against time (will the bugle blow from the barracks?), the breathless dash across the dark room, the clothes flung quickly from invisible hands upon the hooks, black-out – a curious sense of lightness and poetry and companionship is conveyed. *The Spectator*, 13 October 1939

Ignace (France, Gray Film, 1939). Director: Pierre Colombier. Fernandel, Charpin, Dany Loris, Raymond Cordy.

Stanley and Livingstone/Only Angels Have Wings

Stanley and Livingstone lost all chance of being a good film when the producers gave it that title. A pity, because it begins well: a tough newspaper reporter defeats the American military authorities in Indian territory during a rising, and is summoned back to New York by his live-wire proprietor, who snaps out a new assignment at the other end of the world. 'Ever heard of Livingstone?' 'Do you mean the new bar-tender at Joe's?' The fatal name has been spoken; this isn't the story of *a* missionary lost in Africa, and a hard-boiled reporter sent across the world to find him, and prove that a rival paper (the London *Globe*) is wrong when it declares him dead. This is history (though what a Miss Eve Kingsley, a dewy colleen, with whom Stanley falls in love in Zanzibar, can be doing in history I don't know).

History is responsible for the dreary travel sequences shot by Mrs Martin Johnson in Uganda – with the stock lions, giraffes, hippopotami. Most of the film, indeed, consists of long shots of stand-ins moving across undistinguished scenery, while Mr Spencer Tracy reads out extracts from Stanley's diary – into which thoughts of Miss Eve Kingsley oddly intrude (credit for the very remarkable 'historical research' is given to two gentlemen called Hal Long and Sam Hellman). Finally Mr Tracy finds Sir Cedric Hardwicke, and learns Christianity from him – Mr Tracy is always a human being, but Sir Cedric is an elocution lesson, a handclasp. . . . The picture ends with a meeting of the Royal Geographical Society, which refuses to admit Stanley's claims until an opportune telegram arrives from Zanzibar, conveying Livingstone's last messages. Stanley's girl hadn't realized his love, she's married into the London *Globe*, and Stanley, ignoring cables from the *New York Herald*, returns to Africa to carry on Livingstone's work.

History, by which I no longer mean the researches of Hal and Sam, tells us how he carried on that work: the heavily armed ferocious forays, the massacre of natives who had learnt not to trust his Führer's temperament, the disastrous expedition to rescue Emin Pasha (who like Livingstone had no desire to be rescued), the unpleasant sexual rumours which drifted back to London clubs. Mr Tracy, learning not to strike a black, listening to Sir Cedric conducting 'Onward Christian Soldiers', has little in common with the filibuster, poisoned by a childhood in a Welsh workhouse, who replied to the Aborigines Protection Society at a dinner-party: 'He would undertake to provide them with seven tons of Bibles, four tons of Prayer Books, any number of surplices, and a church organ into the bargain, and if they reached as far as longitude 23° without chucking some of those Bibles at some of the negroes' heads he would ——.'

Only Angels Have Wings has everything a good film needs except a good story. It is admirably acted by Mr Cary Grant, Miss Jean Arthur, Mr Thomas Mitchell and Mr Richard Barthelmess (who makes another sombre and impressive return to the screen: he did it before in *Four Hours to Kill*; what happens to him in between returns?), and it is quite magnificently directed by Mr Howard Hawks – who made *Scarface*. Unfortunately, Mr Hawks has written his own story, a sentimental tough tale of a third-rate air line trying to make both ends meet somewhere near the Andes, the girl who steps off a cruise and stays behind (Miss Arthur) and a pilot who once parachuted from his plane and left his mechanic to die (Mr Barthelmess). At the airport, where he arrives with his wife seeking a new job under a new name, he meets the mechanic's brother (Mr Mitchell), and of course the wife was once engaged to the boss (Mr Grant), who is now forcefully loved by Miss Arthur. It's a regulation muddle which needs the regulation devices to untangle it – storm, sacrifice, heroism, redemption. What does remain in the memory is the setting – drab, dusty, authentic, and a few brilliantly directed scenes, as when a young pilot is trying to land in a ground fog; those below can't see the plane, but they can hear his engine and talk to him by telephone, warn him as he overshoots and hear from the vulcanite the regular record of his doomed descent – 1,000 feet, 500, 200, a long-drawn-out waiting for the inevitable crash.   *The Spectator*, 20 October 1939

Stanley and Livingstone (USA, 20th Century-Fox, 1939). Director: Henry King. Spencer Tracy, Cedric Hardwicke, Richard Greene, Nancy Kelly.
Only Angels Have Wings (USA, Columbia, 1939). Director: Howard Hawks. Cary Grant, Jean Arthur, Richard Barthelmess, Rita Hayworth, Thomas Mitchell.

Nurse Edith Cavell/French Without Tears/'Arf a Mo' Hitler

Mr Herbert Wilcox proceeds on his applauded course. As slow and ponderous and well protected as a steam-roller, he irons out opposition. We get from his films almost everything except life, character, truth. Instead we have flags, anthems, leading articles, a tombstone reticence. It would be unfair to call his Way of a Neagle vulgar showmanship (though a certain lack of taste may be suspected in the portmanteau title of his company, Imperadio), for there is seldom anything vital enough to be called vulgar in the successive patriotic appearances of this rather inexpressive actress. Miss Neagle looked nice as Queen Victoria, she looks just as nice as Nurse Cavell: she moves rigidly on to the set, as if wheels were concealed under the stately skirt: she says her piece with flat dignity and trolleys out again – rather like a mechanical marvel from the World's Fair. This is not, I daresay, Miss Neagle's fault: I remember how attractive she was in tight breeches as Nell of Old Drury – then she was allowed a little vivacity, almost an allure: she had not in those days been crowned.

There is very little to say about her latest picture – it is all exactly as you would expect: Belgians sing Anglican carols in the Brussels streets: Germans, who are distinguished by a foreign accent, are all brutes in boots (except for the one regulation officer who is always inserted in such films to show the measure of our impartiality): there is a comic Cockney soldier and a sensitive and sissy one: Miss Neagle recites 'Abide with Me': there is a ceremony in Westminster Abbey, all organ notes and flags and memory, and the ghost of Miss Neagle recites 'Patriotism is not enough. . . .'; Mr Wilcox has undoubtedly given us the works. Who are we to complain that Miss Cavell was not young and lovely (Miss Neagle may consent to be an old Queen, but hardly to be a middle-aged commoner), or to protest that no film could have more contradicted her most famous utterance? Hatred and bitterness are certainly here in good measure; when the drums of propaganda begin to beat again we can hardly expect a popular film producer to stand aloof seeking the tragic values in Miss Cavell's story. Nevertheless, one regrets a little that the English creative spirit has never risen higher in her commemoration than a statue cut in soap and an emotional melodrama. Of the two, one prefers the statue: it seems a little truer to the staid heroism, the Anglican rectitude, the clinical love for patients and mankind.

French Without Tears is a triumph for Mr Anthony Asquith. After the first ten minutes his witty direction and firm handling of the cast (Mr Ray Milland has never acted so well as this before) conquer the too British sexuality of Mr Rattigan's farce. There is always something a little shocking about English levity: the greedy exhilaration of these blithe young men when they learn that another fellow's girl is to join them at the establishment where they are learning French, the scramble over her luggage, the light-hearted badinage and the watery and libidinous eye – that national mixture of prudery and excitement – would be unbearable if it were not for Mr Asquith's civilized direction (unlike most adaptations from stage plays it is the padding that is memorable). The situation is saved, too, by the Navy; Mr Rattigan must be given credit for the sketch of a stiff, shy Commander who finds himself dumped down from his ship into this adolescent kindergarten, and Mr Roland Culver for a brilliant performance. One's enjoyment of the picture (rather reluctantly one admits that it is enjoyable) is a little impaired by the too punctual laughter of feminine addicts.

Let nobody be put off by the title, *'Arf a Mo' Hitler*. This short documentary picture is an interesting record of British army training dramatized against an international background. An admirable eye for satirical effect has set the Aldershot Tattoo with its fireworks and costumes against the grim mechanized advance into Prague. The odd period caps and blazers and bicycles of Sandhurst, the incredible little bristly Crimean moustaches of cadet officers – these belong to the same fantastic world as the shots of Van de Lubbe, hunched and beaten and imbecile between his warders. *The Spectator*, 27 October 1939

Nurse Edith Cavell (USA, Imperadio Pictures, 1939). Director: Herbert Wilcox. Anna Neagle, George Sanders, Edna May Oliver.
French Without Tears (GB, Two Cities/Paramount, 1939). Director: Anthony Asquith. Ray Milland, Ellen Drew, Janine Darcey, David Tree, Roland Culver, Guy Middleton.
'Arf a Mo' Hitler (GB, British Paramount News, 1939). Director: G. T. Cummins.

The Lion Has Wings

A lion with wings would be no odder an exhibit than this documentary picture of the Royal Air Force constructed by Mr Alexander Korda with the help of little fictional scenes acted by Mr Ralph Richardson, Miss Merle Oberon and others; of irrelevant shots from Mr Korda's unfortunate historical picture *Fire Over England*; and of sequences, showing the Central Control Room of the Air Defence, from the admirable recruiting picture of two years' back called *The Gap*. All the first half of the picture is excellent, from the opening words of the commentary, 'This is Britain where we believe in freedom', with the shots of oast houses and country churches and grazing cattle, on to the new workers' flats and the new hospitals and the new schools and the words: 'Is all this to stop because one man wants to dominate the world?' It is propaganda of an intelligent kind; England at peace is contrasted with Germany preparing for war; there are amusing cuts from beach donkeys to German cavalry; from the mathematical ranks of the Brown-shirts, the guardians of one life, to the King strolling unprotected down a Scottish country lane. One cut is magnificently dramatic and a fine example of reticence: from the small dapper Dollfuss with his pale puzzled waxen features, like those of a tailor's dummy, as he pronounces in broken English 'Good-baye' into the micro-phone, straight without explanation to the coffin and the bearers and the aftermath of murder. The management of sound, too, is excellent: over the shots of swimmers in a bathing-pool suddenly breaks the music of a military band before we cut to the goosestep and the grey lines; Hitler, in close-up, addressing a Nazi rally, is cut quickly in and out with bookies hurling their impassioned advice, hucksters wheedling. From England at peace we go to England arming: superb shots of the Air Force – shadows racing across tarmac, lifting on to the roofs of hangars and racing on; grey planes moving in formation over a whole watery countryside; planes diving and twisting among the cumulus, carrying smoke like carnival ribbons straight across the sky; the making of the guns; the balloon barrage; the war.

With the war the film loses force and authenticity: we soon begin to tire of the fake elocutionist voices of trained actors. The Germans, I believe, have remarked that the Kiel battle was fought in the Denham film studios (rather tamely fought, it may be noted), and we become aware of some point in the jest as we watch imaginary battles between fighter squadrons and raiders, (who for some reason are called 'bandits'), in which all the deaths are German and all the heroics English. It would be a serious error, I think, to exhibit this film in the United States until we have shown in the air as well as in the studio that we can save London from the raider: imaginary battles are all very well in a thriller – they are unpleasantly out of place in a documentary, and smack of bravado. One curious effect of using an old propa-ganda film may be noted: the shots from *The Gap* contradict the whole theme. *The Gap* was made to show that unless recruiting improved the raiders must get through: so now we watch an actor frenziedly biting his nails in a control-room which has become part of a picture preaching invincibility. This dreary uncon-vincing fictional battle, however, is only the worst failure in tact and taste: almost as bad are scenes which introduce Mr Ralph Richardson as an Air Force officer, Miss Merle Oberon as a voluntary worker and Miss June Duprez as a nice boy's sweetheart. Americans are unlikely to laugh at the massed salute of the Nuremberg Rally – power and discipline are seldom humorous – but they will not, I imagine, restrain their laughter when Miss Oberon pulls Miss Duprez to attention in the drawing room beside the radio set as 'God Save the King' follows Mr Chamberlain's announcement of war or hide their smiles when Miss Oberon whispers to Mr Richardson, 'Darling, are we ready?' The film ends on a note as false as the opening was true. Miss Oberon in nurse's uniform is speaking for all the women of England, telling the world, through United Artists, that we are fighting for 'Truth, and beauty, and fair play, and ——' with whimsical hesitation and a professional quaver, 'kindliness.' As a statement of war aims, one feels, this leaves the world beyond Roedean still expectant.   *The Spectator*, 3 November 1939

The Lion Has Wings (GB, Alexander Korda, 1939). Directors: Adrian Brunel, Michael Powell, Brian Desmond Hurst. Ralph Richardson, Merle Oberon, June Duprez, Anthony Bushell, Bernard Miles, Flora Robson.

Daughters Courageous/Poison Pen

Daughters Courageous has three stars, and one of them is the cameraman, Mr James Wong Howe. Mr Howe is the best cameraman in the industry: he is an incomparable manufacturer of what the industry badly needs – the glittering cellophane packets which give a kind of desirability to the suppressed sobs and the cheeriness and the good hearts you find inside. One can say of Mr Howe's films that, in spite of directors and scenario-writers, they are always lovely to look at.

The other stars are Mr John Garfield and Mr Claude Rains. It is unnecessary to differentiate between the four daughters: they just belong – with their jollity and innocence – to the absurd tale: they add nothing to it. Their mother is a dress-designer; she has been forced to work because her husband walked out on her when the children were small; she is terribly understanding. Now she's taken up with a nice prosperous businessman, and as they celebrate (a contented family party) her engagement, and the husband-to-be sits at the head of the table carving the roast, the old husband walks in. He is Mr Claude Rains – so the story suddenly seems to contain genuine misery, disappointment, bitterness. He takes the stock Ishmael character – with the cynical wisdom and the traveller's tales – and transforms him into something you might really meet on a wet pavement with a gold nugget to sell, making two ends meet round his hopelessness. The scene after dinner when he sits apart by the radio, and the respectable youths drop in and the girls cluster round his successor lighting his pipe and filling his glass, and he silences every conversation by turning the dial and reminding them in a burst of music of his uncomfortable presence – this scene is finely acted. We know, of course, what his banal destiny is to be: how he will charm his daughters cunningly back into affection: and how he will be forced to walk out on them all again rather than ruin their settled futures (what do these Ishmaels use instead of money?): we know every stage of the routine fear-jerker; but Rains surprises us into belief, with that small triangular withered face which can suggest almost any emotion with a movement of the scaly and weather-beaten eyeball. Mr Garfield, too, acts with the venom of real conviction his parallel part of the anti-social youth with whom the youngest daughter falls in love and who finally accompanies Mr Rains into voluntary exile. The film should be very popular: it is so easy to watch, and perhaps the muddled morality is not nowadays noticeable. I confess it seemed a little odd to me, when we cut from the mother and the new husband swearing their vows binding 'till death us do part', to husband number one packing his bag and making his noble unobtrusive exit.

Daughters Courageous: Gale Page, Claude Rains, Priscilla Lane, Donald Crisp, Fay Bainter, Rosemary Lane, Lola Lane
Poison Pen: Flora Robson

November 1939

Poison Pen is a deplorable example of an English film which tries to create an English atmosphere. The story is about an anonymous letter-writer in a small town who causes a suicide and a murder and turns out to be the rector's sister. Miss Flora Robson acts the unconvincing part as it deserves, turning on a little routine passion at the close as you would a geyser. The dialogue is appalling, full of unnecessary words, like a charade: 'Do you want a porter?' 'Oh, no, I can manage, thank you.' 'We've got the car outside.' 'What a lovely morning'; and the background of the picture is as quaint and false as a Broadway tea-shop. Everybody – from the postman to the Squire – is a character: the villagers – who have oddly assorted accents – are such simple creatures that they crowd into the Post Office to listen to a private call from Australia: the ignorant patronage of men who have spent their lives among the sets of surburban studios is spread thickly over the English countryside.   *The Spectator*, 10 November 1939

Daughters Courageous (USA, Warner Bros, 1939). Director: Michael Curtiz. John Garfield, Claude Rains, The Lane Sisters, Fay Bainter.
Poison Pen (GB, Associated British, 1939). Director: Paul S. Stein. Flora Robson, Robert Newton, Belle Chrystal, Ann Todd.

The Frozen Limits

The Frozen Limits seems to this reviewer the funniest English picture yet produced; more than that, it can bear comparison with the Lloyds and Keatons of Hollywood, with *Safety Last* and *The General*. The credit is not all the Crazy Gang's: that rather repulsive troupe tumble through it – in furs, feathers, nightshirts – with appalling vigour; they seize the comic spirit and impose a kind of mob rule; you may easily be disgusted by the browsing and sluicing; the circus smell of sawdust and human skin. It is all noises and shouts and unintelligible wisecracks. They break through the scenery as if it were a paper hoop. Everything comes to pieces in their boisterous hands. But if you have no sympathy with that savage tribe you will still enjoy the direction of Mr Marcel Varnel and the script of Mr J. O. C. Orton.

The Crazy Gang, bankrupt performers on Hampstead Heath, pick up a newspaper which tells them of a gold-rush to Red Gulch, Alaska. It must be a recent paper, because the Prime Minister, Mr Chamberlain, is saying that England must be prepared – 'he's only talked like that lately'. But when they arrive in Red Gulch on an old horse bus the place seems deserted. When they knock on the Sheriff's door the whole house collapses like a mummy exposed to air: *East Lynne* is advertised outside the theatre, a spider-web drapes the box-office, and the only human being they can disinter is Mr Moore Marriott, of the thin beard and the piping voice and the exultant eye. He is manager, box-office clerk, commissionaire rolled into one: a mad relic of the pioneering days who lives there with his niece, dreaming of the gold he thinks he once discovered and sleep-walking to find it. He admits them to the ruined theatre and makes them pick their way past the legs of an imaginary audience, and how well the Crazy Gang clown it: the sharp exclamation, the muttered apology, the twisting of the back, the little twitters of impatience and irritation in a dark theatre. The truth at last dawns on them – the Chamberlain they read about carried a monocle and not an umbrella: they are two wars too late.

Nevertheless, there *is* gold. When the pioneer walks in his sleep that night he

The Frozen Limits

brings back a lump of ore in his pail: the Crazy Gang take it to the nearest town and, using it to pay for their drinks, unintentionally start a new gold-rush. Red Gulch swarms back to life again, but the Crazy Gang, who fear the boom won't last, are caught salting the diggings with the pioneer's lump. Bill McGrew – a cat among mice – threatens them with lynching unless gold is struck before next midday, so the old pioneer must walk again and lead them to his seam. Fill him up with cheese, but that's not enough. He needs a full moon, and a cardboard one is dangled outside the window while Flanagan rocks him to sleep with a lullaby:

> Got a full tum-tum.
> Got a full moon.

Meanwhile the Mounties are riding to the rescue – a delightful touch this, as they trot slowly through the mountains, singing a song in complacent tenor voices about 'always getting our man', straight out of a Nelson Eddy picture. Back in Red Gulch the pioneer walks, but the villains have heard of the ruse, and to outwit them six ancient pioneers in nightshirts must wander through the town with pails and candles. It would be wrong to tell more: of the forced wedding, with one of the gang impersonating the bride, of the wild chase up and down the curtains and beams of the ancient theatre, of how the Mounties do at last arrive and arrest the wrong man, and of how the gold is discovered. It isn't often that one dwells on the story of an English film, but just as there is always an undertone to the best clowning, the drumming of the rain that rains every day, so this farcical tale of a temporary town abandoned to the beetle and the rat has an odd touch of poetry: the

253

ancient melodrama, the bus which runs only in an old man's mind, the long-vanished better people who must be bowed to in their carriages. It is as if a troupe of clowns had suddenly with raspberries and rude gestures and the tang of the ring on their clothes irrupted into a tale of Mr De La Mare's, all silence, spider-web and vacancy. *The Spectator*, 17 November 1939

The Frozen Limits (GB, Gainsborough, 1939). Director: Marcel Varnel. The Crazy Gang, Moore Marriott.

Juarez

Juarez (pronounced, so the programme tells us, War-ezz) is what is known in the trade as a distinguished film: it follows *Pasteur* and *Zola* and might easily have died of distinction as *Zola* did. Listen to what happened in Warner's studios, if we are to believe the publicity-writers, when it was decided to make the picture. A Doctor Herman Lissauer assembled as complete a bibliography as he could, and within one month turned in to the unfortunate producers and director '372 books, documents, pieces of correspondence and albums of rare and authentic [*sic*] photographs'. Three writers – one of them with the picturesque name of Aeneas MacKenzie – got to work on this material, though, as the credit titles refer to a play of Werfel's and Miss Bertita Harding's *The Phantom Crown*, from which they could learn all they needed to know for this rather superficial picture, one imagines the 372 books, documents, etc., soon went into store. Meanwhile, the art director was drawing 3,643 sketches, the construction department was making 7,360 blueprints (they might surely have done with less, since the same Mexican village set seems to have been used for Vera Cruz, Matamoros and Queretaro), the directors were making a tour of Mexico and Miss Bette Davis was cutting her hair three inches shorter. Presumably the directors looked in at Oaxaca on their trip, but the sight of the ruined convent there did not suggest any alteration in their portrait of Juarez as a Liberal democrat of the Abraham Lincoln school.

It must be admitted, however, that a quite impressive film has emerged from all the muddle – perhaps the muddle wasn't really as great as the publicity department makes out, and the two parts of Juarez and Maximilian are well written and admirably acted by Mr Paul Muni and Mr Brian Aherne (Mr Muni's make-up is extraordinarily impressive: he is an Indian to the very shape of the skull and the stony Aztec profile). I have not usually been an admirer of Mr Aherne's acting: his personality has always seemed to go with a pipe and Harris tweeds and a boundless complacency, but here he nearly acts Mr Muni off the set. With his forked and silky beard, the blond whiskers and curls, the gentle worried inflexibility, he is every inch a Hapsburg, and the film is his from that first puzzled inquiry at Vera Cruz – 'Why are the streets so empty?' – to his long, careful frock-coated stride up the rocky hill of the death-place. (Miss Bette Davis's Carlota simply does not exist beside him.) Mr Muni as the whitewashed Juarez has a smaller and easier part: he has only to be simple, kindly, ruthless from the best ideological motives: he is preaching to the converted. He hasn't got to put over such an unfashionable doctrine as the divine right of kings to be the servant of their people, and when he defines democracy to General Porfirio Diaz every Left Book Club heart will beat a little faster (who cares or knows about the ruined schools and churches?). Many of my colleagues have objected to the dialogue, which they call stilted: it seemed to me to go admirably with the stiff dated Hapsburg court set down, like a millionaire's purchase from Europe, with its gold-leaf and scarlet hangings, its ushers and rules of precedence, in the dry savage countryside, where we watch a vulture peck at a child's body in a ruined village. The cameramen have for once resisted the temptation to make Mexico picturesque – there are hardly any cactuses and no sky-lined peons. *The Spectator*, 24 November 1939

Juarez (USA, Warner Bros, 1939). Director: William Dieterle. Paul Muni, Bette Davis, Brian Aherne.

Golden Boy/On the Night of the Fire

Perhaps because the original play did not seem to me of great importance – a well-told sentimental story of a boxer who wanted at heart to be a violinist, and broke his hand and killed himself in one of those convenient Green Hat car smashes – the film of *Golden Boy* pleased me. The crusty amusing Odets dialogue is still there – we have the fatal fight that the stage could not give us, and if the ending is now a happy one, with the boxer comforted by his girl, who assures him that his hands will one day get back all their musical skill, does it matter very much? Was the symbolism of the play so significant? Wasn't it really a bit of hooey? *Golden Boy* has been directed by Rouben Mamoulian, and apart from the foggy sepia tones which do justice only to Mr Menjou's lounge suits, it has all the vigorous hard-hitting close-up effect one expects from the director of *City Streets* (let's forget and forgive *Queen Christina* and the rest). Mr Menjou as the boxer's manager, with his desperate humour, his unfortunate sexual life, and his recurring disappointments ('Ah, sweet misery of life!') has one of the best parts he has played since *The Front Page*, and Mr William Holden almost persuades us to believe in the boxing violinist. But the real stars of the picture are Mr Mamoulian and Mr Joseph Calleia. You can tell the quality of a director by his close-ups, and I would put the final boxing-match, when the Golden Boy, with hate in his gloves for the sport and his exploiters, kills his black opponent in a cruel knock-out, among the finest sequences of the talking film. It is shot almost entirely in close-up, close to the fighters and close to the audience, back and forth from the plugging gloves to the febrile blondies with their moistened lips, the stout complacent backers at the ringside, and screaming Harlem in the gallery; it is shot subjectively, with hate in the lens as well as in the gloves. And then there is Mr Calleia: Mr Calleia is being groomed these days for sympathetic stardom. The anarchist in *Five Came Back*, with his bloodshot canine suffering eyes, was meant to prepare us for his Father Damien. Here he is back in one of his old gangster parts – the rigid back, the graceful functional body carried like a gun, a haunting picture of a lonely crook who wants to own a champ.

On the Night of the Fire is about a barber who steals some money and then is driven by blackmail to murder. It has been extravagantly praised – an odd thing for those of us who heard the ribald laughter at the Press show. Based on Mr F. L. Green's unconvincing novel, it aims at more than thriller rank; it is meant to be all destiny and the furies in a grim depressed industrial town. The book has been very closely followed – far too closely, for Mr Green's romantic brain seemed to contain no knowledge of how men really act. Fantastic police methods; sudden reversals of character; mobs who are whipped up with the speed of Elizabethan drama – it seems even more unreal upon the screen. Nor is it helped by acting or direction. A lot of aitches carefully and symmetrically dropped never disguise the classy origins of Mr Ralph Richardson, Miss Diana Wynyard and Mr Romney Brent,

Golden Boy: Barbara Stanwyck, Sam Levene, Joseph Calleia, Don Beddoe, Adolphe Menjou, Edward Brophy

while Mary Clare as a half-witted old ragpicker reminds us in her mummery of a hard-working hostess determined to make her dumb-crambo party go. The director has taken most of the dreary story in medium long shots, the camera firmly placed as it were in the front row of the stalls. Watching the dull distances, the ineffective angles and the bad lighting, I found myself wondering – as I have wondered before at Mr Brian Desmond Hurst's *Ourselves Alone* and *Riders to the Sea* – what constitutes promise in an English studio. Can it be that well-worn shot of a gramophone-needle scraping to a close as a man dies out of sight? The second-rate cinema mind has always been attracted to symbolism – the apple blossom falling in the rain, the broken glass, all the sham poetic ways of avoiding the direct statement, which demands some insight into the way men really act.

The Spectator, 1 December 1939

Golden Boy (USA, Columbia, 1939). Director: Rouben Mamoulian. William Holden, Barbara Stanwyck, Adolphe Menjou, Joseph Calleia.
On the Night of the Fire (GB, G & S, 1939). Director: Brian Desmond Hurst. Ralph Richardson, Diana Wynyard, Romney Brent, Mary Clare.

The Marx Brothers at the Circus/Disputed Passage

The old crazy sets have gone now for good, that air of a world run up like a pioneer village overnight at the least expense. We must regretfully accept the fact that, thanks to the Metro millions, the Marx Brothers are finally imprisoned in the Hollywood world. I prefer the circus to the opera and the races – there is no Miss Maureen O'Sullivan here to bring our enjoyment crashing down with the whisper 'Silly' as Groucho lopes lecherously past. There *are* young lovers and a story that runs carefully from A to B – Mr Kenny Baker with his soprano speech and his plump eye-sockets plays a rich Newport young man who shocks his relatives by managing a circus and musically loving an equestrienne ('We've got it oh so bad, but isn't it good. . . . Don't know fish from cake, Don't know if its doughnut or a wedding-cake . . . two blind loves'), there's a villain who wants to own the circus and hires a strong man and a dwarf to rob the manager of the takings, and Groucho, the small-town lawyer with his old umbrella, his stained frock-coat, his wild gleam and erratic intelligence, is on the trail, *ventre à terre*. He may be cramped by the classy direction, by the fine circus sets and the exciting shots of freight-trains moving against a dark sky, the admirable Mervyn LeRoy dope, but he manages all the same to break away to the padded silken side of Madame Dumont (one of Newport's 400) stretched as usual on her Pompadour couch as though she had never moved an inch since the delectable days of *Horsefeathers* and *Duck Soup*.

This is Groucho's film: Chico and Harpo are a long way behind: Groucho singing about a woman tattooist – 'Lydia, oh Lydia, that encyclopaedia': Groucho putting on the dingy tails ('It would take a magician,' he complains, 'to get into this suit', and Chico replies, 'I got it from a magician'), unearthing the white rabbit, the flags of all nations (Harpo pulls out a toy rifle and a band plays), a pigeon ('It's all right. It's a homing pigeon.' 'Then I'll keep a light burning in my pocket.'): Groucho stuck upside-down on the ceiling in suctional boots: Groucho undressing coyly behind the circus lady's screen, hanging up his combined black stockings and long pants: Groucho bearding Madame Dumont in her bedroom. Impossible to explain all the stages to the superb climax when Madame Dumont is shot protestingly out of a cannon, and Groucho, Harpo, the villain and a murderous ape cling to the flying trapeze while she hurtles towards them in her Newport robe and her bursting seams.

Is it, when you come to think of it, a much odder story than *Disputed Passage*, which is about a great surgeon and his great pupil, and how the pupil falls in love with a Chinese girl (but she's only Chinese by upbringing, so the tale is eugenically sound), and how the surgeon tries to break the romance in the cause of science (but really it's because his wife died years ago of appendicitis), and his pupil in the last twenty minutes quarrels with him, pursues the girl to China and gets bombed by Japanese: his life's despaired of, the great surgeon arrives by plane and operates, 'science has done everything it can', the girl turns up too, all's well, and the surgeon admits – for dubious reasons – that there must be a soul. A prologue shows the author, Mr Lloyd Douglas – who wrote that other medical marvel, *Magnificent Obsession* – penning a few lines in his library to the producers: 'Dear Paramount, thank you for preserving the full flavour of my story. . . .' I should describe the flavour as a rather nauseating blend of iodine and glucose.

Mr Douglas's heart-wounds look a bit shabby in this mined, torpedoed world.

December 1939

The Paramount News, with its remarkable record of the rescue by the *Independence Hall* of the survivors of the *Yorkshire* – the broken ship diving out of sight, the white drifting faces on the water – beat any so-called 'serious' film off the screen. No Hollywood tragedy can afford comparison with the beaten puzzled faces of the Lascar sailors (their heads are bandaged because their officers had to knock them out with life-preservers before pitching them overboard in lifebelts), the orphaned child who looks as if she's missed a party, the coffin pitched into the sea wrapped in another country's flag – there's got to be a flag.

The Spectator, 15 December 1939

The Marx Brothers at the Circus (USA, M-G-M, 1939). Director: Edward Buzzell. The Marx Brothers, Margaret Dumont, Florence Rice, Kenny Baker, Eve Arden.
Disputed Passage (USA, Paramount, 1939). Director: Frank Borzage. Dorothy Lamour, Akim Tamiroff, John Howard.

First Love/Our Neighbours – the Carters

First Love is an honest fairy-tale, based even to the slipper and the midnight sanction on *Cinderella*: it doesn't for a moment pretend to be life, this story of the Deanna Durbin orphan with a golden voice who comes to live, when she leaves school, with her rich morose uncle, her hazy and eccentric aunt who dabbles in astrology, and their children – a spoilt society beauty and a backboneless youth who has been conserving energy all his life against an emergency that he is determined shall never turn up. Miss Durbin, of course, wins the hearts of the trampled domestics, even of her soured uncle (Mr Eugene Pallette looking very much like Mr Tod, the badger, with his broad back and twitching nostril, as he disappears regularly to ground), and at the great ball of the season the local police force come to her aid, outwitting the wicked cousin who is determined, through jealousy, that she shall stay at home. Her relatives are all side-tracked into a magistrates' court while she arrives at the ball in the Commissioner's car, wins her coveted prince and leaves a slipper in her hurried midnight exit. The whole tale is carried superbly off: even the butler might sprout pantomime wings at any moment; and as for Miss Durbin's first real affair, it is managed with infinite tact (the halting talk about auxiliary engines on the penthouse roof and the first kiss and the hurried conversational recovery – 'What is a Diesel?'). There is nothing at all to resent in the picture; it is admirably directed, amusingly written, and acted with immense virtuosity by a fine cast. It isn't true: the world is nobody's oyster – no young girl will ever in this way oust the *prima donna* at her first ball and snatch the season's prize, but that doesn't matter, because there is nothing shabby or hypocritical in the dream which Miss Durbin expresses with the drive of irresistible conviction.

The Carters belong to a fairy-tale of very different quality. This *does* pretend to be life – from the awful bluff note on the programme: 'Here's the Carters – the grandest family you've ever met', it tries with blasts of loyalty, cheeriness and good-fellowship to put across a fake idea of middle-class virtue. A genuine subject – the defeat of the small family druggist by the cut-price store – is lost in the appalling sentimentality – all the more appalling for the expert mechanized acting of Mr Frank Craven. No family like this has ever existed: it doesn't even represent, like *First Love*, a natural human hope, but directed with great competence, it makes its effect – the easy tears of middle-aged women all around.

The Spectator, 22 December 1939

First Love (USA, Universal, 1939). Director: Henry Koster. Deanna Durbin, Robert Stack, Helen Parrish, Eugene Pallette.
Our Neighbours – the Carters (USA, Paramount, 1939). Director: Ralph Murphy. Fay Bainter, Frank Craven.

Remontons les Champs-Elysées

How unbearable these films of M. Sacha Guitry would be if they were not so successful. One remembers the superb impertinence with which a few years ago this elderly actor and playwright stalked into the studios, ignoring all rules, all unities, all the painstaking calculations of worthy directors who had been learning all their lives from experience, and began to make pictures which challenged by their very triviality (we had become so used to epics); like his plays, they were nothing at all except mediums for that sagacious hollow voice, that swinging monocle and the conqueror's gait.

Now with his latest picture we can see that he has learnt nothing humdrum and lost nothing valuable. He is the only director who can make films as personal as essays: he might be described as the Montaigne of the screen – we can almost watch him think as he shoots: a momentary pause as a new idea strikes him, and then away with plot, continuity, turn the cameras over here, switch on those lights, scrap that part and read this one. What we seem to see is not a finished product of the creative mind but the act of creation itself, as M. Guitry plays with the pageant of French history. Le Roi Soleil steps like a young conqueror into his coach and out again the other side, withered and monkeyish and old – it is as if M. Guitry had just at that moment thought of that. Foremen are urging on the lazy workmen who are building the Café des Ambassadeurs – 'in those days men were encouraged to work': an idea strikes M. Guitry: in a flash of the eyelid it is the other way about, the foremen sprout twentieth-century cloth caps as they try to make their men go slow: another flash and we are back in the days of Louis-Philippe. It has nothing to do with the story, with continuity, but M. Guitry can leave all that to others: his aim is to catch ideas on the wing.

The framework of his picture is a simple one: M. Guitry plays an elderly school-master (if he can ever be said to play anything but himself) who talks to his pupils with remarkable broad-mindedness about the history of the Champs-Elysées: a rare schoolmaster this, in whose veins, as we soon begin to learn, flows the blood of Louis XV, of Marat and of Napoleon – a model Frenchman, royal, revolu-tionary, bourgeois, and perpetually amorous. (All his ancestors have fallen in love at fifty-four and died at sixty-four, and as this is his sixty-fourth birthday, he must rapidly unload his knowledge.) Most of the picture is in monologue with little acted scenes, and M. Guitry plays his ancestors at ardent fifty-four – with Napoleon III thrown in as good measure. Never was genuine patriotism expressed so lightly, wittily, scandalously, or with more real dignity; and the impudent direction touches poetry when the beaten Napoleon dismisses his carriage and walks alone for the last time up the Champs. 'I cannot believe,' M. Guitry says, 'that Napoleon and Bonaparte were the same man. How interesting if they had met there . . .', and there, as the idea strikes him, the meeting crystallizes between the misty trees, the young revolutionary and the tired old Emperor. 'We couldn't even love the same woman.'   *The Spectator,* 29 December 1939

Remontons les Champs-Elysées (France, Cinéas, 1938). Director: Sacha Guitry. Sacha Guitry, Raymonde Galle. [US title: *Champs-Elysées*.]

Remontons les Champs-Elysées: the Bal Mabille reconstruction

Mr Smith Goes to Washington

Here is Capra, without the help of Riskin, back to his finest form – the form of
Mr Deeds. It has always been an interesting question, how much Capra owed to his
faithful scenario-writer. Now it is difficult to believe that Riskin's part was ever
very important, for all the familiar qualities are here – the exciting close-ups, the
sudden irrelevant humour, the delight – equal to that of the great Russians – in the
ordinary human face. (Claude Rains has not got an ordinary human face, and for
that reason he seems out of place and histrionic, great actor though he is, in a
Capra film.)

The story is regulation Capra in praise of simplicity and virtue and acting
naturally. As a fairy-tale it is a little Victorian: it is not that we are less moved by
virtue in these days, but we are more aware of how the author cheats – virtue is
not bound to win, and the easy moral of a Capra tale comes dangerously close to a
Benthamite apothegm about honesty being the best policy. Young Jefferson
Smith, acted with a kind of ideal awkwardness by James Stewart, is appointed a
Senator to fill an unexpired term: he is a youth leader whose guilelessness is

considered useful by the other State Senator, Joseph Paine, and his business boss, Jim Taylor. They are putting over a tricky piece of graft and they don't want a new Senator who can see his way. So Smith goes up to Washington with his naïve ideals and his patriotism (he knows Lincoln's speeches off by heart) and his sense of responsibility: he feels rapture at the sight of the Capitol dome, stands like a worshipper below the bony marble fingers of the Lincoln statue, and Paine entertains him and side-tracks him.

Then suddenly Smith's secretary, with all the harsh, don't-give-a-twopenny-curse charm of Miss Jean Arthur, opens his eyes to the real Washington, where you can't look round a monument without starting a grafter. He refuses to be a party to fraud and Jim Taylor (Edward Arnold) proceeds to break him – papers are forged, witnesses perjure themselves, he is declared by a Committee of the Senate unworthy to hold his seat. 'Beautiful,' says a reporter at the framed inquiry, 'that Taylor machine.' But Smith won't surrender: when the Senators refuse to listen to him, he takes advantage of the Constitution and holds the floor for twenty-three hours, hoping that his State will support him – in vain because the newspapers have been bought by Taylor. This constitutional battle of one man against the Senate is among the most exciting sequences the screen has given us. But it is a fairy-tale, so Smith wins: Joseph Paine, like a Dickensian Scrooge, is caught by conscience, and I imagine it is easier for us, than for an American who knows his country's politics, to suspend disbelief.

It is a great film, even though it is not a great story, acted by a magnificent cast, so that Capra can afford to fling away on tiny parts men like Eugene Pallette, Guy Kibbee, Thomas Mitchell and Harry Carey. A week later one remembers vividly the big body of Pallette stuck in a telephone-box, the family dinner of the weak crooked Governor (Kibbee) whom even his children pester over the nomination, the whole authentic atmosphere of big bland crookery between boss and politician – the 'Joes' and the 'Jims', the Christian names and comradeship, the wide unspoken references, and one remembers too the faces chosen and shot with Capra care – worried political faces, Grub Street faces, acquisitive social faces and faces that won't give themselves away.   *The Spectator,* 5 January 1940

Mr Smith goes to Washington (USA, Columbia, 1939). Director: Frank Capra. James Stewart, Jean Arthur, Edward Arnold, Eugene Pallette, Thomas Mitchell, Guy Kibbee.

The Real Glory/Twenty-one Days

This, we are tempted to exclaim at *The Real Glory*, forgetting for awhile men like Duvivier, who have brought a mature intelligence to the film, is what cinema should be: a simple story of adventure and sudden death, and will they arrive in time? Every value which exists in a boy's story has been put cunningly into this film – self-sacrifice, misunderstanding, heroism, and if it were not for the intrusion of a couple of females about a third of the way through, it could hardly be improved. It is directed by Henry Hathaway, who made *Bengal Lancer*, and the star is Gary Cooper, with David Niven and others sparkling in the background. I can't remember the women's names – one of them had a sweet and pallid charm which reminded me of Heather Angel: I, too, much resented their presence, dressed up in spotless Sargent dresses, in this dangerous outpost of the Philippines.

The American army has withdrawn, leaving a few white officers to train the native levies, and make them fit to fight for their own independence. 'In twenty-four hours,' the senior officer protests, 'we shall be screaming for help', because the Moros are up under their pirate leader, and are only waiting for the Americans to withdraw before they burn, kill, rape and enslave the frightened Philippinos. The last boats leave, watched by the despairing natives, and the Catholic priest greets the retiring Commander: 'We who are about to die salute you.' The isolation of the almost defenceless town of Mysang is admirably conveyed. The pirates' aim is to provoke the ill-trained troops into the jungle after them, and so they send assassins to cut down the American officers one after another. The most exciting action shots I have seen for a long while on the screen are of the first assassination: the huge half-naked shaven swordsman levering himself up on to the jetty, the towns-people fleeing at the sight of a Moro face, and then his controlled fanatic charge across the deserted quay right to his mark unstopped by bullets. It isn't necessary to give away any more of the story – the ambush and the cholera epidemic, the diverted river, and the last great scene of the assault against a weakened garrison, the pirates catapulted from trees into the fort, while help comes rushing down the dynamited river on rafts. Mr Cooper as the military doctor, who arrives with a present of orchids and a colonel's gallstone for his friends, has never acted better. Sometimes his lean photogenic face seems to leave everything to the lens, but there is no question here of his not acting. Watch him inoculate the girl against cholera – the casual jab of the needle, and the dressing slapped on while he talks, as though a thousand arms had taught him where to stab and he doesn't have to think any more.

Perhaps I may be forgiven for noticing a picture in which I had some hand, for I have no good word to say of it. The brilliant acting of Mr Hay Petrie as a decayed and outcast curate cannot conquer the overpowering flavour of cooked ham. Galsworthy's story, *The First and the Last*, was peculiarly unsuited for film adaptation, as its whole point lay in a double suicide (forbidden by the censor), a burned confession, and an innocent man's conviction for murder (forbidden by the great public). For the rather dubious merits of the original the adaptors have substituted incredible coincidences and banal situations. Slow, wordy, unbearably sentimental, the picture reels awkwardly towards the only suicide the censorship allowed – and that, I find with some astonishment, has been cut out. I wish I could tell the extraordinary story that lies behind this shelved and resurrected picture, a story involving a theme-song, and a bottle of whisky, and camels in Wales. . . . Meanwhile, let one guilty man, at any rate, stand in the dock, swearing never, never to do it again. . . .   *The Spectator*, 12 January 1940

The Real Glory (USA, Samuel Goldwyn, 1939). Director: Henry Hathaway. Gary Cooper, David Niven, Andrea Leeds.
Twenty-one Days (GB, London Films, 1939). Director: Basil Dean. Laurence Olivier, Vivien Leigh, Leslie Banks, Robert Newton, Hay Petrie. [US title: *Twenty-one Days Together*.]

The Light That Failed/The Old Maid

These two pictures succeed admirably in what they attempt – to jerk the waiting tear out of its duct. Human nature is seldom more incomprehensible than in its sympathies; art which is supposed to enlarge them has left us, after all these centuries, reading with casual interest of the casualties in a wrecked train, or passing over a street accident altogether ('no news today'), though both are within range of our experience. But tell a story about a great artist who receives a spear slash in the Sudan, and a long time later goes blind just after painting the picture

The Light that Failed: Ida Lupino, Ronald Colman

of his career – a picture which he doesn't know has been spoiled with turpentine by his angry model, and who later, when he does learn the truth, goes out, blind as he is, to the Sudan, hits on his old newspaper friends and an English square at the moment of attack, and dies happily and quickly with a bullet in the right place – tell a somewhat unusual anecdote of that kind, an anecdote which can hardly appeal to the personal experience of anyone in the audience, and you will have every tenth man and woman weeping in the dark. Take, too, the subject of *The Old Maid* – churned out, it may be noted, by the late Edith Wharton at a time when she must have forgotten the lesson of the Master: you wouldn't say that story either was likely to happen twice on the same planet. A younger sister (Bette Davis) loves the man her sister (Miriam Hopkins) has jilted: he goes off to the Civil War and is killed, leaving her pregnant: so in order to hide her child she opens a home for war orphans. But she becomes engaged to his sister's brother-in-law (the whole story reads like the table of forbidden degrees), and her sister learns of the child: she stops the marriage on the wedding-day, pretending that sister Davis has consumption. Then her own husband dies, and for rather inadequate reasons sister Davis comes to share her home, and it isn't long before her child is calling sister Hopkins 'Mummie' and sister Davis 'Auntie'. Then we skip the years and find sister Davis a typical old maid, disliked by her child, who finds her harsh and unsympathetic (this is to hide the awful truth from her), and it all ends with the daughter's marriage and a farewell kiss to poor auntie at the instigation of kind mummie. This story will undoubtedly prove a winner: in a world of bombed towns tears fall with delirious ease over this rather improbable life of an old maid.

Kipling's novel has been reproduced with great fidelity, and the period is admirably caught, with Norfolk jackets and Sargent hats and gentlemen's rooms: even the pictures painted by Helder are period – big action canvases in the style of the *Illustrated London News*, and we can well imagine the masterpiece, *Melancholia*, as the Academy picture of the year. This is intelligent – it is easier to sympathize with a popular artist we can believe in than in a great unlikely genius. Ronald Colman's Helder is agreeable, but his voice has a way of breaking into insincerity, of giving up the ghost of acting altogether (perhaps the Kipling dialogue is too much for him, admirable coloured stuff though it is), and he is sometimes acted right off the set by Walter Huston as his friend Torpenhow and by Ida Lupino, with her lovely barmaid features, as the vicious little cockney model. Newspapermen will feel envious at this picture of correspondents who really went to Khartoum with Kitchener, or to Kandahar with Roberts, instead of watching endless football-matches and ENSA entertainments behind the lines.

Great actresses choose odd mediums, and perhaps Miss Davis is a great actress – she seemed so in her early pop-eyed appearances, all nerves and nastiness (you remember *Of Human Bondage*). Her performance in *The Old Maid* is of extra-ordinary virtuosity – as the young girl, and the secret mother, and the harsh prim middle-aged woman with her tiny lines and her talcum. It is like a manual of acting for beginners in three lessons, but beside Miss Lupino's vivid outbreak it has the dryness of a textbook. The whole picture is very lavish and competent, with a New World moral outlook which is summed wonderfully up in a phrase addressed by sister Hopkins to sister Davis: 'If Tina is to be made happy her position must be made unassailable, financially and socially.'

The Spectator, 19 January 1940

The Light That Failed (USA, Paramount, 1939). Director: William Wellman. Ronald Colman, Walter Huston, Ida Lupino.
The Old Maid (USA, Warner Bros, 1939). Director: Edmund Goulding. Bette Davis, Miriam Hopkins, George Brent, Donald Crisp, William Lundigan.

The Stars Look Down/Escape to Happiness

Dr Cronin's mining novel has made a very good film – I doubt whether in England we have ever produced a better. Mr Carol Reed, who began some years ago so impressively with *Midshipman Easy* and then became involved in the cheap little second features that were regularly churned out by the smaller English studios, has at last had his chance and magnificently taken it. Since this is the story of a mine disaster his work will inevitably be compared with Pabst's in *Kameradschaft*: he can bear the comparison. When the miners who are on strike advance against the butcher who has refused meat to a sick woman, and when the siren blows for the accident and the children rush across the cement school playground to the rails, and when we listen to the condemned imprisoned men – the youth who was to have been played in a football trial on Saturday and who refuses to believe that Saturday has ever come and gone in their darkness: the old miner feeding the new young hand with cough lozenges: the man with religious mania and the boozer's muttered confession – we are aware of direction which is every bit as good as Pabst's. If the film – constructed authentically though it is of grit and slagheap, back-to-back cottages, and little scrubby railway stations – fails to remain in the memory as long as *Kameradschaft*, it will be because there is too much story drowning the theme: the particular is an uneasy ally in literature of the general. The theme is the dangers of private ownership: Michael Redgrave plays a miner who gets a scholarship and leaves the pits, and he expresses this theme in two speeches – at a college debating society and a meeting of union representatives: the theme that there will always be owners ready to take a gamble sometimes, while the miner takes a gamble always. It isn't so dramatically effective a theme as Pabst's, and the punch is a little pulled. The owner responsible for the disaster has a stroke, repents and dies – this, I imagine, is pure Cronin. Once before Mr Reed tried his hand at a documentary story – *Bank Holiday*. It was highly praised and was full of 'characters', but it smelt of the studio. Here one forgets the casting altogether: he handles his players like a master, so that one remembers them only as people. Miss Lockwood alone as the studious miner's disaster of a wife remains an actress to the bitter end.

Escape to Happiness is one of those pictures of unhappy passion among the artistic and the successful, with smart white-wood sets, grand pianos, good beach clothes and Riviera fishing-villages in which it is natural to expect Miss Bergner to appear, turning somersaults and dying of a weak heart. . . . Only in that case the lovers, I suppose, would escape to the Tyrol. Mr Leslie Howard acts the part of a famous composer and violinist, happily married, with a small girl whom he adores: he falls in love with her music-teacher, a promising young pianist, there are clandestine meetings, she decides it's best to leave him for ever – and instead they are off, first on professional tour and then on passionate holiday. But, as you will expect, the pull of his family is too strong, so she leaves him again for his own good and he creeps back home to see his child and stays. There's nothing really wrong in the story: the only falsity is at the end, when the child is knocked down by a car as she runs to meet her father, and in the dialogue which treads in boots the beaten literary path: life, we must admit, often follows these lines, though perhaps less elegantly. It is in its way a good film: the awful sense in the man of a divided personality is sometimes well conveyed, and the first parting is directed

The Stars Look Down: Emlyn Williams

with miserable truth. But the film is most worth seeing for the new star, Miss Ingrid Bergman, who is as natural as her name. What star before has made her first appearance on the international screen with a highlight gleaming on her nose-tip? That gleam is typical of a performance that doesn't give the effect of acting at all, but of living – without make-up. Mr Howard with his studied inflexions can't help seeming a little false beside the awkward truth of this young actress, and I am afraid we shall regretfully remember this first picture after the grooming and the training have done to her what they did to Sten.

The Spectator, 26 January 1940

The Stars Look Down (GB, Grand National, 1940). Director: Carol Reed. Michael Redgrave, Margaret Lockwood, Emlyn Williams, Linden Travers.
Escape to Happiness (*Intermezzo*) (USA, Selznick International, 1940). Director: Gregory Ratoff. Leslie Howard, Ingrid Bergman, Edna Best.

The Arsenal Stadium Mystery/Pièges

A detective-story must be one of the hardest jobs a director can be assigned, because there's got to be a lot of talk. He must be on his toes all the time to snatch out of the pages of dialogue any opportunity for visual wit. A thriller is compara-

Pièges

tively easy: a gun is photogenic: bodies fall easily in good poses: the camera can move at the speed of a G-man's car, but in a detective-story it has to amble at the walking pace of the mind. Mr Thorold Dickinson, who will be remembered for his promising first film *The High Command*, has admirably succeeded in keeping his detection alive as well as obscure – this picture is as good to watch as either of the *Thin Man* films, and he gives us wit instead of facetiousness – wit of cutting and wit of angle. The action takes place mainly in the offices and changing-rooms at the Stadium: we listen to managers addressing their teams on strategy (one of them is Mr George Allison himself, who deserves a film contract for the vivid way in which he plays George Allison): we watch Mr Emmett of the canned Gaumont voice commenting on a match: we get to know what the jars in the treatment-room contain – the sterilized horsehair and the rest: we learn where to look for a phone-box and which passages lead to the ground. Then one of the Trojans – an amateur team – falls dead in the middle of a match with the Arsenal, and we move to Scotland Yard, but a Yard as undramatic and familiar as the Arsenal rooms. A police pantomime is in rehearsal, and Mr Leslie Banks as Inspector Slade is coaching the beauty chorus. The whole film is kept on that pleasant level of the unexpected. Cross-examinations are made leaning over putters in a practice-room: Inspector Slade borrows a Turkish fez from the pantomime box as he talks to the Home Office pathologist on the phone. The cutting is excellent – 'It's a desperate job', Slade says when the blonde friend of the murdered man is discovered dead on her bed with the poison bottle he has been seeking in her hand, 'two murders in two days', and immediately we cut to the bobbing heads of the Arsenal team at practice, as flippant as balloons in the park. The explanation of the murder depends on another death outside the story and a Coroner's report, and Mr Dickinson's skill is never more evident than in his grim sad dramatization of the dull typewritten pages.

For a while it seemed as if in *Pièges* we were to have another *Carnet de Bal* – a series of episodes amusing, ghastly and sorrowful hung round a woman's neck. A dance-hostess disappears – she is one of eleven disappearances, but this time there is a clue, for she told a friend that she was answering one of those intimate suggestive little advertisements that mention 'companionship'. Her friend helps the police by answering in turn all the doubtful advertisements in the Paris Press – and when von Stroheim looms sadly and secretively up at the dark street-corner rendezvous we hopefully expect a whole series of studies of the lonely, the shy and the warped – the advertisers who are 'broad minded' or lovers of music, who offer 'artistic' employments. But after the von Stroheim episode – a beautifully acted sketch of a mad dress-designer – we plunge into a rather broken-backed *roman policier*, with white-slavers and a homicidal maniac and Maurice Chevalier confessing to murders he never committed for fear of a life sentence. Chevalier seems a little out of place as a rich impresario – he can't help looking like a waiter or a chauffeur of immoderate charm, but there's Jean Renoir and a lovely new actress, Marie Déa, and all sorts of admirable minor parts – a sinister and pathetic manservant, a white-slaver from Athens with a barber's gentility and a sense of his rights, and a police detective who looks like Oscar Wilde. If it's not the film that the Stroheim episode seemed to promise, at least it goes easily, excitingly, amusingly down. *The Spectator,* 2 February 1940

The Arsenal Stadium Mystery (GB, G & S Films, 1940). Director: Thorold Dickinson. Leslie Banks, Greta Gynt, Anthony Bushell.
Pièges (France, Spéva Films, 1939). Director: Robert Siodmak. Maurice Chevalier, Marie Déa, Erich von Stroheim, Jean Renoir.

The Wizard of Oz/ Africa's Skyways

The Wizard of Oz is an American drummer's dream of escape. The book has been popular in the States for forty years, and has been compared there to *Alice in Wonderland,* but to us in our old tribal continent the morality seems a little crude and the fancy material: the whole apparatus of Fairy Queen and witches and dwarfs called Munchkins, the Emerald City, the Scarecrow Man without a brain, and the Tin Man without a heart, and the Lion man without courage, rattles like dry goods. Once a drummer always a drummer, and the author of this fantasy remained the agile salesman, offering his customers the best material dreams – nothing irrational: the Wizard of Oz who sends the dreaming child with her three grotesque friends to capture the witch's broomstick turns out to be a Kansas conjurer operating a radio-electric contrivance. But if we regard this picture as a pantomime, it has good moments: the songs are charming, the Technicolor no more dreadful than the illustrations to most children's books, and the sepia prologue on the Kansas plain, when the child runs away from home to save her dog from a spinster neighbour, and the tornado comes twisting across the horizon,

The Wizard of Oz: Jack Haley, Ray Bolger, Judy Garland, Bert Lahr

is very fine indeed. Miss Judy Garland, with her delectable long-legged stride, would have won one's heart for a whole winter season twenty years ago, and Miss Margaret Hamilton as the spinster-witch, with her bicycle and her broomstick and her incredible razor-edged face, can compete successfully with a Disney drawing. The whole picture is incredibly lavish, and there's a lot of pleasure to be got these days from watching money spent on other things than war. Incidentally, the British Board of Film Censors have given this picture a certificate for adults only. Surely it is time that this absurd committee of elderly men and spinsters who feared, too, that *Snow White* was unsuitable for those under sixteen, was laughed out of existence? As it is, in many places, parents will be forbidden by the by-laws to take their own children to *The Wizard of Oz*.

Africa's Skyways, a documentary made by Strand Films, is for the most part routine travelogue, shots of flying-boats, mail, passengers, beauty-spots, but when we reach Durban something happens: the camera swings from the subject of Imperial Airways to record a horrifying vision of the Rand, the awful squalor of the mining compounds of Johannesburg, the hollow-chested queues for the daily ration of food (including one-sixth of an ounce of coffee per head), the heart-breaking mine-dances, with spears and shields that look as though they had come out of a pawn-shop, the sense of a hopeless exile, and a dying memory of tribal dignity.

The Spectator, 9 February 1940

The Wizard of Oz (USA, M-G-M,1939). Director: Victor Fleming. Judy Garland, Bert Lahr, Ray Bolger, Jack Haley, Margaret Hamilton, Billie Burke.
Africa's Skyways (GB, Strand Productions, 1940). Director: Donald Taylor.

Dark Rapture/Destry Rides Again/The Hunchback of Notre-Dame

Dark Rapture is a film shot by an American expedition to the Belgian Congo – it ends abruptly in a bush fire which destroyed wagons, cameras, everything but these priceless reels of exposed celluloid: the word 'priceless' is used with intention. There has never been a film of Africa to equal this: it should be seen by all those who have watched *African Skyways* with its picture of the Rand compounds, the heartless industrialization and the dingy despair, for this is as near as we can get to what Africa was before the white man came: the wide rapid river, the dense tangled forest and the volcanic mountains that set the cameras trembling have preserved something for the tribesmen here. One carries away from the cinema a sense of innocence, of human dignity reduced to its essentials, no robes or decorations, just the skin and bone and hank of hair. The birdlike, whistling, attenuated voices of the pygmies go wandering deeper and deeper into the heart of darkness; they camp for a night in their makeshift huts of twigs and leaves and then go on, without possessions except their tiny childish bows, until a river stops them. They cannot swim or use canoes: every time they reach water they must accomplish an engineering feat equal to that of the designers of the Sydney Bridge – a man is catapulted on a long vine cable a hundred and fifty feet through the air to the opposite trees and then his fellow workers scramble over: the bridge finished they abandon it and go on, without purpose except the pursuit of food, wandering in a kind of theological Limbo like unbaptized children. Remember that these are the people whom Stanley with his Maxim gun and his Remingtons called 'vicious dwarfs'. With another tribe we watch the initiation of the boys (how was permission obtained to photograph this ceremony?): the little naked boys squat in a scared row while the old men grimly watch to see that everything is as it always was, that no child escapes the fear and pain they suffered, like parents at a commemoration: we see the set small desperate face during the circumcision standing out like something human among the peering masks. Then we cross the hot vibrating mountains and come down into the territory of giants, huge lobelias and heather forty feet high and men of seven feet – an aristocratic race which came centuries ago from Egypt; with fine thin Nephertite features the King's wives hobble, each under twenty pounds of anklets; the Court Poet recites before the sacred cows with their enormous Viking horns two yards between the tips – the beginning of a civilization nipped by the frost from Europe before it had time to spread. Then we watch almost in close-up – an extraordinary sight this – the snaring of the elephants with ropes – sensitive papillon ears, a lightning defence with the trunk. It is impossible to exaggerate the beauty of this film; perhaps it is not a picture for anthropologists: the impressions it gives are rapid, general, uninstructed, aimed at the imagination rather than the intelligence, but anyone who sees it is likely to lose his palate for cinema fiction that week.

Destry Rides Again is the first sufferer: a rather tired Western with a rather tired Dietrich. They have tried to turn Time back and put her exactly where they found her, before the slinky dresses and the long cigarette holders, in the tough husky world of *The Blue Angel*. But time tells ungallantly in the muscles of the neck: there is no falling in love again, even if we wanted to. James Stewart acts magnificently as the Sheriff who won't use a gun, but the picture doesn't take itself quite seriously enough – as though these incongruous actors, and Mischa Auer, Una Merkel, Allen Jenkins, Charles Winninger, were playing Western just for fun. They don't belong

Dark Rapture

to the same world as Brian Donlevy, who has run crooked gambling joints for as long as we can remember and must feel odd in any Eastern clothes.

   The Hunchback will appeal strongly to amateurs of the Gothick school – in its shocking way it's really very fine. The racks and scourges and spiked cords are handled with love, and Laughton's make-up is more horrifying than Chaney's was seventeen years ago – we've toughened in the interval.

 The Spectator, 16 February 1940

Dark Rapture (USA, Armand Denis Productions, 1939). Director: Armand Denis.
Destry Rides Again (USA, Universal, 1939). Director: George Marshall. Marlene Dietrich, James Stewart, Charles Winninger, Brian Donlevy, Una Merkel, Jack Carson.
The Hunchback of Notre-Dame (USA, RKO, 1939). Director: William Dieterle. Charles Laughton, Maureen O'Hara, Edmond O'Brien.

Ninotchka/On Your Toes/A Chump at Oxford/These Children Are Safe

Seeing Garbo has always seemed to me a little like reading Carlyle: good, oh very good, but work rather than play, and a new apprehension was added by the slogan 'Garbo laughs' (no slogan has been plugged so relentlessly since 'Chaplin talks'). One expected the laughter to creak a little with greatness; but this is not merely a Garbo film, it is a Lubitsch film, and the result is enchanting – from the first

On Your Toes: Eddie Albert, Vera Zorina

appearance of the three Russian stooges, all celluloid collar, Adam's apple and secretive boyishness, who arrive in Paris as a trade delegation to offer a Grand Duchess's jewels for sale. They are too innocent to survive in the sly capitalist Lubitsch world of nubile cigarette-sellers and unlimited champagne, and they soon find themselves corrupted and outwitted by the Grand Duchess's lover (Melvyn Douglas), so that a special envoy has to be sent from Moscow to supersede them. The envoy, of course, is Garbo, a veteran Sergeant of the Polish War, with a granite face and an unbecoming hat and an uncompromising suspicion. 'How are things in Russia?' the delegates winningly inquire, and the tombstone voice replies, 'There have been many successful mass-trials. There will be fewer and better Russians.' The story, of course, is of her seduction, too – by capitalist elegance and by Mr Douglas, whose glittering foxy-faced pursuit is a little luscious and long-drawn. The Grand Duchess is forced to steal the jewels and make a bargain – the jewels for Russia without a lawsuit in return for the envoy's prompt departure, and there is a fine satirical little scene when Mr Douglas tries in vain to get an Intourist visa to follow her. The sequence in Russia – Ninotchka's reunion party with the stooges in the shared room with the shared eggs and neighbours going through all the time to the shared lavatory – is hardly comedy at all: it would be the bleakest tragedy if there were not, of course, a happy ending.

On Your Toes has been changed without any loss from musical comedy to straight comedy. It is the story, many will remember, of a young American composer and ex-hoofer who gets mixed up with an impecunious Russian ballet company, and it ends with the production of his Slaughter on Tenth Avenue, in which he dances under a Russian name watched by a couple of comic assassins in the stage box, who have orders to shoot when he stops dancing (his namesake was a traitor to some Russian cause or other). The dialogue has wit: Zorina, who played the prima ballerina in London, acts well, looks lovely, and dances beautifully, and the photography of the ballet sequence is really magnificent. We are left happily wondering why we don't have ballet specially written for the screen. The moving camera and the changing emphasis of the cut and the close-up can offer something new.

Laurel and Hardy are together again – this is better news than anything the papers print. *A Chump at Oxford* ranks with their best pictures – which to one heretic are more agreeable than Chaplin's; their clowning is purer; they aren't out to better an unbetterable world; they've never wanted to play Hamlet. Laurel here is given more opportunity than usual for straight acting; a blow on the head brings back a lost memory, and instead of an American hobo sent to Oxford by a benefactor, he becomes Lord Paddington, an all-round athlete, who disappeared years before.

These Children Are Safe, Alexander Shaw's film of the evacuation, deserves far more space than it can be given here. Admittedly, it dwells most on the favourable side – we see nothing of the slums to which the children sometimes went, and little of the dirt and disease they sometimes brought with them; it is more a lyrical than a documentary film. One remembers afterwards the superb choice of faces in close-up, worried LCC faces, unhealthy bored women's faces, and breaking through all the time the absurd and beautiful faces of children; a sense of happiness and release, and room to play in; the sound of voices singing: 'Do you know the muffin-man who lives in Glory Lane?' The sense of poetry is much rarer in film direction than the sense of humour, let us welcome it whole-heartedly when it is there.

The Spectator, 23 February 1940

Ninotchka (USA, M-G-M, 1939). Director: Ernst Lubitsch. Greta Garbo, Melvyn Douglas, Ina Claire, Bela Lugosi, Sig Ruman.
On Your Toes (USA, Warner Bros, 1939). Director: Ray Enright. Zorina, Eddie Albert, James Gleason, Alan Hale.
A Chump at Oxford (USA, Hal Roach, 1940). Director: Alfred Goulding. Stan Laurel, Oliver Hardy, Harry Langdon.
These Children Are Safe (GB, Strand Productions, 1940). Director: Alexander Shaw.

Sherlock Holmes

It is a pleasure to meet a well-mannered criminal again; we have suffered so long from 'Siddown you', and 'I said, Siddown'; at the Regal we are in 1894, and people say 'Pray be seated', and 'Precisely, Holmes.' In an admirable opening scene Dr Moriarty stands in the dock awaiting with his usual composure the verdict; this, as he expects, is an acquittal, delivered by both judge and jury with undisguised regret, and with a peevish reference to the laws of evidence. At this moment Sherlock Holmes bursts into the court with some last-minute evidence – inadmissible, of course, and Moriarty is turned loose again. This is a brisk and promising beginning to a story which is not only exciting, but, more important, atmospheric-

Sherlock Holmes: Nigel Bruce

ally correct; one feels Conan Doyle might have collaborated when he was not quite in his best form (as when he was writing *The Lion's Mane*, for instance); we are projected straight away – as Holmes shares a hansom with Moriarty from the Old Bailey – into that London of cobbles, mud, fast cabs and gas-lamps; lost London, one was going to say, of Ford Madox Ford's remembrance – of dimmed crescents, dark crowded interiors, and far too many fogs. (We know a darkness now, but it is less terrifying perhaps than the alternate gas-jet and shadow of those streets.) This is the *atmosphere* conveyed, I should make clear, and not the effect of the photography, which is very beautiful.

Dr Moriarty is, one feels, the central figure in the film, in spite of its title; his attempt on the Crown Jewels has the right stable financial touch. Acted by George Zucco, he is viciously correct – a man in the stern suave tradition represented by Colonel Moran ('the second most dangerous man in London'), who, it will be remembered, tilted back his silk hat to take better aim at Holmes with his new compressed-air shotgun, and by Sir George Burnwell (who also made an attempt to steal a crown). He is, of course, savage to inferiors, but at least once he is contradicted, and he takes it good-humouredly: 'Alas, poor Higgins; there was nothing left of him but his boots.' '*One* boot, Sir.' This air of having only just missed the best clubs is enhanced by the cut of the beard; he seemed a lesser man when he shaved it off in order to disguise himself as a police sergeant. Basil Rathbone is physically made for the part of Holmes; one feels he was really drawn by Paget, but mentally he forgets that he belongs to the end of a century, and probably met Wilde at first nights; one can't imagine this Holmes, indolent, mystical, or untidy (there were tobacco-jars and not – shouldn't it have been? – a Turkish slipper on the chimney-piece). Nigel Bruce as Dr Watson almost thumps a tail, and Miss Ida Lupino acts well and looks exquisite as the usual frightened caller in Baker Street.

The Spectator, 8 March 1940

Sherlock Holmes (*The Adventures of Sherlock Holmes*) (USA, 20th Century-Fox, 1940). Director: Alfred Werker. Basil Rathbone, Nigel Bruce, Ida Lupino, George Zucco.

The Proud Valley

It is unfortunate for everybody concerned in *The Proud Valley* that *The Stars Look Down* preceded it: if that fine film had not set a standard this picture of a Welsh mining village would have seemed a worthy, if rather dim, little picture: one might have been tempted to overpraise it for the sake of a few authentic scenes with a GPO touch – the meeting, for example, of the miners' choir to prepare for the Eistedfodd. No picture of a mining district ever seems to be complete without a disaster (we have two in this picture): the warning siren is becoming as familiar as the pithead gear shot against the sky – and that has joined the Eiffel Tower and the Houses of Parliament among the great platitudes of the screen; and yet a far worse tragedy in a district like this must be just inaction. This, perhaps, is the theme of the picture – women pretending sickness when the rate-collector calls, credit petering out at the general store, but too many red herrings scent the story line beside the disasters: colour prejudice is dragged in for the sake of Mr Paul Robeson who plays the part of a big black Pollyanna, keeping everybody cheerful and dying nobly at the end (Mr Robeson's fat sentimental optimism seemed to me a little revolting); and the theme dies out altogether at the close with patriotic speeches and crisis posters and miners dying for England. The direction of the quiet documentary scenes is good, but Mr Pen Tennyson, who may have been handicapped by an undistinguished cast and a wobbly script, seems ill at ease with drama.

The Spectator, 15 March 1940

The Proud Valley (GB, Capad, 1940). Director: Penrose Tennyson. Paul Robeson, Edward Chapman, Edward Rigby.

APPENDIX

The Shirley Temple Libel Action

The review of *Wee Willie Winkie* which is missing from this volume (p. 176) was the subject of a celebrated libel case in which Shirley Temple and 20th Century-Fox sued Graham Greene and *Night and Day*, together with the magazine's printers and publishers. The case appeared before the King's Bench on 22 March 1938, with Greene *in absentia*, and on 23 May 1938, the following account of the hearing appeared among the Law Reports of *The Times*. Graham Greene was at the time in Mexico on a writing assignment. It is perhaps worth mentioning in connection with the 'beastly publication' that *Night and Day* boasted, as well as Graham Greene as film critic, Elizabeth Bowen as theatre critic and Evelyn Waugh as chief book reviewer. It appears to have been intended as a sort of English equivalent of *The New Yorker*, and would seem to have foundered after six months of life more because of its too highbrow tone than because of the refusal of 'every respectable news distributor in London' to handle it. Of contemporary comments on the libel, perhaps the most pertinent came from the pen of Godfrey Winn, himself the victim of some uncharitable comments in a review by Greene (see p. 179), who thought the review 'a queer one, because it was not a criticism of Shirley's clever acting at all, but one which introduced potential audience reactions – reactions which were entirely alien to Shirley's lovable and innocent humour'.

HIGH COURT OF JUSTICE

KING'S BENCH DIVISION
LIBEL ON MISS SHIRLEY TEMPLE: "A GROSS OUTRAGE"
TEMPLE AND OTHERS v. NIGHT AND DAY MAGAZINES, LIMITED, AND OTHERS
Before the LORD CHIEF JUSTICE

A settlement was announced of this libel action which was brought by Miss Shirley Jane Temple, the child actress (by Mr. Roy Simmonds, her next friend), Twentieth-Century Fox Film Corporation, of New York, and Twentieth-Century Fox Film Company, Limited, of Berners Street, W., against Night and Day Magazines, Limited, and Mr. Graham Greene, of St. Martin's Lane, W.C., Hazell, Watson and Viney, Limited, printers, of Long Acre, W.C., and Messrs. Chatto and Windus, publishers, of Chandos Street, W.C., in respect of an article written by Mr. Greene and published in the issue of the magazine *Night and Day* dated October 28, 1937.

Sir Patrick Hastings, K.C., and Mr. G. O. Slade appeared for the plaintiffs; Mr. Valentine Holmes for all the defendants except Hazell, Watson, and Viney, Limited, who were represented by Mr. Theobald Mathew.

SIR PATRICK HASTINGS, in announcing the settlement, by which it was agreed that Miss Shirley Temple was to receive £2,000, the film corporation £1,000, and the film company £500, stated that the first defendants were the proprietors of the magazine *Night and Day*, which was published in London. It was only right to say that the two last defendants, the printers and publishers, were firms of the utmost respectability and highest reputation, and were innocently responsible in the matter.

The plaintiff, Miss Shirley Temple, a child of nine years, had a world-wide reputation as an artist in films. The two plaintiff companies produced her in a film called *Wee Willie Winkie*, based on Rudyard Kipling's story.

On October 28 last year Night and Day Magazines, Limited, published an article written by Mr. Graham Greene. In his (counsel's) view it was one of the most horrible libels that one could well imagine. Obviously he would not read it—it was better that he should not—but a glance at the statement of claim, where a poster was set out, was quite sufficient to show the nature of the libel written about this child.

This beastly publication, said counsel, was written, and it was right to say that every respectable news distributor in London refused to be a party to selling it. Notwithstanding that, the magazine company, with the object no doubt of increasing the sale, proceeded to advertise the fact that it had been banned.

Shirley Temple was an American and lived in America. If she had been in England and the publication in America it would have been right for the American Courts to have taken notice of it. It was equally right that, the position being reversed, her friends in America should know that the Courts here took notice of such a publication.

"SHOULD NOT BE TREATED LIGHTLY"

Money was no object in this case. The child had a very large income and the two film companies were wealthy concerns. It was realized, however, that the matter should not be treated lightly. The defendants had paid the film companies £1,000 and £500 respectively, and that money would be disposed of in a charitable way. With regard to the child, she would be paid £2,000. There would also be an order for the taxation of costs.

In any view, said counsel, it was such a beastly libel to have written that if it had been a question of money it would have been difficult to say what would be an appropriate amount to arrive at.

Miss Shirley Temple probably knew nothing of the article, and it was undesirable that she should be brought to England to fight the action. In his (counsel's) opinion the settlement was a proper one in the circumstances.

Mr. VALENTINE HOLMES informed his Lordship that the magazine *Night and Day* had ceased publication. He desired, on behalf of his clients, to express the deepest apology to Miss Temple for the pain which certainly would have been caused to her by the article if she had read it. He also apologized to the two film companies for the suggestion that they would produce and distribute a film of the character indicated by the article. There was no justification for the criticism of the film, which, his clients instructed him, was one to see which anybody could take their children. He also apologized on behalf of Mr. Graham Greene. So far as the publishers of the magazine were concerned, they did not see the article before publication.

His LORDSHIP.—Who is the author of this article?

Mr. HOLMES.—Mr. Graham Greene.

His LORDSHIP.—Is he within the jurisdiction?

Mr. HOLMES.—I am afraid I do not know, my Lord.

Mr. THEOBALD MATHEW, on behalf of the printers, said that they recognized that the article was one which ought never to have been published. The fact that the film had already been licensed for universal exhibition refuted the charges which had been made in the article. The printers welcomed the opportunity of making any amends in their power.

His LORDSHIP.—Can you tell me where Mr. Greene is?

Mr. MATHEW.—I have no information on the subject.

His LORDSHIP.—This libel is simply a gross outrage, and I will take care to see that suitable attention is directed to it. In the meantime I assent to the settlement on the terms which have been disclosed, and the record will be withdrawn.

INDEX

Index

Index